MODELLING THE LEGAL DECISION PROCESS FOR INFORMATION TECHNOLOGY APPLICATIONS IN LAW

Law and Electronic Commerce

Volume 4

The titles published in this series are listed at the end of this volume.

Modelling the Legal Decision Process for Information Technology Applications in Law

by

Georgios N. Yannopoulos

Preface by Chris Reed

KLUWER LAW INTERNATIONAL

THE HAGUE / BOSTON / LONDON

A C.I.P. Catalogue record for this book is available from the Library of Congress.

ISBN 90-411-0540-9

Published by Kluwer Law International,
P.O. Box 85889, 2508 CN The Hague, The Netherlands.

Sold and distributed in the U.S.A. and Canada
by Kluwer Law International,
675 Massachusetts Avenue, Cambridge, MA 02139, U.S.A.

In all other countries, sold and distributed
by Kluwer Law International, Distribution Centre,
P.O. Box 322, 3300 AH Dordrecht, The Netherlands.

Printed on acid-free paper

Printed in the Netherlands.

στο *Νίκο*, τη *Μαρία* και τη *Λητώ*

*(to **Niko**, **Maria** and **Lito**)*

Οὐκοῦν εἴ τίς τινα μηχανὴν ἔχοι πρὸς τοῦτο,
ἔργῳ καὶ λόγοις τίνα τρόπον διδάξειεν ἂν ἕτερον
εἴτε μείζονα εἴτε ἐλάττω περὶ τοῦτ' ἔχειν ἔννοιαν,
ὅπως χρὴ φυλάττειν καὶ ἐπανορθοῦν νόμους, οὐκ ἂν
ποτε λέγων ἀπείποι τὸ τοιοῦτον πρὶν ἐπὶ τέλος ἐλθεῖν;

Plato, The Laws, 769E

"Thus, if someone had a machine (device) with which he could teach another by deed or word to understand, in a greater or lesser degree, how he should observe or amend laws, he should finish what he has to say, and not leave the work incomplete"

TABLE OF CONTENTS

xiv

LIST OF FIGURES

LIST OF TABLES

CHAPTER 1

CHAPTER 3

PREFACE

For many years lawyers and computer scientists have dreamed of using information processing technology to predict, facilitate or emulate legal decision-making, and have investigated how this dream might be fulfilled[1]. The course of those investigations has been more prolonged than most researchers expected; not because the technology has failed to deliver[2] but because the legal decision-making process has turned out to be more complex than was previously thought.

Early research[3] concentrated on rule-based expert systems, and was based on a very simple model of the legal decision-making process:

$$R \times F = D$$

(i.e. rules (R) applied to the facts of a case (F) produce the decision (D)[4]).

This model assumes that the law consists of clearly-stated, published rules, and that the task of the judge is merely to identify[5] the applicable rules, and then to apply

---

1   The seed from which this work is generally recognised to have grown is LOEVINGER, "*Jurimetrics: the next step forward*", (1949) 33 *Minnesota Law Rev.* 33.

2   In scientific fields, decision-making technology proved effective many years ago - see e.g. BUCHANAN & SHORTLIFFE, *Rule-Based Expert Systems* (Addison Wesley: Reading, Mass. 1984) [medical diagnosis].

3   A useful review of the field prior to 1990 can be found in SERGOT, *The Representation of Law in Computer Programs*, COMPLEX 1/91 (Tano: Oslo 1991).

4   For an analysis of the defects of this model see SUSSKIND, *Expert Systems in Law: a Jurisprudential inquiry* (Clarendon Press: Oxford 1987).

5   In its most extreme form, the model further assumes that the translation of the law into production rules is a linguistic, rather than a legal, task, and that this translation can be effected by a person who has no legal training - see SERGOT *et al*, "*Formalisation of the British Nationality Act*" in YEARBOOK OF LAW, COMPUTERS AND TECHNOLOGY Vol. 2 (Butterworths: London 1986).

them. In jurisprudential terms this could be described as a strong positivist position, assuming that the law is merely a set of production rules which can be discovered from the primary source material, and that provided these rules are identified in their entirety the system will be a complete representation of the law in that area.

This approach to the problem of legal decision-making is generally recognised (at least by lawyers) to be inadequate[6], as it models only a small part of the judicial function.[7] It now seems that purely rule-based expert systems can only be useful within limited domains of the law, and only useful to a limited class of users.

Once the defects of purely rule-based expert systems had been discovered, research turned to investigating ways of replicating the decision-making process in areas where production rules were inadequate. These inadequacies are most obvious where the law exhibits "open texture"[8], rather than being expressed as clear rules. Techniques have been developed for the automation of non-rule based reasoning which appear to be able to cope with open textured law, including case-based reasoning[9], reasoning by analogy[10] and neural networks.[11]

---

[6]   See LEITH, *"Fundamental errors in logic programming"* (1986) 29 COMPUTER JOURNAL 3.

[7]   For example it completely ignores issues such as:

- the judgmental questions involved in deciding which rules are applicable;

- how a judicial decision is reached if there are no directly applicable rules;

- that some "rules" do not have binary, "yes" or "no" answers. In these cases the so-called rule cannot work on binary data but requires an assessment of one party's behaviour in relation to the norm. Questions such as, "Did the defendant take reasonable care?" are not really yes/no questions. The court is required to assess the range of human behaviour on the continuum from totally reasonable to totally unreasonable, and to decide where on that continuum the defendant's behaviour lies. A rule- based system cannot answer such questions, but most areas of the law contain many of these questions, e.g. whether a person has taken reasonable care.

[8]   HART, *The Concept of* Law (Clarendon Press: Oxford 1961).

[9]   SKALAK & RISSLAND, "Arguments and Cases: an inevitable intertwining", 1 *Artificial Intelligence and Law* 113.

[10] ASHLEY & RISSLAND, *"Toward modelling legal argument"* in MARTINO & SOCCI (EDS.), *Automated Analysis of Legal Texts* (North-Holland: Amsterdam 1986).

[11] ZELEZNIKOW & STRANIERI, *"The Split-up System: integrating neural networks and rule-based reasoning in the legal domain"*, PROCEEDINGS OF THE 5TH INTERNATIONAL CONFERENCE ON ARTIFICIAL INTELLIGENCE AND LAW (ACM Press 1995) 185.

As a result of this progress in research, automated legal decision-making systems have been produced which are useful in the practice of law, but which are useful only within a precisely delineated legal domain and subject to stated limitations. Their users are generally experienced lawyers who can recognise the constraints and limitations under which these systems operate. These systems should more accurately be described as legal assistants than as legal decision-makers[12].

The final step which remains to be taken is the combination of the different methods of automated reasoning to produce systems which can automate the legal decision-making process from start to finish. To achieve this end, it is necessary to analyse how that decision-making process operates, the types of reasoning which are appropriate at each stage, the sources from which relevant information should be sought and the points at which non-legal information or understanding is required.

A legal decision-making system which is based on such an analysis should exhibit the "deep structure" which has been argued to be essential if such systems are to succeed.[13] It is this analysis which Dr. Yannopoulos's book undertakes.

Chapter 1 develops a model of the complete legal decision-making process. The chapter:

- identifies the actors involved in making legal decisions and clarifies their differing roles;

- explains and justifies the methodology used for constructing the model; and

adopts a systems analysis approach to the formalisation of the legal decision-making process.[14] This enables him to distinguish the various steps of collecting

---

[12] Whilst it might be acceptable to offer a pure rule-based system to a lawyer not experienced in that area of law, leaving him to supplement its lack of judgmental ability with his own legal expertise, it would clearly be unacceptable (and perhaps unethical) to market such a system to those who lack that expertise. And even the expert lawyer would be at a loss if the area covered by the system were so far outside his own experience that he could not supply the right kind of expertise.

[13] McCARTY, "*Intelligent Legal Information Systems: Problems and Prospects*" in CAMPBELL (ED.), *Data Processing and the Law* (Sweet & Maxwell: London 1984).

[14] This is particularly well-illustrated by the pseudo-code description of the methodology which is reproduced as an addendum to the Chapter.

and processing information which are necessary, and to indicate branching points and recursive loops which are essential to processing the flow of information through that process.

The resulting model, illustrated in graphical form in Chapter 1.10, demonstrates the flow of information through the entirety of the legal decision-making process, from fact collection (e.g. from the lawyer's client) to delivery of judgment.

Chapter 2 concentrates on expert systems in law, the area where the majority of research has focused. It discusses their use in relation to the model, and identifies those parts of the decision-making process where expert systems technology is appropriate to process the information flow and those where alternatives such as information retrieval or document assembly systems need to be integrated into the processing.

The model of Chapter 1 is not purely theoretical; the initial draft was subject to empirical testing as part of Dr. Yannopoulos's involvement in the EC-funded *Nomos* project, the results of which were used to refine the draft model into the form set out in Chapter 1. The *Nomos* project and the empirical testing are examined in Chapter 3, which also discusses the effectiveness of knowledge acquisition via natural language processing of legal texts.

Chapter 4 presents the author's general conclusions. Perhaps the most important of these is that the majority of research into legal expert systems to date has concentrated on the formalisation of knowledge in a particular legal domain, rather than on what the user of the system requires; an answer to his or her legal question.

The merest glance at the graphical representation of the model of Chapter 1 indicates that the decision-making process begins with the facts of the problem, which derive from the social, political and economic environment, and ends with the legal decision which has effects in that environment. The information processing between these two stages takes place in the legal system, but if the expert system in question operates solely within the confines of the legal system its results are only usable by practitioners within that system.

Expert systems of this type are like legal text books; they may focus more precisely on the particular issues of the case than a book, which of necessity analyses the legal issues at a higher level of generality, but the results they produce must still be subject to further processing through the mind of a legal practitioner before the legal decision can be arrived at. As Dr. Yannopoulos states in his Epilogue:

> "As long as such applications cannot offer anything more than books, traditional professions - like lawyers - will not use them."

Researchers who have ambitions to produce true legal decision-making systems, as opposed to systems which merely refine a sub-set of the information required by a decision-making lawyer, will find this book invaluable.

Chris Reed
Reader in Information Technology Law
at the University of London

ACKNOWLEDGEMENTS

This work was submitted as a doctoral thesis to the Faculty of Laws of Queen Mary & Westfield College of the University of London. It was approved by the Examiners, and the Degree of Doctor of Philosophy was awarded in 1996. Many thanks are owed to many people and institutions for the accomplishment of this book and previously for the Ph.D. Thesis.

I feel heavily indebted to my supervisor *Chris Reed* for his patience and his support and guidance during all these years. With his constant encouragement and sympathy to all my problems, including personal ones, he is not only a knowledgeable teacher, supervisor and – now – boss, but also a dedicated friend. Special thanks are owed for the Preface of this book that he kindly wrote. I also thank *Jilly Reed* for proof-reading some of the conclusions. At the Information Technology Law Unit, *Lorraine Mulpeter* creates a warm working environment and she is invaluable in overcoming the everyday bureaucratic difficulties as well as those that were related to the Ph.D. research and to this publication.

Professor *Jon Bing* with his support and comments was the main motivator to publish the thesis. For the long years of my research I have greatly benefited from the discussions with him and Professor *Peter Seipel*, whenever I met them, even in social events. I would particularly like to express my gratitude for their constant help and encouragement.

I also owe thanks to Kluwer Law International for assuming the responsibility of this edition, and especially to Mrs *Annebeth Rosenboom* for her patience.

The constructive criticism of *Richard Susskind* and *Robin Widdison*, the Ph.D. Examiners, has been vital for improving certain points of this book, and I wish to express my thanks for their academic contribution.

Shortly before this publication *Philip Leith*, *Peter Wahlgren* and *John Zeleznikow* have found the time to supply invaluable remarks for this book and I cordially thank them.

The main source of funding for the Ph.D. research was a scholarship from the Greek Scholarship Foundation (*Ίδρυμα Κρατικών Υποτροφιών - IKY*). I must thank them for their contribution, as well as Professor *Dionysia Kallinikou*, who was the scholarship supervisor. I am also very grateful to my professors at the University of Athens: Professor *Michalis Stathopoulos*, Professor *Giorgos Philokyprou* and Professor *Antonis Pantelis* who constituted the supervising committee of my initial research in Greece and helped me to articulate many of the introductory questions.

My gratitude is also expressed to the personnel of the Norwegian Research Centre for Computers and Law in Oslo, to Professor *Jean-Louis Bilon* and the personnel of the Institut de Recherche et d' Études pour le Traitement de l' Information Juridique in Montpellier, and to the personnel of the Istituto per la Documentazione Giuridica in Florence. They have all been extremely helpful and hospitable during my visits there. These visits were sponsored by a Grant from the University of London (Central Research Fund).

Finally, I would also like to thank all the academic and professional lawyers that have answered my questionnaires and generally all the people that have helped me in many ways.

For all these years my family has been my stable point of reference, and without their help this study would have never been possible. They deserve a special mention and this book is dedicated to my parents *Niko* and *Maria* and to my sister *Lito*, for their endless moral and material support.

Bayswater, 20 September 1997

G.N.Y.

0. PROLEGOMENON

0.1 INTRODUCTION

0.1.1 The Background of the Ph.D. Research

The *Information Crisis in the area of Law,* first described by SIMITIS[1] in the early seventies, is still reigning in the nineties.[2] This is an observation made not only by experts but by any well-intentioned observer.[3] On the *macro level,* the administration of Justice is characterised as a bureaucratic, cumbersome and non-flexible institution, which usually reproduces the malfunctions of the administrative infrastructure of the subject (state or international organisation) which enforces it. This observation refers mostly to the deficiencies of the 'information' system, but nevertheless adds more arguments to the criticism concerning the substantive *justice-giving* function of every judicial system, which is absolutely affected by these deficiencies.

---

1   SIMITIS S., *Informationskrise des Rechts und Datenverarbeitung*, Karlsruhe, 1970.

2   See recently SUSSKIND defining hyperregulation as "legal information of unmanageable quantity and complexity". SUSSKIND R., *The Future of Law*, Clarendon Press, Oxford, 1996, p. 71.

3   The following thoughts are based on the study of the Legal/Justice systems of UK, USA, France, Germany, Italy, Greece and the EEC, of which I am aware. I think that they are characteristic representatives of the vast majority of both common and civil law systems. Furthermore, personal contacts with lawyers from other countries, such as Norway, Sweden and the former Soviet Republics have been used as a source of information.

1

After field research on two separate occasions (winter 1990 and summer 1994) amongst London's law firms and from the experience gained in academic institutions the author is convinced that this 'crisis' still dominates two decades after it had first been established. This research initially intended to examine some of the specific problems that arise whenever Information Technology meets Law and *vice versa,* mainly from a Lawyer's point of view. In the early nineties expert systems seemed one of the potential tools that could improve legal information systems.

In January 1992, and while trying to refine these ideas, I was faced with the unique opportunity to work as the Legal Expert and Analyst for the implementation of the *Nomos-Advisor* legal expert system within the framework of the *Nomos*[4] *Project* (an EEC project funded under the Esprit initiative). Briefly, the aim of the project was to assist the implementation of expert systems by providing tools that perform 'automatic knowledge acquisition' from legal texts in Italian and French. *Nomos-Advisor*, the legal expert system, of which I drafted the legal analysis, used *Nomos's* results as an input in order to validate the mentioned methodology.

The biggest false assumption made when attempting to model automatically acquired legal knowledge is that methodological and procedural legal knowledge is also contained in the text of law. Although the legal profession intuitively knows the falsity of this assumption, researchers in the area of automatic knowledge acquisition are still confident in implementing systems that use only the text of laws as their main source of knowledge. Knowledge engineers are then forced to make their own interpretations of this knowledge, thus resulting in erroneous and legally unacceptable interpretations of the law.

It was obvious from the first stages of the project that *Nomos* was also following this flawed hypothesis. To solve the problem a draft methodology of 'teaching' law to the other members of the implementation team by drafting sketches showing all the possible connections of the elaborated text with other parts of the legal system was developed. After the completion of the *Nomos* project (November 1992) it was decided that the results, including the expert system itself (especially the methodology to refine the knowledge base of *Nomos-Advisor*), should constitute the empirical material of my Ph.D. Thesis. Additionally, this material was used to

---

[4] See the whole implementation in detail in *Chapter 3*. For the terminology see *Chapter 2*.

promote the above draft methodology to a full scale model which was tested against the results of the *Nomos-Advisor* prototype.

The main observation was that computerised applications in law (expert systems, information retrieval, document assembly etc.) are usually built around a specific piece of legislation. Such a fragmentary approach to the law cannot produce legally 'correct' results because it ignores the effect of other connected parts of the law. Therefore, researchers must adopt an extended view of the legal phenomenon, which, in practice, entails that the analysts of these applications must be legally educated and continuously aware of both the theoretical differences and the practical consequences that different legal theories and methodologies impose. Furthermore, the analysis must be undertaken in the light of the legal system as a whole, trying to create an integrated legal sub-system that can support practical problem solving. The main argument of the Ph.D. Thesis and of the present book is that in order to implement applications following these guidelines, *some kind of model representing the legal decision process as a whole* must be followed. If this methodology is not applied, legally erroneous results may arise from otherwise technically 'perfect' computer applications.

0.1.2 A Profile of this Book

The title of the book: *Modelling the Legal Decision Process for Information Technology Applications in Law* mirrors a mixture (1) of the initial ambition to conduct research in legal information systems and (2) of the empirical findings of the *Nomos* project. Initially, an attempt is made to provide some methodological tools by tackling the problem of terminology and defining the epistemological position of this study between law and computer science (*Prolegomenon*). The term *Information Technology Applications in Law* is favoured amongst others and it is emphasised that the newly developed discipline of Information Technology and the Law lacks a stable theoretical and methodological background.

Then the archetype, which was drafted from the initial sketches and guidelines, is elaborated in the form of a full scale model. This is a general model of the legal decision process, encapsulating a '*minimum requirements configuration*' for building Information Technology Applications in Law from a jurisprudential point of view (*Chapter 1: Modelling the Legal Decision Process for Information Technology Applications in Law*). This model is intended to be used as a 'checklist' that can depict a compact picture of the full course of the Legal Decision Process

3

and can provide a clearer view of the methodological rules so that future researchers, especially non-Lawyers, will avoid the omission of important elements of the process.

Secondly, feedback from the *Nomos-Advisor* implementation is used to reduce the scope of the model to the application of legal expert systems and to emphasise the specific problems arising. (*Chapter 2: Applying the Model to the Creation of Legal Expert Systems*). The analysis is extended to explain basic terminology and methodologies used later in the third chapter.

Thirdly, the whole process of implementing the fully functional prototype legal expert system *Nomos-Advisor,* which constituted the empirical testbench of the Ph.D. Thesis, is described. (*Chapter 3: Empirical Investigation*). This prototype used the Italian VAT Law as a source and was tested with real life cases. Finally, conclusions derived from the implementation and the consultation sessions are used to confirm the theoretical assumptions and the main argument of the thesis, and, consequently, to evaluate the proposed model (*Chapter 4: Synthesis - General Conclusions*) followed, in the closing section, by a general discussion about the future of Information Technology Applications in law *(Epilogue).*

0.2 THE EPISTEMOLOGICAL PROBLEM

Interdisciplinary research involving the sciences, and especially technology, has always been the Achilles' heel of Lawyers. Until recently it was a *sine qua non* condition, for all jurists, to devote a large part of every thesis, essay or article to a brief (sometimes naive) introduction to the 'scientific' or 'technological' details of the subject, together with an apologia explaining why and how a theorist from the legal discipline deals with sciences. All authors included the standard citations about the second industrial revolution, the explosion of information, the benefits of using computerised information systems and the usefulness of modern technology.

Nowadays, fortunately, it is not necessary to apologise for undertaking research in the multidisciplinary topic of *'Computers and Law'*. After four decades of research and intellectual debate on the issue, a large wealth of bibliography is available to introduce newcomers to the field and provide the excuses. Any kind of introduction to Information Technology, or any 'exposé' of the 'miracles' computers can achieve, is outside the scope of this book. It is believed that in the nineties, a mature audience of computer literate[5] lawyers has been created which is not reluctant to accept research initiatives into more profound issues of '*Computers and Law*', and that such an audience is familiar with the basics of technology as well as with computer usage in the law office.

Nevertheless, although the waters are no longer deep, one cannot yet submit that they are properly charted. The application of scientific methods to the Law, according to the classic definition by LEE LOEVINGER,[6] and under whatever name (*Computers and Law, Cybernetics and Law, Information Technology and Law, Legal Informatics* etc.), has always been examined as a phenomenon arising from pragmatic situations, and thus never succeeded in obtaining a '*de jure*' recognition.

With only a few brilliant exceptions,[7] through the forty years of debate on the issue neither a general theory nor a compact methodology has been developed. Furthermore, until today researchers have not even agreed on terminology and on whether or not this field constitutes a new discipline. Consequently, while in normal interdisciplinary research the researcher is familiar with the solid background of two or more disciplines, in the case of law meeting computer science the researcher is confronted with an absolute vacuum.

Therefore, the writing of this prolegomenon has not been led by the desire to develop just another doctrine, but by two emerging needs: (1) to outline a general theory and a compact methodology and (2) to interpret the existing terminology for the subject. This framework could provide a stable workbench for this research and a navigation chart for future explorers.

---

5   It has been recently postulated that nowadays "[l]awyers must be trained to work digitally in a digital world or they may as well shut shop tomorrow". SUSSKIND R., *The Future of Law*, Clarendon Press, Oxford, 1996, p. 256.

6   LEE LOEVINGER, *Jurimetrics: The Next Step Forward*, in MINNESOTA LAW REVIEW, Vol. 33, p. 455, April, 1949.

7   Starting with the classics: the works of LEE LOEVINGER, LYCIEN MEHL and VICTOR KNAPP as well as the edition of *Jurimetrics* by BAADE (ED.), New York 1963. One should also mention the countless writings of JON BING since the seventies, the landmark monograph of PETER SEIPEL *Computing Law* (Stockholm, 1977), the works of WILHELM STEINMÜLLER, HERBERT FIEDLER, MARIO LOSANO, VLADIMIR VRECION, SPIROS SIMITIS and in the late eighties the articles of GIANCARLO TADDEI-ELMI.

0.3   THE HISTORY

> "Knowledge, like other, is one, but each separate part of it which applies to some particular subject has a name of its own; hence there are many arts, as they are called, and kinds of knowledge, or sciences."[8]

> "Thus every intellectual activity is either *practical* or *productive* or *speculative*."[9]

The debate between Platonic and Aristotelian dualism concerning the nature of Knowledge, as characterised by the above quotations, has dominated the evolution of human thought for the past 25 centuries. PLATO in *'Theaetetus Sophist'* defends the unity of knowledge and of methodology applicable to all disciplines, while, on the other hand, ARISTOTLE in his *'Metaphysics'* distinguishes between Philosophy and Sciences. In ELMI'S words, in one of the few contributions dealing with the epistemological aspect of the issue in question, "those gnosseological dichotomies have since then exhausted the minds of philosophers and scientists in a continuous effort to find answers to metaphysical questions".[10] Is it then knowledge unitary or pluralistic? And what kind of methodology or methodologies can be applied to every or all of the disciplines? ELMI characterises *Legal Informatics* (his terminology) as the last link in the chain; a new discipline, which must also find or try to find answers to those queries.[11]

Certainly, the issue in question is one of the latest fruits of intellectual thought, and 'the enthusiasm for Cybernetics' and 'the back of logical neopotivism' in the late forties played their role in accelerating those developments, but, of course, without the technological advance the discussion about 'modern uses of law' would have

---

[8]   PLATO, *Theaetetus Sophist* 257C42, Loeb edition 1977, Translation by H.N.Fowler.

[9]   ARISTOTLE, *Metaphysics* 1025b25, Loeb edition 1933 Translation by H.Tredennick. The *verbatim* translation should be "practical, poetic or theoretical" and corresponds greatly to the Latin distinction between *Prudentia, Ars,*and *Scientia*. See also SOURLAS P., *Fundamental Issues of Legal Methodology,* Athens 1986 (in Greek).

[10]   See ELMI-TADDEI G., *L' Informatique Juridique entre la Philosophie et la Science: "Autonomie et Interdisciplinarité"* in LES ANNALES DE L' IRETIJ, No.1, Montpellier, 1989, p. 195 and also ELMI, *L' Insegnamento Dell' Informatica Giuridica in Italia,* in INFORMATICA E DIRITTO, Vol. 1, p. 188, 1989 where a brief analysis of the two theories can be found.

[11]   The debate is now more than ever interesting in the light of the recent efforts of scientists to develop Grand Unified Theories (GUIs) especially on the provenance of the Universe. See also CALDWELL M.E., *Jurisprudence in Interdisciplinary Environments* in JURIMETRICS, March 1968 with some interesting points on today's specialisation against *homo universalis*.

stayed a theory. However, it can be argued that originally the conditions matured back in the 18th century when the Aristotelian tradition characterising jurisprudence as *prudentia* recessed due to the theory of Natural Law,[12] thus permitting to other dimensions of the legal phenomenon, such as the social and practical, to show themselves. At this stage, it must be made clear that – as most legal researchers know - the debate over the character of jurisprudence is very lengthy and still on-going. Therefore, for the purposes of this study references to the different theories will be made only to the extent to which they affect its contents. It is also known that *Law* in all its aspects has always been the most reluctant discipline to adapt to modern methods and to change its consolidated positions.[13]

Irrespective of the stimuli that lead someone to undertake research in this field, it is a duty to refer to LEE LOEVINGER as the father of *Jurimetrics*, whose article *"Jurimetrics, the Next Step Forward"* in MINNESOTA LAW REVIEW vol.33, 1949 is considered to be the cornerstone of the issue in question. Furthermore, one could pay tribute to the early pioneers of the field, amongst others, COLIN TAPPER,[14] VITTORIO FROSINI, LAYMAN ALLEN,[15] PETER SEIPEL,[16] LUCIEN MEHL,[17] EJAN MACKAAY, SPIROS SIMITIS[18] and JON BING.[19] However, many authors omit to refer to the scientists who contributed to the post-war development of computer technology, which turned the romantic dreams about the interaction between Law and Computers into a tangible reality. On that point special tribute is owed to

---

[12] See SOURLAS P., *Fundamental Issues of Legal Methodology,* Athens 1986 (in Greek) p. 54.

[13] For instance, it took many decades to recognise *Sociology* and *Methodology of Law* as separate disciplines.

[14] TAPPER C., *Lawyers and Machines*, in THE MODERN LAW REVIEW, Vol. 26, p. 121, March, 1963.

[15] ALLEN L., *Symbolic Logic: A Razor-edged Tool for Drafting and Interpreting Legal Documents*, in YALE LAW JOURNAL, 66, p. 833, 1957.

[16] SEIPEL P. , *Computing Law*, Liberfoerlag, Stockholm, 1977.

[17] MEHL L., *Automation in the Legal World: From the Machine Processing of Legal Information to the "Law Machine"*, Symposium on the Mechanisation of the Thought Process, National Physical Laboratory, U.K., 1958.

[18] SIMITIS S., *Informationskrise des Rechts und Datenverarbeuitung*, Karlsruhe, 1970.

[19] BING J., *A Model of Legal Information Retrieval as Part of the Decision Process*, in INFORMATICA E DIRITTO, Vol.2, No.3, p. 259, 1976.

ALAN TURING, the mathematician who first referred to the General Problem Solving Machine and hence also to legal problems.[20]

0.4   THE TERMINOLOGY

While the attempt to define the possible discipline of the interaction between Computers and Law has not led to generally acceptable results, the situation in relation to defining terms is even more disappointing. Notwithstanding the efforts of academics in several law schools[21] to teach the subject, the discipline has never been generally accepted as a full subject into legal curricula. For this reason their efforts have always been fragmentary and have never led to the development of a standard unified terminology.

On the other hand, the already mentioned fact that Lawyers are computer - though not necessarily keyboard – illiterate,[22] multiplies the misunderstandings, thus closing the vicious circle and increasing the traditional gap between Law and Sciences. It is characteristic that, during the preliminary research concerning this investigation (see *infra* Chapter 1), conducted from October 1990 till May 1991 among twenty of London's large and medium-sized Law Firms, only 2 out of the 20 people questioned understood the scope and the goal of this research. The rest, all ranked amongst the Firms' 'Computer Lawyers',[23] exhibited a range of misunderstandings in response to the statement that this research is dealing with *Computers and Law*.

The results were identical four years later: during another field survey, concerning the use of CD ROMs by Law Firms, towards the end of the Ph.D. research (August 1994), lawyers still had not improved their knowledge of Information

---

[20] See his known paper of the fifties TURING A, *Computing Machinery and Intelligence* in MIND 49, p. 433, 1950.

[21] SUSSKIND emphatically claims that "the teaching of law in absence of IT is gradually becoming a misrepresentation of legal practice and legal process". SUSSKIND R., *The Future of Law*, Clarendon Press, Oxford, 1996, p. 258.

[22] See LEITH P., *The Computerised Lawyer: A Guide to the Use of Computers in the Legal Profession*, Springer-Verlag, 1991.

[23] I.e dealing with the in-house computer applications in law and not with substantive Information Technology Law issues.

Technology. In the most extreme examples, those questioned were not sure whether or not their firm possessed a machine which could access CD ROMs, while others insisted that their present system of providing information manually was better than one in which lawyers could mess up their computers.

Furthermore, in every day life, both academics and practitioners, as well as other researchers, do not seem to have clarified the basic distinctions of the topic. This vague situation provides a fertile ground to charlatans[24] who under the cover of the wide term *'Computer Law'* or *'Computers and Law'* or *'Legal Informatics'* pretend to possess the secrets of every aspect of the discipline, from substantive law issues to specific computer applications.

As a starting point, the RECOMMENDATION NO.R(80)3 of the COUNCIL OF EUROPE on *Teaching, Research and Training in the field of 'Computers and Law'* states that we need at least three terms to define the discipline. The same line is followed by most authors[25] in the field. However, disagreement and confusion arise from the words used to describe those three terms. First of all, there is an emerging need to describe the whole of the discipline (see *infra* 0.5) which by assumption will be called the T-TERM which then, in the late professor VANDENBERGHE'S words, presents a diptych,[26] having on one side computer applications in law (T2-TERM) and on the other issues of substantive law regulating computers and modern technology (T1-TERM)

0.4.1 The T-Term: *Information Technology and the Law*

Up to now a compound term to describe the interaction between Law and Computers and *vice versa*[27] as a new discipline has not been developed. The previously introduced terms: *Jurimetrics, Legal Cybernetics* and in Italian:

---

24 Characteristic definition by WESSEL M. *What is "Law, Science and Technology Anyway?"* in JURIMETRICS, Spring 1989, p. 259.

25 SEIPEL P. , *Computing Law*, Liberfoerlag, Stockholm, 1977, p. 132 see also FROSINI V., *Computer Law in the 80s* in COMPUTER LAW & PRACTICE, July/August 1986.

26 The vast majority of authors agree on this notion see also VANDENBERHGHE, *Software Oracles* in OSKAMP - KASPERSEN (Eds.) *Amongst Friends in Computers and Law,* Kluwer 1991 and also BING, *Information Law,* in MEDIA LAW AND PRACTICE, 1981 p. 220.

27 SEIPEL P. , *Computing Law*, Liberfoerlag, Stockholm, 1977, p. 132.

Giuscybernetica, although they retain their historical value, have never been generally accepted, and have been criticised for covering only specific areas of the subject.

Therefore, contrary to the methodological rule that forbids the use of compound terms[28] in order to define a discipline, the T-TERM cannot avoid the use of the conjunction: AND.[29] Since most authors agree on the second part of the term (Law, or at least the adjective Legal) the question is simply what word should be adopted for the first part of the term. Initially *'Computers and Law'* was adequate, but with the expansion of technology and, especially, telecommunications the demand for broader terms became urgent. *Information* and *Information Science* were proposed, but those two terms included elements of Information Theory and other legal meanings of Information, causing both to be rejected as being too broad and including irrelevant matters.[30]

It is obvious that the term to be used should cover the technological aspects of information, e.g. the processing of information. It should include hardware, software and communications and, finally, it should not sound unfamiliar to the ears of the audience. According to the OXFORD DICTIONARY OF ENGLISH (1987):

> *Information Technology* is the branch of technology concerned with the dissemination, processing and storage of information, especially by means of computers... and the convergence of telecommunications and computing technology is generally known in Britain as Information Technology,

while,

> *Information Science* is that branch of knowledge which is concerned with the procedures by which information especially that relating to technical or scientific matters is stored, retrieved and disseminated... and investigates the properties and behaviour of information, the forces governing the flow of information and the means of processing information for optimum accessibility and usability... and it is often used to imply the application of science and technology ... to handling information generally.

---

[28] It is worth to note the effort of SEIPEL in his *Computing Law,* Stockholm, 1977 to introduce unsuccessfully the term *'Computing Law'.*

[29] See also the RECOMMENDATION NO.R(80)3 of the COUNCIL OF EUROPE, comments, title, where the terms *Computers and Law* and *Applications of Computers in the Legal Field* are introduced.

[30] See on that the *Preface* of REED in REED C. (Ed.) *Computer Law,* Blackstone Press, 1990 and also FROSINI V., *Computer Law in the 80s* in COMPUTER LAW & PRACTICE, July/August 1986.

Therefore, the only term to satisfy the aforementioned conditions for the first part of the T-TERM is *Information Technology* and hence *Information Technology and the Law*.

0.4.2 The T1-Term: *Information Technology Law*

The strong tradition of the term 'Computer Law' as well as the pragmatic value of the term *Information Technology Law*[31] compel it as the most appropriate T1-TERM. The tradition ensures that the term will be understood by Lawyers while, pragmatically, *Information Technology Law* covers the broader needs of developments such as telecommunications.[32] The problem lies in the extent to which the *legal usage of computers* and the *legal regulation of computer usage*, i.e. substantive computer law, can be classified under that term.

This classification is dependent – in the first place - on the legal system in use and on many other factors. The most crucial problem is whether *Information Technology Law* can be accepted as a separate, legal or non-legal *discipline*. Attempting to draft this classification falls outside the scope of this study, but two points should be mentioned: First, in connection with the two other terms (T and T2), *Information Technology Law* should also function as a shelter for 'homeless' issues that might arise from unpredictable technological developments.[33] Second, a possible classification of *Information Technology Law* should always bear in mind the relevant classification (sub-terms etc.) of the other half of the diptych (the T2-Term) and try to be consistent with them.

0.4.3 The T2-Term: *Information Technology Applications In Law.*

Although the term *Informatika* appears in some early Russian texts[34] it was only in 1966 that the French Academy accepted the artificial term *Informatique*,[35] made

---

31 See also BING J., *Information Law* in MEDIA LAW & PRACTICE, p. 237, 1981.

32 See also REED C., *Preface*, in REED (Ed.) , *Computer Law*, 1990.

33 This hypothesis (made in early 1993) is now confirmed in view of Internet Law finding a place under Information Technology law.

34 See OXFORD DICTIONARY OF ENGLISH (1987): *Informatics*.

from a synthesis of the words *information* and *automatique*,[36] in order to cover what in English is known as *Computer Science*.

Originally, the term *Informatique Juridique* was used to describe the electronic processing of legal information. The same terms, under the strong influence of WIENER'S *Cybernetics*[37] and SHANNON'S *Theory of Information*[38] were also introduced in other languages, to describe the same phenomenon e.g. the use of computers (read *Information Technology*) and computer oriented methods in law:[39] *Informatik* in German, *Informatica* in Italian and hence *Rechtsinformatik* and *Informatica Giuridica* respectively.

The transplant of those terms caused two major problems. Firstly, the terms were developed differently in each country by expanding or narrowing their field of interest, until their initial meaning was lost. From a methodological point of view it is not considered correct to raise insurmountable barriers between the terms T, T1 and T2 since their fields often overlap,[40] but in that case, *'informatique juridique'* (and its translations) turned into a 'keyword' for every possible problem, thus abolishing every distinction. It is still believed by many continental lawyers that all aspects of Information Technology and Law, varying from Legal Expert Systems to substantive issues of Data Protection, are *'informatique juridique'*. The same, but to a lesser degree, occurs for English-speaking lawyers with the term *'Computer Law'*.

Secondly, in an effort to translate the above mentioned terms into English the term *Legal Informatics* was introduced. Whether the term tries to represent the initial pure meaning of *'informatique juridique'* or its later, corrupted version, the choice is wrong because the OXFORD DICTIONARY OF ENGLISH (1987) states that:

---

[35] Coined by Philippe Dreyfous in 1962. See also INTZESSILOGLOU V., *Ilektroniki epexergasia tou dikeou (Electronic Processing of the Law)*, Thessaloniki 1989, (in Greek).

[36] For more details see also FROSINI V., *Computer Law in the 80s* in COMPUTER LAW & PRACTICE, July/August 1986, p. 196.

[37] WIENER N., *Cybernetics*, MIT 1961 (revised edition of the 1949 first edition).

[38] CHANNON C.E. *A Mathematical Theory of Information*, Boston 1948.

[39] *Sic* SEIPEL, *Computing Law*, Stockholm 1977, p. 123.

[40] Consider for example the case of legal norms regulating legal expert systems or expert systems producing legal regulations.

Informatics is the discipline of science which investigates the structure and properties (not specific content) of scientific information, as well as the regularities of scientific information activity, its theory, history, methodology and organisation.

According to this definition, the content of the information, which is of vital importance to legal applications, is not covered by the term. Furthermore, it can be argued that pragmatically the term was never adopted by the English-speaking audience,[41] and it certainly cannot be found in any British law school curriculum. Beside the conditions set in the previous paragraph, the T2-TERM should also contain an 'umbrella' function to cover any future technological development that might fall into its jurisdiction. It is, therefore, evident that the term, which can solve the aforementioned problems, which complies with the set conditions, and, which remains consistent with the T-TERM, is *Information Technology Applications In Law*.[42]

0.5   THE DISCIPLINE[43]

0.5.1 The Creation of the Paradigm

All the prerequisites set by KUHN[44] for the formation of the *'paradigm'* of *Information Technology and the Law*, such as the circulation of specialised journals, the creation of societies and the claim for a special place in the curriculum, have been present since the sixties, and were finally established in the

---

[41] It is characteristic that during two conferences on *Artificial Intelligence and Law* (in Oxford 1991 and Amsterdam 1993), which I have attended, the English-speaking participants have never used this term, while there was only a limited use from continental participants. Nevertheless it is worth mentioning that the computer laboratory at Queen Mary & Westfield College (built in 1992) is called the *'Informatics Laboratory'*.

[42] See also the proposal of SEIPEL for *Lex Computationis* (T1-Term) and *Computatio Legis* (T2-term) in SEIPEL P., *Introduction*, in SEIPEL (Ed.), Kluwer, Computer/Law Series, 1990, p. 4.

[43] The structure of this paragraph will follow the one of SEIPEL, *Computing Law*, Stockholm, 1977. The purpose of this choice is not to object his ideas, but mostly to show that in the methodological area not much improvement has been achieved for the past twenty years.

[44] See the well known essay of KUHN T., *The Structure of Scientific Revolutions*, University of Chicago Press, 1962.

seventies and eighties.[45] In particular, the creation of Institutes or Research Centres (whether connected or not with Universities) devoted exclusively to the cultivation of *Information Technology and the Law* has led to the development of a group of 'opinion leaders' in the field, which - at least in Europe - exercise great influence over every aspect of the discipline.[46]

In the United States the *Jurimetrics Journal*[47] has gained continuous international acceptance as a direct descendant of LOEVINGER'S *"Next Step Forward"*, thanks to the efforts of LAYMAN ALLEN, while in Europe the above mentioned centres also produce journals with international dissemination (such as COMPLEX and INFORMATICA E DIRITTO). In the UK one could refer to the two existing societies: the *Society for Computers & Law* and the *British & Irish Legal Education Technology Association* and to six journals (although most of them deal with substantive *Information Technology Law* only):

1. COMPUTERS & LAW,

2. TOLLEY'S COMMUNICATIONS LAW (a merger of Media Law and Practice with Computer Law & Practice),

3. COMPUTER LAW AND SECURITY REPORT

4. LAW TECHNOLOGY JOURNAL,

5. INFORMATION AND COMMUNICATIONS TECHNOLOGY LAW (Formerly, Law, Computers and Artificial Intelligence) and

6. INTERNATIONAL JOURNAL OF LAW AND INFORMATION TECHNOLOGY

---

[45] More recently SUSSKIND refers to a new Legal Paradigm within *legal practice* in connection with Information Technology. This is different that the one analysed here, which rather concerns the legal academia and education. SUSSKIND R., *The Future of Law*, Clarendon Press, Oxford, 1996, p. 41.

[46] If referring to persons there is a duty to mention LEE LOEVINGER, referring to Institutions one should mention (for Europe) the *Norwegian Research Centre for Computers and Law* (NRCCL), the Swedish Law and Informatics Research Institute (IRI), the *Institut pour le Traitement de l' Information Juridique* of the University of Montpelllier (IRETIJ) and the *Centro per la Documentazione Giuridica* in Florence (IDG).

[47] For a complete list of the journals see in the bibliography.

Two more journals have emerged on the Internet: the JOURNAL OF INFORMATION LAW & TECHNOLOGY and the WEB JOURNAL OF CURRENT LEGAL ISSUES.

It should be noted that the academic background behind those activities is not very strong, especially in the area of courses and teaching. Although in most cases these journals reflect only individual efforts, it can be argued successfully that a paradigm for *Information Technology and the Law* has been established.

In the late seventies, SEIPEL has argued convincingly[48] that the concept of paradigm[49] can also be applied to the legal science. He underlines that the sole difference of the natural sciences 'paradigm', compared to that developed in Law, is that the latter is mostly affected by social needs, which tend to be the most important factors. This theoretical construction is not, however, widely accepted. Although a part of the legal scientific community has worked for more than twenty years on those problems pointing out the social and scientific needs that emerge from the introduction of *Information Technology and the Law* as a discipline, the vast majority of legal scholars have been reluctant[50] to accept it as a separate discipline, and the long debate firstly over the need for such a discipline and secondly over its classification (as legal or non-legal) continues.

0.5.2 *Information Technology and the Law* as a Discipline

The debate on whether or not legal science should deal with scientific problems is a long-standing one.[51] The research described in this book was undertaken *ad hoc* to investigate scientific problems within a legal environment. It would, therefore, be contradictory to defend the position that lawyers should not interfere with the sciences. At the other end, the exaggeration of 'involvement' produces a

---

[48] See SEIPEL, *Computing Law*, Stockholm, 1977 p. 180 where he includes a brief analysis of the paradigm concept applied to the Swedish legal scholarly activities.

[49] As described in KUHN T., *The Structure of Scientific Revolutions,* University of Chicago Press, 1962, p. 19.

[50] See LOEVINGER'S disappointing conclusions in *Science, Technology and Law in Modern Society* in JURIMETRICS, Fall 1985, p. 1. There is also poor response of the law schools (at least in the UK) to introduce separate courses for computers and law.

[51] See both SEIPEL P. , *Computing Law*, Stockholm, 1977 and ELMI G.T., *L' Informatique Juridique entre la Philosophie et la Science: 'Autonomie et Interdisciplinarité'* in LES ANNALES DE L' IRETIJ, No.1, Montpellier, 1989, p. 195.

monotonous and fruitless repetition of the "emerging need to introduce the discipline". This attitude verifies SEIPEL'S fears twenty years ago that "...by developing paradigms, legal informatics will probably set itself apart from other fields of knowledge and gain recognition as an independent discipline but this is not a *goal in itself...*".[52] Indeed, these fears are proving day by day to be most realistic, since for twenty or so years *Information Technology and the Law* has continued to be a discipline *in being*, which can claim neither standard terminology nor a structured methodology, and what remains is "random activities and lack of interest in methodological issues".[53]

It has been documented[54] that, in order to produce the paradigm, uncertainty and conflict must dominate the scientific area for a specific period of time. For *Information Technology and Law,* this hesitation could have been desirable in the seventies but it is not acceptable in the nineties. Today, the 'undefined social needs' that usually strengthen every argument in favour of scientific evolution, are concretely articulated: There are clear demands from academia, practice and clinical legal education to introduce *Information Technology and the Law* into the legal curricula. Additionally, most authors agree on the need for integration, proposing a united discipline covering and resolving all the aspects of the problem,[55] both *substantive law* and *Information Technology applications in law*.

Under this pressure, there are not many alternatives to follow: the demand for the development of an autonomous, integrated and mature discipline of *Information Technology and the Law* should be supported.

In order to define a possible method – for introducing the discipline in legal academia and practice - there is always a danger, that ideological debates will divert the already defined needs into endless discussions. This is a phenomenon that has been perceived in other social sciences and may lead to the stalemate of creating an *ad hoc* 'demand for the demand'. It is, therefore, better to follow the

---

52 SEIPEL P. , *Computing Law*, Stockholm 1977, p. 252 (italics added).

53 SEIPEL P. , *Computing Law*, Stockholm 1977, p. 296.

54 KUHN T., *The Structure of Scientific Revolutions,* University of Chicago Press, 1962.

55 See also the interesting opinion of SEIPEL (in SEIPEL P. , *Computing Law*, Stockholm 1977) of a piecemeal approach which is appropriate to the structure of law schools. Even that approach would be welcome as first step, since in most law schools (at least in the UK) the field is not taught at all.

same policy as the one for the *Terminology*: The methods should arise, *ex necessitate*, from the pragmatic situation rather from theory. A point to be observed, for *Information Technology and the Law*, is that this 'demand' to introduce the discipline does not aim to provide simply one more scientific 'tool'.[56] It will be shown in the next chapter, that *Information Technology and the Law* is not only a 'tool' but it will - perhaps already does - exhibit some of the basic principles and functions of the legal phenomenon like the knowledge of law, equity, and the newly developed 'right to information'.

0.5.3 The Interdisciplinary Environment

As illustrated by SEIPEL, "*computing law*[57] cuts across practically every field of substantive and procedural law, and of computer science and economics". Given the present disappointing situation, it would have been easy to attach *Information Technology and the Law* to any of the above branches in order to provide the necessary academic environment. Nevertheless, that approach, although driven by practical reasons, lacks methodological basis and presents the danger of creating a kind of 'promiscuous' discipline which changes its characteristics according to its temporary host.

Instead, it has been proposed by ELMI[58] that parts of *Information Technology and the Law* should follow the *interdisciplinary integrated model*. This model proposes that distinct and autonomous disciplines should each be integrated but they should keep the relationships and the interdependence between them. Parts of this representation (especially *Information Technology Law*) follow the multidisciplinary model, which simply proposes the juxtaposition of the *results* of two disciplines. However, the diversity and the complexity of the different fields entails that the existing global models about the links, the interactions and the forms of dependence

---

[56] The theory of *Information Technology and the Law* being only a 'tool' is the main argument of the 'null' approach supporters, who claim that computers are nothing more than a tool (e.g. like a typewriter) in the hands of lawyers. see also SEIPEL P. , *Computing Law*, Stockholm 1977, pp. 227 & 273. In view of the recent technological developments I think that this opinion is obsolete.

[57] SEIPEL P. , *Computing Law*, Stockholm 1977, p. 137. *Computing Law* is the term used for *Information Technology and the Law*.

[58] For a detailed analysis on the position of IT and Law within the multidisciplinary environment see ELMI, *L'Informatique Juridique entre la Philosophie et la Science* in LES ANNALES DE L' IRETIJ, No. 1, Montpellier 1989, p. 195.

17

between disciplines cannot suit today's epistemological situation.[59] ELMI argues that modern epistemology needs to be more pragmatic - in his words 'descriptive, decentralised and local' abandoning the old fashioned *multi-, trans-* and *inter-*disciplinary dogma.

This is not just a theoretical discussion but has practical consequences when intra-legal interdisciplinary problems occur. As emphasised by SEIPEL,[60] only an integrated discipline that can assume responsibility and secure advanced interdisciplinary research between *information technology* and *legal science* will be able to solve them. To be consistent with those thoughts, it must be clearly exposed that the legal side should be the dominating one, and thus *Information Technology and the Law* should be characterised as a *legal* discipline. As already stated, this characterisation arises from practical needs and does not intend to take a stand in the long debate over the classification of sciences. It is beyond doubt that the non-legal part of *Information Technology and the Law* cannot deal with legal problems or impose solutions on the law and, therefore, is incapable of taking the above mentioned responsibility.

0.5.4 The Basis, the Boundaries, the Structure

Drawing sharp theoretical dividing lines is not in accordance with the spirit of this study, which deals with a specific pragmatic problem. Flexibility will be the rule whenever a prescriptive definition is needed, and therefore, an additional classification of the possible fields or branches of the discipline will not be attempted. Many classifications from reliable sources[61] exist, where the careful reader can always detect a secure place for the object of this book.

---

[59] See the very interesting article of VANYO J.P. , *The Legal System can it be Analyzed to Suit the Scientist?* in JURIMETRICS, Winter, 1973, p. 100 especially on the interrelation of disciplines.

[60] SEIPEL P. , *Computing Law*, Stockholm 1977 pp. 137, 216, 255.

[61] Mostly from the relevant journals. SEIPEL (*Computing Law*, Stockholm 1977) presents many of them. In the author's opinion, the most extensive classification, including a very rich bibliography, is the one presented in the second semester of each year in the bibliographical edition of INFORMATICA E DIRITTO (although some of the proposed 'branches' can be disputed).

Concerning the basis[62] of the discipline it can be argued that the first definition by SEIPEL introducing the "interaction between *Computers* and *Law*"[63] should be expanded to the 'interaction between *Information Technology* and *Law*' in order to include, as already stated, all future technical developments and telecommunications.

SEIPEL'S detailed analysis of the boundaries of the discipline of *Information Technology and the Law* has tried successfully to defend the character of a discipline '*in being*'. *Information Technology and the Law* should, according to his expectations, and those of many others, have reached the stage of maturity by the eighties. Subsequently, BING has pointed out that "...the discipline is not a matter of definitions but a choice of strategies...".[64] It is a common belief that this alternative has not appeared yet and therefore, we are obliged today to follow the same course of argument: We must apply an extensive strategy in pursuit of all the possible fields of interest of *Information Technology and the Law*.

To strengthen the above argument, it could be added that since these early descriptions a large wealth of literature has been generated (see *infra* Chapter 1) but the same considerations still puzzle researchers, especially because no standard methodology has yet been developed. The example of *Artificial Intelligence and Law* is characteristic: the question whether *Artificial Intelligence and Law* constitutes a branch of the above described discipline or a separate discipline in itself is still pending. There are, of course, numerous earlier writings, but if we hypothesise that the starting point for practical applications in this field is the writings of BUCHANAN & HEADRICK,[65] twenty-five years later WAHLGREN[66] is still demanding a stable theoretical background and a methodology for *Artificial Intelligence and Law*.

---

[62] For some interesting early aspects see FIEDLER H., *Grundprobleme der Juristischen Informatik*, in DATANVERARBEITUNG IM RECHT, Vol. 3, 1974.

[63] SEIPEL P. , *Computing Law*, Stockholm 1977, p. 292.

[64] BING J., *Information Law* in MEDIA LAW AND PRACTICE, p. 237, 1981.

[65] BUCHANAN B. & HEADRICK TH., *Some Speculation About Artificial Intelligence and Legal Reasoning*, in Stanford Law Review, Vol. 23, No. 40, November, 1970.

[66] WAHLGREN P., *A General Theory of Artificial Intelligence and Law*, in PRAKKEN H., MUNTJEWERFF A.J. AND SOETEMAN A. (Eds.), *Legal Knowledge Based Systems the Relation with Legal Theory*, PROCEEDINGS OF THE JURIX CONFERENCE, Koninklijke Vermande, Amsterdam, 1994.

0.6 CONCLUSION TO PROLEGOMENON

This prolegomenon has attempted to find a golden mean between two contradictory positions. The first would be to add one more hysterical voice to those already crying out for "an emerging need for *Information Technology and the Law*" without, however, taking any necessary step towards that goal. A pure, strict set of rules and unmoveable barriers defining *Information Technology and the Law*, its possible structure, its position within the legal science as well its boundaries, would leave no doubt to the reader of what *Information Technology and the Law* should be. The second position would be to write down a pathetic introduction which ignores the problems, adding some romantic historical remarks and the well known myths of integration.

However, rather than adopting either of these positions it seemed more useful to inform the reader and let him draw his/her own conclusions. The route chosen was to present an outline of the methodological and structural problems, not in the sense of a simple encyclopaedic juxtaposition or in order to impose solutions but to show that this study is (and shall remain) aware of those difficulties.

It is postulated that *Information Technology and the Law* is still *'in being'*, demanding originality and scientific autonomy. BING emphatically claims that "...the new area may contain heterogeneous legal issues... and may be of temporary use, to be abandoned when the rate of development tapers off...".[67] This remark, combined with the dynamic characteristics of both the consisting disciplines leaves no room for standardisation. A lot of practice and experience will be needed before the attainment of standards and final definitions. It is hoped that future scientific work, conferences, seminars and continuous research will provide *Information Technology and the Law* with the infrastructure that it currently lacks, and with more sophisticated terminology.

---

[67] See BING J., *Information Law* in MEDIA LAW AND PRACTICE, 1981, p. 237.

1. MODELLING THE LEGAL DECISION PROCESS

1.1   INTRODUCTION

1.1.1   Initial Background

The very first thoughts about the Ph.D. research and this book were developed in the late eighties when the author was working for an on-line legal database company, providing support to customers on both legal and technical questions. In the technical field, users were instructed how to use the communications programs in order to get connected and how to use the interface program of the database in order to get information. In the legal field, the support was focusing on how to modify the queries of the users in order to reach the desired result. Even with the help of the support personnel, users often failed to find the information they were seeking. An over-simplified hypothesis would be that the deficiencies in the *recall* and *precision* rates - to use information retrieval terms - were justified by the restrictions of the Boolean[1] techniques upon which the database was built.

The main observation, however, was that even if the Boolean restrictions were to be overcome by manually instructing the users to modify their queries, still the database could not reach a high level of quality in providing legal information. Therefore, the initial stimulus was the speculation that a large part of the deficiencies of that database were due to a distorted and fragmentary view of the

---

[1]   See a detailed analysis *infra* in section 1.7.7 The Search for Legal Sources.

legal decision-making process. This misconception was reproducing neither the true way lawyers 'think' nor the full path of their thought.

Supported by a post-graduate research grant from the *Greek State Scholarship Foundation (IKY)* in 1990 the author began a study of Information Technology Applications in Law, examining the specific problem of legal decision-making in connection with legal information systems. Two arguments constituted the basis of this research: first, that the *Information Crisis*[2] is a given problem of everyday legal practice and second, that only electronic[3] information systems could help to master this situation. Therefore, the first target was to verify the above speculation, and to demonstrate that a more integrated view of the legal phenomenon could improve the quality of legal information systems. The second step would be to find specific tools that could facilitate the envisaged improvement.

From a sentimental point of view, the reason behind the desire to improve legal information systems was the first hand experience of the 'agony' of lawyers in their search for legal information and the embarrassment at the obvious 'under-use' of modern electronic information systems.

1.1.2   Field Research

Field research was conducted on two separate occasions (winter 1990 and summer 1994) in order to verify the basic arguments of the Ph.D. research, i.e. the existence of a *Crisis* in legal information and its connection to the use of computerised systems. The first survey was conducted in winter 1990 amongst London's law firms and providers of information systems for lawyers. In details (see *Table 1-1* in page 23) the survey which concerned the use of information systems by lawyers has shown that:

1. The computer department (in large firms) or computer retailers (in the case of small firms and individual practitioners) decides about the implementation of information systems within the lawyer's office. Unlike the information systems

---

2   As described by SIMITIS S., *Informationskrise des Rechts und Datenverarbeitung*, Karlsruhe, 1970, i.e. roughly a bulk of information more than the lawyer can manipulate.

3   Through personal communication my attention was called to the remarkable fact that in 1992 some Judges (in the UK) were still hand-writing their decisions.

of other professions (especially in the sciences) in law firms it is computer managers, usually with no legal education, who decide and provide information systems to be used by lawyers.

Firm	Use of IT	Use of AI
Barlow Lyde Gilbert	Separate Law Library & Law Librarian, Solicitors not directly using IT for informational purposes. Newsletter everyday.	None
Clifford Chance	IT Department for in-house systems and for all applications: internal management, office automation, informational purposes	Legal Expert System for EEC Competition Rules under development, (1990)
Freshfields	IT Department for in-house systems and for all applications: internal management, office automation, informational purposes	None
Richards Butler	Separate Law Library & Law Librarian, Solicitors not directly using IT for informational purposes	None
Masons	Separate Law Library & Law Librarian, Solicitors not directly using IT for informational purposes	Some research mainly because of individual interest
Linklaters & Paines	IT Department for in-house systems and for all applications: internal management, office automation, informational purposes	None
S.J. Berwin	Separate Law Library & Law Librarian, Solicitors not directly using IT for informational purposes	None
Slaughter & May	Not responded	None
CREST project	Public Sector, Administration of Justice	None
Butterworths (Lexis)	Legal database, same conclusions on its direct use by solicitors	None
Context	Legal database. Effort to sell the product (EEC Celex Legislation) both on-line and off-line via CDs	Some applications under development (1990)

Table 1-1: Informal research amongst Law Firms concerning the use of IT and AI
(October - December 1990)

2. The different information resources are fragmented around the firm and in most cases there is no central policy as to what sources must be bought and especially how they can be used by the firm. Normally, in large firms the law librarian bears the enormous task of coordinating all these resources and of providing information sometimes for more than 200 practitioners. Because of the misunderstandings in communication quite often the practitioner must

reformulate his/her query to the librarian and *vice-versa*. This situation is causing a continuous feedback, leading to a vicious circle.

3. According to the survey, the most important finding was that lawyers are not directly using information resources except through the above mentioned librarian. It appears that in both legal professions lawyers are still - if not keyboard illiterate as in the eighties - at least illiterate in using complicated hardware and software (such as CD-ROMs). The result is that the vast majority of information needs rests on the shoulders of an intermediate person (the law librarian*)*. The integrated user-friendly system, as it has been proposed since the eighties[4], has not yet reached every legal desk.

After these findings[5] it was evident that the lawyer is not in direct contact with the legal sources and legal information. Therefore the initial argument of the *Information Crisis* was focused on the noticeable fact that the information flow in a legal environment contains this surprising gap. The second step would be to investigate the specific tools which could close or at least narrow this gap.

In the early nineties the idea of expert systems was expanding in the bibliography and was in the vanguard of computer technology. The idea of such a system appeared to promise a tool which could be used to improve the information flow in a legal environment[6]. Therefore the research moved towards introducing an 'intelligent' interface between the user and existing on-line legal databases that could amplify the use of traditional retrieval systems. The challenging idea of an integrated workstation encapsulating all kinds of resources (databases, expert systems, telecommunications and office automation: word-processing, local databases, spreadsheets, time billing systems etc.) situated on top of the legal desk, appeared very attractive.

---

[4] See especially BING J. *Computer Assisted Working Environment for Lawyers. Part I: The Concept and Design of Integrated Workstations for Lawyers*, in 7th COLLOQUY ON THE USE OF COMPUTERS IN THE ADMINISTRATION OF JUSTICE, Lisbon 11-13 October 1988, Report to the Council of Europe, 12 February, 1988.

[5] For a comparison with the United States see *The Chicago-Kent Large Firm Survey and Statistical Analysis on the use of Computers* (1992-94) (www.lawkent.edu).

[6] That is why the first survey (see *Table 1* in page 23) contains a column about the use of Artificial Intelligence (AI).

1.1.3   The Generation of the Need for a Model

As explained in the Preface, in 1992 the author was invited to participate in the *Nomos* project, an EEC Esprit Phase II project, which was providing tools that perform 'automatic knowledge acquisition' from legal texts in Italian and French. This experience gave the author the opportunity to test the already developed ideas about legal information systems and their improvement and to identify new theories. *Nomos-Advisor* was a prototype legal expert system whose purpose was to solve legal problems in the application of the Italian VAT law. *Nomos-Advisor* was the peak of the *Nomos* project because it used *Nomos's* results as an input in order to validate its methodology. The author worked for one year in a post combining both the notions of the *'domain expert'* and the *'knowledge engineer'*, trying to improve and refine the above mentioned 'input', which was used as a *'knowledge base'* for the prototype expert system.. Explanations about the technicalities and the terminology of expert systems and Artificial Intelligence are given in Chapter 2 (*Applying the Model to the Creation of Legal Expert Systems*) while the whole course of implementation of the *Nomos-Advisor* prototype expert system is exposed in Chapter 3 (*Empirical Investigation*).

It will be shown in detail in Chapter 3 (see especially section 3.3 The Puzzle of the N-A Prototype) that the whole project was built upon a series of false assumptions and deficiencies. However, the crucial factor that led to the development of the general model described in this Chapter (1) was the embarrassment caused by the fact that a multi-million ECU project could not produce legally acceptable results. It is known even to first-year law-students that legal reasoning cannot be performed by using only parts of legislation. Therefore, in theory, researchers and especially *knowledge engineers*[7] must adopt an extended view of the legal phenomenon and acquire basic legal skills in order to develop legal applications.

Immediately after having studied the general analysis of the project and without any need to enter its internal details, the flagrant observation was that the whole project was built around a specific piece of legislation (the Italian VAT law) without any reference to other parts of the law and the legal system. Furthermore, the final 'product' of the project was restricted only to a few articles of the Italian VAT law.

---

[7]   These are persons responsible to create the *Knowledge Base*, one of the essential parts of an expert system, such as the envisaged *Nomos-Advisor* system. For Artificial Intelligence terminology and methods see also Chapter 2.

Such a fragmentary approach could not endorse 'valid' legal reasoning and was showing the lack of fundamental legal skills. The biggest false assumption was that methodological and procedural legal knowledge are also contained in the text of a certain statute.

Therefore, in order to proceed with the implementation of the envisaged application (the *Nomos-Advisor* legal expert system) a method needed to be developed which should cover these deficiencies. In practical terms, the author had to 'teach' law to the other members of the implementation team, to write down 'checklists' with all the necessary components of the legal decision process and to draft sketches showing all the possible connections of the elaborated text with other parts of the legal system. It was these draft 'checklists' and sketches that produced the idea of creating a full scale theoretical model of the legal decision process.

Nomos indicated that producing expert systems in isolation from a model of the legal decision-making process was worse than useless. The purpose of the remainder of this Chapter is to present such a model and furthermore to support the argument that such a model *must* be used in all attempts to produce automated legal decision-making tools (including non-expert systems tools).

From the methodological point of view the basic parts of the model described in this Chapter were produced in parallel with the development of the *Nomos-Advisor* prototype upon which most of the assumptions expressed here were tested. This explains why most of the *'Examples'* in Chapter 1 refer to the *Nomos* project while the *'Link to the Model'* notions in Chapters 2 and 3 are used to show the connections of the model to expert systems and to the project. Therefore, the core of the model described here was used as a guide and at the same time refined by using feedback from the empirical results. However, the final theoretical version as exposed in this Chapter (1) was developed after the end of the project.

1.1.4 Research in Legal Information Systems

The next step of the Ph.D. research was to scrutinise existing bibliography in order to find the relevant works in the field. The classic of its kind, *Legal Decisions and*

26

Information Systems[8] by JON BING and TRYGVE HARVOLD was the first attempt to analyse the legal decision process from an information systems perspective. Although their testbed had been the trivial information retrieval systems of the seventies, the experiment proved successful and their monograph has been the strongest methodological point of reference for Information Technology Applications to the Law for nearly 15 years. The BING-HARVOLD model with subsequent amendments[9] was chosen *ex necessitate* as the basis for the model proposed here, because it was the only existing model at the time that the initial research started. Furthermore it seemed a working model - at least with many applications in the area of information retrieval - and many of its aspects coincided with my empirical findings. Finally, it was widely accepted from the authors in the area of Information Technology Applications in Law and did not suffer any fundamental defects apart from the use of outdated hardware.

Attention should be drawn to the fact that it was not until the nineties that a systematic generic analysis of the legal decision process for Information Technology Applications in Law appeared. In 1991 PHILIP LEITH with his *Computerised Lawyer,*[10] tried such an approach, although more from the point of *sociological jurisprudence*, while STUART NAGEL (ED.) in his *Law, Decision Making and Microcomputers*[11] collects some interesting opinions from leading scholars in the field and MITAL & JOHNSON[12] go into advanced technical details of legal applications. These three latter sources refer also to more recent technological achievements, namely AI and Law and Legal Expert Systems. RICHARD SUSSKIND,[13] in turn, focuses on the specific jurisprudential problems that occur while building *Expert Systems in Law.*

---

[8] BING J. & HARVOLD T., *Legal Decisions and Information Systems*, Universitetsforlaget Oslo, 1977.

[9] See BING J., *Handbook of Legal Information Retrieval*, North Holland, Amsterdam, 1984, BING J., *Legal Decisions and Computerized Systems*, in SEIPEL (Ed.), Kluwer, Computer/Law Series, 1990 and BING J., *Rules and Representation; Interaction between Legal Knowledge Based Systems and the General Theory of Legal Rules*, in BLUME (Ed.), Kluwer, Computer/Law Series, 1991.

[10] LEITH P., *The Computerised Lawyer, A Guide to the Use of Computers in the Legal Profession*, Springer-Verlag, London 1991. See especially chapters 5 through 9.

[11] NAGEL S.(Ed.), *Law, Decision Making and Microcomputers*, Quorum Books, New York 1991.

[12] MITAL V. & JOHNSON L., *Advanced Information Systems for Lawyers*, Chapman & Hall, London, 1992.

[13] SUSSKIND R., *Expert Systems in Law*, Clarendon, Oxford 1987.

After the completion of the *Nomos-Advisor* project, PETER WAHLGREN, a Swedish researcher, in his monograph on *Automated Legal Reasoning,*[14] has provided a contribution to the methodological basis of Artificial Intelligence and Law. He set out, for the first time, the jurisprudential framework within which an acceptable *legal knowledge engineering procedure* should be developed and introduced a model[15] of the legal reasoning process.

The criteria for choosing the above works as reference startpoints were (1) their relevance to the model proposed here, in that they discussed specifically the problems of the intersection of computer applications and law and (2) the fact that they recognised the need for a description of the whole legal information system, rather than confining themselves to a discrete part of that system or to a particular application. This last criterion is acting as a strong filter because in most cases existing works fall in the same pitfall of describing fragmentary small scale applications without any consideration for the legal system as a whole.

1.1.5   Research in Artificial Intelligence and Law

Because the testbench of this study has been an Artificial Intelligence application, the *Nomos-Advisor* prototype (see *infra* Chapter 3), it was necessary to take into account the work in the field of Artificial Intelligence and Law.[16] After the landmark paper of BUCHANAN & HEADRICK,[17] various fragmentary attempts appeared in the late seventies and in the eighties trying to connect Artificial Intelligence (known also as AI) and/or its methods to the Law. Some of these also include analyses of the legal decision process under the aforementioned

---

[14] WAHLGREN P., *Automated Legal Reasoning: A Study on Artificial Intelligence and Law*, Kluwer, Computer/Law Series, 1992.

[15] GORDON has also built an *Artificial Intelligence Model of Procedural Justice* based on article 9 of the United States Uniform Commercial Code and has identified some of the most obscure points and problems that occurred during this effort. GORDON T., *The Pleadings Game: An Artificial Intelligence Model of Procedural Justice,* unpublished PhD Thesis, Fachbereich Informatik, Technische Hochschule, Darmstadt, 1993.

[16] For a historical review of legal theories in connection with AI see SAMUEL G., *The Challenge of Artificial Intelligence: Can Roman Law Help us Discover whether Law is a System of Rules ?,* in LEGAL STUDIES , Vol. 24, p. 25, 1992.

[17] BUCHANAN B. & HEADRICK TH., *Some Speculation About Artificial Intelligence and Legal Reasoning,* in STANFORD LAW REVIEW, Vol. 23, p. 40, November, 1970.

perspective. One could start with BRYAN NIBLETT[18] and his *Advanced Course* on *Computer Science and the Law* and continue with MARTINO'S[19] two editions on 1. *Deontic Logic, Computational Linguistics and Legal Information Systems* and 2. *Automated Analysis of Legal Texts*, both based on the proceedings of conferences held in Italy in 1981 and 1985 respectively. Some later efforts take the form of specific monographs such as ANNE GARDNER'S, *An Artificial Intelligence Approach to Legal Reasoning*, (MIT Press, Cambridge Mass, 1987), KEVIN ASHLEY'S *Modeling Legal Argument* (MIT Press, Cambridge Mass., 1990)[20] and TREVOR BENCH - CAPON'S (ED.), *Knowledge Based Systems and Legal Applications*, (Academic Press, London, 1991) where one can find a summary and classification of most of the known research projects until 1991.

Since 1987, the five International Conferences on Artificial Intelligence and Law, in Boston (1987), Vancouver (1989), Oxford (1991), Amsterdam (1993) and Maryland (1995) have constituted the internationally recognised forum for scientific debate in the area of AI and Law. Their proceedings (see the Bibliography) have included various contributions many of which have crucially affected this research. Furthermore since 1992 the International Association of Artificial Intelligence and Law edits the ARTIFICIAL INTELLIGENCE AND LAW Journal, which also contains numerous papers affecting this work.

In terms of bibliographic reference the final input for the Ph.D. Thesis were the proceedings[21] of the last Jurix Conference, held in Amsterdam in December 1994. The main subject of the conference was *"the Relation of Legal Knowledge Based Systems with Legal Theory"*. For the first time it was possible to collect the

---

[18] NIBLETT B., *Computer Science and the Law, an Advanced Course,* Cambridge University Press, 1980.

[19] MARTINO A.A (Ed.), *Deontic Logic, Computational Linguistics and Legal Information Systems,* North-Holland Publisher, 1982 and

MARTINO A.A. - SOCCI-NATALI F. (Eds.), *Automated Analysis of Legal Texts,* North Holland, Edited versions of Selected Papers from the International Conference on Logic, Informatics, Law, Florence September 1985, North Holland, 1986.

[20] RISSLAND'S, *AI & Law: Stepping Stones to a Model of Legal Reasoning,* in YALE LAW JOURNAL, Vol. 99, p. 1957, 1990, should also be mentioned here.

[21] PRAKKEN H., MUNTJEWERFF A.J. AND SOETEMAN A. (Eds.), *Legal Knowledge Based Systems the Relation with Legal Theory,* PROCEEDINGS OF THE JURIX CONFERENCE, Koninklijke Vermande, Amsterdam, 1994.

opinions of the leading scholars in the field on this crucial matter and, consequently, to update and clarify some of the views exposed here.

For publishing this book SUSSKIND'S[22] *Future of Law*, KATSH'S[23] *Law in A Digital World*, NATHANSON'S[24] *What Lawyers Do* and TISCORNIA'S,[25] *Il Diritto Nei Modelli dell' Intelligenza Artificiale* were taken into consideration. Again the criteria for choosing the specific works, referred to, in each section were their relevance to the model and their recognition of the need for a full description of the legal information system. In the case of legal theory and jurisprudence, first year text-books were used in order to show that some of the knowledge needed to build the model is a *sine qua non* qualification of a legally educated person. In the case of sociological jurisprudence only works referring to the introduction of modern technology were included.

1.1.6 The Aims of the Modelling

The first remark is that the model proposed here is an attempt to *describe* what actually happens rather than to *prescribe* a method for reaching legal decisions. In that sense it can not be claimed that this is the only model, or the most accurate or the most complete. Other researchers may perceive things differently, or examine in detail other aspects of the legal decision process. However, given the existing bibliography (see *supra*), the model proposed here seems more complete than any other produced so far. Furthermore, the basic argument of this book is not so much to use *the* specific model proposed here but to promote the idea of using *a* model representing the legal system as a whole.

The cornerstone of representing law in another form and hence also of modelling for Information Technology applications is considered to be ALLEN'S[26] famous

---

[22] SUSSKIND R., *The Future of Law*, Clarendon Press, Oxford, 1996.

[23] KATSH M. E., *Law in a Digital World*, Oxford University Press, New York, 1995.

[24] NATHANSON S., *What Lawyers Do: A Problem-Solving Approach to Legal Practice*, Sweet & Maxwell, London, 1997.

[25] TISCORNIA DANIELA, *Il Diritto Nei Modelli dell' Intelligenza Artificiale*, CLUEB, Bologna, 1996.

[26] ALLEN LAYMAN E., *Symbolic Logic: A Razor-edged Tool for Drafting and Interpreting Legal Documents*, in YALE LAW JOURNAL, Vol. 66, p. 833, 1957.

article in the late fifties. He proposes the use of symbolic logic as an intellectual tool in order to master human experience. Here, however, as explained in the *Prolegomenon,* the main aim is not only to "facilitate investigations concerning automation",[27] which is always desirable, but in particular to support theoretically the needs that emerged from the practical findings of the *Nomos-Advisor prototype.*

This perspective, of the theoretical support, could possibly coincide with a subset of the *General Theory of Artificial Intelligence and Law,* very recently proposed by WAHLGREN. Especially, it coincides with the proposed *Generality Criterion* that "contributions that are submitted to this area should be possible to relate to clearly defined research goals, accepted methods, and basic components of a general uncontroversial nature."[28] It also complies with his *Particularity Criterion* that "any theory that should be able to contribute to practical undertakings with Artificial Intelligence systems must be of a very specific kind and if the aspects of particularity are not met, *it will not be possible to develop applications reflecting any authentic characteristics of the law or legal reasoning"*.[29]

Nevertheless, the model attempted here is also trying to cover other IT applications in Law such as information retrieval, document assembly etc. Some of these applications are not following - at least for the time being - Artificial Intelligence[30] (known also as AI), but nonetheless they are interconnected with the legal decision process. In that sense the proposed modelling, although emerging from an Artificial Intelligence application (the *Nomos-Advisor* prototype legal expert system), has a wider scope than WAHLGREN'S *General Theory of Artificial*

---

[27] WAHLGREN P., *Automated Legal Reasoning: A Study on Artificial Intelligence and Law,* Kluwer, Computer/Law Series, 1992, p. 145.

[28] WAHLGREN P., *A General Theory of Artificial Intelligence and Law,* in PRAKKEN, MUNTJEWERFF & SOETEMAN (Eds.), PROCEEDINGS OF THE JURIX 94 CONFERENCE, Koninklijke Vermande, Amsterdam, 1994, p. 84.

[29] WAHLGREN P., *A General Theory of Artificial Intelligence and Law,* in PRAKKEN, MUNTJEWERFF & SOETEMAN (Eds.), PROCEEDINGS OF THE JURIX 94 CONFERENCE, Koninklijke Vermande, Amsterdam, 1994, p. 84 (emphasis added).

[30] See also the considerations of OSKAMP that "a model giving more general guidelines will make it possible to make the choices consciously. This can improve the range of applications of the system. It also offers the possibility to reuse parts of the knowledge bases. By this I mean that a careful ordering and representation of the knowledge could make it possible to use part of the knowledge base for expert systems that perform different tasks within the same domain" in OSKAMP A., *Model for Knowledge and Legal Expert Systems,* in ARTIFICIAL INTELLIGENCE AND LAW, Vol. 1, No. 4, 1993, p. 246 and also see the initial endeavours of the *Nomos* project in Chapter 3.

Intelligence and Law (see also *infra* 1.3.1 The Rule of Integration), exceeding the limits of Artificial Intelligence techniques.

Therefore, it must be emphasised that the following analysis is not exclusively an investigation of the methods of Artificial Intelligence in conjunction with Law and hence not solely a study of *legal knowledge engineering*. Under this term we must classify all the methods trying to transform part of law and legal knowledge into something 'understandable', and therefore suitable for use by computers by applying AI techniques (see also Chapter 2). In most practical cases, e.g. applied expert systems, this takes the form of a *knowledge base*, which - to state some presumed known terms (see *infra* 2.2.1) - together with the *inference engine* and the *user interface* are the three essential parts of an expert system. This procedure is often called *formalisation* and it has been at the centre of research on Artificial Intelligence and Law, where numerous investigators are trying to answer the question of *how* to formalise law and legal knowledge. That is, at least, what the majority of research projects presented during the five International Conferences on Artificial Intelligence and Law show.

These studies, however, have been limited to the AI and Law field while this chapter is not solely dedicated to these methods. Rather, it endeavours to be an inquiry into the interdisciplinary field of Information Technology Applications in Law which tries to draft theoretically a general model of the legal decision process. This corresponds to the description of BING almost twenty years ago:

> "[t]he purpose of presenting this model of the legal decision process is twofold: Firstly, it is an attempt of relating the different elements of a legal decision in a coherent and systematic manner. Secondly, *it is an attempt of constructing a frame for discussing legal information systems as part of the decision process.*"[31]

The main difference here is that such a model could potentially be used in many IT Applications in Law and not only for Information Retrieval as in the BING-HARVOLD model or solely for AI Applications in Law (for the purpose of this model see also *infra* 1.3.4 The Rule of Content). At the same time the advantage is that the model proposed here also shows the possible 'points of insertion' of these different technologies (such as AI, information retrieval, document assembly etc.).

---

[31] BING J., *A Model of Legal Information Retrieval as Part of the Decision Process*, in INFORMATICA E DIRITTO, Vol. 2, No. 3, p. 259, 1976 (emphasis added).

The following methodological rules (*infra* 1.3) define the course of argument of the generalised model. Furthermore, they elaborate the aims already exposed and they set the boundaries of this effort. It is more important, however, that they play at the same time another role: they depict the objectives which guided this study and are, therefore the justification for many of the choices made during the course of this research.

1.2   DEFINITIONS AND CONVENTIONS

Legal texts, and particularly statutes have a preamble or a preliminary part where definitions are given, especially if the legal meaning of a word is substantially different from the one used in everyday life. Therefore, among lawyers it is a habit to search for these 'definitions' in order to better understand the scope of application of the law. Thus, definitions are targeted by all researchers who want to build Information Technology Applications in Law, in order (a) to understand the scope of the proposed model and its limits in future applications and (b) to become conscious of the subtle differences - of which sometimes even lawyers are ignorant - that may be crucial when building such applications.

> **Example:**
> From the *Nomos-Advisor prototype* it emerges that we must clearly define the qualifications of the user of the application. If the user of an IT Application is legally educated then the provision of cure to legally trivial problems - for instance what constitutes mobile or immobile property - can be omitted. Otherwise the 'application' must include a much wider range of occasions in order to cover the needs of a layman. The second case leads to a considerable augmentation of the data volume (either as 'knowledge base' for AI applications or simply 'computer' data) which cannot be ignored by the analyst.

Until now the term lawyer has been used for the person who is legally educated. In the following paragraphs the terms *Lawyer, Client, Norms, Legal Reasoning, Legal Problem* and *Legal Decision* will be discussed.

1.2.1   Lawyer

One of the necessary components of a legal - or *stricto sensu* of a normative - system is the provision of cure to the *Legal Pathology* i.e. the problems caused by deviations or infringements of the substantive rules that the system imposes. This usually takes the form of methodological or procedural rules (in contrast to *substantive rules*) that permit and define such a cure. Persons entitled to *cure* or to *advise on the cure* of the aforementioned *Pathology* will be called **Lawyers,** for the purposes of this study.

> **Constant 'Lawyer':** A person entitled by the legal system to cure or to advise on the cure of the Legal Pathology.

This definition is very similar to that of BING & HARVOLD where "[L]awyer denote[s] all persons working with legal problems, regardless of their formal education or degree",[32] while WAHLGREN introduces the narrower "[c]riterion of qualification that the decisions made by the persons involved, in their normal work situation must concern legal rules".[33] In both cases, the authors try to expand the *verbatim* meaning of the word 'lawyer' in order to include as many legal professions as possible, e.g. judges, prosecutors, in-house lawyers, administrators, civil servants etc. In the same vein ZELEZNIKOW & HUNTER articulate that "therefore 'Lawyer' is not limited only to those practitioners who have formal qualifications and are practising pursuant to the various rules regulating legal practice. We use the term to include anyone who is dealing with law in its many facets."[34] and they continue by adding a taxonomy of six categories of lawyers i.e. 1.Legislative lawyers, 2.Judicial Lawyers, 3.Barristers, 4.Solicitors, 5.Academic Lawyers, and 6.Community Lawyers.

It is not necessary to diversify to that extent the tasks that lawyers perform.[35] In this particular case, another discipline could be more helpful: by borrowing the examples and the terminology from medicine (*cure* and *advise on the cure*), the lawyer's tasks may be classified under these two broad categories. The adopted definition attempts a broader coverage of the notion of a 'lawyer' for persons

---

[32] BING J. & HARVOLD T., *Legal Decisions and Information Systems*, Universitetsforlaget Oslo, 1977, p. 17.

[33] WAHLGREN P., *Automated Legal Reasoning: A Study on Artificial Intelligence and Law*, Kluwer, Computer/Law Series, 1992, p. 146.

[34] ZELEZNIKOW J. & HUNTER D., *Building Intelligent Legal Information Systems, Representation and Reasoning in Law,* Kluwer, Computer Law series, 1994, p. 13.

[35] SUSSKIND uses the same distinction (lawyer - judge) in order to identify the way (forward or backward) legal expert systems can reason through the law. SUSSKIND R., *Expert Systems in Law*, Clarendon, Oxford 1987, p. 210.

entitled to take legal decisions so as to satisfy the needs of the whole 'legal world'. Furthermore, it represents the two basic courses of argument a Lawyer performs (see *infra* 1.2.3 Norms, Legal Problem and Legal Reasoning). The clear advantage, if we accept this definition, is that the foreseen Information Technology Applications in Law, which will follow this model, will be accepted and used by a wider range of users.

Simultaneously, this definition emphasises the differences of the two main directives in the legal decision process. First, under the notion of *'persons entitled'* we must include all persons, whom the legal (normative) system authorises to act as Lawyers. This characterisation can vary from the most restricted version of an exclusive *de jure* authorisation, allowing only persons qualified - and only those qualified as such - according to the rules of the system, to act as lawyers to the expanded version of a free *de facto* recognition, i.e. anyone can decide or advise on legal issues and therefore as a Lawyer. In most modern state imposed legal systems, the rule is that only qualified persons (e.g. only those registered on the rolls of the Law Society, an Inn or Bar association, only Judges etc.), can act as Lawyers, whilst in other normative systems (e.g. within organisations) and for their internal purposes, the situation may differ, especially in the case of advice-giving.

> **Example**
> Disciplinary action in organisations (such as schools, the army or large companies) is usually taken by persons (teachers, officers, managers etc.) without legal education but qualified by the organisation to impose 'legal' decisions. In these cases advice-giving is usually left to the laymen. This assertion of course does not disqualify a layman from giving legal advice to another layman without any legal or ethical binding

Second, the notion of *'persons that cure or advise on the cure'* denotes in particular that legal decision-making persons authorised to apply justice (*to cure*) have different objectives from those who consult on the application of justice (*to advise on the cure*). The former will be called the *Judge*, playing the *Justice-giving* role of a Lawyer, and the latter will be called *Counsel*, playing the *Justice-consulting* role of a Lawyer. This is not merely a distinction of persons, as we know it, but rather represents two faces of a coin: it is the functions and attitudes that differ since the two roles may appear in the same person, as for example when a Judge (or a Justice-giving person) advises the attorneys before taking his/her decision.

The *Justice-giving* person is obliged to find a legal decision as a remedy to the legal problem, strictly guided by the rules of the system. The *Justice-consulting* person is also 'obliged', under the rules of professional ethics, to find, or in most cases to predict, a legal decision within the framework of the legal system, but *in favour* of his/her client. For example, this includes the means for acquitting the client in a criminal case, to help him/her win a civil case, or to give the 'best' legal advice for the interests of the client when he/she is obliged to undertake legal risk etc. (see also *infra* 1.3.7 The Rule of Oscillation and Legal Problem Solving). The latter case can be expanded so as to also include the case of hypothetical advice for training or teaching purposes.

Given the seriousness of the matter, the legal system sets strict criteria for the qualification of a person to the above roles, especially in the case of Judges. These criteria do not necessarily refer to any sort of a particular legal or formal education but rather to the fact of abiding by the methodological (procedural) rules of the system. It is a common practice that in many legal systems, public servants even of a lower rank (e.g. police officers, administrators etc.) are entitled to take legal decisions.

> **Constant 'Judge'**: A *Lawyer* obliged to find a legal decision abiding by the rules of the legal system in order to cure the *Legal Pathology*

> **Constant 'Counsel'**: A *Lawyer* obliged to find or predict the 'optimum' legal decision in favour of his *Client* abiding by the rules of the legal system and professional ethics

Example:
In Italy, Inland Revenue Tax Commissioners / Inspectors, are entitled to decide on the payable amount of the tax, to impose penalties, to characterise transactions etc.

It should be added that, the meaning of the above 'obligation' is that the Lawyer must not refuse to make a decision for problems brought in front of him/her.[36]

---

[36] This obligation in the case of the Judge is often described in civil law systems as the *'déni de justice'* doctrine. See also WAHLGREN P., *Automated Legal Reasoning: A Study on Artificial Intelligence and Law*, Kluwer, Computer/Law Series, 1992, p. 164.

1.2.2 Client

The Client is the person that experiences the problem and notifies it to the Lawyer. Sometimes, however, he/she may be self-motivated, either as a working hypothesis or mainly in order to deal with legal problems that arise at a later stage.

> **Example:**
> *Experiencing the problem*: A *Client* is caught tax-evading
> 1. *Self-motivated working hypothesis*: *What if* I don't pay any tax? *What if* I move my assets abroad?
> 2. *Prediction of legal problems*: How can I pay less?

It should be noted, however, that the observation of BING & HARVOLD[37] that "the initiative by the client presupposes that he is aware of the legal nature of the problem" is not quite accurate, to the extent that the (layman) Client is usually only aware of the fact that a certain problem must be dealt with by a Lawyer[38] and is not aware of its nature. It is very common in every day practice for the Client to furnish the Lawyer with personal or social problems,[39] rather than legal ones.

> **Example:**
> Someone who has problems in his/her tax payment emphasises to his/her Lawyer that he/she wants to 'pay less'. This person is only aware that he/she must contact a Lawyer to seek help. He/she knows nothing about the legal nature of the problem i.e. tax evasion, criminal offences etc. He/she usually explains to the Lawyer the problems of everyday life, recession etc.

Constant 'Client': A person presenting his/her problem to a Lawyer

Furthermore, it should be stressed that the 'client' notion should be extended in order to include the case where a legal issue is brought to the attention of a Lawyer in the form of a 'situation' rather than from a physical person, like, for example, when a prosecutor institutes a prosecution in view of an impenetrable crime.

---

[37] BING J. & HARVOLD T., *Legal Decisions and Information Systems*, Universitetsforlaget Oslo, 1977, p. 17.

[38] Of the same view is SUSSKIND, who characterises this phenomenon as the paradox of reactive legal service, SUSSKIND R., *The Future of Law*, Clarendon Press, Oxford, 1996, p. 23.

[39] For a recent insight on the professional conduct of lawyers and a characteristic example see NATHANSON S., *What Lawyers Do: A Problem - Solving Approach to Legal Practice*, Sweet & Maxwell, London, 1997, p. 55.

To this point, it should be added that one of the important qualifications of a lawyer-Counsel is to establish good communication with the client and to develop skills for successful interviews.

1.2.3   Norms, Legal Problem and Legal Reasoning

Although in jurisprudence[40]   the discussion about norms and their validity is endless, it could be deducted that norms are conditional statements, issued by an authoritative body, expressed in the form   *if p then q*. The first part of the condition is known as *antecedent (protasis)* and the second as *consequent (apodosis)*. In most legal systems the doctrine of valid sources (see *infra* 1.8.1) prescribes what can be considered as a valid norm at a certain time.

Norms: Conditional statements in the form *if p then q*

BING & HARVOLD used a pragmatic definition, claiming that a "legal problem is a problem to whose solution legal argumentation may contribute".[41] WAHLGREN, however, uses a wider criterion accepting that *"Legal Reasoning* is used as a collective label for a number of mental processes leading to a legal decision. Some of these mechanisms focus on the event that has initiated the current issue and concerns situation-identification, interpretation and fact evaluation. Other aspects of legal reasoning include law-search, and involve choices between available rules and arguments. The process also comprises a constant evaluation of possible decisions and formalisation activities."[42]

It would be realistic to base a possible definition for 'legal reasoning' on the acceptance of the use of *legal interpretation* and the *legal syllogism* (see *infra* 1.7.6 Reasoning with Rules and The Legal *Syllogism*) as the determining factor. This solution shows that a decision (or a claim) is justifiable according to the law in force. In other words, this *subsumption* of real facts to existing rules should be the

---

[40]   The discussion about norms is confined to the minimum necessary. The literature about norms is gigantic and beyond the scope of this study.

[41]   BING J. & HARVOLD T., *Legal Decisions and Information Systems*, Universitetsforlaget Oslo, 1977, p. 18.

[42]   WAHLGREN P., *Automated Legal Reasoning: A Study on Artificial Intelligence and Law*, Kluwer, Computer/Law Series, 1992, p. 146.

'hard core' of the notion of 'legal reasoning'. This 'hard core' is continuously evaluated by the legally important parameters (such as methodological rules) which are always in the mind of the Lawyer. Otherwise, even a layman can perform a law search (like an ordinary library search) or can identify and interpret legal facts without 'reasoning legally'.

> **Constant 'Legal Reasoning':** a mental process encapsulating *legal interpretation* and the *legal syllogism* in order to conclude legal decisions

From these thoughts emerges the more general definition for a legal problem:

> **Constant 'Legal Problem':** Problems that need legal reasoning as a solution

From the vast amount of bibliography concerning legal reasoning, one division is of importance to this model because it could reveal the course of argument that a lawyer is performing in order to solve a legal problem: The division between (1) legal reasoning treated as the process *to reach* the legal decision and (2) legal reasoning analysed as trying to find arguments in support or *to justify*[43] a decision.[44] Opinion is divided as to which method lawyers are following to conclude their decisions. Sometimes there is no clear distinction between the roles, which are overlaid. However, the target in all cases is to conclude a rational decision according to the legal system in use, even if the Lawyer must use interpretation to create special regulations deriving from a given piece of legislation.(See also *infra* 1.3.7 The Rule of Oscillation and Legal Problem Solving).

SUSSKIND[45] has recently expanded the notion of legal problems in order to include a managerial pre-emptive approach to dispute resolution. I believe that this can be technically covered, for this model, under the broad definition of Legal Decision

---

[43] For arguments in favour of the justification theory see ALEXY R., *Legal Expert Systems and Legal Theory*, in FIEDLER *et al.* (Eds.), Attempto Verlag, Tübingen, 1988, p. 69.

[44] See also the detailed analysis of WRÓBLEWSKI J., *Legal Expert Systems and Legal Reasoning*, in MARTINO (Ed.), North Holland, 1992, p. 382.

[45] He supports that many clients adopt a proactive rather than reactive approach for dispute resolution and instruct their lawyers accordingly. SUSSKIND R., *The Future of Law*, Clarendon Press, Oxford, 1996, p. 24.

(infra). However, I think that the professional and ethical rules of the legal professions should be a safe borderline in defining the extent of any "managerial" piece of advice.

1.2.4   Legal Decision

WAHLGREN restricts the notion of legal decision to "the result of the legal reasoning process" distinguishing, however, that "legal decisions may be, for instance visible in the way that they have a direct effect due to formal reasons (e.g. the decision of a judge closing a court proceeding, or the decision of a solicitor performing a transaction on behalf of a client). On the other hand, legal decisions may also be indirect and their effects may be hidden due to the fact that they are elements of complex situations. This is what happens in the usual counsel situation, with or without trial or connection to a dispute, and also in the legal teaching situation. The advice, the argument, or the description of the law is founded on a previous decision of the lawyer concerning the ways in which to handle the issue of the situation at hand."[46]

For the purposes of this model, the Legal Decision must be considered under the broader BING & HARVOLD[47] notion of a conclusive opinion or advice that is formulated at the end of the process rather than the typical decision of courts, bodies or persons entitled to take such decisions. Under this perspective the 'conclusive' character of the legal decision can be highlighted so as to encompass also the problem of the recursion of the process already correctly emphasised by WAHLGREN:

> It should be stressed that in many situations (e.g. during negotiations or court proceedings) legal decisions are tentatively suggested in an argumentative manner and often reformulated, e.g. when the opposing party produces obstacles in the form of new information and counter-arguments. In other words, there is a close relation between the legal decision and the legal reasoning process due to the fact that a legal decision may give rise to more

---

[46] WAHLGREN P., *Automated Legal Reasoning: A Study on Artificial Intelligence and Law*, Kluwer, Computer/Law Series, 1992, p. 147.

[47] BING J. & HARVOLD T., *Legal Decisions and Information Systems*, Universitetsforlaget Oslo, 1977, p. 15.

or less foreseeable effects, of which some may challenge and provoke the decision in such a way that a transformation is motivated.[48]

Attention should be paid, however, to the fact that even in the case of simple informal advice, before the stage of reaching a 'legal decision', the Lawyer (especially the Counsel) must take into consideration the procedural or methodological rules that are applied in order to formulate a *quasi* formal decision because in most cases these technicalities affect his overall course of argument and because he/she is trying to predict the official behaviour of a Judge.

> **Constant 'Legal Decision':** A conclusive and integrated piece of advice for the Client

Example:
If petitions to the Inland Revenues Offices are only to be written on special forms it is not worth advising the Client to call in and ask the Clerk to reduce his tax, or to simply write a complaints letter. This was also the case in the *Nomos* project where special petitions (instanzas) had to be obtained.

1.3   METHODOLOGICAL GUIDELINES

1.3.1   The Rule of Integration

The methodological limitations in defining *Information Technology Applications in Law*, outlined in the *Prolegomenon*, show only one aspect of the problem. One of the major deficiencies, however, is that the *Legal Information System* is not examined under the light of modern systems' theory, which demands the integrity of applications. Most IT Applications in Law, such as information retrieval, decision support systems, automatic drafting of legal documents etc., have been, up to now, only fragmentary efforts designed *ad hoc* to solve specific problems and have never incorporated and adapted to the whole legal decision process.[49] That

---

[48] WAHLGREN P., *Automated Legal Reasoning: A Study on Artificial Intelligence and Law*, Kluwer, Computer/Law Series, 1992, p. 147.

[49] See also MOLES R. N., *Logic Programming - An Assessment of its Potential for Artificial Intelligence Applications in Law*, in JOURNAL OF LAW AND INFORMATION SCIENCE, Vol. 2, No. 2, 1991.

might be a good start for a planned 'bottom up' methodology prepared to build integrated legal information systems, but this has not yet been achieved. The only exception, confirming the rule, is the aforementioned work by WAHLGREN, which being jurisprudential as the author confesses,[50] examines the legal reasoning process as an integrated whole.[51]

Concerning the former situation, the large gap between lawyers and technicians as well as the lawyer's traditional illiteracy in technical matters, is often put forward as an excuse. Nevertheless, the technocratic manner in which Law has been treated by the above applications, thus leading to completely erroneous results,[52] has been screened as frequently. Despite the legal profession's negative attitude to change and technological innovation, this lack of integration is one of the basic reasons that lawyers have not yet trusted modern technology as much as other professions have done. It is characteristic that the percentage of Lawyers using electronic information retrieval systems is the same as referred to by BING & HARVOLD,[53] and by LEITH[54] fourteen years later!

> **Rule 1:** The Legal Decision Process must be treated as an integrated whole seen through the eyes of a 'Lawyer'

This rule does not suggest strictly that the modelling must be carried out by legally educated persons, but introduces the rather wider idea that "the whole legal process can be understood only if we move away from the academically (and popularly) constructed perception of law being about abstract rules, and towards a fuller

---

[50] WAHLGREN P., *Automated Legal Reasoning: A Study on Artificial Intelligence and Law*, Kluwer, Computer/Law Series, 1992 p. 21.

[51] See, however, GREENLEAF G., MOWBRAY A. & TYREE A., *The DataLex Legal Workstation, Integrating Tools for Lawyers*, PROCEEDINGS OF THE 3RD INTERNATIONAL CONFERENCE ON ARTIFICIAL INTELLIGENCE AND LAW, Oxford, June 25-28 1991, ACM Press, 1991, p. 215, where a workstation combines expert systems, hypertext and free text retrieval into one tool.

[52] WAHLGREN speaks about "...various misconceptions of the nature of law..." and quotes LEITH P., *Legal Expert Systems, Misunderstanding the Legal Process*, in COMPUTERS AND LAW 49(1986) where severe criticism about these applications can be found. WAHLGREN P., *Automated Legal Reasoning: A Study on Artificial Intelligence and Law*, Kluwer, Computer/Law Series, 1992 p. 30.

[53] BING J. & HARVOLD T., *Legal Decisions and Information Systems*, Universitetsforlaget Oslo, 1977.

[54] LEITH P., *The Computerised Lawyer, A Guide to the Use of Computers in the Legal Profession*, Springer-Verlag, London 1991. See especially chapters 5 through 9.

understanding of what goes on in the real world of the barrister"[55] and I shall add: *of the Lawyer*. To be more specific, the integration described here must be defined from the point of view of the active legal practitioner.

Example:
This rule was used during the knowledge engineering phase of the *Nomos-Advisor* prototype in order to identify some of the missing parts of the knowledge base and mainly to clarify the misconceptions of linguists.

1.3.2   The Rule of the Legal System

A fortiori, these phenomena occurred in the case of AI and Law, which demands stronger technical skills. SUSSKIND discovered that half of the 19 major AI & Law projects (before 1987) had no reference at all to jurisprudence and only two referred explicitly to jurisprudence as a source.[56] Similarly WAHLGREN concludes that:

Most apparent in the field of AI and Law is perhaps that the submitted contributions - with a few exceptions - are *remarkably technically oriented*. The studies in various detailed aspects of legal knowledge representation and the elaboration of various logical systems have often been major objects of concern.

At the same time comparatively little attention is given to studies on the *jurisprudential aspects* and the practical consequences of automation. Assumptions about the nature of legal reasoning are in many cases implied or completely tacit.[57] (Italics added)

In many of these applications a jurisprudential analysis was not only missing, but law was examined outside the context of the whole legal system and was treated as if it were a guinea-pig. Furthermore, it was not confessed that this was another scientific experiment, but in most cases it was claimed that systems built in such a

---

[55] MORISON J. & LEITH P., *The Barrister's World and the Nature of Law*, Open University Press, Milton Keynes - Philadelphia, 1992, p. 19.

[56] See SUSSKIND R., *Expert Systems in Law*, Clarendon, Oxford 1987, appendix I. This fact is also emphasised by WAHLGREN P., *Automated Legal Reasoning: A Study on Artificial Intelligence and Law*, Kluwer, Computer/Law Series, 1992. p. 24.

[57] WAHLGREN P., *Automated Legal Reasoning: A Study on Artificial Intelligence and Law*, Kluwer, Computer/Law Series, 1992, p. 141.

way could actually give legal advice and thus could produce legal implications.[58] It is contended that without an analysis of jurisprudence, all these projects fall solely in the domain of computer science and *not at all* in the legal domain.[59]

It is well known that every Legal System has its own philosophical and methodological basis that determines its principles, purposes and functions. For the purposes of this model, SUSSKIND'S comment for the specific case of Legal Expert Systems that

> "[i]t is beyond argument, however, *that all expert systems must conform to some jurisprudential theory because all expert systems in law necessarily make assumptions about the nature of law and legal reasoning.* To be more specific, all expert systems must embody a theory of structure and individuation of laws, a theory of legal norms, a theory of descriptive legal science, a theory of legal reasoning, a theory of logic and the law, and a theory of legal systems, as well as elements of a semantic theory, a sociology and a psychology of law (theories that must all themselves rest on more basic philosophical foundations). If this is so , it would seem prudent that the general theory of law implicit in expert systems should be explicitly articulated... "[60]

should be paraphrased to: *all information technology applications in law must conform to some jurisprudential theory*.

To achieve the same target, on a theoretical level, WAHLGREN[61] insists "[t]hat system development and system implementation in the field of law must be often adjusted to certain frameworks, of which some may be visible only to those who are legally trained". The same idea has been expressed earlier by BING & HARVOLD who emphasise the 'rule of law' as a justification for improvement in

---

[58] See *infra* Chapter 2, 2.4.3 and MOLES R. N, *Logic Programming - An Assessment of its Potential for Artificial Intelligence Applications in Law*, in JOURNAL OF LAW AND INFORMATION SCIENCE, Vol. 2, No. 2, 1991.

[59] Authors are still not certain about the qualities of differnet domains and they tend to parallel law to other disciplines (e.g. engineering, medicine etc.) for the purposes of developing models of problem solving. See for example VALENTE A., *Legal Knowledge Engineering, A Modelling Approach*, IOS Press, Amsterdam, 1995, pp. 27-29.

[60] SUSSKIND R., *Expert Systems in Law*, Clarendon, Oxford 1987, p. 20 (emphasis added).

[61] WAHLGREN P., *Automated Legal Reasoning: A Study on Artificial Intelligence and Law*, Kluwer, Computer/Law Series, 1992, p. 30.

legal information systems"[62] and later by BING insisting that "[w]e realise that in working with the problems of designing legal expert systems we have returned to basics: We are working with the problems formerly seen as belonging to the philosophy of law or the theory of norms. But these problems have now ceased to be academic, they have become vital to the design of computerised decision and expert systems...".[63]

It is beyond argument that a jurisprudential theory, be it 'positivism', 'realism', 'Marxism', 'the rule of law', 'the idea of a social or universal justice' or any other theory must consolidate the basis of each Legal Information System. Under this hypothesis only *lawyers*, in the sense of people having legal training, are well suited for this task. Otherwise the result would be technically correct, in terms of Information Technology, but legally unacceptable. It must be emphasised here that this does not refer to the known difference between 'pragmatists' and 'purists'[64] i.e. to the old question whether we must build a working practical system (pragmatists) or a theoretical model (purists), but only to the *internal consistency* between a Legal System and a supporting Legal Information System.

Furthermore, legal methodology logically precedes any other investigation, because it determines the method of applying law. Therefore, *Information Technology Applications in Law* must also be based on a particular legal methodology and it is unacceptable to encourage the use of the methodology of other disciplines for legal applications. *We must never forget that IT is a means designed to help the users and not a goal in itself.*

To summarise, the next methodological rule of the model under question is that, if we decide to investigate and improve the Legal Information System by using modern technology, that must be done by means of a legally, not a technically, oriented analysis.[65] Furthermore, the repercussions from the surrounding social,

---

[62] BING J. & HARVOLD T., *Legal Decisions and Information Systems*, Universitetsforlaget Oslo, 1977, p. 227.

[63] BING in SEIPEL (Ed.), *From Data Protection to Knowledge Machines*, Kluwer, Deventer, 1990, p. 250.

[64] See SUSSKIND, *Pragmatism and Purism in AI and Law,* in AI & SOCIETY, Vol. 3, p. 28, 1989.

[65] See SUSSKIND R., *Expert Systems in Law*, Clarendon, Oxford 1987, p. 23 and WAHLGREN P. , *Automated Legal Reasoning: A Study on Artificial Intelligence and Law*, Kluwer, Computer/Law Series, 1992, p. 28.

political and economical environment should never be neglected. Two of the purposes of this analysis are (a) to show - and represent in the model - that any Legal Information System, applied to the actual legal decision process, must be unbreakably attached to a certain legal theory, and (b) to put legal reasoning outside a closed symbolic system since norms can only be interpreted as part of a legal system.[66] Consequently, all IT (including AI) applications to the Law, considered within the context of such a system, must remain consistent with that theory.

> **Rule 2:** Any Information Technology Application in Law is part of a legal system and must abide by the jurisprudential theory that supports it.

> **Rule 3:** Any Information Technology Application in Law must abide by the substantive, procedural and methodological rules of the legal system

Example:
These rules were used in the *Nomos-Advisor* prototype in order to identify the parts of law that should be included by using hypertext as well as to determine the general reasoning attitude of the expert system.

It should be noted that compliance with Rule 3, may prove cumbersome in view of the introduction of Information Technology in the legal field. Because it is not hard to generally abide by the procedural and methodological rules, but it is very laborious to change and adapt those rules to the requirements of Information Technology (an over simplistic example: to amend all legislation requiring written forms to electronic ones). Therefore, the transformation envisaged to take place in legal practice[67] may not simply be a matter of change of business strategy or personal attitudes but an immense enterprise involving institutional changes in the whole legal system.

---

[66] BING J. & HARVOLD T., *Legal Decisions and Information Systems*, Universitetsforlaget Oslo, 1977, p. 31.

[67] See SUSSKIND R., *The Future of Law*, Clarendon Press, Oxford, 1996, p. 3.

1.3.3   The Rule of Practicality

The basic thesis of this model is even more ambitious and enthusiastic than the *pragmatist* one.[68] Information Technology must be used in Law in order to produce applications with practical effects. This does not rule out the use of theory or theoretical models, used to create the founding in interdisciplinary research, but as was emphasised in the *Prolegomenon*, Information Technology in penetrating the Legal world has to overcome many barriers. Among others, IT must appear convincing to a profession, notorious for its reluctance to change, such as lawyers. Moreover, it is believed that the theoretical discussion cannot be of any help to that point. Only accurately designed practical applications, and not the 'randomly made' blueprints that terrify lawyers with their irrational results, can prepare the path for the full introduction of modern IT techniques into the old-fashioned legal office and can facilitate the everyday practice of the legal profession.

BING & HARVOLD, as early as 1977, argued that

> "[J]ustifying the change in technology, one might argue that the new information system is more efficient - making legal research less time-consuming and consequently cheaper in the long run. This is obviously not the main motivation behind the creation of better information systems. We have several times pointed out that the new technology represents a basic change influencing the research habits of lawyers. Comparing the state of research before and after the introduction of the new technology, one will find a difference in *quality*. A different type of research is conducted; the lawyers do not confine themselves to doing what they were doing before the change; they do more or something else. These changes in the quality of legal research may not adequately be translated into quantitative terms (time or money). And it is precisely these changes in *quality* that they are very often pointed out as *the chief justification for introducing the new technology*.[69] (emphasis added)

This was clearly reflected in the *Nomos* project (see *infra* Chapter 3). While the initial goal of the project was to confront the *quantity* of EEC legislation and cases, the target of the *ad hoc* application concerning the application of the VAT law was

---

[68] See the views about *Pragmatism* in SUSSKIND R. *Pragmatism and Purism in AI and Legal Reasoning*, in AI & SOCIETY, Vol. 3, p. 28, 1989.

[69] BING J. & HARVOLD T., *Legal Decisions and Information Systems*, Universitetsforlaget Oslo, 1977, p. 225.

the improvement of the *quality* of the decisions made by public servants at an otherwise very busy (in terms of *quantity*) department of the Italian Ministry of Finance.

Quality improvement should be the main purpose of Information Technology, acting, I shall repeat, as a means to help other disciplines. The use of IT should not be a goal in itself. To be more specific, in the case of Legal Information Systems, it should be remembered that the target is not to develop 'perfect' systems from a computer science point of view. It is expected that this gain in quality is only helpful as far to achieve the main goal i.e. to improve – I think dramatically - the legal system itself.

Therefore, it must be stressed that the proposed model tries to represent the legal decision-making process as a whole, i.e. from the birth of the legal problem to the achievement of a practical legal decision (see *Figure 1-9* page 118). To avoid the risk of misunderstandings, this does not refer to the *stricto sensu* legal reasoning process, i.e. the *legal syllogism* in its classical form (of (1) major premiss (sentence), (2) minor premiss (sentence), (3) subsumption and (4) conclusion), which, nevertheless is included in that process (see *infra* 1.7.6).

The reason for this approach is, in the first place, to find the possible and feasible points of insertion of IT - and more specifically AI - applications within the legal decision process, and specify some of the essential characteristics of these types of applications. However, the innermost desire, which sets out this methodological guideline, is to use the model in order to build applications that could be of practical use. Besides, many of the conclusions exposed in these theoretical considerations were derived from the practical implementation of the *Nomos-Advisor* prototype. From these thoughts emerges the next methodological rule:

> **Rule 4: The model of the Legal Decision Process will be used for practical applications**

Example:
The intended purpose of the *Nomos-Advisor* prototype was to be able to answer legal questions at front-end Internal Revenues offices in Italy.

This rule depicts the possibility of IT applications to produce practically exploitable results, i.e. legal consultations that have meaning and are logically consistent, and it does not in any case restrict the use of the application to practitioners only.

1.3.4   The Rule of Content

Among the *cognoscenti* of the AI and Law field, it is beyond question that the vast majority[70] of the papers and the scientific debate deal mainly with the possible means of *formalising* the Law or, in a more strict sense, with the norms. In other words, most of the research is trying to answer the question of *how to represent* the Law in a computer oriented method (*formalisation*) and little attention has been given to the question of *what to represent* (see also *infra* 2.4.1)

The reason for this does not lie in the naive hypothesis that if we know *how* to represent something (Law in our case) then it is easy to represent *whatever* we like, but mainly in the lack of jurisprudential analysis, as exposed in 1.3.2 (The Rule of the Legal System). Otherwise, if jurisprudence was the basic source, it would have been obvious that the first parameter to determine would be *what* to represent.

From this issue emerges the next methodological guideline of the modelling that will be attempted here: The proposed model of the Legal Decision Process is mainly dedicated to the description of *what* must be represented in an Information Technology Application in Law. This is somewhat similar to the intentions of BING & HARVOLD, in that their model is not a description of a psychological process but merely "[i]t is a description in principle of the different elements of a decision process, as they may be sorted out after a decision has been made".[71]

Similarly, it has been asserted that "[o]ur general conclusion is that research in the field of artificial intelligence should start from models of human knowledge and human knowledge processing not from the knowledge representation and processing formalisms that are available".[72] In that sense, this model does not wish to develop a new legal theory or methodology, nor wishes to change, modify or evaluate any of the existing legal theories or methodologies. It does not even claim for itself the title of a methodology for building IT Applications in Law, because the enumeration of the elements of the Legal Decision Making Process, is neither

---

[70] See for example the Proceedings of the five AI & Law Conferences.

[71] BING J. & HARVOLD T., *Legal Decisions and Information Systems*, Universitetsforlaget Oslo, 1977, p. 16.

[72] DE VEY MESTDAGH in KRACHT D. - DE VEY MESTDAGH C.N.J - SVENSSON J.S. (Eds.), *Legal Knowledge Based Systems: An Overview of Criteria for Validation and Practical Use*, Koninklijke Vermande BV, Lelystad, 1990, p. 103.

exhaustive nor exclusive, and in that sense stays open to all possible enhancements and improvements.

The sketch merely encapsulates what shall be called the *'minimum requirements configuration'* for building IT Applications in Law. Therefore, the model described here must be considered, at the first glance, only as a checklist. This 'checklist' can (a) depict a compact picture of the full course of the Legal Decision Process, (b) provide a clearer view of the methodological rules affecting the process (c) sketch the intervention of the surrounding environment (d) play the role of a handy 'memory' tool, especially to non-Lawyers, in order to avoid the omission of important elements of the process.

> **Rule 5: Determine *what* to represent**

These estimations were evaluated during the empirical investigation of the *Nomos-Advisor* prototype (see Chapter 3) where such lists have been used by the research team in order to determine the parts of law that should be included for representation. This 'checklist' methodology has helped the project's team and may also help future researchers. As explained, the character of the model is *descriptive*, depicting an actual situation. It may, however, be endeavoured, at a second level, to expand this initial sketch to a full scale methodology. Such methodology could guide the building of the aforementioned applications but it is should not in any case attempt to prescribe a formalised method for reaching legal decisions.

1.3.5   The Rule of Checklist

During the course of building this model many computer oriented techniques will be used: The model itself resembles a flowchart, the enumerated 'steps' might be taken for program instruction lines and the 'functions' look like program routines. The use of the above techniques, which could even support the extreme position of characterising this model as: *The Legal Decision Process as a checklist for Information Technology Applications In Law* was followed consciously under the concept of the previously mentioned 'checklist'. BING & HARVOLD are very close to this position by arguing for their information retrieval model by saying that "[t]hese elements [of the decision process] will be represented by intuitive leaps of the mind, and it may consequently seem somewhat non-realistic to attempt to portray them in a model. Also, the model grossly understates the interaction between the different elements when a problem is being worked out in the mind. The content of any element may not be determined until the decision is made - only then is a balance established which makes it possible to analyse the decision. But - for the representational reasons - the process will be described as a sequential process with one beginning and one end."[73]

Rule 6: Use the results of rule 5 as a checklist

The choice, however, to represent the model proposed here as a sequential process, does not necessarily entail that this 'modelling' is just a traditional flowchart having a 'Start' and an 'End'. WAHLGREN states that "[T]he law affects all parts of society and a legal system must be able to cope with problems occurring in all sectors of human activity. It is, therefore, obvious that legal problem solving must be based to some extent on principles of a *general nature*".[74] That leads to the examination of the next methodological rule concerning legal problem solving.

1.3.6 The Rule of Rule-Based Deduction

The previously referred to task of *internal consistency* entails that the model must be able to adopt as many legal theories[75] as possible. Many arguments can be put for and against different legal theories, predominantly between the main two: *positivism* and *realism*. The legal background for building this model was the positivist one: It is believed that law is a set of imposed rules, that rules define the legal reasoning process and that legal reasoning is attached to a deductive process i.e. a process in which predetermined premises are used to derive conclusions. MACCORMICK emphasises that:

> "Whoever would deny that strictly deductive reasoning is a genuine and important element in legal justification...must show that there is some alternative theory which can equally well account for rules about the burden

---

[73] BING J. & HARVOLD T., *Legal Decisions and Information Systems*, Universitetsforlaget Oslo, 1977, p. 16.

[74] WAHLGREN P., *Automated Legal Reasoning: A Study on Artificial Intelligence and Law*, Kluwer, Computer/Law Series, 1992, p. 31 (italics added).

[75] For a classification of the different projetcs in the AI & Law Conferences see VALENTE A., *Legal Knowledge Engineering, A Modelling Approach*, IOS Press, Amsterdam, 1995, p. 9.

of proof and related matters...It is not contended that such reasoning is all that is involved in legal justification..."[76]

SUSSKIND articulates that "it seems undeniable that the distinguishing characteristic of the overwhelming majority of the systems [referring to those expert systems existing in 1987] is their dependence on deductive inference procedures. In consequence, all those objections to deductive legal reasoning that pervade the jurisprudential literature seem to be germane to legal knowledge utilisation".[77] And to justify exactly the same issue WAHLGREN states that

> "a rule-based *description* of legal reasoning does not say anything about the outmost nature of the process. In other words, the analysis of legal reasoning that is outlined here is not intended to address the question as to whether or not the process will be eventually and in its ultimate meaning turn out to be rule-based. The objective of this exploration is to develop a jurisprudentially sound model of legal reasoning that may facilitate investigations concerning automation. The reason why a rule-based approach is preferred is thereby merely the fact that rules provide a feasible (easily understandable and traditionally well established) way to describe how lawyers (and people in common) appear to reason."[78]

And, finally, ALCHOURRÓN & BULYGIN postulate that "[l]egal reasoning, which purports to show that a decision (or claim) is justifiable according to the law in force, is essentially deductive in character or at least can be reconstructed as a logical inference, in which on the basis of two kinds of premises, normative and factual, a conclusion is reached which states that certain legal consequences are applicable to a particular case. This inference shows that a decision to apply those consequences to this particular case is legally justifiable."[79]

It must be confessed, however, that following the positivist approach is not a sign of approval of the said theory but rather emerges from the need to comply with the already exposed practicality considerations. The model presented here is closer to the one described by FIEDLER:

---

[76] MACCORMICK N., *Legal Reasoning and Legal Theory*, Clarendon Press, Oxford, 1978, p. 52.

[77] SUSSKIND R., *Expert Systems in Law*, Clarendon, Oxford 1987, p. 25, see also pp. 163-203.

[78] WAHLGREN P., *Automated Legal Reasoning: A Study on Artificial Intelligence and Law*, Kluwer, Computer/Law Series, 1992, p. 145.

[79] ALCHOURRÓN C. & BULYGIN E., *Limits of Logic and Legal Reasoning*, in MARTINO (Ed.), 1992, p. 9.

"in contradiction to a merely "deductive" conception, legal decision-making here is conceived essentially as a process of modelling, a process of constructing conceptual models of a specific structure. This specific structure, of course, incorporates deduction: *the model to be constructed deductively connects sets of facts and legal rules as premisses to the legal decisions as the conclusion*...[t]he difference form the merely deductive conception mentioned above is that the modelling conception of legal decision-making incorporates the mutual adaptation and reshaping of facts and rules and stresses the tentative, and in part heuristic, character of the drafting process."[80]

Four clarifications are needed here:

First, we must distinguish between the rule approach referring to the legal system as a set of rules and to rule-based representations of law upon which the above explanation of WAHLGREN is based (see more in 2.2.2 Knowledge Representation).

Second, the notion of 'deduction' has a wider meaning and should not be confused with 'monotonic' logical deduction, where a conclusion that has been justified cannot be overturned by the addition of new information. ALCHOURRÓN & BULYGIN emphasise on this point that "[t]his does not mean that a decision can actually be deduced from the premisses; *deciding is an act of will and as such is not determined by logic*".[81]

Third, this methodological rule does not entail the denial of Case-Based-Reasoning (CBR) i.e. reasoning by the example of previous cases. Simply, for the practical aspirations of this model it is assumed that even in the latter case of CBR, the decisions can be used as material from which to deduce rules.[82]

---

[80] FIEDLER H., *Expert Systems as a Tool for Drafting Legal Decisions*, in MARTINO & SOCCI-NATALI (Eds.), North Holland 1986, p. 608 (emphasis added) the same author later proposes "the change of the leading paradigm of judicial decision making from deduction to modelling" in FIEDLER H., *Legal Expert Systems and the General Theory of Law*, in FIEDLER et al. (Eds.), Attempto Verlag, Tübingen, 1988, p. 13.

[81] ALCHOURRÓN C. & BULYGIN E., *Limits of Logic and Legal Reasoning*, in MARTINO (Ed.), 1992, p. 9 (emphasis added).

[82] For a characteristic example involving various methods for reaching a legal decision see SMITH J.C & GELBART D., *Legal Reasoning, Legal Theory and Artificial Intelligence*, in THE PROCEEDINGS OF THE INTERNATIONAL CONFERENCE ON COMPUTERS AND LAW, RESEARCH, DEVELOPMENT AND EDUCATION, Association Quebecoise pour Le Development de L'Informatique Juridique, Montreal, 1992, Vol. C2.2, p. 1-11.

Fourth, on the important question whether this deduction is used to reach or to justify legal decisions the model will try to include both aspects as expressing the two aspects of a coin.

> **Rule 7:** Follow rule-based deduction to reach or justify legal decisions

Example:
This rule was used in the *Nomos-Advisor* prototype in order to identify the connection of the Conceptual Graphs representation to expert systems production rules and the points where human intervention was needed.

Moreover, this rule should not lead to the naive hypothesis that just the inclusion of rules in an information system can produce legally correct results. As early as 1987 GREENLEAF *et al.* have argued that applications, adopting the strict rule-based methodology of sciences, were erroneous because "most other domains which have been the subject of expert systems are largely concerned with the causal relationships between physical processes and objects. The rules in such a domain are intended to model the physical process, even though the modelling might not necessarily be at the level of fundamental mechanisms. It is the formulation of these rules...which is the exercise of expertise."[83]

In this model, intuitive positivist ideas acquired during legal education and professional experience could be put forward as excuses for choosing the same approach, that is the acceptance of a rule-based legal system as opposed to rule scepticism.[84] However, as in all parts of this study, the moderate views followed entail that the acceptance of the set of rules axiom should not lead to the other extreme that law is just mechanical rule application. In support, SUSSKIND concludes that "for every conclusion drawn, and, consequently, during every consultation with an expert system, there must ultimately be some human

---

[83] GREENLEAF G., MOWBRAY A., TYREE A., *Expert Systems in Law: The Datalex Project*, in PROCEEDINGS OF THE FIRST INTERNATIONAL CONFERENCE ON ARTIFICIAL INTELLIGENCE AND LAW, Boston, 1987, p. 10.

[84] Rule scepticism is one of the streams of the American Legal Realism school of thought, which is based on the philosophical theory of pragmatism. The latter defends that epistemological and ethical judgements are subjective and cannot be verified as true or false. According to the realists legal rules are not the major determining factor in reaching a judicial decision, but are mere rationalisations of a decision reached for other reasons. Realists support that the judge first reaches a tentative conclusion and then tries to find a premiss in the form of a legal rule or rules which will justify the conclusion. The father of realism is Oliver Wendell Holmes and one of the most known rule sceptics is Jerome Frank.

judgement".[85] Apart from these human interventions, feedback from the social environment is also affecting the process. (see also *infra* 1.4.2 The Input: Socially Related Facts).

1.3.7 The Rule of Oscillation and Legal Problem Solving

Having agreed the previous rule and for practical purposes, it is necessary to examine the direction towards which the rule-based deduction will move. The problem of curing legal pathology is often transposed as a problem of defining legal reasoning. The question of the nature of legal reasoning, about which much has been written, leads, in turn, to the old question of how to define the nature of law. On this specific point SMITH has argued that

> "[m]edical, dental and engineering schools would generally not offer courses on the nature of medicine, dentistry or engineering because the practice of these professions seldom raises the kind of foundational questions which drives one back to basic theory about the discipline. Such issues, however, often arise in the legal practice, consequently, these are exactly the kind of question a course in jurisprudence asks about law. *In law there is no consensus about what law is, nor about the true nature of legal reasoning,* but it is nevertheless needed if legal rationality is to be self-conscious. Furthermore, lawyers have no body of scientific knowledge which lies at the core of their discipline...[r]ather law rests upon sets of fundamental values about which there is a great deal of societal dissensus"[86]

The obvious conclusion is that legal problem solving, without denying its character as a rational activity, does not resemble other 'problem solving' techniques both in its goals and methods. First, the target is neither stable nor clear, as for example, in medicine where the ultimate goal is, according to the Hippocratic oath, to cure the patient and save lives, or in mathematics where one has to prove the theorem. In sciences, generally, one is trying to find the truth while law is trying to solve social conflicts.

---

[85] SUSSKIND R., *Expert Systems in Law*, Clarendon, Oxford 1987, p. 203.

[86] SMITH J.C., *The Application of Expert Systems Technology to Case-Based Law*, in PROCEEDINGS OF THE FIRST INTERNATIONAL CONFERENCE ON ARTIFICIAL INTELLIGENCE AND LAW, Boston, 1987, p. 84.

In Law, the task of the **Judge** (or any *justice-giving* person) is to use executable legal decisions having binding force or any other means by which the legal system arms him in order to cure the legal pathology.[87] On the other hand, the task of the **Counsel** (or any *justice-consulting* person) is to predict this behaviour and to defend, according to the profession's ethics, the interests of the client. This is, interestingly, depicted by BERMAN & HAFNER[88] as 'indeterminacy', i.e. the ability to justify both sides of a legal question, using accepted legal principles to reach mutually inconsistent results and this holds true even in cases where there is agreement on the facts and the applicable rules of law. That is to explain that the typical layman's view that the Judge wants to convict the accused, while the Counsel wants to acquit him is not the rule and in modern legal practice many extreme situations have seen the light of publicity.

Example:
Many times, according to the guidelines of the Counsel, the defendant Client pleads guilty to a charge in a court of a lesser degree in order to avoid the cumbersome and expensive procedure in a higher rank court which may also lead to a worse decision for him. Or, in a divorce case the Client wants to get as much as possible of the common properties but to pay as little as possible maintenance cost etc.

MORISON AND LEITH submit two extreme examples: First, the one of 'Goliath chasing David' when "a large business organisation may, for commercial or competitive reasons, wish to pursue a smaller rival through all stages of courts regardless of the objective merits of the particular case. With insurance companies, there may be pressures of various sorts depending on the institutional goals and policies of the moment."[89] Second, the effort to work on a particular aspect of the law in order to alter it.[90]

---

[87] See, however, the different opinion of WAHLGREN, that his model could also be adapted to other domains. He suggests that medical or psychological diagnosis, presents similarities with legal reasoning, at least as far as it concerns the 'matching' of previous cases. WAHLGREN P. , *Automated Legal Reasoning: A Study on Artificial Intelligence and Law*, Kluwer, Computer/Law Series, 1992, p. 389.

[88] BERMAN D. & HAFNER C., *Indeterminacy: A Challenge to Logic-based models of Legal Reasoning*, in YEARBOOK OF LAW COMPUTERS & TECHNOLOGY, Vol. 3, 1987, p. 3.

[89] MORISON J. & LEITH P., *The Barrister's World and the Nature of Law*, Open University Press, Milton Keynes - Philadelphia, 1992, p. 73.

[90] MORISON J. & LEITH P., *The Barrister's World and the Nature of Law*, Open University Press, Milton Keynes - Philadelphia, 1992, p. 74, referring also to the example of claims in Northern Ireland against the Department of Environment and other bodies, for injuries caused by tripping

Nevertheless, the hypotheses that legal problem solving resembles purely a strategy or risk management techniques are not widely accepted, and the above examples were used to show how diversified the opposing arguments in a legal case can be. It is true that Lawyers take strategic or risk management decisions[91] (see also *supra* the 'pleading guilty' example) but the grounds of their *legal* decisions are based on those small 'portions' of legal reasoning, which this model is trying to capture. Curing the legal pathology is mainly based on the provisions and the methods that the legal system imposes for such a cure and, therefore, it is thereby affected. The following oversimplified example will show how the same facts could produce different results.

> **Example:**
> In a particular legal system a Law imposes VAT on certain transactions. Given the complexity of modern life the Statute by the time of its enforcement was not able to predict all possible transactions and therefore it includes a classification procedure: Employees above a certain rank (Judges) at Internal Revenue Offices are entitled by the system to take decisions and to characterise unclassified cases brought to them by citizens (Clients), as *subject* or *not subject* to tax. Let us now examine the results that may occur under different factual situations.
>
> **Fact:** A poor and homeless citizen **C** performs a certain transaction **T** (not included in the text of the Law) and wants to know if it is subject to tax. The results can be seen in *Table 1- 2*

This example does not try to enter the complexity (see *infra* 1.7) of legal - or specifically teleological - interpretation but attempts to emphasise that in legal problem solving, or, otherwise, for the cure of the Legal Pathology, factors other than the facts of the case in question affect the course of argumentation, and that, consequently, identical facts may lead to different legal decisions.

---

over paving stones that have been inadequately maintained. Barristers involved in this work were encouraged to look out for individual cases that could be used to develop the law in a way that restricted liability.

[91] See also the views of SUSSKIND that risk management and similar assessments will predominate legal practice, as we know it. I think that, although this vision presents realistic aspects, it is mainly influenced by the example of big law firms dealing with big corporations and it ignores small scale practices. More importantly it does not analyse aspects of Criminal Law – which the present model tries to cover - where negotiation and risk management is not always possible. SUSSKIND R., *The Future of Law*, Clarendon Press, Oxford, 1996.

Second, Law differs[92] in the method followed to solve the problem. Unlike the sciences (see *infra* note 86) where axioms through forward chaining (a term borrowed from AI) are used to prove theorems, in Law 'input facts' can be used in many ways and deductive reasoning, although accepted previously as a rule, can not always provide a solution.

	Initial Presumption of the Legal System	Methodology used by the Judge	Result
Case 1	In favour of taxation	Bound to reach a 'Just'[93] decision	T subject to tax
Case 2	In favour of taxation	Bound to reach a 'Just & Fair' decision	T not subject to tax
Case 3	In favour of taxation	Free to decide	Unpredictable
Case 4	Against taxation	Bound to reach a Just decision	T not subject to tax
Case 5	Against taxation	Bound to reach a 'Just & Fair' decision	T not subject to tax
Case 6	Against taxation	Free to decide	Unpredictable

Table 1- 2 : The same facts can produce different legal results

This entails that the basic hypothesis of this model is based on a rule-application deductive approach. Nevertheless, the model also tries to encapsulate elements of teleological interpretation, approaching the completely opposite theory of legal realism, and stays open to neighbouring disciplines like systems theory and the sociology of law. That is the main reason for accepting 'input' - which affects the 'process' - from the surrounding social phenomena, but again this does not translate into choosing arguments at random, which represents the other extreme.

Example:
This notion was used in the *Nomos-Advisor* prototype in order to introduce

---

92 See also the example about the indeterminacy of the "canons" of interpretation of ALEXY that "a rule such as "Interpret every norm so that it can achieve its purpose" leads to divergent outcomes when each of two interpreters has a different view as to the purpose of the norm in question." ALEXY R., *A Theory of Legal Argumentation, The Theory of Rational Discourse as Theory of Legal Justification, (English Translation),* Clarendon press, Oxford, 1989.

93 This distinction is used for the purposes of this simplified example. *Just* meaning the decision that transparently applies published laws and *Fair* the one that modifies these rules for the individual case taking into account other factors such as social repercussions (in our case the fact that C is poor and homeless). It is out of the scope of this research to examine the case where the Judge is not obliged to take a decision.

sources other than the statute i.e. in the example of the poor citizen having to pay tax, the Goliath chasing David case etc.

The issue refers to the debate (see for example the known differences between HART[94] and DWORKIN[95] on the freedom that the legal system appoints to the Judge, especially in the case of gaps) between positivists and realists, on whether legal reasoning is only deductive reasoning applying rules or justificatory discretion. This issue has been thoroughly examined by legal philosophers and is essential for the overall structure of a legal system. In order to justify the bridging of the gap WAHLGREN asserts that:

> "Wasserstrom deserves, however, to be recognised for having provided a major theoretical break through by introducing a model of legal reasoning based on a dichotomy. In the model, two phases in the legal decision making were recognised: a *process of discovery* and a *process of justification*, leaving room for both activities connected to rule application (in the process of justification) and for considerations of evaluation and individual factors in each case (in the process of discovery). Wasserstrom provided in this way a theoretical foundation where arguments of deductive and non-deductive reasoning did not need be in conflict with each other. In consequence, it may be alleged that the debate on whether or not legal reasoning is rule-guided has lost much of its importance."[96]

The aim of this study is to show not only the static nature of legal reasoning but also its dynamic aspect i.e. the course of argumentation.[97] Towards that direction ENGISCH[98] successfully introduced the notion of an interplay[99] between facts and

---

[94] According to HART, in a case of "open texture", the Judge is free to decide anything, his/her decision is not determined by the law but by his convictions and his views in political morality. HART H.L.A., *The Concept of Law*, Clarendon Oxford, 1961 and HART H.L.A., *Positivism and the Separation of Law and Morals*, in HARVARD LAW REVIEW, Vol. 71, 1958.

[95] According to DWORKIN the Judge is not free to decide but he/she is bound by the 'principles' of a legal system which can always lead to the right answer to a legal problem. DWORKIN RONALD, *A Matter of Principle*, Clarendon Press, Oxford, 1986 and DWORKIN RONALD, *Taking Rights Seriously*, 1977 (6th impression) Duckworth & Co., London, 1991.

[96] WAHLGREN P., *Automated Legal Reasoning: A Study on Artificial Intelligence and Law*, Kluwer, Computer/Law Series, 1992, p. 65.

[97] See, however the considerations of SUSSKIND concerning *backward* and *foreword* chaining, for a possible expert systems methodology. SUSSKIND R., *Expert Systems in Law*, Clarendon, Oxford 1987, p. 213.

[98] ENGISCH K., Einführung in das juristische Denken (Introduction to Legal Thinking), p. 252, Greek Translation, Athens, 1981. The English version of the maxim is taken from the English translation

norms. "[T]he judge", he says, "is making a retrogressive movement of his eyes back and forth, between the facts of the real life and the norms". This idea of an oscillation, either in the older form of a pendulum or of a modern electronic oscillator, both seeking the point of equilibrium, will also dominate the model described here. Therefore, although the arrows (see *Figure 1-9* in page 118) might deceive the viewer, the whole process is not a linear one-way course from 'facts' to 'decision', nor do there exist standard points of 'departure' and 'arrival'.[100] This metaphor also embodies the use of input beyond deductive reasoning and leaves the model free of dogmatic references.[101]

> **Rule 8: Oscillate between law (legal rules) and real facts in order to reach a decision**

1.4   THE INPUT OF THE PROCESS

Historically, the first legal retrieval system is considered to be John F. Horty's Information Retrieval System designed for the health statutes of Pennsylvania around 1956. The systems that followed in the legal field,[102] were technically oriented to the big mainframe computers of the era. In most cases they were applications of text databases. Their 'model', trying to represent a trivial legal information system, was affected by the known 'flowcharted' scheme of a traditional information system (*Figure 1- 1*).

---

of ALEXY R., *Theorie der juristischen Argumentation* (A Theory of Legal Argumentation), Oxford University Press, 1989.

[99] See also ALEXY R., *Theorie der juristischen Argumentation* (A Theory of Legal Argumentation), Oxford University Press, 1989, p. 228.

[100] See also BING J. & HARVOLD T., *Legal Decisions and Information Systems*, Universitetsforlaget Oslo, 1977, p. 16 stating that their model "will be described as a sequential process for representational reasons".

[101] See also WARNER arguing that "[t]his conventional articulation of the problem solving process ignores the need for parallel problem solving...the design of a useful Law Machine must take the parallel nature of legal reasoning into account" in WARNER D. R. JR., *Toward a Simple Law Machine*, in JURIMETRICS JOURNAL, Vol. 29, p. 451, Summer, 1989.

[102] For a historical review see WAHLGREN P., *Automated Legal Reasoning: A Study on Artificial Intelligence and Law*, Kluwer, Computer/Law Series, 1992, p. 123 and BING J., *Handbook of Legal Information Retrieval*, North Holland, Amsterdam, 1984.

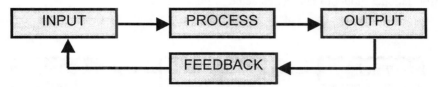

Figure 1- 1: A Typical Information System

To be more specific, if we follow a systemic approach adopting roughly the idea of a 'closed' system, i.e. a relatively autonomous system that is not accepting input from sources other than those specified, we can briefly explain the above terms: *'Input'* being in this case the insertion of data into an information system, *'process'* being the arithmetical and/or logical calculations that the system is capable of performing and *'output'* being the results that this process could produce. A *'feedback'* function is also provided to show the recursive capability of the system, i.e. the ability to re-elaborate already obtained results.

It is obvious that this model has been generated by system analysts who have a strong IT background. Nevertheless, the above scheme has also constituted the basis of many of the automation systems targeting the legal office of the eighties. As WAHLGREN puts it: "although the input-output devices and the storage techniques have changed, the underlying principles of most I[nformation] R[etrieval] systems are basically the same today as they were thirty years ago. The I[nformation] R[etrieval] technique has been also successful in many fields outside the legal domain."[103]

Existing models suffer fundamental defects in adopting the traditional path of 'legal problem solving', but nevertheless they want the Lawyer to be presented primarily with either a *'situation'*[104] or with *'facts'*,[105] which he is obliged to elaborate

---

[103] WAHLGREN P., *Automated Legal Reasoning: A Study on Artificial Intelligence and Law*, Kluwer, Computer/Law Series, 1992, p. 122.

[104] WAHLGREN P., *Automated Legal Reasoning: A Study on Artificial Intelligence and Law*, Kluwer, Computer/Law Series, 1992, p. 153.

[105] BING J. & HARVOLD T., *Legal Decisions and Information Systems*, Universitetsforlaget Oslo, 1977.

towards a certain result. Therefore, it would be better to transform the above informational model to the one depicted in *Figure 1- 2*:

Figure 1- 2: A Typical Legal Information System

At that time (mid-seventies), Information Retrieval was the only available form of electronic elaboration of the Law, and this scheme has served for many years especially within this function of the Legal Information System. It is depicted schematically in *Figure 1- 3*.

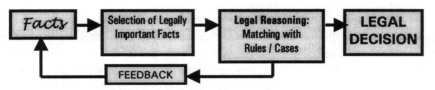

Figure 1- 3: A Legal Information Retrieval System

The most important element of the above scheme is that legal reasoning takes the form of *conceptual matching* with Rules/Cases, including the interim legal decision that a rule/case is relevant/important to the problem in question. This is normal, given that the ultimate goal is to *retrieve* legal material (rules and/or cases) in order to support legal reasoning, to 'find and interpret' the law and hence to conclude the legal decision. It is worth mentioning here that pursuing the opposite route (from the 'decision' to the 'matching') could also fit in the same scheme if we follow the (mainly Realists') view that Lawyers are only looking for supportive material for an already pre-decided legal decision.

Tradition is essential to legal practice and this simple model has traditionally helped lawyers understand modern technology for many years. It was, therefore, decided that it would constitute the core of this model, not out of necessity but out of the true hope to facilitate the introduction of IT into the legal world. It will be shown, however, that this simple model must be enhanced because it does not take into consideration several parameters that crucially affect the legal decision process.

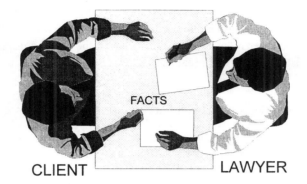

Figure 1- 4
The exchange of facts between a Client and a Lawyer is a human contact

1.4.1   The Input: Human Behaviour

Figure 1-4 is emphatically used to illustrate the most important characteristic of the Client to Lawyer relation: in fact this is a human interaction[106] affected by human behaviour. In the jargon it is often 'customer' driven and it is initiated from the user's starting point which is usually a query involving a human activity. To be more precise, in scientific terms this does not constitute a pure exchange of information between two isolated information systems, but clearly the exchange of ideas between two human beings. Therefore all the usual problems occurring in human communication (bias, misunderstandings, self-motivations etc.) are more than obvious in this situation, where the client usually feels depressed by the legal problem in question.

SUSSKIND underlines that "clients come to their lawyers with their perceived legal problems and the lawyer then reacts to them. There are two known difficulties with this approach: first, by the time the client perceives a problem it may well be too late; and second, it is unlikely, in any event, that clients will be able to perceive all

---

[106] UK residents might recall the advertising sign of Legal Aid.

63

their legal problems"[107] while LAURITSEN from a different perspective emphasises that "[the lawyer] must operate in a world of 'noisy' information: information that is often approximate, incomplete, inaccurate, inconsistent, and uncertain. Some of these factual deficiencies flow from the client, who may be forgetful, misinformed, reluctant to disclose information out of pride or embarrassment, or plain dishonest."[108] The other relevant fact at this stage is the specific usage of language as well as the distinction between real and legal facts, by the client.

1.4.2   The Input: Socially Related Facts

The non-legally oriented analysis usually treats the 'Input Facts' as the 'Input Data' in a traditional information system. It is worth repeating that jurisprudence, as a social science, enjoins that the legal phenomenon is indeed a *social phenomenon* and must be treated as such.

LEITH emphasises that "we cannot look at the rule in isolation - we can only see its existence within a social context since it depends upon its interpretation for the context in which it is to be applied"[109] and WAHLGREN similarly argues:

> [T]he types of arguments that may be employed for the justification of a
> legal decision are domain-bound and that the factors which are relevant in
> this aspect of legal reasoning are to a large extent the reflections of the *moral*
> and the *ethical* standards of the *social environment surrounding* the legal
> system[110] (Italics added)

Law, therefore cannot be considered outside that surrounding social, economical and political framework and in our model none of the elements can function outside

---

[107] SUSSKIND R., *Introduction*, in ESSAYS ON LAW AND AI, COMPLEX 7/93, NRCCL, Oslo, 1993, p. 5.

[108] LAURITSEN M., *Knowledge-Based Approaches to Government Benefits Analysis*, PROCEEDINGS OF THE 3RD INTERNATIONAL CONFERENCE ON ARTIFICIAL INTELLIGENCE AND LAW, Oxford, June 25-28 1991, ACM Press, 1991, p. 98.

[109] LEITH P., *Fundamental Errors in Legal Logic Programming*, in THE COMPUTER JOURNAL, Vol. 29, No. 6, 1986, p. 547.

[110] BING J. & HARVOLD T., *Legal Decisions and Information Systems*, Universitetsforlaget Oslo, 1977, p. 230.

a certain social economical and political context.[111] This environment mirrors the dominant philosophical theories, and, consequently, the dominant legal philosophy and methodology that map out the legal interpretation and reasoning. Yet, in the case of 'input facts' the social environment determines their character in two dimensions: (a) as far as the input source (the 'client' as described by BING & HARVOLD) is preoccupied by his background and, therefore, this bias is reflected in the 'facts' while he exposes them to the Lawyer and (b) *vice-versa* the Lawyer's background, and especially his/her knowledge of the legal system affects the interpretation of the 'input facts', biases his/her opinion and furthermore, together with external information from the social environment, continuously guides his reasoning process.

Example:
In case (a) consider the same input 'real' facts supporting the same taxation case: A 'client' wants to pay less tax and this is being presented to the Lawyer by (1) the organised accountancy department of a big corporation producing analytical tables, reports, correspondence etc., and by (2) an average citizen who only wants to pay less producing only the taxman's receipt. The differences in all aspects, i.e. the way of presentation, the data accuracy, the focussing on the legally important details etc. between (1) and (2) are more than obvious.

In case (b) LEITH[112] in the known (David – Goliath) example wants the Lawyer to advise his client, although all procedural and substantive rules are in his favour, not to sue a multi-national for a minor difference. All that has been decided before entering any legal process and just because of that *extra-legal* knowledge of social reality.

The legal phenomenon is adapted to an 'open textured' world in order to cover all the possible aspects of social life (see also Figure 1-5). Therefore, the characterisation of the 'input facts' as 'data' must be reconsidered: Mathematical models are not able to represent a social phenomenon in all its extent. The primary stage of a Legal Information System and the primary step to solve a legal problem, i.e. 'input facts', must be analysed within the social, economical and political framework of both the Client and the Lawyer. Still, even in this case, such an

---

[111] See a similar approach in VALENTE A., *Legal Knowledge Engineering, A Modelling Approach*, IOS Press, Amsterdam, 1995, p. 49.

[112] In LEITH'S words "the Lawyer will not advice a client who cannot get legal aid to sue ICI, say though he might advice ICI to sue the client, whatever the 'rule' of law might say" LEITH P., *Legal Expert Systems: Misunderstanding the Legal Process*, in COMPUTERS & LAW, No. 49, September 1986, p. 30.

analysis does not entitle us to a 'general legal problem mechanism',[113] and many elements of the model used for the purposes of this study stay 'open' towards this framework.

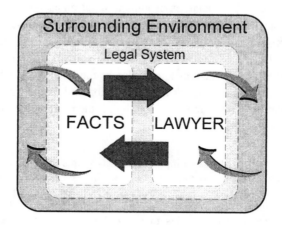

Figure 1- 5
The procedure that initiates the Legal Decision Process is affected by the surrounding environment

The same set of facts can be used, depending on their degree of evidence, to prove an uncertain result, in the case of the criminal Lawyer - that is the person taking legal decisions in criminal cases - who evaluates forensic evidence in order to bring charges against a suspect. They may be used to support an already decided result, in the case of the Lawyer who argues in favour of his client, or a judge who wants to justify his decision. Or, finally, the same facts can be used to support two conflicting opinions, in the case of the two parties in civil litigation.

Input 1: Socially Related facts

Finally, this 'openness' permits the use of broader criteria than the given set of rules which otherwise could be criticised as inflexible and restrictive.

---

[113] WAHLGREN P., *Automated Legal Reasoning: A Study on Artificial Intelligence and Law*, Kluwer, Computer/Law Series, 1992, p. 237.

1.4.3   The Input: Real Facts and Legal Facts

BING & HARVOLD set the scene for the starting point of the model:

> The case - as described by the proven facts - is the lawyer's starting point
> ... To us it is important to stress that our model takes the *facts* of the case,
> rather than the legal *norms* as the point of departure. He [the lawyer] has
> used his legal background knowledge in order to extract the proven facts
> from the totality of the problem. Also he may already have used feedback
> information from later elements in our model of the decision process. But
> generally speaking we may say that *up to this point substantive law has not
> entered into the process.*[114](emphasis added)

It is, therefore, the Lawyer's task to distinguish from the whole set of facts that the
Client will produce, those that are *Legal Facts* from those that are *Real Facts*. He
must then determine those that are really important for the case in question.[115]
With the exception of routine cases (see *infra* 1.6.5 The First Decision and the
Question of 'Easy Cases'), lawyers usually classify the facts in hand during a pre-
processing stage that, due to legal education, is intuitive to all average
practitioners. The same occurs for the selection of the specific branch of law
involved in the case. It is at this time that the legal problem - together with the
decision *whether* such a problem *exists* - is born in the mind of a lawyer. This
reduction of the external world *stimuli* to a set of (legal or real) facts which are
important for the actual legal problem, presupposes right at this early stage that the
user of a Legal Information System must be a Lawyer or at least someone having a
minimum legal background.[116]

This is justified by the fact that the effort to cure the legal pathology is
administered by procedural rules, which, respectively, are based on the
fundamental law (constitution) of each legal system. Therefore, the Lawyer and *a
fortiori* the Judge are not free to examine the real facts, as for example an historian
would examine his sources. Instead, various procedural rules propose the degree

---

[114] BING J. & HARVOLD T., *Legal Decisions and Information Systems*, Universitetsforlaget Oslo,
1977, p. 20.

[115] WAHLGREN P., *Automated Legal Reasoning: A Study on Artificial Intelligence and Law*, Kluwer,
Computer/Law Series, 1992, p. 153 calls this phase *identification*.

[116] See *infra* Chapter 2 on how to use expert systems in 2.4.5.

(to what depth) and the character (obligatory or not) of the examination of the real facts. (See *infra* 1.6.1 The Search for Relevant and Sufficient Facts*)*.

Input 2: Mixed Real and Legal 'Biased' Facts

Example:
This notion was used in designing the user interface of the *Nomos-Advisor* system, and especially to restrict the options of the user while he/she was trying to input questions to the systems. This was achieved through structured menus and pop-up windows.

1.4.4   The Input: Language Dependent Facts

The metaphor of 'Information Flow' is widely used to depict the transfer of information within an informational system, and many methods have been proposed in order to measure, direct, enhance, reduce and generally control this 'flow'. One of the early researchers in the area of IT Applications in Law, RONALD STAMPER,[117] after confessing that he was "the unwitting prisoner of these metaphors...", over-rules his original positions[118] and outlines the dangers of treating information within a Legal Information System as if it were empirical factual data:

> The whole information system, as opposed to the electronic signalling system is based upon the human cultural system. By suppressing awareness of the cultural system, the impression is given that information exists, as a kind of abstract substance, independently of human beings and their social systems
>
> [T]he facts or data are treated as a kind of 'raw' material that the computer can turn into distilled 'information'. It is even normal practice (in computerese) to use the word 'data' in the singular to suggest that 'it' is a substance processed by the computer.[119]

He proposes that instead of using the mis-conceived classic model that encapsulates the 'illusion' of information flow:

Input ➔ Process ➔ Output

---

[117] STAMPER R., *Expert Systems, Lawyers Beware*, in NAGEL (Ed.)

[118] See all his writings in the seventies and eighties.

[119] STAMPER R., *Expert Systems, Lawyers Beware*, in NAGEL (Ed.), p. 24.

it would be better to use a more transparent model in which "Nothing flows but there is a cause-and-effect chain linking one lot of signs to another. Nothing is actually carried by the signs, they only have significance in the context of the social groups of the people who interpret them:

Signs ➔ Encode ➔ Process ➔ Decode ➔ Signs

Interpreter ....➔ (common culture) ...... ➔ Interpreter"[120]

Paraphrasing STAMPER'S argument it can be submitted that Lawyers do not need plumbing skills such as filtering or distilling the 'mystic fluid' of Information. The misconception of 'information flow' has to be abandoned: Every piece of information is subject to the critical eye of the Lawyer - interpreter and acquires significant value only after the decoding process. This notion parallels the linguistic theories where the 'true meaning' is what the members of a community which share a common culture agree as such, given there exists free communication, on equal terms between them.[121] Besides, it is accepted that facts are essentially language-dependent; without sentences there could be no facts.[122] In this case, the legal community is entitled to decode and interpret the meaning of words, or otherwise characterise the meaning of the above mentioned signs. (See also *infra* 1.7 Interpretation)

Input 3: Language Dependent Facts

Again, we should be careful with this concept of the identification of the 'true meaning' and the characterisation of signs. If this characterisation is seen as the main task to be performed when building Information Technology Applications in Laws, it is likely that as a result other elements of the process will be neglected. This, for example, happened in the *Nomos* project (see *infra* Chapter 3) where the linguistic analysis was quite elaborate but other parts of the process, of equal or greater importance, were omitted.

---

[120] STAMPER R., *Expert Systems, Lawyers Beware*, in NAGEL (Ed.), p. 25.

[121] See WITTGENSTEIN'S later theory *infra* note 153 and 1.7.1 Decoding the Meaning of Words and Legal Linguistics.

[122] See ALEXY referring to the theory of truth of HABERMAS in ALEXY R., *A Theory of Legal Argumentation, The Theory of Rational Discourse as Theory of Legal Justification, (English Translation)*, Clarendon press, Oxford, 1989, p. 103.

1.5   INITIATING LEGAL THOUGHTS

Since the early descriptions of the seventies, researchers in the area of Information Systems and AI as well as in Cognitive Science have been trying to identify *what is in a Lawyer's mind* when confronting a legal problem, in other words after the above mentioned input has entered the Lawyer's sphere of thought. However, controversy surrounds whether these efforts were also focussing on an understanding of the true way Lawyers work, and, consequently, on the true nature of law, or rather constitute a reprint of already perceived (and therefore biased) views. In one (of the few) empirical research about the profession of Barristers in the UK, MORISON AND LEITH[123] support the latter argument. They emphasise the widely held, but erroneous, belief that law concerns the close analysis of texts (a view held by many AI researchers, including the *Nomos* project team), they argue that law has more to do with persuasion, rhetoric and negotiation and they provide a new prospect of what lawyers actually do.

The latter argument, especially in the sense of perceiving a more realistic view of the law, is significant for the purposes of our model; first, because following the rule of practicality (*supra* 1.3.3) we must identify exactly what Lawyers do and, second, because the (even biased) perceptions and the everyday practice of the legal profession affect legal reasoning.

In the opinion of a senior counsel, quoted by MORISON AND LEITH: "...almost certainly most cases, are really argued about the facts because everybody knows the law, the law is fairly obvious... a running down case, a factory case there is not much law about... It is in a minority of cases therefore where the law counts in the sense that there are two views of the law... There are three situations I suppose: one - there is no argument about the law, it is only about the facts two - there is law but it is fairly clear, where do these facts fit in the legal framework? The third and much less frequent one is what is the law? Cases where the law is generally uncertain are more interesting, intellectually more satisfying. Broadly speaking, a QC is used where there is a point of law or where *a lot of money* is involved... For

---

[123] MORISON J. & LEITH P., *The Barrister's World and the Nature of Law*, Open University Press, Milton Keynes - Philadelphia, 1992.

example I spent 7 or 8 hours this weekend on one particular aspect of a case I'm doing next week." [124]

In the same vein, the argument could be extended to the whole notion of a 'Lawyer', pointing out that nowadays in many cases the work of a 'Lawyer' is just a mechanical reproduction of known procedures. This is not, however, a philosophical position, for which a more detailed analysis will follow in the next chapter, but, rather, a remark from the practical point of view, in order to define the pre-process stage of legal decision making. [125]

1.6   THE PRE-PROCESS

In the light of the above thoughts, it can be seen that when a lawyer is confronted with facts which constitute a legal problem he/she elaborates them in an intuitive pre-process. The intuitive character of this pre-process is owed, together with other parts of the legal reasoning process, to legal education. The important part of this pre-process is the first decision whether a given set of real facts constitutes a legal problem 'worth' not only entering the legal reasoning process but generally occupying the Lawyer's time.

This first decision on the nature of the legal problem does not concern legal philosophy but deals with the economics [126] of the case and the tasks of everyday professional legal practice. Questions about the complexity and the cost/benefit analysis of the case must be answered now, otherwise valuable time could be lost. It may be wrongly perceived that this is the rule for *Counsels* but experience shows that many *Judges* are also guided by thoughts such as their daily workload, their special experience in a given case etc.

---

[124] MORISON J. & LEITH P., *The Barrister's World and the Nature of Law*, Open University Press, Milton Keynes - Philadelphia, 1992, p. 46 (emphasis added).

[125] It is interesting to see the effort of ALEXY to 'decompose' the process of legal justification into a number of 'steps' in ALEXY R., *A Theory of Legal Argumentation, The Theory of Rational Discourse as Theory of Legal Justification, (English Translation)*, Clarendon press, Oxford, 1989, p. 228.

[126] See the early description of HOLLANDER A. & MACKAAY E., *Are Judges Economists at Heart?*, in CIAMPI (Ed.), North Holland 1982 and the recent views about risk management and pre-emption of SUSSKIND R., *The Future of Law*, Clarendon Press, Oxford, 1996.

It should be mentioned that, in most cases, this pre-process does not involve any consultation of legal or other information sources but is rather an elaboration of knowledge already possessed by the lawyer. This emphasises the importance of the general knowledge background and skills that a Lawyer acquires. It is obvious that at this pre-process stage much depends on his/her ability to memorise certain parts of the law and, consequently, a large part of legal education is dedicated to this goal.

The said pre-process takes place almost automatically, but for practical reasons the course in a Lawyer's mind, after the initial input of the real facts will be examined in a step by step manner. At the same time, the examined steps (1.6.1 to 1.6.5) are considered to be the minimum necessary elements of this pre-process.

1.6.1   The Search for Relevant and Sufficient Facts

This is a recurrent process, which could have the character - in IT terms - of a subroutine. BING realistically describes that "[t]he initial extraction of relevant facts or circumstances is *tentative*. The lawyer has available, as a latent resource, the full bag of details comprising the problem as part of the world, with all its parties, witnesses and documents. At any time, the lawyer may refer back to this wealth of details, sift through them once more for extracting new facts to replace or supplement those made available in the first selection."[127] The Lawyer is obliged - sometimes by Law - to make an exhaustive inquiry into all the relevant facts of the legal problem in question. He / She must be skilled enough to disregard unnecessary information. Furthermore, it may be the case that the Lawyer will need to go back and obtain more facts, even in the middle of the process, in order to complete inadequate information. Especially, **Judges** must clearly be convinced of the real facts that took place or concern a legal problem, otherwise they are not able to grant justice.

> **Example:**
> If a Judge does not know whether a caravan is permanently attached to the ground he/she is not able to choose the relevant legal rule and consequently to decide that the said property is mobile or immobile and hence its owner liable to different kind of taxation. At other times he/she may have a clear

---

[127] BING in SEIPEL (Ed.), *From Data Protection to Knowledge Machines*, Kluwer, Deventer, 1990, p. 228.

picture of the real situation (that e.g. the caravan is not attached) but he/she may not be convinced that the owner tells the truth about ownership.

[Pre-Process]: Step 1: Reduce the Input Facts to those Relevant and Sufficient for the Legal Problem

This is, however, guaranteed in most legal systems by imposing strict procedural rules, usually based on the fundamental law (constitution) of the system. As explained before, the Lawyer and *a fortiori* the Judge are not free to examine the real facts. Under a formal procedure (civil, criminal or administrative), various procedural rules propose the degree (to what depth) and the character (obligatory or not, permitted or not) of the examination of the real facts.

Example:
In a civil law legal system like the Greek or the German, the Judge is *free* to decide about the truth of the real facts in a criminal case, while he is *bound* by the facts that the parties produce and prove (*onus probandi*) in a civil case. Sometimes he/she cannot search for more facts due to procedural rules e.g. because a witness is a relative to the parties or the accused, or in 'delicate' cases where more important human rights prevail (for example in cases of rape etc.)

Notwithstanding the case of the Judge being obliged to search for these facts, there exists, however, a real possibility that the Lawyer must play at this stage the role of a confessor in order to extract all the facts from the Client. WAHLGREN characteristically refers that "components of the description may be disputed and mutually exclusive or inconsistent facts appear. This is, for example an ordinary situation for a judge listening to opposing parties in trials. Likewise, the concepts used in situational descriptions may be vague."[128] This situation could reach an extreme when the client, is may not be producing all the facts or is misleading the Lawyer, falsely expecting a better result. Therefore, as mentioned before, not only the bias and misunderstandings of human contact, but also human behaviour itself affect this stage.

Example:
A Client is ashamed to confess that he/she was drunk when driving, or he/she tells lies because he/she wrongly believes that the punishment will be severe, while the case from the legal point of view is much simpler.

---

[128] WAHLGREN P., *Automated Legal Reasoning: A Study on Artificial Intelligence and Law*, Kluwer, Computer/Law Series, 1992, p. 154.

This extreme example, however, does not entail the use of purely sociological methods in order to find and apply the law[129] but emphasises the variety of facts that the Lawyers must take into account, as well as the importance of the depth of his/her search.

For reasons of complete coverage, it could also be mentioned that, due to existing rules, the examination of some facts may be prohibited, especially in the case of personal information, data protection issues etc.

1.6.2 Disqualifying Facts

Parallel to the above search, the Lawyer is thoroughly looking for disqualifying facts, i.e. legally related facts that immediately solve the problem or rule out the use of the legal reasoning process. WAHLGREN characterises this strategy of "finding one disqualifying fact that excludes whole situations, or eliminates a large number of possibilities" as "the most effective method in initial identification phases."[130] It is here that experienced Lawyers show their skills and that most of the *rules of thumb* and *heuristics* find appropriate ground. For the substantive issues this takes effect while formulating the legal problem, but in most cases the question of the economics of the case prevails. Therefore, apart from the substantive issues and at the same time, the Lawyer is obliged to examine a huge bulk of procedural and administrative disqualifying rules. The extent of this obligation can vary according to the legal methodology used: sometimes it is imposed by law, at other times by professional ethics and at others it is left to the discretion of the person handling the problem.

> **[Pre-Process]: Step 2: Check if the Input Facts trigger Substantive, Procedural or Administrative Disqualifying Rules**

Example:
In the *Nomos-Advisor* prototype, under the Italian VAT law regime, if a

---

[129] see also the considerations of WAHLGREN about infringing the principle of predictability, WAHLGREN P., *Automated Legal Reasoning: A Study on Artificial Intelligence and Law*, Kluwer, Computer/Law Series, 1992, p. 67.

[130] WAHLGREN P., *Automated Legal Reasoning: A Study on Artificial Intelligence and Law*, Kluwer, Computer/Law Series, 1992, p. 161.

transaction had taken place in certain areas of Italy, it was immediately a disqualifying fact for taxation purposes.

Examining formal procedural rules[131] before entering the substantive issues is a good policy, since in many cases this disqualifies the further investigation of a case. It can be noted here that it is a common practice for courts to insist on disqualifying procedural rules in order to avoid entering the full legal process. Sometimes a 'Counsel' does the same (within professional ethics) in order to win a case already lost in the substantive issues.

1.6.3 The Selection of the Branch of Law and of the Course of Argument

The last important question in the mind of the Lawyer, during this pre-process, is where in the Legal Framework these facts fit. This is important because it is the first stage during which the huge volume of law and legal knowledge, at least as this is perceived by the Client, is reduced by the Lawyer to specific branches and hence sources of Law; here it is decided which major cases and statutes are involved and which are the implications:

Example:
An average practitioner knows almost immediately whether the violation of certain tax legislation implies criminal offences, or whether in a car crash in a civil law country both criminal and administrative (for the Traffic Code violation) as well civil (for the remedies) laws are involved.

WAHLGREN tries to combine this step of the pre-process with the previous ones by arguing that "[f]rom a broader perspective the initial activities within legal reasoning may be seen as a search process following two lines. The lawyer must try to form a general description of the case which includes a search for relevant facts. At the same time he must search for a legal proposition that will enable him to form a legal rule that is applicable in a given case, i.e. a rule that contains a description of a similar situation. The objective of the process is to be able to

---

[131] For an interesting approach to annex procedural rules into a model of legal reasoning see BERMAN D. & HAFNER C., *Incorporating Procedural Context into a Model of Case-Based Legal Reasoning*, in PROCEEDINGS OF THE 3RD INTERNATIONAL CONFERENCE ON ARTIFICIAL INTELLIGENCE AND LAW, Oxford, 25-28 June 1991, ACM Press, 1991, p. 12.

subsume the specific situation under a general description of a situation in the legal-system."[132]

It can be argued, however, that for most Lawyers this is an automatic intuitive procedure. Especially in the case of Judges, strict procedural or courts administration rules narrow the field of application and, mostly, their 'input' are cases concerning a specific branch of Law. Nowadays, Counsels are highly specialised so they are commissioned to practice on certain types of cases, and therefore, on certain branches of Law. Even 'General Practitioners', as in the case of high street solicitors in the UK, that deal with a wide spectrum of cases, are capable of performing successfully this initial characterisation. Further considerations and more complex legal peculiarities that will arise are to be resolved later.

Of particular interest is the observation that the Lawyer and especially the Judge must have an extended view of the totality of legal rules and cases that affect the legal problem. BING emphasises that "[t]he lawyer may lack a detailed understanding of the relevant legal rules, but he or she probably will have some *general* understanding of that area of law. And even if that is lacking the lawyer has a general understanding of what types of facts or circumstances the law recognises".[133]

In civil law systems, dominated by the positivist approach, the Lawyer tries to submit the facts of a real life case to a general and abstract legal rule. In common law systems, he/she tries to identify the similarities of a real life case to a case already decided. Although the basic units of these systems differ (rules v. cases), in both cases the Lawyer must have a general view of the legal sources which he/she is immediately scanning in order to reduce them to a subset relevant to the legal problem in question. In view of this, WAHLGREN asserts successfully that

> "despite different legal traditions the *functions* of the legal systems are to a large extent similar. That is to say that, although on the surface exist huge differences in the way the legal order is perceived and described, an important function of the legal order in both positivism and realism is to

---

132 WAHLGREN P., *Automated Legal Reasoning: A Study on Artificial Intelligence and Law*, Kluwer, Computer/Law Series, 1992, p. 150.

133 BING in SEIPEL (Ed.), *From Data Protection to Knowledge Machines*, Kluwer, Deventer, 1990, p. 228.

provide effective fact recognition and fact classification assistance in legal reasoning. In addition, there is little doubt that initial legal identification is possible due to the fact that legal classification schemata of a general nature are reflected to a large extent in the background knowledge of lawyers."[134]

This choice (and the choice of a course of argumentation) within a legal system, can explain why the control of hyperregulation envisaged by SUSSKIND[135] is not an easy task. For, selecting information in the area of legal problem solving is not simply a matter of distinguishing the relevant from the irrelevant from the huge amount of sources, but a more complicated process involving little steps of legal reasoning leading to those initial judgements.

This initial judgement is not final, nor it is absolutely correct. It may be the case that the search for further real facts, or the false understanding of the facts, will result in involving more or other branches of law, so that the final subset of legal sources will be different. But still, the important fact here is that in the vast majority of legal problems the scene has already been set: The lawyer knows that it definitely concerns a criminal case, a civil case, a tax case, a divorce maintenance case, etc.

The same considerations apply to the course of argument that the Counsel will take in favour of his/her client (see *supra* 1.3.7 The Rule of Oscillation and Legal Problem Solving) or that the Judge will follow in order to grant justice. No matter how complicated this course is, its basic lines are decided here, as well as, in the case of Lawyers, the final goal that will satisfy the 'client'.

> **Example:**
> In the previously mentioned divorce case the Lawyer is immediately aware of the necessary steps to be taken in order to get the best result in favour of his/her Client i.e. to obtain more of the common properties (if any) and to pay less maintenance.

[Pre-Process]: Step 3: Select the Branch(es) of Law Involved and the Course of Argument

---

[134] WAHLGREN P., *Automated Legal Reasoning: A Study on Artificial Intelligence and Law*, Kluwer, Computer/Law Series, 1992, p. 160.

[135] SUSSKIND R., *The Future of Law*, Clarendon Press, Oxford, 1996, p. 98.

1.6.4   The Effect of Background Knowledge

This term will define all the *extra-legal* political, social, economical[136] or other knowledge that affects this first decision of the Lawyer. With big City firms charging around £200 per hour and high street practitioners around £100 (in the UK) and with similar prices elsewhere, the economical aspect[137] of a case always comes first. The next barrier considered is also economical as judicial costs are high and the process time consuming which is similar for every authoritative justice-giving body.

SUSSKIND insists that "lawyers will be retained not just to crystallise in legal terminology a deal already agreed on by the parties but *as advisers on all aspects of legal risk management*"[138] and recently he has elaborated this idea, speculating a full scale change of the legal paradigm toward strategy and risk management.[139] Earlier, but, in the same vein, ZELEZNIKOW & HUNTER have introduced (for Australia and England) the 'costs indemnity rule':

> "This rule provides *a very strong disincentive to initiating baseless litigation*. Thus, unless one has a very strong case, a potential plaintiff will be advised to drop any threatened litigation, since upon losing the case, he or she will be up for both sets of legal costs. Therefore within the system only hard cases are ever likely to be appealed."[140]

Notwithstanding any objections for the above views, in pragmatic terms, cases 'not worth' their money at the initial phase will not pass the threshold of a Lawyer, and if they do, they have little chance to proceed further. This has, of course, raised issues of social policy and social justice. Discussions about Legal Aid in the UK are very polarised and the same situation exists for similar schemes in other countries. After all, this is clearly a problem of the justice-giving function of

---

[136] HOLLANDER A. & MACKAAY E., *Are Judges Economists at Heart?*, in CIAMPI (Ed.), North Holland 1982.

[137] See also NAGEL S., *Legal Ethics and Decision-Aiding Software*, in MARTINO (Ed.), 1992, with analytical tables of the Client and Lawyer profits for various hours worked in a US environment.

[138] SUSSKIND R., *Introduction*, in ESSAYS ON LAW AND AI, COMPLEX 7/93, NRCCL, Oslo, 1993, p. 5 (bold added).

[139] SUSSKIND R., *The Future of Law*, Clarendon Press, Oxford, 1996.

[140] ZELEZNIKOW J. & HUNTER D., *Building Intelligent Legal Information Systems, Representation and Reasoning in Law*, Kluwer, Computer Law series, 1994, p. 57 (emphasis added).

modern societies and justice itself, but this is the cynical reality. Legal problems falling outside these considerations and given the lack of time of practitioners, will only be examined by academics or be given as an exercise to law students.

If the economical aspect is the strongest filter for examining a legal problem, other factors play a role as well. The administration of justice is one of them, its bad organisation forcing Judges to issue 'fast' decisions when they have a bulk of cases to handle etc. Social knowledge is another (see *supra* 1.3.7 the example of the poor and homeless citizen).

The overall education and culture of the Lawyer has been proposed as another factor. MORISON AND LEITH have empirically found, for the case of Barristers, in the UK, that "If an advocate regularly operates in a particular area he or she will develop the sorts of skill, personal relationships and initial knowledge that make it a difficult or even perverse choice for a solicitor to choose someone from outside." They furthermore emphasise the effect of specialisation, by adding that "although most barristers aim to litigate on both sides - to appear for the plaintiff as well as the respondent in civil matters and to prosecute as well as defend in the criminal courts - this sometimes becomes difficult in view of the type of service that solicitors require"[141] For practitioners, in general, even inside information from the rumours in the Law Courts has been brought to our attention, concerning the opinion Lawyers have about the certain Judges handle certain cases etc.[142]

In all these cases the conclusion is that, law being an open system, all the possible parameters affecting a legal problem must be considered. Especially, it is crucial to feed such parameters into the practical Information Technology applications that are being proposed here.

---

[141] MORISON J. & LEITH P., *The Barrister's World and the Nature of Law*, Open University Press, Milton Keynes - Philadelphia, 1992, p. 60.

[142] See also LEITH P., *The Computerised Lawyer, A Guide to the Use of Computers in the Legal Profession*, Springer-Verlag, London 1991. p. 221 and OSKAMP stating the following example "published law says A, but the expert knows that one specific judge in 9 out of 10 cases says B in such circumstances" OSKAMP A., *Model for Knowledge and Legal Expert Systems*, in ARTIFICIAL INTELLIGENCE AND LAW, Vol. 1, No. 4, 1993, p. 250 see also the extreme example for manipulating a decision in SCHILD U. J., *Open-Textured Law, Expert Systems and Logic Programming*, unpublished Ph.D. Thesis, University of London, 1989, p. 133, where in trials that the judge was appointed according to the initials of the parties some parties have changed their names in order to avoid a certain judge.

[Pre-Process]: Step 4:Consider carefully the Background Pragmatic Knowledge

This notion is self-restricting to the pragmatic motivations and it is somehow narrower than the 'background knowledge' described by WAHLGREN which represents the general experience and qualifications of a Lawyer. In detail, his/her "immediate recollection of relevant legal categories", his/her ability to "recall a large number of previously instanced facts" and his/her awareness "of how different elements are interrelated with each other in the legal system".[143] WAHLGREN'S thoughts about *moral* and *practical considerations* in which he acknowledges that "elements of a subjective nature are essential for the outcome of legal reasoning"[144] more closely coincide with this 'background pragmatic knowledge', but they are examined in the completely different part of law-search in his model.

1.6.5   The First Decision and the Question of 'Easy Cases'

It is high time for the Lawyer, after elaborating in his/her mind the previous steps, to draft his/her first decision. It is well known that some legal problems are automatically interpreted and solved in the legal mind without further considerations, while others need further mental elaboration and interpretation. Similarly WAHLGREN states: "This is for instance the case in situations in which the nature of the upcoming issues can be easily determined in advance and in which the law is stable and clear. In many fields of the law this is not an unusual situation. ... The same applies to many other kinds of legal issues of frequent occurrence, like for example cases concerning inheritance, traffic incidents, various taxation issues, etc. ... The fact that rule applications may be arrived at with little or no effort does not, of course mean that the underlying principles of reasoning cannot be of a complicated nature."[145]

---

[143] See WAHLGREN P., *Automated Legal Reasoning: A Study on Artificial Intelligence and Law*, Kluwer, Computer/Law Series, 1992, p. 156.

[144] See WAHLGREN P., *Automated Legal Reasoning: A Study on Artificial Intelligence and Law*, Kluwer, Computer/Law Series, 1992, p. 175.

[145] WAHLGREN P., *Automated Legal Reasoning: A Study on Artificial Intelligence and Law*, Kluwer, Computer/Law Series, 1992, p. 148.

The difficulty in discussing this topic lies in the use of a known term in order to describe something subtly different: The *Hartian 'easy' cases* classification is used here in a rather broader[146] sense.[147] For the purposes of this study, 'easy' cases are separate from those automatically decided and not in need of interpretation. Those are the cases that the Lawyer, by using the above pre-process criteria, does not allow to follow the route of interpretation. The Lawyer immediately decides how he/she will deal with them and advises the client accordingly.[148] The reason for this characterisation is that these 'decisions' constitute a conclusive and integrated piece of advice (*supra* 1.2.4) and hence must be considered as a remedy to the legal pathology.

If (depicted by the conventional diamond shape in *Figure 1- 6*) the lawyer, after the cumulative consideration of steps 1-4 of the Pre-Process, 'feels' that this is a 'hard case' his/her thought enters the next stage of examining the meaning of law i.e. *Interpretation.* Otherwise, he concludes what will be called 'final legal arguments' (see *infra* 1.9.1) and he omits the stage of Interpretation.

For reasons of complete coverage, an extreme case must be reported, in which a Counsel initiates a full judicial and/or administrative procedure for an 'easy' case, in order to make more personal financial gains for the reasons explained in 1.6.4 above. In that instance the case is 'easy' and follows the 'easy' route in the mind of the Counsel, while it appears 'hard' to the eyes of the Client. It is not, however,

---

[146] See also the distinction of GARDNER that *easy cases* are those whose verdict could not be disputed by knowledgeable, rational lawyers, while *hard cases* pose questions about which lawyers might disagree. GARDNER A., *An Artificial Intelligence Approach to Legal Reasoning*, Mit Press, Cambridge Mass, 1987. A similar approach is that of HAGE *et al.*, where 'hard cases' are connected with the procedure that leads to their determination and that the decision -making process is determining whether a case is 'hard' HAGE J., LEENES R. & LODDER A., *Hard Cases: A Procedural Approach*, in ARTIFICIAL INTELLIGENCE AND LAW, Vol. 2, No. 2, 1994, p. 114.

[147] A novel approach is taken by MCCARTY L.T., *On the Role of Prototypes in Appellate legal Argument*, in PROCEEDINGS OF THE 3RD INTERNATIONAL CONFERENCE ON ARTIFICIAL INTELLIGENCE AND LAW, Oxford, June 25-28, 1991, ACM Press, 1991, p. 187, where "[t]he task for a lawyer or a judge in a 'hard' case is to construct a theory of the disputed legal rules and legal concepts that produces the desired legal result, and then to persuade the relevant audience that this theory is preferable to any theories offered by an opponent. Empirically, legal theories seem to take the form of *prototypes* and *deformations*, and one important component of a persuasive argument is an appeal to the *coherence* of the theory thus constructed.".

[148] Concerning Information Technology Applications in Law, 'easy' cases could be different depending on the application. In information retrieval an 'easy' case could be one about which the Lawyer knows all the relevant information (i.e legislation, case-law, precedents etc.); in expert systems it could be one that the lawyer immediately knows the solution etc.

easy to prove whether this is against professional ethics, and, moreover, to force a Counsel to think in a certain way. For the purposes of the model, therefore, we must stay with the initial rule that the Counsel abides strictly by professional ethics.

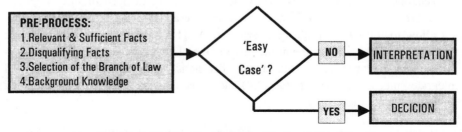

Figure 1- 6: The First Decision about 'Hard' and 'Easy' Cases

[Pre-Process]: **Case 1:** from Steps 1-4 it is an 'Easy Case'
THEN Conclude Final Legal Arguments
Case 2: from Steps 1-4 it is NOT an 'Easy Case'
THEN START INTERPRETATION

ZELEZNIKOW & HUNTER[149] have introduced a further distinction between 'hard cases' i.e. "cases that require application of difficult and often contradictory legal concepts" and *'impossible cases'* i.e. "cases, which we as a society cannot afford to leave to computers, even if they ever become capable of resolving them". This may be correct when considering the *stricto sensu* functions of a legal expert system, but it is not acceptable for the purposes of this model. The task of a legal system, upon which this model is based, is to provide cure and a means of cure for every type of the legal pathology.

1.7   INTERPRETATION

A substantial part of the legal literature of all legal systems has been devoted to *Interpretation* and its elements. Sometimes this occurred to such an extent that the term became surrounded by mystery and confusion, and laymen think of it as a

---

[149] ZELEZNIKOW J. & HUNTER D., *Building Intelligent Legal Information Systems, Representation and Reasoning in Law,* Kluwer, Computer Law series, 1994, p. 59.

magic melting pot where the whole of legal knowledge is amalgamated. Of course, the limits of characterisation of Legal Interpretation *per* se are wide and can vary from a 'deep philosophical investigation' to a 'mechanical reproduction of elaborated knowledge'. It is not feasible to search for the truth, which would also presuppose the support of a certain philosophical school of thought and hence of the superiority of a certain legal system, and could lead to the ancient question whether Law is *art* or *science*.

Even after the reduction of the legal sources to those relevant to the case and to the course of argument, the lawyer must still search a volume of legal material in order to 'match' the facts to the antecedent of legal rules. The problem is that in modern societies, given the complexity of life, law is trying to cover as many aspects as possible of this complexity and to regulate many individual cases. Under this perspective, law presents itself in a general and abstract character. As a consequence, in *'hard'* cases the automatic 'matching' of the facts to the law is exceptional. The rule is that the Lawyer is not able to immediately subsume the facts to the rule and he/she must perform a further mental elaboration in order to *interpret* the content of the law. Taken together, *Legal Interpretation* is a standard logical procedure that all Lawyers perform during their everyday practice, the way they have been trained to, in order to identify the meaning of the legal rules.

> **[Interpretation] Definition:** The Logical Procedure performed by Lawyers in order to identify the Meaning of Law

The phase of interpretation and the phase of rule application are distinct in the analysis of legal reasoning. Indeed, one must first identify the meaning of normative sentences and then apply it. However, this distinction is not that clear on a pragmatic level, when both actions are performed simultaneously by the Lawyer. The following analysis will try to give a simplistic overview of the process.

1.7.1 Decoding the Meaning of Words and Legal Linguistics

The first phase in the logical procedure of Interpretation includes an interrelated and not always distinct phase: the phase of the *Linguistic Decoding* of the input facts. The core of every theoretical or practical activity within positive law, and the first stage of all interpretational phases, is the understanding of the meaning of linguistic expressions through which the legislator communicates the content of the enforced law.[150] It should be noted that in contrast to sciences, where although objects, observations and experiments can be conceived by means of the language, they still exist outside it, in law, the positive law can only be conceived within the language. It is impossible for law to exist outside the language. Language is a constituting and not a descriptional element of rules, e.g. the sign "no smoking" does not just depict the will of the person that wrote it, but is a rule in itself.

The division of language in three branches: *syntactics* which examine the typical interrelation of signs between them, *semantics* which examine the correspondence of signs to their meaning and *pragmatics*, which examine the use of signs within certain aspects of human activity can also be applied to legal language.

The *syntactics of legal language* are trying to identify the typical interrelations between the signs themselves and between the sentences, in order to qualify them as valid, or not for legal discourse. They also examine the typical logical structure of legal sentences.

Example:

(a) Between the sentences (Italian VAT Law, article 7§3):

(1) "The supply of services is considered to be effected within state Territory
when
(2) the services are supplied by subjects having their domicile within that territory

it is important to identify the logical structure behind "*when*" as 'condition' in order to interpret the first sentence as 'consequent' as and the second as 'antecedent'.

(b) Within the sentence "*with exception* to the previous paragraph", the logical structure behind "*with exception*" must be identified.

The *semantics of legal language* embody mainly the identification of the meaning of positive law. Furthermore, the contextual interpretation of legal rules (see *infra* 1.7.6) is contained. The *pragmatics of legal language* is mainly addressing the problem of understanding the 'real facts' under consideration. Teleological interpretation, in which the legal rule is examined as a part of social environment, can be attached to this category.[151]

---

[150] See also SOURLAS P., *Themeliodi Zitimata tis Methodologias tou Dikeou*, (*Fundamental Issues of Legal Methodology*, in Greek), Athens 1986, p. 70.

[151] See for example HAGE supporting the view that "which interpretation is legally correct is *the law*", in HAGE J., *Teleological Reasoning in Reason-Based Logic*, in PROCEEDINGS OF THE 5TH

Interpretation always starts from interpreting the meaning of words. The notion of Language Dependent Facts (*supra* 1.4.4) is also significant here. STAMPER emphasises that:

> [D]ifferent meanings are made by different agents in the process of interpretation, a more appropriate view for the treatment of law. An oversimplified notion of meaning is not a sound basis for legal expertise, which is pre-eminently concerned with the resolutions of disputes about meaning.[152]

It is in WITTGENSTEIN'S later writings[153] that the theory of 'communication act' is developed. The meaning of the words ought to be found in the communication act that is performed in every instance. This theory connects, for the first time, the meaning of a word with its use. WITTGENSTEIN uses the expression 'language games' to denote that, like in a game, an element is not defined with external linguistic rules but by describing the functions that this element can perform, e.g. in order to define what a 'bishop' is in chess, we can say that it is the piece that can only move diagonally, can capture another piece etc. In the same manner, the meaning of an expression is the set of its valid uses in certain circumstances and for certain goals. Therefore, the understanding of a word can be conceived not only in its *syntactic* and *semantic* dimension but also in its *pragmatic* dimension, since every new use and communication act is defining the meaning.[154]

> **[Interpretation] Step 1: Decode the meaning of words, in their *syntactic*, *semantic* and *pragmatic* dimension**

Remark:
During the Nomos-Advisor implementation (see *infra* chapter 3) due to its linguistic origins great attention was paid to the *syntactic* and *semantic* meaning of signs contained in a specific legal text, but not to the *pragmatic*

INTERNATIONAL CONFERENCE ON ARTIFICIAL INTELLIGENCE AND LAW, University of Maryland, 21-24 May 1995, ACM Press, 1995, p. 19.

[152] STAMPER R., *Expert Systems, Lawyers Beware*, in NAGEL (Ed.), p. 30.

[153] WITTGENSTEIN L., *Philosophische Untersuchungen*, Oxford 1953, see also LEINDELNNER-RUPERTSBERGER E., *Linguistics, Wittgensteinian Linguistic Philosophy and Artificial Intelligence*, in SINDING-LARSEN (Ed.), COMPLEX 7/88, OSLO, 1988.

[154] See also the interesting construction of WRÓBLEWSKI concerning those three dimensions (syntactic, semantic and pragmatic) of legal rules in connection with the consistency of a legal system WRÓBLEWSKI J., *Computers and the Consistency of Law*, in INFORMATICA & DIRITTO, No. 1, 1990, p. 8.

meaning. Many components of the process such as procedural and heuristic knowledge were omitted.

The problem of various different meanings is not a defect of natural languages but is inherent to the language as means of communication. Under this assumption, vagueness in language can be resolved by the use of definitions, which, nevertheless, cannot resolve all ambiguities. First, because defining the meaning of words entails the use of other words included in the definition (*definiens*), which in turn must be defined, a process which cannot go on endlessly. Second, it is impossible to define all the words of a language, since this would only lead to the development of a different 'artificial' language.

The conclusion, in connection with this modelling, is that it is impossible to develop '*substantive definitions*', i.e. definitions that rely only on the substance of the defined word (definiendum). It is only possible to develop '*definitions of use*', i.e. for a limited number of uses (like for example the 'constants' in the beginning of this modelling). It is obvious that the more delimited the number of uses, the more effective is the definition. Even so, it is not *a priori* certain, that the claimed definition is still valid. It must be borne in mind that the application of semantic rules is a convention, and, as such, the relation between words and objects is also conventional. The original author may have deviated from the definition or may have invalidated its use for the creation of a word. In this case, the conditions of the *ad hoc* use of the word must be re-examined. It is, therefore, clear that *definitions that can automatically replace the definiendum by the definiens, and thus radically solve the problem of conception, do not exist.*[155]

Concerning the use of language in law, two main problems may arise: that concerning the meaning of the legal utterances, and that of vagueness. The latter will be examined in the next paragraph while for the first it must be emphasised, *that the utterance of sentences in law is not trying - in most cases - to describe what is simply happening but to express a rule, demanding compliance with its normative content.*

Example:
The phrase "State Territory is considered to be the one subjected to Its sovereignty..." (Italian VAT Law Article 7§1) is not a general declaration

---

[155] See also SOURLAS P., *Themeliodi Zitimata tis Methodologias tou Dikeou*, (*Fundamental Issues of Legal Methodology*, in Greek), Athens 1986, p. 75 (emphasis added) and also the Conceptual Graphs representation in Chapter 3.

for a special qualification of the Italian soil, but within the framework of a taxation law it is a command as of what constitutes the place within which an activity can be taxed.

1.7.2　The Core Problem of Interpretation

In a classic analysis, HART tries to reveal the deep reason behind the need of interpretation by saying that

> Plainly this world is not our world; human legislators can have no such knowledge of all the possible combinations of circumstances which the future may bring. This inability to anticipate brings with it a relative indeterminacy of conduct (e.g. a rule that no vehicle may be taken into the park), the language used in this context fixes necessary conditions which anything must satisfy if it is to be within its scope, and certain clear examples of what is certainly within its scope may present to our minds... When the unenvisaged case does arise, we confront the issues at stake and can then settle the question by choosing between the competing interests in the way which best satisfies us. In doing so we shall have settled a question as to the meaning, for the purposes of this rule, of a general word.[156]

MACCORMICK generalises that "on any view of law and in any type of legal system which involves the use of 'valid rules', the problem of interpretation must on occasion arise".[157] WAHLGREN, departing from the theoretical model and approaching everyday legal practice, emphasises the obligatory character of interpretation by saying that "all the actual instances of legal reasoning must include the establishment of a connection between a legal proposition and a conceived rule"[158] as well as the difficulties in establishing this connection. The real issue, however, arises when such a connection cannot be established, and the core problem, for a practical modelling, is to overcome this difficulty.

In interpretation, such a difficulty arises when we encounter one of the three main shortcomings: (a) 'vagueness' (b) 'conflicts' or (c) 'gaps' (all three known also by the Latin maxim *discrepationes legitimae)*.

---

[156] HART H.L.A., *The Concept of Law*, Clarendon Press, Oxford, 1961, p. 125.

[157] MACCORMICK N., *Legal Reasoning and Legal Theory*, Clarendon Press, Oxford, 1978, p. 72.

[158] WAHLGREN P., *Automated Legal Reasoning: A Study on Artificial Intelligence and Law*, Kluwer, Computer/Law Series, 1992, p. 189.

Vagueness refers to the situation when the text of the legal rules leaves ambiguities about their meaning. This is due mainly to the following: (1) not all the words of a legal rule have a certain predetermined meaning, (2) law has no unified terminology for all of its branches, (3) law uses a meaning wider or narrower than the meaning used in the activity which law is intended to regulate and (4) that the law intentionally leaves a margin of a very wide interpretation in order to cover as many cases as possible. It has been said, that in law only numbers are not vague.

Examples (1-4):

1. What is the meaning of 'real estate' for the purposes of Art. 7§2 of the Italian VAT Law ? (The definition can be found in the Italian Constitution Art. 42 and the Italian Civil Code Arts. 832, 840 and 2643)

2. The differences of the meaning of 'domicile' as taken by Art.7§3 of the Italian VAT Law (concerning the legal seat of companies) and as taken by general company law.(The meaning is different for taxation law than for company law)

3. When we must try to cover the cases of 'caravans' fixed to the ground by the word 'immobile property'(Art. 7§4a of the Italian VAT Law) (The meaning of the word "caravan" is narrower and has to be subsumed to immobile property)

4. When the law refers generally to '*supply of services*' (Art. 7§3 of the Italian VAT Law) (A large number of meanings can be subsumed under "supply of services")

Conflicts arise when two conflicting to each other rules are trying to regulate the same facts. *Gaps* we encounter when law leaves unregulated a certain case although it regulates similar cases.

Example:
The Italian Vat Law regulates the supply of energy like electricity (Art. 7§4a in combination with Art. 4) but not the supply of atomic energy

It is important to understand that 'not regulating' a case may be intentional on behalf of the legislator, therefore the crucial factor is whether 'similar' cases demand regulation.

From legal text-books it is apparent[159] that the goals of any legal order are the same: (a) clarity of its rules, (b) consistency of its rules and (c) complete coverage. It must be emphasised that these goals are not solely logical prerequisites of any legal system but, moreover, they constitute practical guidelines that inspire the Lawyer on *how* to interpret. Nevertheless, the specific route taken in order to reach these goals differs in every legal order, depending on the legal system (see *supra* 1.6.3) and, especially, on the power that the legal system appoints to the Judge for covering the gaps. Furthermore, legislators must take care to maintain the consistency when drafting laws, in order to reduce the above defects. It has also been postulated that in view of Information Technology Applications in Law, legislators should restrict themselves to use, in law, words with only one meaning.[160] This can never be totally achieved - in technical terms - while it will also lead to the denial of basic functions of a legal system, like the flexibility in regulating social relations.

This problem is partly resolved[161] by the use of 'definitions' which reduce the ability and the powers of the Lawyer to decide the degree of applicability of a law, since he/she is obliged to use the word with the strict meaning that the law explains. Experienced legislators even define how wide the scope of definitions shall be, by stating, for example, that these definitions only apply to this particular law etc. Still, even the most experienced legislator, like in every other aspect of a language, cannot foresee every future use of a word. The problems of vagueness can only be resolved within the *pragmatic* dimension of the language, by defining expressions in correlation with the specific circumstances, and with the individuals that use them.

The majority of the jurisprudential works are devoted to the manner in which to solve these difficulties and complications of interpretation. It has, however, to be admitted that as part of legal education, the perception of Legal Interpretation together with its basic elements gradually becomes second nature to newly qualified lawyers. From personal experience, the famous canons of interpretation by FRIEDRICH CARL VON SAVIGNY[162] and the Legal Methodology of LARENZ[163] are

---

[159] See for example ARAVANTINOS I., *Eisagogi stin Epistimi tou Dikeou*, (*Introduction to the Law*, in Greek), Sakkoulas, Athens, 1983.

[160] See also... Orwell's "1984".

[161] See in Chapter 3 the problem of 'missing definitions'.

[162] SAVIGNY FRIEDRICH CARL VON, *System des heutigen römischen Rechts*, I, 1840.

intuitively followed by most civil law - and especially a Germanic oriented legal system (like the Greek)- devoutly. It is therefore inevitable that legal education and everyday practices of a lifetime will affect the drafting of the practical model attempted here.

1.7.3   The General Rules of Interpretation

Before proceeding, it should be repeatedly emphasised that Interpretation, like any other part of our model, is dominated by the legal methodology of the legal system in question, and therefore, a different methodology or legal theory may impose different interpretational rules. To strengthen the same argument, WAHLGREN comments that "[l]egal subsumption must not be, however, performed haphazardly. Rule application is normally guided by a number of elaborated methodological rules of a formal nature. Methodological rules determine and explain not only the presuppositions for rule applications, but they also determine how rule applications ought to be completed."[164] Antithetically, HART, asserts that "[c]anons of 'interpretation' cannot eliminate, though they can diminish these uncertainties; for these canons are themselves general rules for the use of language, and make of general terms which themselves require interpretation."[165]

The Rule of Practicality (*supra* 1.3.3) entails for this model that some elementary rules, known from first year law school text-books,[166] and affecting the *interpretation* procedure, as a whole, will be examined, particularly, in view of the already described methodological rules of the model. It is, consequently, clear that this is not imposed by any preoccupation towards one or another legal or philosophical system.

The first rule is that Interpretation is not an end in itself, but it is only a means towards curing the Legal Problem, and, thus, applying the Law. This could be

---

[163] LARENZ KARL, *Methodenlehre der Rechtswissenschaft*, (5th edition), Berlin, 1983.

[164] WAHLGREN P., *Automated Legal Reasoning: A Study on Artificial Intelligence and Law*, Kluwer, Computer/Law Series, 1992, p. 150.

[165] HART H.L.A., *The Concept of Law*, Clarendon Press, Oxford, 1961, p. 123.

[166] See e.g. ARAVANTINOS I., *Eisagogi stin Epistimi tou Dikeou*, (*Introduction to the Law*, in Greek), Sakkoulas, Athens, 1983, p. 155.

extended to the case where the Interpretation itself is presented as a legal problem, but again the ultimate goal should be the pragmatic fact of applying the Law.

> **[Interpretation] Rule 1: Interpretation is a means to apply the Law not an end in itself**

The second rule is somewhat narrower than the previous one, focussing mainly on the depth of an 'interpretational investigation' and is depicted in the Latin maxim: *interpretatio cessat in claris,* i.e. interpretation should not go further than the understanding of the meaning of the words to be interpreted.

> **[Interpretation] Rule 2:** *Interpretatio cessat in Claris*

The uncertainty in this case is that, as already noted, the Lawyer (under the notion of *supra* 1.2.1) must be able to identify what is clear and where and when interpretation must stop; it is evident that a layman has a completely different view in understanding the 'legal' meaning of words. For the practical purposes of this model, these two rules entail that certain limits must be set in order to avoid an 'endless loop' - in computer jargon - i.e. a recursive process that will lead continuously, either to extended and more different theoretical aspects of interpretation, if we ignore *Rule 1*, or, to more abstract and deeper meanings of a word, if we overlook *Rule 2*.

1.7.4   A General Condition: Sufficient Interpretation

During this entire mental elaboration, the Lawyer is continuously evaluating the degree and the quality of the process. This results in *interim* arguments concerning the sufficiency of the logical procedure described as Interpretation: If at any stage this procedure has reached a sufficient degree of maturity, i.e. a satisfactory understanding of the meaning of the applicable law, it is time for the Lawyer to direct his/her thought towards applying the law and towards the conclusion of 'final legal arguments' (see *infra* 1.9.1).

Otherwise, the Interpreter must go back to exhaust all the means of Interpretation and to finally search for more legal sources. In both cases, it should be noted that the guideline for taking these decisions will be the legal methodology in use. This guideline will determine how strict the formality criteria for reaching the above decision shall be, as well as the criteria for deciding the degree of certainty and conviction about Interpretation needed. Moreover, it should be clear that these criteria are more indulgent in the case of *Counsels* and stricter in the case of *Judges*. Therefore, in the latter case, the law itself usually prescribes in an exhaustive way their precise use. As WAHLGREN puts it "there exist a large number of formal rules governing the process. Formal aspects do not only set out standards for decision makers. In many cases, formal rules also explicitly point-out and limit the rules of substantive nature that can be applied in a given situation."[167]

> **[Interpretation] Condition: Interpret until Interpretation is sufficient, according to the legal methodology in use.**

Furthermore, this condition must encapsulate all possible considerations for the evaluation of the results.

1.7.5   The Classical Phases of Interpretation

What, then, are the logical steps that the lawyer must take in order to define whether a tank - to use the overused classical example[168] - can enter, for commemoration purposes, a park where, according to the 'law' entrance is prohibited to 'motor vehicles'?

Most legal text-books[169] describe the classical phases[170] of interpretation,[171] therefore the discussion will be confined to the minimum necessary. The *first phase*

---

[167] WAHLGREN P., *Automated Legal Reasoning: A Study on Artificial Intelligence and Law*, Kluwer, Computer/Law Series, 1992, p. 204.

[168] HART H.L.A., *The Concept of Law*, Clarendon Press, Oxford, 1961, p. 125.

[169] At this stage first year law school text-books were used; see ARAVANTINOS I., *Eisagogi stin Epistimi tou Dikeou*, (*Introduction to the Law*, in Greek), Sakkoulas, Athens, 1983, SOURLAS P. , *Themeliodi Zitimata tis Methodologias tou Dikeou*, (*Fundamental Issues of Legal Methodology*, in Greek), Athens 1986 and STAMATIS K., *Isagogi sti Methodologia tou Dikeou*, (*Introduction to Legal Methodolgy*, in Greek), Thessaloniki, 1991.

[170] The number of these phases (or canons of interpretation) remains in dispute. SAVIGNY distinguishes the grammatical, the logical, the historical and the systematic element, while LARENZ distinguishes five criteria: the literal meaning of the statute; the contextual meaning; the regulatory purposes, aims and normative intentions of the historical legislator; objective-teleological criteria; and finally conformity to the Constitution. SAVIGNY F. C., *System des heutigen römischen Rechts*, I, 1840. LARENZ K., *Methodenlehre der Rechtswissenschaft*, (5th edition), Berlin, 1983 for an alternative approach see MACCORMICK N., *Argumentation and Interpretation in Law*, in RATIO JURIS, Vol. 6, No. 2, p. 16, July, 1993.

is that of removing *vagueness*. "Vagueness constitutes a general limitation for effective communication and language whose effects can be reduced but not eliminated by the introduction of technical terms and legal concepts".[172] Therefore, the first stage in this procedure is always the *textual* one, i.e. the understanding of the natural meaning of a concept; by examining the words of the rule the Lawyer tries to identify all the possible meanings of the 'vague' words (*linguistic phase*) and then to choose one of all the meanings.

It is important here to identify the use of words within specialised vocabularies and especially those that have both a legal and an ordinary meaning. In order to complete this first phase, i.e. to choose the proper meaning, the Lawyer must proceed to the second stage, that of *teleological interpretation*,[173] which entails that the decisive criterion for choosing a meaning shall be the *intention* that the Law envisages (*ratio legis*). The important element here is that *this intention cannot be found in the specific wording of a certain rule but has to be detected in the whole system*[174] *of the Law*.

> **Example:**
> In the former example of 'real estate' (Italian VAT Law Art.7) we must investigate the whole legal hierarchy, starting from the Italian Constitution (article 42), the Civil Code (articles 832, 840 and 2643), specific Statute Law etc. in order to detect the *intention of the Law* about this meaning i.e. which factual cases fall within. It is clear that this *intention* cannot be found by just reading and interpreting only the text of the rule in question.

Two types of teleological interpretation are supported: the *objective* in which the lawyer has to determine the objective purpose of the law and the *subjective* where

---

[171] For an alternative classification see MACCORMICK D.N. & SUMMERS S.R., *Interpreting Statutes, a Comparative Study*, Aldershot, Dartmouth Publishing, 1991, note also the case of interpretation specifically prescribed by the legal system e.g. in the UK the *Interpretation Act 1978*.

[172] WAHLGREN P., *Automated Legal Reasoning: A Study on Artificial Intelligence and Law*, Kluwer, Computer/Law Series, 1992, p. 200.

[173] See the innovative - for American jurisprudence - approach of BERMAN & HAFNER to represent the 'purpose of legal rules' and hence teleological interpretation in case-based-reasoning, BERMAN D. & HAFNER C., *Representing Teleological Structure in Case-Based legal Reasoning: The Missing Link*, PROCEEDINGS OF THE 4TH INTERNATIONAL CONFERENCE ON ARTIFICIAL INTELLIGENCE AND LAW, Amsterdam, 15-18 June1993, ACM Press, 1993, p. 50.

[174] See MACCORMICK juxtaposing a series of arguments for an acceptable understanding of a legal text seen as part of a legal system, MACCORMICK N., *Argumentation and Interpretation in Law*, in RATIO JURIS, Vol. 6, No. 2, July 1993, p. 22.

the lawyer must discover the intentions of the legislator when the law was drafted. Also of particular interest are two observations: First, Interpretation can be *extensive* when, based on the *intention* of the Law, it widens the application area of the concept or *vice-versa restrictive* when, again based on the *intention* of the Law, it limits this area. Second, the degree of definition of concepts can vary within a legal system. Most of them are vaguely defined like the 'real estate' and the 'motor-vehicles' in the examples, while others like numbers, signs etc. are more strictly defined. The same considerations exposed earlier concerning the outcome of a legal decision (see *supra Table 1-2* p.58) apply here i.e. depending on the two types of interpretation (extensive or restrictive) the decision may vary accordingly.

> **[Interpretation] Phase 1:**Perform *linguistic* and *teleological* interpretation of the meaning of the rule in order to remove *vagueness.*

The *second phase* is that of trying to exclude *conflicts*, and again includes a first *textual* stage and a second where one specific legal rule is selected amongst two or more. The first stage is somehow different from that previously mentioned, in that the Lawyer does not try to identify the meaning but rather to verify a conflict between two or more legal rules. The second stage is dominated by the known, *three axioms of legal hierarchy* in their Latin maxims:[175] (1) *Lex superior derogat legi inferiori*; (2) *Lex specialis derogat legi generali* and (3) *Lex posterior derogat legi priori*. The order of the laws' hierarchy depends on the status of the issuing authority or to customary practice.

> **[Interpretation] Phase 2:** Select the applicable rule by using the *three axioms of legal hierarchy* in order to exclude *conflicts*

The *third phase* is dedicated to the elimination of *gaps*. In a first *textual* stage the Lawyer must verify that a gap really exists. In a second *conjectural* stage the Lawyer is trying to speculate about the similarities of the non-regulated case with

---

[175] See however, the considerations of ALEXY that "[m]ore significant than the problem of the number of *canons* is the question of their rank order... The difficulty in justifying a rank order is closely related to the difficulties of determining the goal of interpretation. A decision about the goal of interpretation presupposes a theory regarding the function of adjudication, and this in its turn presupposes an answer to the question whether and to what extent rational legal argumentation is possible." ALEXY R., *A Theory of Legal Argumentation, The Theory of Rational Discourse as Theory of Legal Justification, (English Translation)*, Clarendon press, Oxford, 1989, p. 3.

already regulated cases. If a sufficient degree of similarity is established then the gap is eliminated by the use of the regulated case. Otherwise, the Lawyer must use *analogy*, and if that does not succeed, he/she must use the *argumentum a contrario*. As a supplement, the known arguments, *a fortiori*, *a minore ad maius* and *a majore ad minus* can be used. It must be emphasised that this procedure must be carried out in compliance with the general intentions and aspects of the legal system, otherwise the final result is not valid.

> **[Interpretation] Phase 3: Speculate similarities, or use analogy, or, legal arguments to establish similarity with regulated cases in order to *eliminate* gaps**

By *analogy*, the Lawyer is trying to establish similarity with an already decided case (in the sense of a case regulated by law) by replacing the antecedent proposition related to the decided case with the undecided one.

Example:
In the legal proposition: "If the transaction is supply of electric energy it must be taxed.", the notion of *"atomic energy"*, which is not defined in the law, can by analogy replace *"electric energy"* and therefore it can be assimilated that "atomic energy must be taxed". This method was used for filling in the information in the hypertext explanations of the *Nomos-Advisor* prototype.

It is interesting to note that reasoning by analogy may not be permitted by the legal system, like in the criminal law of many European countries (being one of its principles) and/or in some aspects of civil law (for example the Greek Constitution article 78§1 does not permit reasoning by analogy in taxation law).

Argumentum a contario is the logical opposite to reasoning by analogy. In this case the important element is that the given case is *not* comparable to any one regulated by the law. (The previously referred notion of disqualifying facts finds also its place here).

Example:
The article 7§2 (Italian VAT Law) "The transfer of goods is considered to be effected with its territory if its object is real estate or national or nationalised goods...", entails that *a contrario* goods other than real estate or national or nationalised goods are not regulated by this instance of the law.

It has been argued that the other three forms of *a fortiori*, *a minore ad maius* and *a majore ad minus* are not typical logical arguments but rather plausible

95

justifications. Nevertheless, their practical value in legal reasoning has not been contested. In these arguments the problem lies in an intermediary *premiss sentence* which compares the case in question with another similar one and indicates a transition between them.

Examples:

If "persons having their residence" are not subject to taxation then *a fortiori* persons having a temporary residence are not subject to tax.

If "persons having their residence in State Territory" are subject to taxation then by using the *argumentum a minore ad majus* persons having their domicile therein are subject to tax too. In reverse order (domicile - >residence) the same example can be taken for the *argumentum a majiore ad minus*.

1.7.6 Reasoning with Rules and *The Legal Syllogism*

The fundamentals of logic owe their origin to the writings of ARISTOTLE and especially in the *Prior Analytics* of the *Organon*. The *Syllogism* is considered as a form in which, from a given set of propositions, follows another necessary proposition. The basic problem of logic, i.e. the clarification of the consequences between premisses, is of paramount importance for legal reasoning.

Returning to the model, if everything is clear in the mind of the Lawyer, i.e. input facts, applicable and interpreted legal rule, then he/she must find the legal consequences of this rule by performing the *legal syllogism*. This is a logical procedure which consists of 4 parts: (1) The major premiss (sentence), (2) the minor premiss (sentence), (3) the subsumption and (4) the conclusion,

Example:

Major Premiss Sentence: State Territory is considered to be the one subjected to Its sovereignty, with the exception of the Districts of Livigno, Campio d'Italia and of the national waters of the lake of Lugano...(Italian VAT Law, Art.7§1)

Minor Premiss Sentence: A transaction has taken place in the District of Livigno

Conclusion: The transaction is not considered to have taken place in State Territory

Interpretation: Step 2: Perform the Legal Syllogism

By definition, the problem of performing reasoning with rules is one of logic, because it is considered essential to follow elementary logical rules when performing the *legal syllogism*. Since the early description of *'Jørgensen's dilemma'*[176] a large wealth of literature[177] has been generated on this very ability to perform the *legal syllogism*.[178] A group of researchers, having KELSEN[179] as their main representative, completely denies the ability to perform the legal syllogism. They assert that legal rules are willing acts, through which it is attempted to affect the behaviour of other persons. Therefore, legal reasoning is not an objective matter of logic, but a matter of the subjective will of the justice-giving person, who, in turn, has acquired his/her power to form this will from another legal rule. A second group of researchers accepts that legal rules can be characterised, by using a two-values system,[180] as true or false and, therefore, the legal syllogism can be performed. They maintain, however, that the criterion for the characterisation as true or false is the conformity with 'natural' law. Practically, this is achieved by adding descriptive elements to the normative text of a rule and thus enabling the characterisation as true false, e.g. the above example (1.7.1 towards the end) would become

From: *State Territory is considered...*(cannot be true or false)

---

[176] JØRGENSEN J., *Imperatives and Logic*, Erkenntnis, 1937, defended that (i) a sentence can only constitute the premiss of a logical syllogism when it can be characterised as true or false (ii) imperatives (and hence rules) can not be characterised as true or false, therefore, (iii) rules can not constitute the major or the minor premiss sentence of logical reasoning. But it was known that instinctively such syllogisms can be performed like in the following example:

> Promises must be kept (rule - *major premiss sentence*)
>
> This is a promise (*minor premiss sentence*)
>
> ---
>
> This promise must be kept (*conclusion*)

As a result Jørgensen himself was reluctant in accepting this outcome so he proposed to overcome the above position (ii).

[177] See one of the proposed solutions by ALCHOURRÓN C. & MARTINO A., *A Sketch of Logic without Truth*, in PROCEEDINGS OF THE SECOND INTERNATIONAL CONFERENCE ON ARTIFICIAL INTELLIGENCE AND LAW, Vancouver, 1989, p. 165.

[178] This corresponds to SUSSKIND'S notion of 'the argument of truth-value' see SUSSKIND R., *Expert Systems in Law*, Clarendon, Oxford 1987, p. 223.

[179] KELSEN H., *Allgemeine Theorie der Normen*, Wien 1979 (and English translation).

[180] For a recent criticism, exposing also many of Hart's views on the use of logic in law see LOUI P. R., *Hart's Critics on Defeasible Concepts and Ascriptivism*, in PROCEEDINGS OF THE 5TH INTERNATIONAL CONFERENCE ON ARTIFICIAL INTELLIGENCE AND LAW, University of Maryland, 21-24 May 1995, ACM Press, 1995, p. 21.

To: *[According to Italian Law] State Territory is considered...*(can be true or false)

A third group of authors - and amongst them OTA WEINBERGER[181] - mainly endorse the use of *deontic logic.*[182] This group denies the significance of the ability of a legal sentence to be characterised as true or false, in favour of *deontic logic* representing <u>all</u> possible instances of legal linguistic utterances.

Apart from these philosophical considerations, the concern for this model is that practically all lawyers perform the legal syllogism in order to subsume real facts under legal rules. Concerning the representation of law (see *infra* 2.3.2) it is worth mentioning that since law is a prescriptive discipline and not a science, only an informal logic could be adequate. SUSSKIND argues that "any computer system that manipulates entities with deontic content necessarily makes assumptions about, and presupposes a theory of, deontic logic". He stresses, however, that "[t]here are extremely complex philosophical and technical issues involved in the development of deontic logic, however, and it must be noted that there is not any system of deontic logic that commands the degree of general support that many systems of classical logic currently do."[183]

This idea of applying an 'informal logic' opposes the view of WAHLGREN that "nothing of what has been undertaken in this study indicates that deontic logic has any practical significance in the context of automation of legal reasoning"[184] because it is believed that any theory that can adequately represent law should be examined.

---

[181] Amongst many of his writings see WEINBERGER O., *Philosophische Studien zur Logic*, Prague, 1964 and WEINBERGER O., *Rechstlogic*, Vienna - New York, 1970.

[182] The peculiarity of legal rules has led to the development of a specific logic of rules, which differs to classical logic in that it entails more than two values (true or false) in its sentences. The founder of deontic logic is VON WRIGHT G.H.with his work *Deontic Logic*, in Mind, Vol. 60, 1951, who has, nevertheless changed many times the content of his theory. See also JONES A., *Deontic Logic and Legal Knowledge Representation,* in RATIO JURIS, Vol. 3, No. 2, July, 1990, p. 237 and JONES A. & SERGOT M., *Deontic Logic in the Representation of Law: Towards a Methodology*, in ARTIFICIAL INTELLIGENCE AND LAW, Vol. 1, No. 1, p. 45, 1992.

[183] SUSSKIND R., *Expert Systems in Law*, Clarendon, Oxford 1987, p. 225.

[184] WAHLGREN P., *Automated Legal Reasoning: A Study on Artificial Intelligence and Law*, Kluwer, Computer/Law Series, 1992, p. 311.

Another problem is that of subsuming the particular facts under the general descriptions of the law. This is considered merely as a logic problem of classifying the particular under the general, to subsume certain particular facts under the predicates contained in the legal rule. However, SUSSKIND emphasises (for expert systems) that "the process of classifying and subsuming the facts of any case within the terms of the knowledge base cannot be executed by the system, because *an initial human subsumptive judgement based on knowledge of linguistic usage must be made*"[185] LARENZ raises the bid by speaking of the "insight that the application of law is not exhausted by a process of subsumption, but rather requires a wide range of value judgements on part of those applying the law."[186]

Indeed, the problem of subsumption is not a legal one, but rather a problem concerning the empirical use of knowledge. As ALCHOURRÓN & BULYGIN put it "the application of the general terms of a language to particular objects of the world...is the only philosophical problem of the relation of (general) words to things".[187] Similarly, on a more abstract - philosophical level WRÓBLEWSKI argues that "the open question is whether one can find an adequate calculus of formal logic covering the rather complicated relations between epistemic premises, axiological premises and the decision justified by them."[188]

The above observations seem, however, only to identify rather than to resolve the problem. In practical terms, the solution chosen affects the assumptions about the qualifications of the possible users of the applications, and the decision as to which parts of the model could be automated. This conclusion was also confirmed during the *Nomos* project (see Chapter 3) and significantly changed the views about the possible users and the degree of automatisation of the system. It was decided, for

---

[185] SUSSKIND R., *Expert Systems in Law*, Clarendon, Oxford 1987, p. 184 (emphasis added).

[186] LARENZ K., *Methodenlehre der Rechtswissenschaft*, (5th edition), Berlin, 1983 see, however, the analysis of ALEXY for the objectivisation of these value judgements in ALEXY R., *A Theory of Legal Argumentation, The Theory of Rational Discourse as Theory of Legal Justification, (English Translation)*, Clarendon press, Oxford, 1989.

[187] ALCHOURRÓN C. & BULYGIN E., *Limits of Logic and Legal Reasoning*, in MARTINO (Ed.), 1992, p. 10.

[188] WRÓBLEWSKI J., *Legal Expert Systems and Legal Reasoning*, in MARTINO (Ed.), North Holland, 1992, p. 383.

example, that the users must have basic legal skills and that the subsumptive judgements must be made by the user.[189]

1.7.7   The Search for Legal Sources

From the methodological point of view, WAHLGREN, in his model, wants the 'law-search' before interpretation,[190] but the Lawyer, even for 'hard cases', firstly starts interpretation by using memorised law sources, and then, if he/she needs further support, directs his/her thought to the search of legal sources. Without setting sharp dividing lines, this distinction is important because it can help to identify the most important regulations in any given part of law that are automatically used by an experienced practitioner. In turn, this function could provide one more filter of 'disqualifying facts' or 'rules', which, in this case, diminishes the volume of information to be processed.

As explained in section 1.2.3 (in the case of Legal Reasoning), opinion is divided on whether the Lawyer is searching the law in order to apply it or whether he/she is searching the law in order to justify pre-decided arguments. The situation is made more confusing by the different methods, mainly used in Artificial Intelligence applications, known as data-driven and goal-driven approaches. In the first case, possible conclusions are identified, whatever they may be, by applying general principles and rules of law to a specific case. In the latter, the conclusion is predetermined, and the lawyer tries to search out legal arguments in support of this conclusion.[191]

However, SUSSKIND has demonstrated "[i]t is law statements that are at the core of any legal knowledge base, and we derive these statements from law formulations. And my account of law formulations neither prejudices nor

---

[189] I think that Susskind's view for expanding the spectrum of users is premature for the current state-of-the-art in IT. SUSSKIND R., *The Future of Law*, Clarendon Press, Oxford, 1996, p. 281, see also *infra* 2.3.6 The Information Crisis of Legal Decision Making and 2.4.5 Exegisis: how to Create and Use Legal Expert Systems.

[190] WAHLGREN P., *Automated Legal Reasoning: A Study on Artificial Intelligence and Law*, Kluwer, Computer/Law Series, 1992, p. 172.

[191] See also KOERS A. & KRACHT D., *A Goal Driven Knowledge Based System for a Domain of Private International Law*, PROCEEDINGS OF THE 3RD INTERNATIONAL CONFERENCE ON ARTIFICIAL INTELLIGENCE AND LAW, Oxford, June 25-28 1991, ACM Press, 1991, p. 81.

presupposes either theory of the nature of law just outlined. All that I assume is that the law can be expressed in natural language, and that this is possible is 'incontrovertible'."[192] WAHLGREN correspondingly argues that "[*l*]*egal positivism* in contemporary jurisprudence has come to mean a perspective in which *the legal rule system is taken more or less for granted*. The emphasis in works based on positivism is often directed towards the elaboration of methods for manipulating, transforming and applying legal rules. Within the positivism paradigm, *legal dogmatics* (i.e. works aiming to clarify the *content of the law* in specific fields by means of systematisation and interpretation of legal materials) has emerged as a major research approach".[193]

Therefore, it can be successfully submitted that for the purposes of this model, the theoretical differences on this issue are not *per se* important. What is important is the search and systematisation of legal materials that attract the Lawyer's attention.[194] Whether the lawyer's argument moves forward (data-driven) or backward (goal-driven), of paramount significance is the '*matching*', in plain words, of the Lawyer's desire, to certain parts of the legal sources. To achieve this 'matching', certain decisions are taken about the *course of argument* already defined during the pre-process (see *supra* 1.6.3) so as to determine which parts of the legal sources will be considered relevant, and hence retrieved and used.

> **Example:**
> The above divorce Lawyer will start looking for all the rules (statute or case irrelevant) in favour of acquiring as much as possible of the common properties and for all the rules that entitle his/her Client to pay as little maintenance as possible.

This notion closes the 'goal oriented' approach by OSKAMP, that "the goal will define the necessary knowledge and the system will usually backward chain."[195] This important issue, however, is not often taken into consideration while building

---

[192] SUSSKIND R., *Expert Systems in Law*, Clarendon, Oxford 1987, p. 38, and pp. 35-38 for the terminology used.

[193] WAHLGREN P., *Automated Legal Reasoning: A Study on Artificial Intelligence and Law*, Kluwer, Computer/Law Series, 1992, p. 48, (italics added).

[194] On the problem of legal sources see also the distinction of BING between sources and information contained in these sources i.e. to the subjective interpretation that a Lawyer may assign to sources BING J., *Handbook of Legal Information Retrieval*, North Holland, Amsterdam, 1984.

[195] OSKAMP A., *Model for Knowledge and Legal Expert Systems*, in ARTIFICIAL INTELLIGENCE AND LAW, Vol. 1, No. 4, 1993, p. 251.

legal applications, and especially databases. Advances in our understanding of how Lawyers think, and hence of the course of legal argument, have been hampered by the Boolean techniques used in traditional retrieval systems, i.e. the combination of words or expressions to be retrieved by means of the conjunctive 'AND', the disjunctive 'OR' and the negative 'NOT' of the algebra developed by George Boole in 1847.[196] This combination is then used to match the entries of an existing index of words or thesaurus, as it is called. The *'curse of Boolean Algebra'* has also been emphasised by BING[197] since the mid-eighties by denoting that:

> "[u]ser research demonstrates, beyond doubt, that lawyers as average end users cannot handle properly this type of request. What may seem simple in an abstract demonstration becomes obviously cumbersome when trying to translate a problem into a search request. The result is a rather large fraction of improper arguments, where the logic is mixed up, and a strong inclination to use simple requests. Simple here means either only one word or two or more words combined with AND."

The course of argument used in the previous example, as well as generally, asserts that the legal course of argument is not simply a Boolean 'AND' expression. Indeed, it does not represent a query seeking matching entries in an existing index or thesaurus, but rather constitutes a legal argument. ZELEZNIKOW - HUNTER share the same views by saying that:

> "[U]nfortunately, current legal databases such as INFOONE in Australia, and Westlaw and LEXIS in the United States generally retrieve data on keywords. This is inadequate to provide intelligent legal advice, since the very range of material necessary to consult for legal advice cannot be adequately nor accurately represented merely by keywords. Further, the subtlety of legal language and the complexity of legal reasoning cannot be represented in this form. The existing legal information databases use simple Boolean logical operators to retrieve information from the database. Unlike sophisticated database retrieval systems, these commercial legal databases can only retrieve information as atoms, that is simple logical structures, as opposed to usefully extracting free text material"[198]

---

[196] See BOOLE G., *The Mathematical Analysis of Logic*, Cambridge, 1847.

[197] BING J., *The Text Retrieval System as a Conversion Partner,* in YEARBOOK OF LAW COMPUTERS & TECHNOLOGY. Vol. 2, 1986, p. 35, see also BING J., *Designing Text Retrieval systems for 'Conceptual Searching,* in PROCEEDINGS OF THE FIRST INTERNATIONAL CONFERENCE ON ARTIFICIAL INTELLIGENCE AND LAW, Boston, 1987.

[198] ZELEZNIKOW J. & HUNTER D., *Building Intelligent Legal Information Systems, Representation and Reasoning in Law,* Kluwer, Computer Law series, 1994, p. 19.

and in further support they refer to the known BLAIR-MARON[199] full text retrieval study which concluded that users only retrieve a small proportion of the material they really want. Consequently, legal information retrieval systems should not nowadays be based upon closed thesauruses of predetermined terms, but they must adopt modern conceptual techniques including expert systems under the form of intelligent 'front-ends' that would be able to represent the above 'legal course of argument'.

> **[Interpretation]:** **Case 1:** If [Interpretation Steps 1-2] need support from Legal Sources perform SEARCH for sources of substantive and procedural law
> **Case 2:** If [Interpretation Steps 1-2] do need more support check the [Interpretation Condition]

Taken together, this is the phase where the thought of the Lawyer escapes from the previous stage (*interpretation - syllogism*), to the *search for sources* of substantive and procedural law.

1.8   THE CREATION OF THE LEGAL SUBSYSTEM

The volume of legal sources is often proposed as the main reason for introducing Information Technology in the legal field, and it is well known that, historically, the first legal applications were information retrieval systems. This is also the view of laymen who often ask "how do you remember all the law by heart?" Nevertheless, a meaningful question should be: "what is the Lawyer looking for while searching legal sources?"

It is true that legislators and legislative bodies in most modern states are producing a bulk quantity of statutes (even in common law states) under the tendency, after the prevailing positivist ideas and the codifications of the 19th century, to regulate as many aspects as possible of human activity. It is also true that judicial and administrative bodies are issuing a large number of decisions every day, sometimes of equal importance to both civil and common legal systems.

---

[199] BLAIR D. & MARON M.E., *An Evaluation of Retrieval Effectiveness for a Full-Text Document Retrieval System*, in COMMUNICATIONS OF THE ACM Vol. 28, No. 3, March 1985, p. 289.

However, without ignoring the importance of the problem of producing too many laws and legal sources, Lawyers, in most cases, do not have to search the totality of this material. Practically, the Lawyer has already, from the previous phase of selection of the *Course of Argument* (*supra* 1.6.3), 'pin-pointed' certain elements of the legal sources that are relevant to the case or will support his/her argumentation.

A general condition dominates this recursive process of 'search' of the legal sources: that it will be continued until 'sufficient' sources are found. For this goal, the Lawyer must continuously make interim arguments concerning the sufficiency of the sources (see this function depicted in *Figure 1-9* in page 118). Moreover, if the Lawyer at this later stage discovered that the input facts he/she is already using, in order to 'match' them with the sources, are insufficient to find any at all or to 'match' adequate sources in support of his/her argument, he/she must again return to the initial phase of examining the client; he/she must either investigate for new facts or he/she must examine the existing ones more thoroughly.

> **[Search] Condition:** Perform SEARCH until sufficient sources are found. *If* the facts are not sufficient for SEARCH look for more facts.

Within the core of 'search', the so called *doctrine of legal sources* is dominating the methodological questions for where and what to search within the legal system, and defines the valid sources of substantive and procedural law, as well as methodological rules, while two other important, but neglected factors: *heuristic and empirical legal knowledge* as well as *social knowledge repercussions,* fall within the limits of the legal system with the surrounding environment and will be examined separately (see also *Figure 1-8* in page 113).

1.8.1 The Doctrine of Valid Legal Sources

The positivist tradition presupposes a system of clearly defined rules, with an established hierarchy amongst them. This is called *doctrine of legal sources* and helps to identify the rules that the legal system characterises as valid at a certain point in time. SUSSKIND defines that "[t]he formal sources of any developed legal system are those sources that establish or confirm the validity and authority of rules or principles derived from them".[200] The important element for this model, however, is that the doctrine is not only defining the content of what is valid law but it also, by appointing special hierarchical values to its sources it shows the way that an effective law search must follow.

> **Example:**
> A draft hierarchy for civil law systems would be to place first the constitution and then the codes (civil, penal, procedural etc.), then legislation, preparatory works, case law and finally jurisprudence. Therefore, an experienced Lawyer should first look for the constitutional rules and the rules in codes that support his/argument, then the legislation, case law etc. This is not of course absolute and the Lawyer is free to search all sources but it would be abnormal to search, for instance, firstly in preparatory works or in jurisprudence.

As WAHLGREN articulates, "the doctrine of legal sources may be looked upon as a collection of methodological rules or 'managing rules' and as such it is essential for the guidance of law-search in many ways",[201] and he continues that "it is not possible to work out some universal code comprising an elaborated search strategy for legal material based on the hierarchical order of the legal sources".

Nevertheless, hierarchically, the doctrine indicates in the first place the sources of substantive law (constitution, international treaties, statutes, decrees etc. or case law i.e. various types of court judgements), and then those of procedural law that the Lawyer is normally obliged to search; in the second place, it enumerates the 'other' permitted sources such as precedents, parliamentary preparatory works, fair practice, equity etc. that the Lawyer is obliged to search; and finally, it juxtaposes jurisprudence, legal literature etc. that the lawyer may search. The whole process is guided by the methodological rules.

[Search] Step 1: Search the Valid Legal Sources

For a model used for expert systems, OSKAMP uses different categories articulating that "[t]his leads us to the observation that five separate knowledge sources can be

---

[200] SUSSKIND R., *Expert Systems in Law*, Clarendon, Oxford 1987, p. 40, see also his interesting objection in implementing legal expert systems when there exist doubts amongst experts over what sources are valid.

[201] WAHLGREN P., *Automated Legal Reasoning: A Study on Artificial Intelligence and Law*, Kluwer, Computer/Law Series, 1992, p. 173.

distinguished. Three of them, i.e. legislation, case law and knowledge based on legal literature, guidelines etc., find their origin in widely accepted written materials. The fourth, expert knowledge, consists of experiential knowledge that is mostly factual knowledge, relevant to a specific domain. The fifth source, legal metaknowledge, consists of knowledge that makes it possible to optimise the use of the knowledge coming form other sources."[202] These sources can be adapted, by various approaches, to the categories proposed here. Especially, the source described as 'meta-knowledge' can easily be amalgamated with the heuristic and empirical knowledge described in the next paragraph.

An interesting option is proposed by SARENPÄÄ, to introduce a doctrine of the sources of information, i.e. "a doctrine on the content and use of legal information sources. Its goal [would be] to promote optimal use of legal sources."[203] However, all these theories may in practice be hampered by the difficulty in identifying the valid legal sources out of a gigantic corpus of legislation.[204]

Apart from categorisations, however, following the general rule of the legal system (*supra* 1.3.2), two fundamental principles are inherent to this phase: the *principle of legality*[205] and the *principle of equality* before the law.[206] The first principle reflects the demand for *predictability*, i.e. the necessity within a legal system to predict certain results to respective actions, while the second principle entails that cases, similar from the legal point of view should be decided alike. A legal order that does not meet these requirements is condemned to lose its authority. The important consequence for this phase is that the lawyer is not free to go beyond what is stated explicitly in the law. "[I]t is held that every decision requires not merely grounds, but grounds of a special kind: they must be legal. The judge must

---

[202] OSKAMP A., *Model for Knowledge and Legal Expert Systems*, in ARTIFICIAL INTELLIGENCE AND LAW, Vol. 1, No. 4, 1993, p. 248 see also an earlier more technical description in WALKER R, ZEINSTRA P. G.M & VAN DEN BERG P. H., *A Model to Model Knowledge about Knowledge or Implementing Meta-Knowledge in PROLEXS*, in VANDENBERGHE (Ed.), Kluwer, Computer/Law Series, 1989.

[203] SAARENPÄÄ A., *Computers and Legal Life, The Use of Computers in Legal Life and their Role in Legal Thinking*, in BLUME (Ed.), Kluwer, Computer/Law Series, 1991, p. 56.

[204] See also the recent considerations of SUSSKIND about hyperregulation, SUSSKIND R., *The Future of Law*, Clarendon Press, Oxford, 1996, p. 17.

[205] WAHLGREN P., *Automated Legal Reasoning: A Study on Artificial Intelligence and Law*, Kluwer, Computer/Law Series, 1992, p. 214.

[206] See also DWORKIN R., *Law's Empire*, London, 1986, p. 228.

not go beyond the sphere of law, by appealing to non-legal (e.g. moral) norms, except in cases where the law itself authorises him to do so. And then in these cases the ultimate ground for the decision will be a legal norm."[207]

Therefore, the search of sources and hence the whole legal decision making is delimited by these two principles. WAHLGREN stresses that "[i]n individualised instances of the legal reasoning process the necessity to be careful in this respect means that *lawyers must be exhaustive in their activities concerning the processes of law-search* and identification and that it is not wise to terminate these activities if any other, seemingly relevant element has been found. A thorough investigation of the legal material and/or of the current situation may indicate, in many cases, that some additional prerequisite or circumstances must be considered as it may be of great relevance for the outcome of the decision."[208]

From another point of view, SUSSKIND emphasises the need in case-law search to identify the *ratio decidendi*[209] i.e. - in his words - the identification of the rule for which any given case purports to be the authoritative source. He, furthermore, asserts that "although the common law may not be sufficiently represented in terms of rules, it cannot be doubted that it is invariably possible, desirable and necessary to interpret individual cases in the form of individuated rules".[210] This approach views *ratio decidendi* as a general rule or principle contained into the text of the decision that has to be isolated from the surrounding *dictum*. Therefore it can be submitted that case-law can also be covered under the proposed model,[211] which, as said, is based on rules.

[207] ALCHOURRÓN C. E. & BULYGIN E., *Normative Systems*, Springer Verlag, Wien, 1971.

[208] WAHLGREN P., *Automated Legal Reasoning: A Study on Artificial Intelligence and Law*, Kluwer, Computer/Law Series, 1992, p. 216 (emphasis added).

[209] See also BRANTING trying to represent *ratio decidendi*, BRANTING K., *A Reduction-Graph Model of Ratio Decidendi*, in PROCEEDINGS OF THE 4TH INTERNATIONAL CONFERENCE ON ARTIFICIAL INTELLIGENCE AND LAW, Amsterdam, 15-18 June1993, ACM Press, 1993, p. 40.

[210] SUSSKIND R., *Expert Systems in Law*, Clarendon, Oxford 1987, p. 84.

[211] A model for *ratio decidendi* is attempted by BRANTING K., *A Computational Model of Ratio Descidendi*, IN ARTIFICIAL INTELLIGENCE AND LAW, Vol. 2, No. 1, 1994, p. 1.

1.8.2 Heuristic and Empirical Legal Knowledge

These sources of 'legal' knowledge are not encountered amongst the traditional sources. Their usability, although much more appreciated during the Pre-Process, cannot be denied, and they are increasingly important to this pragmatic model.

Empirical legal knowledge is the subjective personal knowledge of law that each lawyer possesses. It contains the overview of the certain legal field that an expert has, as well as the interrelations within different parts of this legal domain. It is obvious that this knowledge will be stronger within the field of specialisation of the lawyer. This kind of knowledge corresponds to SUSSKIND'S *heuristic experiential knowledge*,[212] which he defines as "the informal, judgmental, experiential, and often procedural knowledge" while his *non heuristic knowledge*, i.e. "knowledge about how to go about the administration of law" must be included partly within the doctrine of valid legal sources[213] and partly within *heuristics*. However, empirical knowledge should also contain all kind of predictions about the outcome of a legal decision, which involve probabilistic reasoning, and sometimes take the form of strategy.[214]

> **Example:**
>
> When the client asks about the best form of corporation, in order to pay less tax, and the law provides numerous solutions, the Lawyer must use strategy in order to choose the best solution.

Heuristic Knowledge is what in the jargon is called 'rules of thumb',[215] i.e. hints and tricks about certain procedures, mnemonic codes, automatisation methods for solving complex legal problems etc. SUSSKIND accepts that "*heuristics,* enable the human expert to make educated guesses when necessary, to recognise promising

---

[212] SUSSKIND R., *Expert Systems in Law*, Clarendon, Oxford 1987, p. 57.

[213] Normally in the form of explanatory or transition statutes.

[214] Notwithstanding that 'legal reasoning' must be take into account. See supra 1.3.7 The Rule of Oscillation and Legal Problem Solving and *supra* note 91.

[215] BUCHANAN & HEADRICK define that "[h]euristics (or heuristic rules) are rules of thumb that usually contribute to solutions of problems without in any way providing a guaranteed method for solution. In a chess game, for example, one heuristic rule for winning is to control the centre of the board. There is certainly no guarantee that the player controlling the center will win; yet center control has contributed to winning enough games that it is a guideline for every player." BUCHANAN B. & HEADRICK TH., *Some Speculation About Artificial Intelligence and Legal Reasoning*, in STANFORD LAW REVIEW, Vol. 23, p. 40, November, 1970, p. 46.

approaches to problems, and to deal effectively with errorful or incomplete data".[216]

Heuristics, from the psychological point of view, can be applied when a human expert is confronted with a problem for which he knows no clearly applicable decision procedure, or for which existing procedures are excessively cumbersome.[217]

It is interesting to note, however, that numerous investigators have built legal expert and knowledge based systems, based on a clear distinction between the so called 'public' (i.e. published definitions, textbooks etc.) and 'private' (rules of thumb) legal knowledge. This was purely an 'expert systems' methodology, which restricts the concept of the legal sub-system. This conclusion has subsequently been confirmed by the analysis of the *Nomos* project (see Chapter 3).

On that point, SUSSKIND asserts that the distinction between two sorts of knowledge (public and private) is inappropriate in the case of law, because "although 'public' legal knowledge, appears in the form of legal textbooks, that is, as an orderly presentation, *inter alia*, of descriptive law-statements, such writings are not exhaustive of the category of public legal material. For our formal legal sources - law-formulations - are also to be found in paper and print...[f]urthermore...legal heuristics are sometimes set forth in print".[218]

[Search] Step 2: Search for *Heuristic* and *Empirical* Legal Knowledge

It should be added that empirical and heuristic knowledge, apart from being part[219] of the sources, where the lawyer searches, can themselves help the search procedure. They become[220] *meta-rules* or *meta-knowledge,* which BING & HARVOLD describe as "all norms governing a legal decision process".[221]

---

[216] SUSSKIND R., *Expert Systems in Law*, Clarendon, Oxford 1987, p. 46.

[217] SUSSKIND R., *Expert Systems in Law*, Clarendon, Oxford 1987, p. 91.

[218] SUSSKIND R., *Expert Systems in Law*, Clarendon, Oxford 1987, p. 46.

[219] This is only to declare that *empirical knowledge* and *heuristics* must be part of the sources in a practical model for Information Technology Applications in Law. It does not entail the acceptance of these sources as part of the formal legal ones, according to the previously defined doctrine.

[220] See SUSSKIND R., *Expert Systems in Law*, Clarendon, Oxford 1987, p. 110, describing that "...all those meta-rules that are not meta-law-statements, are, like law-predictions and law-derivations,

1.8.3 Social Knowledge Repercussions

The entrance of 'input' from the social environment to the legal system has already been accepted for practical reasons (see *supra* 1.4.2). It must be noted, however, that this position has already been supported theoretically, as part of the theory of legal discourse, by ALEXY[222] and PECZENIK[223] who submit that social demands can 'spring' from the social environment into the legal system (see *Figure 1-7* - page 111). This, they defend, can take place either during the formulation of legislation or during interpretation, and resembles the transformation of empirical knowledge to scientific knowledge.

[Search] Step 3: Search for Social Knowledge Repercussions

Irrespective of the scientific value of the above theory,[224] even the criticism against accepts that "it presents a procedure of transforming *empirical knowledge* to *normative one*" and that "social repercussions, when they do not constitute the criterion of enforcing the law, show the degree of its effectiveness".[225] Both these conclusions suit the purposes of this model. Therefore, it is partly justifiable to introduce to the model *non-legal* sources of law, that are, nevertheless, apparent in legal decision-making, as ethical and moral rules, rules of conduct and behaviour, cultural values, or different policies. It is irrelevant whether this input will be characterised as a formal legal source or as arguments that support legal decision making

---

instances of legal heuristics: they are informal, judgmental, experiential, and procedural rules of thumb (emphasis added).

[221] See BING J. & HARVOLD T., *Legal Decisions and Information Systems*, Universitetsforlaget Oslo, 1977, p. 19.

[222] ALEXY R, *A Theory of Legal Argumentation, The Theory of Rational Discourse as Theory of Legal Justification*, (English Translation), Clarendon press, Oxford, 1989.

[223] PECZENIK A., *On Law and Reason*, Kluwer, 1989.

[224] This theory has been refined further by McCORMICK N. & WEINBERGER O., *An Institutional Theory of Law, New Approaches to Legal Positivism*, D. REIDEL PUBLISHING COMPANY, Dordrecht, 1986.

[225] See STAMATIS K., *Isagogi sti Methodologia tou Dikeou, (Introduction to Legal Methodolgy*, in Greek), Thessaloniki, 1991, p. 79.

1.8.4   Individuation - The Legal Subsystem

In the words of ATIYAH, "law seems to be a seamless web, a huge network of interrelated rules of common law or case law, and of statute"[226] and this 'web' is constituted of the sources already exposed. LEITH similarly, but from a rather sociological point of view argues that "it is only by having a global appreciation of all the aspects of law which will allow each of these aspects to be properly understood - for law is an interconnected body of practices, ideology, social attitudes and legal texts, the latter being in many ways the least important".[227]

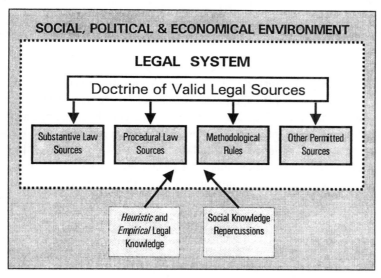

Figure 1- 7: In the search for law the doctrine of valid legal sources is dominating, but non-legal sources are considered too, and they are affecting the creation of the legal subsystem

The Lawyer, however, although aware of this huge network and its interrelations as a matter of legal education, in solving a certain legal problem, is not using the totality of legal sources. For, the general theory and infrastructure of the legal system as a whole lies in the back of his/her head, but the formerly defined *course*

---

[226] ATIYAH P. S., *Common Law and Statute Law*, in THE MODERN LAW REVIEW, Vol. 48, No. 1, p. 1, For the origins of the maxim see KATSH M. E., *Law in a Digital World*, Oxford University Press, New York, 1995, p. 21.

[227] LEITH P., *The Computerised Lawyer: A Guide to the Use of Computers in the Legal Profession*, Springer-Verlag, 1991, p. 213.

of argument, as said, guides his/her search in order to accurately pin-point only the sources needed for the problem in question. Nevertheless, the interrelations and the 'in content' interpretation with the rest of the law still remain intact. SUSSKIND[228] brings to light the long debate about *individuation*, i.e. the division of the law into distinct components, in order to answer the practical question: what is to count as one complete law?[229] The answer is affected by the concept of individuation followed by the Lawyer.

Nevertheless, from a practical point of view and for the needs of this model, in order to achieve completeness, the Lawyer is 'cutting' across and down the whole set of legal sources which can support a separate 'course of argument'.[230] The elementary 'unit' of this system, therefore, is the rule, and the result of the 'cutting' is a set of sources relevant to the above 'course of argument' (see *Figure 1-8* p. 113).

This is closer *mutatis mutandis*[231] to what SUSSKIND describes as the *'legal-subsystem'* in the case of his expert system analysis i.e. "a part of the legal system that contains all the laws of the system valid at a certain time (momentary[232] legal system), together with interpretations, derivations, predictions and meta-rules, based on these formulations".[233] Similarly MARTINO argues that "[w]henever lawyers and other professionals think of a partial legal system, however small it may be, they think of it as a self-sufficient set with the complete capacity to legally regulate any fact or situation belonging to that domain. There are even those who

---

[228] See SUSSKIND R., *Expert Systems in Law*, Clarendon, Oxford 1987, p. 118-128.

[229] SUSSKIND R., *Expert Systems in Law*, Clarendon, Oxford 1987, p. 121.

[230] In practcal terms it is also suggested that "no-one can pretend to have mastery over anything other than small subsets of a legal system" see SUSSKIND R., *The Future of Law*, Clarendon Press, Oxford, 1996, p. 12.

[231] I.e. by adopting the definitions of this model.

[232] See also WRÓBLEWSKI defining the "minimum optimum concept of law" containing only the norms and the "maximum concept of law" containing all facts relevant for decision-making, in WRÓBLEWSKI J., *Operative Models and Legal Systems, in* CIAMPI (Ed.), North Holland, 1982, p. 217.

[233] SUSSKIND R., *Expert Systems in Law*, Clarendon, Oxford 1987, p. 141 and SUSSKIND R. *The Latent Damage System: A Jurisprudential Analysis*, in PROCEEDINGS OF THE SECOND INTERNATIONAL CONFERENCE ON ARTIFICIAL INTELLIGENCE AND LAW, Vancouver, 1989.

always think of it as a consistent set or a set that can be reconstructed in a consisted manner."[234]

Therefore, the legal sub-system for this model[235] would contain part of the formal sources defined by the doctrine of valid[236] legal sources, part of empirical and heuristic legal knowledge, part of social knowledge, and part of methodological rules and interpretation that are relevant to the course of argument.

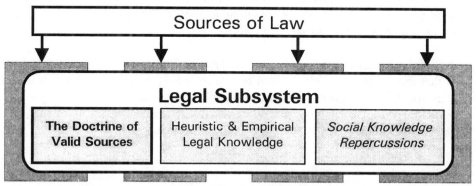

Figure 1- 8: From the total set of sources the Lawyer is isolating those necessary for the creation of the legal subsystem

This coincides with what RAZ describes as "many statutes from all the branches of the law, including civil as well as penal law, contribute to the content of every law" and further on he concludes that "[l]egal philosophy has double task. First, it has to formulate criteria by which to determine the identity of the authoritative legal material... [and second] has to formulate principles of individuation of laws,

---

[234] MARTINO, *Preface* in MARTINO A.A. (Ed.), *Expert Systems in Law*, NORTH HOLLAND, 1992, p. viii.

[235] For a different approach on how to define the legal category for a real fact see SKALAK D., *Taking Advantage of Models for Legal Classification*, in PROCEEDINGS OF THE SECOND INTERNATIONAL CONFERENCE ON ARTIFICIAL INTELLIGENCE AND LAW, Vancouver, 1989, p. 234.

[236] See also the interesting opinion of TISCORNIA "to analyse the legal decision-making process for the purpose of obtaining a model in which the deductive structure that justifies the decision is integrated with other formal aspects of legal reasoning" in TISCORNIA D., *Meta-Reasoning in Law: A Computational Model*, in JOURNAL OF LAW AND INFORMATION SCIENCE, Vol. 4, No. 2, 1993, p. 368.

in order to determine *how much of the matter contained in the whole system goes to make up one law.*"[237]

> **[Search] Step 4: Isolate the sources that support the course of argument and create the *legal subsystem***

MARTINO & GRU call that "small legal system" and, interestingly, argue that the problem is "not only representing law or its interpretation but also the path which a legal professional would take in consulting legislation."[238] which covers the notion of the *course of legal argument*.

A common misunderstanding in many Information Technology Applications in Law is that this spiritual exercise, called otherwise *individuation*, is confused with the standard divisions (statute, section, paragraphs etc.) of legal texts. The legal subsystem, however, does not refer to certain predetermined divisions of law, but rather it is cutting across all kinds of valid legal sources.

1.9   THE OUTPUT: THE LEGAL DECISION

1.9.1   Drafting Final Legal Arguments

The notion of 'legal argument', as an integrated piece of legal opinion, can also be used to cover interim implicit legal decisions that take place before the issue of the final ones.[239] 'Legal arguments' then is the smallest unit of legal advice.

> **Conclude Final Legal Arguments**

---

[237] RAZ J., *The Concept of a Legal System, An Introduction to the Theory of Legal System*, second edition, Clarendon, Oxford, 1980, p. 71(emphasis added).

[238] MARTINO A. & GRU O., *International Sale: An Expert System Prototype*, in MARTINO (Ed.), 1992.

[239] See also WAHLGREN P., *Legal Reasoning: a Jurisprudential Description*, in PROCEEDINGS OF THE SECOND INTERNATIONAL CONFERENCE ON ARTIFICIAL INTELLIGENCE AND LAW, Vancouver, 1989, p. 148.

It is also this part of the model which 'collects' the so decided 'easy cases'. Irrespective of their characterisation, their 'solution' also produces legal arguments.

1.9.2 The Output: Socially Related Result

The nature of Law itself dictates a 'socially accepted' result. LEITH postulates that "the legal process is principally a process of social negotiation; this negotiation occurs, with regard to ouster clauses, in a running battle between the legislators and the judiciary to formalise a clause which will have the desired effect. Thus not only the meaning of the words which are contained within the clause but also the practical effect which they might have has been taken into account".[240]

WAHLGREN, analogously, argues that "[I]n addition to easy access to a more or less comprehensible corpus of legal knowledge, a good understanding of what may be acceptable in the social environment of the intended legal decision as well as experience and knowledge of previous completed rule applications including their effects are doubtless other important aspects of legal expertise...".[241] The essence of this result, be it the rule of law, some other vague legal principle, the welfare of the client, or maybe a universal idea of justice, falls outside the scope of this book, being a matter of legal philosophy. But, what must be stressed is that the Legal Decision itself, as an active part of an 'open textured' social being, is not unique. There are always many potential solutions, and, consequently, many paths that one can follow to reach them. This multitude shows the ability and the flexibility of social sciences to solve human, as opposed to mechanical problems, but also indicates the dangers when a mechanical approach to the social sciences is attempted.

BERMAN & HAFNER, though supporters of automated legal reasoning systems, insist that "[t]he law's indeterminacy does not result from judicial perversity or disdain for logic. Rather, it recognises the reality that law embodies social political and economic realities rather than manifesting neatly arranged symbols of abstract

---

[240] LEITH P., *Fundamental Errors in Legal Logic Programming*, in THE COMPUTER JOURNAL, Vol. 29, No. 6, 1986, p. 549 (emphasis added).

[241] See also WAHLGREN P., *Automated Legal Reasoning: A Study on Artificial Intelligence and Law*, Kluwer, Computer/Law Series, 1992, p. 228.

thought processes".[242] In the scheme (see *Figure1-9* page 118) this 'openness' is depicted by the dotted line, which allows input and output between the surrounding 'environment' and the 'input facts' - 'legal decision'.

[Output]: Socially Related Results

1.9.3   Issuing the Legal Decision

In many legal systems, formal rules predict the exact appearance (oral or written etc.) and the formalities of a legal decision.[243] In many cases, constitutional rules guarantee that a formal legal decision (especially one given by the courts) must be adequately justified or, for example, include appeal guidelines. It is worth noting that many efforts to build Information Technology Applications in Law have been hampered by the fact that the final legal decision had to be issued in a formal way: e.g. bearing a special stamp, or signatures of the witnesses etc.

It is, however, common that lawyers use for many decisions a standard text or a pre-made form in which they complete certain parts. Again, the rules are stricter for Judges and simpler for Lawyers. In some simple circumstances, a legal decision may only be a form completed by a Lawyer and signed by a Judge.

WAHLGREN[244] insists that the legal decision must also be comprehensible to the persons involved, even to laymen, but it is believed that 'explicitness' is the less problematic side of a legal decision, where too often the complaints concern the substantive legal and logical issues.

[Output:] Issue the Legal Decision

---

[242] BERMAN D. & HAFNER C., *Indeterminacy: A Challenge to Logic-based models of Legal Reasoning*, in YEARBOOK OF LAW COMPUTERS & TECHNOLOGY, Vol. 3, 1987, p. 30.

[243] This could have many aspects, in Italy for example the judges of higher courts are obliged by law to 'feed' the decision to the Italgiure information retrieval system.

[244] WAHLGREN P., *Automated Legal Reasoning: A Study on Artificial Intelligence and Law*, Kluwer, Computer/Law Series, 1992, p. 227.

1.10   SYNTHESIS OF A MODEL - CONCLUSIONS OF CHAPTER 1

Once all the steps discussed in this chapter are synthesised, we are presented with the picture in *Figure 1-9* (page 118). The reason for this complicated scheme is the desire to depict the whole legal process under the 'checklist' notion already described. To summarise the arguments expressed above, the following points should be emphasised:

1. This model is not just a simple narration about a typical information system but rather tries to represent the full course of a certain human mental transaction, that of legal decision making. It is, however, an attempt to describe what actually happens, and not to prescribe a method for reaching legal decisions. In that sense, it can be characterised as *descriptive*.

2. The basic argument does not assume that the model is the only one possible. Furthermore, it does not defend the correctness or the completeness of the model but rather supports the thesis that such a model needs to be developed and must be used.

3. The model was developed in parallel with the *Nomos-Advisor* prototype. Most of its parts were tested with this prototype and at the same time refined by using feedback from the empirical results.

4. The procedure is not a one-way linear 'input-output' system. Legal decision making as a social phenomenon remains open to feedback from its surrounding social, political and economical background so that *stimuli* can enter from both ends of the model. Furthermore, the route is not predetermined and the arrows are only indicative.

5. This modelling is attempted from the practical jurisprudential point of view. This explains why at the core of this procedure lies the notion of *legal reasoning* and *legal interpretation*, as a basis for practical legal information technology applications. However, given the previously mentioned 'openness', the model can accept any other valid form of legal reasoning, such as case based reasoning, free interpretation etc.

6. The model tries to stay as neutral as possible to the prevailing legal theories, but emphatically insists that any practical information technology application in law must be based on the sound background of *a* legal theory.

117

7. This model endeavours to be used as a 'checklist' that can depict a compact picture of the full course of the Legal Decision Process, and provide a clearer view of the methodological rules so that future researchers, especially non-Lawyers, will avoid the omission of important elements of the process.

8. The enumeration of the elements of this checklist is neither exhaustive nor exclusive but rather depicts the *'minimum requirements configuration'* for building Information Technology Applications in Law.

9. Under this endeavour, it should be noted that many of the elements affecting the Legal Decision Process can be found within the legal system, but others also exist outside the legal system. In that sense, the model also depicts the interrelations with the surrounding environment.

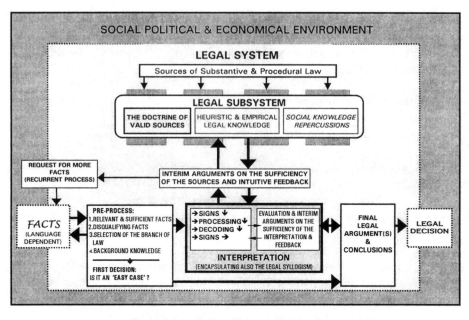

Figure 1-9: Modelling the Legal Decision Process

In this configuration and from a rather 'technical' point of view the model has a number of uses: First, it enables one to determine *where* in the legal decision process one can use automated systems. Second, it enables one to determine the input and output functions, how they should be discovered, and thus what the limitations of the system are. Third, it enables one to determine what *type* of automated decision-making tools can be used in the two distinct but interrelated levels:

The *lower level* represents the 'deductional' character of the core of legal reasoning, including interpretation and the legal syllogism (see *Figure 1-9* page 118). This level is suitable for introducing rule-based expert systems, case-based expert systems, and reasoning by example methods, neural networks and generally applications that perform legal reasoning.

The *upper level* represents the 'matching' function of the search of legal sources. This level is suitable for all kinds of information retrieval applications, document storage systems, hypertext applications etc. Applications that use legal reasoning to improve the performance of information retrieval, like 'intelligent' front-ends, 'intelligent' conceptual retrieval methods etc. appear to combine the characteristics of both levels and could be placed as a bridge between them.

A number of these issues will be examined in detail in the next Chapter (2). The analysis, however, will concentrate on the application of the model to rule-based expert systems. This particular kind of applications will be used in order to reduce the scope of the model, and to test the conclusions of Chapter 1. The reason for choosing this example amongst the multitude of automated decision support systems lies in the fact that the *Nomos-Advisor* prototype of the *Nomos* project was a typical example of a rule-based expert system.

ADDENDUM TO CHAPTER 1

The Legal Decision Process as a Checklist for Information Technology Applications in Law

[CONSTANTS]

Lawyer:	A person entitled by the legal system to cure or to advise on the cure of the Legal Pathology.
Judge:	A **Lawyer** obliged to find a legal decision abiding by the rules of the legal system in order to cure the *Legal Pathology*
Counsel:	A **Lawyer** obliged to find or predict the 'optimum' legal decision in favour of his/her **Client** abiding by the rules of the legal system and professional ethics
Client:	A person presenting his problem to a Lawyer
Norms	Conditional statements in the form *if p then q*
Legal Reasoning:	A mental process encapsulating *legal interpretation* and the *legal syllogism*
Legal Problem:	Problems that need *legal reasoning* as a solution
Legal Decision :	A conclusive and integrated piece of advice for the Client

[RULES]

1. The Legal Decision Process must be treated as an integrated whole seen through the eyes of a **'Lawyer'**
2. Any IT Application in Law is part of a legal system and must abide by the jurisprudential theory that supports it.
3. Any IT Application in Law must abide by the substantive, procedural and methodological rules of the legal system
4. The model of the Legal Decision Process will be used for practical applications
5. Determine *what* to represent
6. Use the results of rule 5 as a checklist
7. Follow rule-based deduction to conclude or justify a legal decision
8. Oscillate between law (legal rules) and real facts in order to reach a decision

[INPUT]

1. Socially related facts
2. Mixed real and legal 'biased' facts
3. Language dependent facts

[PRE-PROCESS]

1: Check that the Input Facts are Relevant and Sufficient for the Legal Problem
2: Check if the Input Facts trigger Substantive, Procedural or Administrative Disqualifying Rules
3: Select the Branch(es) of Law Involved and the Course of Argument
4: Consider carefully the Background Pragmatic Knowledge
        Case 4.1: IF from Steps 1-4 it is an 'Easy Case'
                THEN Conclude **FINAL LEGAL ARGUMENTS**
        Case 4.2: IF from Steps 1-4 it is **NOT** an 'Easy Case'
                THEN Start **INTERPRETATION**

[INTERPRETATION]

   Definition: The Logical Procedure performed by Lawyers in order to identify the meaning of the law

   CONDITION: Interpret until Interpretation is sufficient, according to the legal methodology in use.

     Rule 1: Interpretation is a means to apply the Law not an end in itself

     Rule 2: *Interpretatio cessat in Claris*

     Step 1: Decode the meaning of words in their syntactic, semantic and pragmatic dimension

       Phase 1:   Perform *linguistic* and *teleological* interpretation of the meaning of the rule in order to remove **vagueness**

       Phase 2:   Select the applicable rule by using the *three axioms of legal hierarchy* in order to exclude **conflicts**

       Phase 3:   Speculate similarities, or use *analogy*, or, *legal arguments* to establish similarity with already regulated cases in order to eliminate **gaps**

     Step 2: Apply the rules by performing the **Legal Syllogism:**

          Articulate Major Premiss sentence
          Articulate Minor Premiss sentence
          Subsume

          Conclude

    Case 1: IF [Interpretation Steps 1-2] need support from Legal Sources
       THEN Perform **SEARCH**
    Case 2: IF [Interpretation Steps 1-3] do not need more support
  THEN check the **CONDITION**

[SEARCH]

 Condition: Perform SEARCH until found sources are sufficient to create a *legal sub-system*.

   IF the facts are not sufficient for SEARCH look for more facts.

  Step 1: Search the sources following the doctrine of *Valid Legal Sources*

  Step 2: Search for *Heuristic* and *Empirical Legal Knowledge*

  Step 3: Search for *Social Knowledge Repercussions*

  Step 4: Isolate the sources that support the course of argument and create the *legal sub-system*

[Conclude FINAL LEGAL ARGUMENTS]

[OUTPUT]

  Condition: Socially Related Results
    ISSUE THE LEGAL DECISION

122

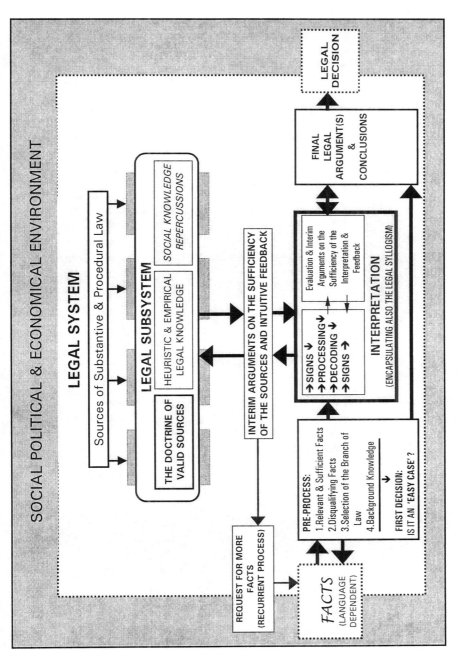

Figure 1-9: Modelling the Legal Decision Process

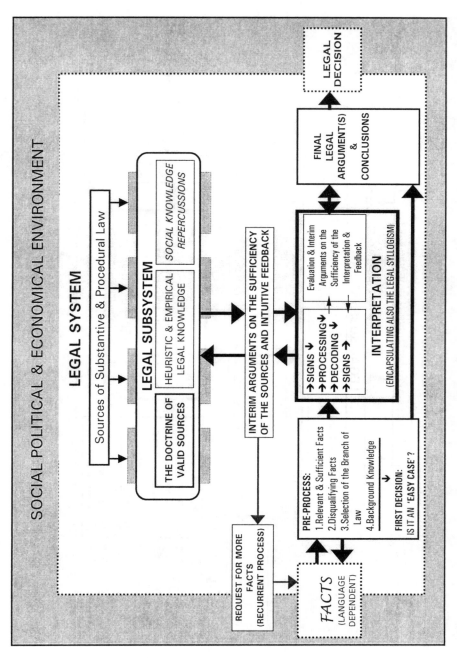

Figure 1-9: Modelling the Legal Decision Process

2. APPLYING THE MODEL TO THE CREATION OF LEGAL EXPERT SYSTEMS

2.1   INTRODUCTION

The model described in Chapter 1 is of a general character, targeting all possible Information Technology Applications in Law. However, as already explained, and as will be shown in detail in Chapter 3, the empirical testbench of this study was the creation of a legal expert system. The results of the experimental stage have revealed the need to identify and describe the special problems arising when attempting to use the model in connection with methods of Artificial Intelligence, and particularly to examine the specific problems of expert - or better, knowledge-based - systems. The empirical input from this Artificial Intelligence application was generalised to the theoretical model of Chapter 1. Therefore, Chapter 2 will, by reducing the general model to the level of expert systems, act as a 'bridge' to the specific application of Chapter 3.

It should be explained, however, that this chapter is not a full scale analysis of the implementation of expert systems, but rather highlights particular problems that occurred when an expert system was introduced into the model. In that sense, only a brief encyclopaedic description of the essential elements of expert systems is set out in the following paragraphs, mainly to explain terms and procedures to those not familiar with Artificial Intelligence techniques. Next, the chapter tries to find possible points of insertion of expert systems into the model and discusses their feasibility from a theoretical standpoint. Finally, from the numerous problems that the implementation stage revealed (described in Chapter 3), four special issues, considered to be major drawbacks in the design of expert systems for legal reasoning, are examined in detail.

2.2   PARTICULAR TECHNICAL CHARACTERISTICS OF EXPERT SYSTEMS

The general idea to produce computer programs that could solve human problems is very old. However, it was in the fifties that developments have led to coining the term 'Artificial Intelligence'[1] (now widely known as AI) for defining computer applications that could emulate certain aspects of human expertise in a specific domain of knowledge. In the sixties and seventies such applications, called 'expert' systems, were produced in the fields of medicine[2], chemistry[3] and geology.[4] Before proceeding, it should be clarified that "[t]here is no computer system in all of the artificial intelligence community which has anything approaching 'intelligence', as it is understood in the human world. Artificial intelligence merely seeks to understand some aspects of the way humans reason, and, hopefully, simulate these aspects. Researchers use the expression 'intelligent system' as a shorthand for any computer system which uses some or all of the techniques to be found within any of the sub-areas of artificial intelligence research. None of the researchers yet believe that these systems are intelligent as the layperson understands it; they simply know that the system uses artificial intelligence techniques and is therefore an 'intelligent system'."[5]

The typical definition is that *knowledge-systems*, as opposed to *data-systems,* incorporate active knowledge about an application. They do not depend on a fixed model or algorithm, but can produce solutions to novel situations. An *Expert System* is a knowledge-based system that incorporates enough knowledge to reach

---

[1]   By JOHN MCCARTHY circa 1956, see also FEIGENBAUM E. - FELDMAN J., *Computers and Thought*, Mcgraw-Hill, New York, 1963.

[2]   The DENDRAL system for definition of organic chemistry combinations by FEIGENBAUM & LEDERBERG, see BUCHANAN B. & SHORTLIFFE E., *Rule Based Expert Systems*, Addison Weshley, Reading MA, 1984.

[3]   The MYCIN system for diagnosing bacterial infections, by BUCHANAN B. & SHORTLIFFE E. (Eds.), *Rule Based Expert Systems: The MYCIN experiments of the Stanford Heuristic Programming Project*, Addison Weshley, Reading MA, 1984.

[4]   The PROSPECTOR system, for mineral exploitation.

[5]   ZELEZNIKOW J. & HUNTER D., *Building Intelligent Legal Information Systems, Representation and Reasoning in Law*, Kluwer, Computer/Law Series, 1994, p. 82.

expert levels of performance, or, "emulates the behaviour of a human expert within a limited legal domain".[6]

Since the fifties, in the area of Law, the scientific debate around 'Jurimetrics', i.e. the application of scientific methods to the Law.[7] In that era 'Jurimetrics' consisted of statistical methods, used to predict judicial behaviour. This implementation has produced the basis for the future use of computers for legal reasoning and hence for the creation of legal expert systems. It was, however, the pioneers of expert systems in other disciplines, BUCHANAN AND HEADRICK,[8] that proposed, for the first time, a method for using Artificial Intelligence techniques for legal reasoning, by applying their DENDRAL system to legal problems.

Recent developments, however, suggest abandoning the use of the term 'expert systems' in favour of the term 'knowledge-based systems', in an effort to emphasise the distinct character of the body of knowledge of those systems, as opposed to their - if any - expertise. The critics[9] argue that a system called 'expert' is not a substitute for knowledge, but, rather, an aid to the process.

Of the same opinion is SUSSKIND, by arguing that "[expert systems] are used as high-level intellectual aids to their users, which explains one of their alternative epithets: intelligent assistants", he concludes, however that "[t]hey differ from Intelligent Knowledge Based Systems (IKBS) in that the latter may recognise speech, perceive images, or indeed solve problems in a fashion that undoubtedly is dependent on knowledge, yet that requires no particular human expertise. Only those IKBS that embody a depth and richness of knowledge that permit them to perform at the level of an expert in a particular (and normally highly specialised) domain, therefore, ought then to be designated expert systems".[10] Indeed, the core aim of a knowledge-based system is broader: It does not try to solve *ad hoc* legal

---

6   REED C., *Expert Systems*, in REED (Ed.), *Computer Law*, Blackstone, 1990.

7   See the classic article of LEE LOEVINGER, *Jurimetrics: The Next Step Forward*, in MINNESOTA LAW REVIEW, Vol. 33, p. 455, April, 1949 and the writings of LAYMAN ALLEN.

8   BUCHANAN B. & HEADRICK TH., *Some Speculation About Artificial Intelligence and Legal Reasoning*, in STANFORD LAW REVIEW, Vol. 23, p. 40, November, 1970.

9   See for example WAHLGREN P., *Automation of Legal Reasoning, A Study on Artificial Intelligence and Law*, Kluwer, Deventer, 1992, p. 109.

10   SUSSKIND R., *Expert Systems in Law: a Jurisprudential Inquiry*, Clarendon Press, Oxford, 1987, p. 9.

problems but rather to automate a whole set of legal tasks by incorporating both legal knowledge and reasoning strategies.[11]

2.2.1 General Prerequisites of an Expert System

As explained, the following analysis is not a deep investigation of the methodology to build knowledge based systems but an encyclopaedic outline of terms and procedures, mainly in order to prepare the reader for Chapter 3. Briefly, the main components that we expect to find in most expert systems are:

- A representation of a body of domain specific knowledge. The classic example is to represent this knowledge in the form of rules, so the system is often categorised as *rule-based*.

- An appropriate mechanism for using this body of knowledge by reasoning with facts and rules.

- A mechanism to generate explanations and to justify the advice given.

- A mechanism to complete the above body of knowledge, by adding, for example, new rules, or as it is called meta-knowledge.

- An interface, in order to communicate with the user, possibly with a limited 'natural language' processor.

To implement this classic configuration, expert systems are presented using:

- A *knowledge base* which is the 'storage tank' to include the body of knowledge,

- An *inference engine* which is the said mechanism of inferences and explanations, and

- A *user interface* to communicate with the user.

---

[11] Notice however, that an expert system providing advice and guidance is also a subset of a knowledge based system. The distinction is based on the tasks that the systems perform. See also the considerations of AIKENHEAD M., *Legal Knowledge Based Systems: some observations on the future*, in WEB JOURNAL OF CURRENT LEGAL ISSUES, 1995, in endnote 1 and the definition of SCHILD *"Legal Advisory Systems"* in SCHILD U. J., *Open-Textured Law, Expert Systems and Logic Programming*, unpublished Ph.D. Thesis, University of London, 1989, p. 17.

The person who possesses the expertise is called *domain expert* while the person who is trying to extract this knowledge and transform it into the knowledge base representation is called *knowledge engineer*.

A system configured in this manner is therefore expected[12] to:

- Solve an important problem that would otherwise have to be solved by a human expert. The goal is not necessarily to design a program that reasons in the same way as a human, but whose outputs are, with certain constraints, as intelligent as those of a human reasoner[13].

- Be flexible in integrating new knowledge incrementally into its existing store of knowledge

- Assist its operator to elicit, structure and transfer knowledge

- Present its knowledge in a form that is easy to read

- Provide explanations of its advice

- Reason with judgmental or inexact knowledge about the nature of a task or how to do the task efficiently

- Deal with simple sentences in natural language

It should be noted that the above methodology has its roots in the first practical expert systems.[14] The method is mainly scientific but it was also used for systems in the legal field and, indeed, for the first commercially available legal expert system.[15] This, consequently, shows that, through time, the methodology for knowledge-based applications in law was not developed *ad hoc*, as it would be endeavoured, but rather was based on existing paradigms from the scientific disciplines (such as medicine, or geology).

---

[12] WALKER A., *Knowledge Systems, Principles and Practice*, IBM JOURNAL, Vol. 30, January, 1986, p. 3.

[13] See ASHLEY K., *Modelling Legal Argument*, MIT Press, Cambridge Mass., 1990, p. 1.

[14] See *supra* notes 2, 3,.4.

[15] CAPPER P. & SUSSKIND R., *Latent Damage Act, The Expert System*, Butterworths, London, 1988.

2.2.2 Knowledge Representation - The Knowledge Base

It is evident that the above 'body of knowledge' is not directly understandable by the machine, but has to be transformed to another 'computer oriented' form.[16] Therefore, in order to use knowledge in a machine the first step is to choose a way of representing it. From the time of HOHFELD,[17] different schemes have been proposed for representing legal knowledge in some other form and there exists a plethora of so-called representation languages. These include:

- *Logical representation schemes*, which use logic to represent the knowledge base;

- *Procedural representation schemes*, where knowledge is represented as a set of instructions for solving a problem;

- *Network representation schemes* where knowledge is represented in graphs with a system of *nodes* and *arcs*: the nodes represent evidence or hypotheses about something and the arcs represent causal linkages and relations among the nodes;[18] and finally,

- *Structured representation schemes*, which extend the above network scheme to complex data structures consisting of *slots* with attached values.[19]

The procedure of transforming legal knowledge into a structured form understandable by computers is often called *formalisation*.

Several of these representations stand somewhere between natural language and programs.[20] According to the expert systems gurus' dogma: what is needed is a

---

[16] The transfer of knowledge from the knowledge sources to the computer program is called *knowledge acquisition*. For the specific problems of legal knowledge acquisition see *infra* 2.4.2.

[17] HOHFELD, WESLEY & NEWCOMB, *Fundamental Legal Conceptions as Applied in Judicial Reasoning*, Edited by Walter Wheeler Cook from the 1913 article, 23 YALE LAW JOURNAL, Yale University Press, New Haven, 1963.

[18] Semantic networks and Conceptual Graphs, SOWA'S method of representing natural language, which is described in detail in Chapter 3, are very much similar to this method.

[19] See details in ZELEZNIKOW J. & HUNTER D., *Building Intelligent Legal Information Systems, Representation and Reasoning in Law*, Kluwer, Computer/Law Series, 1994, p. 96.

formalisation that should be easy to (a) read, to (b) add to and (c) to change knowledge. The method should also (d) support explanation generation and, in addition, should be able (e) to separate *declarative* from *procedural* knowledge.

Some of the proposed methods[21] make use of a *hierarchy*, in which lower items are normally assumed to inherit some of the properties of higher items,

e.g. vehicle → car → cabriolet etc.

Some notations are used without explicit reference to a hierarchy, like *rules* and *nets*. Others, such as *frames* and *objects,* are built around the hierarchical notion. A *frame* looks like a form, which we can fill in with specific knowledge content and then may have a place in a hierarchy of forms. An *object* is a process, like a mathematical black box, that receives a message, changes its internal state, and sends out a message.

From the technical point of view, the selection of the representation method is also dependent on the inference engine (see *infra* 2.2.3). However, this may lead to serious distortions of the knowledge base, because in order to increase the programs 'technical efficiency' and compliance with the inference engine, important elements of legal knowledge are omitted. Finally, the mainstream expert systems' methodology requires a certain uniformity in the knowledge base, so that the 'units' of knowledge can be introduced or eliminated easily, in order to obtain an update function for when the knowledge changes.

Returning to the purposes of this study, it should be noted that as early as 1974, BAUER-BERNET has stressed that "[f]ormilization of an empirical discipline will not transform it into a formal discipline! Formal rules need continuous empirical corroboration".[22] In the same vein REED argues that "[o]ne of the major criticisms

---

20 See also the *'isomorphism'* proposal i.e. the as much as possible closeness of the formalised 'knowledge base' to the original knowledge by BENCH-CAPON in all his writings and especially BENCH-CAPON T. & CONEN F., *Exploiting Isomorphism: Development of a KBS to Support British Coal Insurance Claims* in PROCEEDINGS OF THE 3RD INTERNATIONAL CONFERENCE ON ARTIFICIAL INTELLIGENCE AND LAW, Oxford, June 25-28 1991, ACM Press, 1991.

21 For a detailed description see MITAL V. & JOHNSON L., *Advanced Information Systems for Lawyers*, Chapman & Hall, London, 1992, p. 66.

22 BAUER-BERNET HÉLÈNE, *Effect of Information Science on the Formation and Drafting of Law*, in JURIMETRICS JOURNAL, Summer, 1974, p. 244.

levelled at I[ntelligent] K[nowledge] B[ase]s is that they encapsulate only the 'surface structure' of a domain of law, and do not exhibit any of the 'deep understanding' that a human lawyer will possess. This can be seen, for example, in an expert system which advises a small business on its tax liabilities. Effective tax advice requires not only an understanding of laws relating to taxation, but also an understanding of principles of accounting, the structure of the client's business, the nature of its activities, and the expertise of its staff."[23]

At the first instance, it appears that the proposed – science oriented - representation techniques are insufficient for the construction of legal expert systems. Therefore, other means for representing knowledge must also be examined. Furthermore, in legal applications, more attention must be paid to the empirical input (see also infra 2.4.1 Enigma I: What Legal Knowledge for a Knowledge Base?). The long discussion about choosing the right kind of representation loses its meaning if the knowledge to be represented is not correct or complete.

2.2.3   The Inference Engine

The classic configuration of a knowledge system entails that knowledge should be represented in the form of rules, and then such a system is called a rule-based system. The *rules* in an expert system environment are often represented in the form:

If [Condition A] [AND] [Condition B] THEN...

or in the form of the Horn clauses:

RESULT q IF a AND b AND c AND d...

In this scheme Condition A will be trying to match something in the knowledge base and the THEN / RESULT part specifies an action to be done. These kind of rules are also called 'production rules'. More often, these rules are accompanied by 'confidence values' in order to perform '*inexact*' reasoning.

---

23 REED C., *Expert Systems*, in REED (Ed.), *Computer Law*, Blackstone, 1990, p. 223.

An E-MYCIN[24] rule for example reads:

IF "plant is wilting" AND
    NOT "leaves have yellow spots"
        THEN "there is not enough water" : 60

Fuzzy logic, which can represent a multiple of truth values between 0 and 1, and together with probability techniques is then used to produce a result. The number 60, in the above example, indicates that we have a 60% or 0.6 confidence in the rule and it is used in a numerical form of judgmental reasoning. Fuzzy logic also provides certain rules for combining these rules and making complicated calculations.

The *inference engine* is defined as the mechanism which processes these rules in order to solve a problem. *Deductive reasoning*, a process in which a set of predetermined premises known as *axioms* is used to derive conclusions, is fundamental to rule-based expert systems. The *inference engine* uses many methods to manage the rules for deduction, the best known being *forward* and *backward* chaining. In forward chaining, the inference engine combines rules in order to reach a conclusion. In backward chaining a conclusion is asserted and then the inference engine searches the knowledge base to find all the rules that support this conclusion. These two methods may also be combined. By 'browsing' through the rules contained in the knowledge base, the system is delimited, however, to solving only those problems which can be decided in a finite number of steps.

It is obvious that this deductive mechanism and its connection to logic and logic methods are fundamental to expert systems. SUSSKIND & CAPPER,[25] however, expose a number of inherent drawbacks in this rule-based approach and suggest that such systems will not be used by laymen, but rather by qualified experts.

Expert systems are expected to be transparent in their function. Therefore, the inference engine must be able to trace the facts of the case in question, and the rules that it is using, and provide a reasonable *explanation* for their use.

---

[24] MYCIN was an expert system for diagnosing bacterial infections. Its basic system, without the knowledge base, was used like a 'shell' under the name E-MYCIN (empty MYCIN) see BUCHANAN B. & SHORTLIFFE E. (Eds.), *Rule Based Expert Systems: The MYCIN experiments of the Stanford Heuristic Programming Project*, Addison Weshley, Reading MA, 1984.

[25] SUSSKIND R. & CAPPER P., *The Latent Damage System, A First Generation Expert System in Law*, in MARTINO (Ed.), North Holland, 1992.

Practically, in rule-based systems, this takes the form of showing to the user the chain through the rules and a list of the facts that confirmed (or not) the rules.

For informational purposes, however, it should be noted that a large part of recent research in AI and Law is targeting the use of alternatives to the use of rules. One such method is *Case Based Reasoning (CBR)*,[26] where problems concerning 'new' cases are solved, not by using rules, but by analogy with previous cases or examples stored in the system's knowledge base. This method has gained ground in Common Law jurisdictions, where arguing with cases plays a primary role in legal practice. It must not be confused, however, with way common law functions with precedents and cases.

Case Based Reasoning uses two basic inference methods, in contrast to rule-based deduction (followed by the model described here): (1) either a solution is drawn from previous cases or (2) a new case is evaluated by comparison to previous cases. The main difficulty with CBR systems is that in order to fulfil the above inference methods they use symbolic representations of the cases, which can be subjective and biased. Furthermore, it is cumbersome to keep large case-bases together with complicated case representations. However, CBR, although falls outside the scope of this chapter to be examined in detail, appears a promising technique in supplementing rule-based expert systems especially in the area of explanations, analogical reasoning and retrieval of similar cases.

Another method, being in experimental stage,[27] is the use of *neural nets*, named after the neuron cells in the brain. This is a computer model simulating the structure of a biological nervous system providing many input and output channels connected in a complex way, in contrast to the single channel of existing systems. Successful use of computerised neural networks has been reported in the field of pattern recognition, while in the area of law there have been attempts to use them

---

[26] For examples in CBR see SKALAK D. & RISSLAND E., *Arguments and Cases: An Inevitable Interwining*, in ARTIFICIAL INTELLIGENCE AND LAW, Vol. 1, No. 1, 1992 and ASHLEY K., *Case-Based Reasoning and its Implications in Legal Expert Systems*, in ARTIFICIAL INTELLIGENCE AND LAW, Vol. 1, No. 2, 1992, p. 113. For a detailed analysis see in the bibliography GARDNER A., *An Artificial Intelligence Approach to Legal Reasoning*, MIT Press, Cambridge Mass, 1987 and ASHLEY K., *Modeling Legal Argument*, MIT Press, Cambridge Mass., 1990 see also all the writings of ASHLEY, BERMAN, HAFNER and RISSLAND.

[27] For an introductory discussion see REED in REED (Ed.), *Computer Law*, Blackstone Press, London, 1990 and REED C., *Expert Systems and Legal Expertise*, in Computer Law & Practice, Vol. 5, p. 122, 1989.

as a method of solving legal problems based on previously decided cases. Although not yet widely commercialised, neural nets appear promising for legal applications in the area of fuzzy reasoning,[28] i.e. reasoning with uncertain data, or reasoning with means other than the traditional logical rules and in the field of reasoning by example. The latter could have great potential in solving the problem of matching a current situation with already decided cases.

2.2.4 PROLOG v. Shells

To implement an expert system, special programming languages such as PROLOG[29] and LISP[30] are used. *PROLOG* is the main programming language for so called 'logic programming' and was adopted by the Japanese as the basis of their Fifth Generation Project concerning human reasoning. While it was first implemented to support natural language processing, it works essentially as an efficiently executable part of mathematical logic, thus being of interest to expert system reasoning. Furthermore, it contains some declarative features from computational mathematics logic, and some procedural aspects from conventional programming. Many of the mechanisms one needs for an expert system are inherent in the language and many inference engines for expert systems are similar to the PROLOG inference engine.

The other solution is to use an *expert system shell*, "[which provides the researcher] with a ready-made inference mechanism upon which to construct his expert system, thereby removing the need for him to design, and write the code for, his own inference engine. Shells are created by removing the domain-specific knowledge of an existing expert system and leaving the inference sub-system, which can then, in turn be applied to a different problem domain."[31] Expert system

---

[28] For a recent example with rule-based reasoning see ZELEZNIKOW & STRANIERI, *The Split-up System: Integrating Neural Networks and Rule-Based Reasoning in the Legal Domain*, in PROCEEDINGS OF THE 5TH INTERNATIONAL CONFERENCE ON ARTIFICIAL INTELLIGENCE AND LAW, University of Maryland, 21-24 May, 1995, ACM Press, 1995, p. 185.

[29] *PROgrammation en LOGique.*

[30] *LISt Processing.*

[31] SUSSKIND R., *Expert Systems in Law: a Jurisprudential Inquiry*, Clarendon Press, Oxford, 1987, p. 155.

shells date back to MYCIN[32] which, without its knowledge base, became E-MYCIN (empty MYCIN) and was used as an expert system shell. This system was written in LISP. The advantage of shells is that the developer does not have to build the system 'from scratch' and no particular experience is necessary. Generally, shells are rule-based and provide limited inferencing in the form of forward and backward chaining.[33]

2.2.5 The User Interface

The user interface is an often neglected part of legal information systems. Developers do not realise that a poor interface is one of the main causes for the under-use of information systems by lawyers. Currently, most systems have a simple interface, which does not encourage the usually computer-phobic lawyers to use the system. In the worst scenario, this interface is a simple line editor accepting 'yes' or 'no' to the posed questions. In some more sophisticated applications the user is presented with menus, graphics and hypertext.

It is believed that future trends – especially graphic interfaces - in computer technology will also improve this neglected aspect. In the meantime, potential analysts should be careful to (1) decide the number and the complexity of the questions asked to the user; (2) design interesting screens and menus; (3) follow an appearance resembling that of paper-based textual material and (4) ensure the coordination between the different components of the system.[34] Further enhancements should include the ability of the user to browse back and forth through the system, to back-track the questions and the conclusions of a session, as well as the ability to save and print the session.

WIDDISON[35] has emphasised the need, not only to enhance the user interface, but also to make it resemble traditional legal research tools. He argues, further, that

---

32 See supra note 24.

33 See also WATERMAN D.A., *A Guide to Expert Systems*, Addison-Weshley, Reading MA., 1986.

34 For a detailed analysis see WIDDISON R., PRITCHARD F., & ROBINSON W., *Expert Systems meet Hypertext: The European Conflicts Guide*, in JOURNAL OF LAW AND INFORMATION SCIENCE, Vol. 3, No. 1, 1992, p. 90.

35 WIDDISON R., *Expert Systems: the Forgotten Dimension*, in COMPUTERS AND LAW, Vol. 3, No. 1, March, 1992, p. 33.

"[i]n a subject like law, expert systems users cannot be expected to answer questions without consulting relevant primary and secondary text materials. It is generally accepted by software developers that users must have fast, context sensitive, on-screen access to a database of such text materials during consultations... Such an approach gives developers the flexibility to build environments that have a familiar 'look and feel' to users. Text materials can be given the appearance of paper based books with electronic 'pages' that can be accessed read and skipped through in the normal way. The electronic pages can be designed to look much like their paper-based equivalents, and can be 'footnoted' in an apparently conventional way."

It is believed that one of the major obstacles in the advancement of technology in the legal environment is the predominating – from the time of the law school - 'book culture' (see *infra* 2.3.6 The Information Crisis of Legal Decision Making). Under this hypothesis, the adoption of the above technique i.e. the trick of 'electronic books', could substantially familiarise lawyers with modern technology[36].

2.2.6 Hypertext

Maintaining links with other relevant materials is an inherent difficulty of rule-based expert systems. To tackle this problem, numerous researchers[37] have proposed the use of *Hypertext* in combination with knowledge-based systems.[38] *Hypertext* is a collective name used for the management of many aspects of information such as text, graphics, sound, video etc. Hypertext is trying to place information in a more enhanced structure than that of a book, or other paper form, which are the traditional methods preferred in a legal environment.

---

[36] See for example the legal advisory system LEDIA, which is an electronic textbook providing information on the legal aspects of EDI (Electronic Data Interchange) in MITRAKAS A., *A Legal Advisory System Concerning Electronic Data Interchange within the European Community*, COMPLEX 6/96, Tano, Oslo, 1996.

[37] See for example ZELEZNIKOW J. & HUNTER D., *Building Intelligent Legal Information Systems, Representation and Reasoning in Law,* Kluwer, Computer/Law Series, 1994 and MOWBRAY, GREENLEAF & TYREE, *The Privacy Workstation*, in YEARBOOK OF LAW COMPUTERS AND TECHNOLOGY, Vol. 6, p. 178, 1992.

[38] See also the technical descriptions in MITAL V. & JOHNSON L., *Advanced Information Systems for Lawyers*, Chapman & Hall, London, 1992, chapter 9, p. 143.

In its simplest form, hypertext consists of textual material which is retrieved by 'links' between words and phrases in documents.[39] These 'links' are referred to as 'vertical', when a particular word, called a 'hotword', is linked with a particular node or nodes; or as 'horizontal' when they cross-reference nodes.[40] Hypertext provides a powerful method of document presentation because users can selectively display and read the information that they want, without looking at irrelevant information (compare with the formulation of the legal sub-system *supra* section 1.8). Hypertext is particularly suited for the legal domain, because most legal texts contain reference to other sources, such as other decisions, precedents, statute etc. and furthermore, legal texts in most cases cannot be interpreted without reference to these other sources. 'Jumping' from decision to decision and, then to statute, and then to precedent and back is a method often used by lawyers.

One of the problems associated with hypertext, is that of keeping a huge network of 'links' up to date, which do not cover the semantic but rather the syntactic meaning of words. Another problem, known as 'lost in hyperspace', is when the user is not able to find his/her way within this network of links.[41] Therefore, the user must be always guided through the information.

In connection with the model of Chapter 1, developers must be careful to link all the proposed nodes of legal decision making, especially in the area of the legal sub-system. Also apparent is the problem of the so-called *rich* and *poor* links, where crucial information is contained in a badly labelled node. It is obvious that potential developers, after assigning the values for the creation of the legal sub-system (see section 1.8), should also be careful in introducing the pointers for a hypertext system.

---

[39] See also the analytical description of WAHLGREN P., *Hypertext and Legal Structures*, in MARTINO (Ed.), 1992.

[40] See also DAYAL S. & MOLES R., *The Open Texture of Language: Handling Semantic Analysis in Legal Decision Support Systems*, in JOURNAL OF LAW AND INFORMATION SCIENCE Vol. 4, No. 2, 1993, p. 343.

[41] For an interesting solution see MACAULAY M., *Mapping Legal Hypertext Systems*, in CONFERENCE PRE-PROCEEDINGS, 7TH BILETA CONFERENCE, 1992.

2.3   PLACING EXPERT SYSTEMS INTO THE MODEL

2.3.1   Possible Points of Insertion of Expert Systems

The problem of inserting expert systems into the model lies more in the effort to keep the internal consistency of the model, by abiding to the rules and the interconnections, rather than finding these 'points of insertion'. The latter are otherwise determined by the current technological state-of-the-art and are relatively easy to identify. For that purpose, i.e. identifying the possible points of insertion the described model presents three different parts:[42] (1) the core part of legal reasoning including legal interpretation, (2) the part of formulating the legal sub-system and legal information retrieval and (3) the two side parts of input and output.[43]

Into the *first part*: Traditional rule-based expert systems - with the limitations that will be exposed - could be applied, adjusted to solve 'hard cases'. Furthermore, expert systems could help with methodological and procedural rules, by continuously reminding users either (1) the rank of triggering those rules or (2) by pointing out the sufficiency of interpretation. The question of the sufficiency of 'facts' could also be tackled by using an expert system as a 'checklist'. As explained in Chapter 1, the model is open to many solutions, and the use of other technologies in this part is not ruled out. Therefore, any other method for legal reasoning is acceptable provided that it observes the interconnections and the general restrictions of the model. In that direction, *Case Based Reasoning* (CBR) techniques, or *Neural Nets* could substitute rule-based expert systems in this part of the model. It is anticipated, however, that *mutantis mutandis* adaptations must be

---

[42] See also the categorisation of SUSSKIND R., *Artificial Intelligence, Expert Systems and the Law, A European Appraisal*, in ESSAYS ON LAW AND AI, COMPLEX 7/93, NRCCL, Oslo, 1993. These ideas were later elaborated into the *Legal Information Continuum* in SUSSKIND R., *The Future of Law*, Clarendon Press, Oxford, 1996, p. 86.

[43] See also LEITH P., *The Computerised Lawyer: A Guide to the Use of Computers in the Legal Profession*, Springer-Verlag, 1991 about *primary* and *secondary* legal information retrieval and Oskamp distinguishing between "what may be seen as two levels into which legal practice may be divided. The first level is that of what could be called 'first aid' legal help, i.e. straight legal advice and information. At the second level the case is taken to court, where the judge will have to give his judgement to that specific case." OSKAMP A., *Knowledge Representation and Legal Expert Systems*, in VANDENBERGHE (Ed.), Kluwer, Computer/Law Series, 1989, p. 197.

made to the notions of *Legal Interpretation* and the *Legal Syllogism* because CBR is following a different inference method than the rule-based deduction proposed by the model. Furthermore, a number of the methodological guidelines of the model must be adapted accordingly in order to favour the use of cases and examples against rules.

Into the *second part*: Systems involving conceptual retrieval, i.e. a different organisation of data bases in order to retrieve information more effectively, could be applied.[44] These could follow knowledge-based systems methodology. Another possible use is the implementation of front-ends, i.e. systems that facilitate the search in existing databases by improving the interface and by formulating the query of the user. In that case, front-ends can use knowledge-based systems techniques. Again, the methodology is not restricted to rule-based expert systems. In particular, matching techniques and similarity criteria developed for Case Based Reasoning can be used for improving the structure of existing and future databases.[45] It must be repeated, however, that the considerations of the previous paragraph concerning the interrelations with the other parts of the model must be taken into account.

Into the *third part*: Document assembly systems[46] could help in the initial phase of facts input by introducing automatic completion forms. Expert systems could be used here in guiding the drafting of legal documents, and in restricting fill-in forms. In the output phase, i.e. in issuing the legal decision, expert systems could create checklists, explain rules, draft documents etc. It should be remembered, however, that the legal working environment is also an ordinary office. As such,

---

[44] For an example in conceptual retrieval and neural networks see SCHWEIGHOFER, WINIWARTER & MERKL, *Information Filtering: The Computation of Similarities in Large Corpora of Legal Texts*, in PROCEEDINGS OF THE 5TH INTERNATIONAL CONFERENCE ON ARTIFICIAL INTELLIGENCE AND LAW, University of Maryland, 21-24 May, 1995, ACM Press, 1995, p. 119.

[45] See RISSLAND, SKALAK, & FRIEDMAN, *BankXX, A Program to Generate Argument through Case-Based Search*, in PROCEEDINGS OF THE 4TH INTERNATIONAL CONFERENCE ON ARTIFICIAL INTELLIGENCE AND LAW, Amsterdam 15-18 June 1993, ACM Press, 1993, p. 117 and recently RISSLAND & DANIELS, *A Hybrid CBR-IR Approach to Legal Information Retrieval* and RISSLAND & FRIEDMAN, *Detecting Change in Legal Concepts*, in PROCEEDINGS OF THE 5TH INTERNATIONAL CONFERENCE ON ARTIFICIAL INTELLIGENCE AND LAW, University of Maryland, 21-24 May, 1995, ACM Press, 1995, pp. 52 & 127.

[46] See also LAURITSEN M., *Technology Report: Building Legal Practice Systems with Today's Commercial Authoring Tools*, in ARTIFICIAL INTELLIGENCE AND LAW, Vol. 1, No. 1, p. 87 and GORDON T., *A Theory Construction Approach to Legal Document Assembly*, in MARTINO (Ed.), North Holland, 1992.

this part of the model is strongly connected with general office automation, and the number of possible applications is endless.

An important difference between the parts of the model is hidden here: (1) Systems which perform functions in the first part of the model must be capable of sound legal reasoning techniques in order to produce reliable and trustworthy results; while (2) systems in the other parts can act as delimited assistants to legal decision making and the final decision will remain a task of the user. However, the most consequential issue, for any particular application, is the task to comply with the internal consistency between the three, interrelated, parts of the model. The findings of the *Nomos* project, in connection with the methodology of the model proposed in Chapter 1, indicate that an expert system incorporated in the first part (attempting to reason with rules) must additionally take into consideration (a) the legal sources appearing in the second part and (b) factual information and sociological input from the third part.

> **Link to the Model:**
> The scheme of the model and the checklist must be used in order to identify
> all possible connections. Systems inserted into one of the parts of the model
> must not be built in isolation but in relation to the other parts.

Establishing these connections requires the maintenance of an immense knowledge base, which presents additional practical difficulties. The following paragraphs will examine these problems depending on the character, the peculiarities and the limitations of each kind of application, i.e. *legal reasoning*, *information retrieval* and *office automation*.

2.3.2   For Legal Reasoning

It could be argued that Legal Reasoning, being the core task of a knowledge-based system, dominates all aspects of a legal decision-making system i.e. even in the case of information retrieval or office automation. That is the purpose of interconnecting all the parts of the model and presenting them within the same framework (see *Figure 1-9*). The core procedures must encapsulate legal reasoning if the final aim is for the application to be consistent with the rules of the model.

> **Link to the Model:**
> Most of the rules of the model and especially the *Rule of Integration* and the
> *Rule of Practicality* must be applied here in order to identify if the insertion

> of an expert system is feasible. All the parts of the model referred to in the
> *Checklist* must be taken into consideration

Otherwise, these applications will never be placed within the informational system of the legal office, and, therefore, will not be used. The argument is the same for applications that are simply research experiments. Elementary scientific methodology entails that even basic research must have as input an accurate set of data, and parts of the law, used for 'experimentation' divorced from their place in the legal decision process are not accurate statements of law. In the case of legal information systems, applied research is used in the everyday tasks of legal or other practice as well as in academia,[47] because "law cannot be viewed without the working and practical concerns of the solicitor, barrister and the private citizen".[48]

There is no doubt, that from the theoretical speculations of the early seventies which were initiated in the landmark article of BUCHANAN & HEADRICK,[49] a range of applications have been created on a *practical level*,[50] i.e. the theoretical considerations were applied by actually building such applications and evaluating their results. Nevertheless, it cannot be submitted that these legal expert systems were without problems, which will be examined later (see *infra* 2.4). However, apart from the thesis that legal reasoning dominates every aspect of knowledge-based systems, the general question raised is whether such systems, to be incorporated in the model, can be implemented in the core part of legal decision making, and, indeed, produce legal decisions. In terms of the model, this is translated to whether expert systems can be inserted into the core part in order to perform legal reasoning, and to solve 'hard cases'. This part is depicted in the model (*Figure 1-9*) with the sketch for *Interpretation*, *Legal Syllogism* and *Final Legal Arguments*.

---

[47] See the same idea supported by WAHLGREN P., *A General Theory of Artificial Intelligence and Law,* in PRAKKEN, MUNTJEWERFF & SOETEMAN (Eds.), Proceedings of the Jurix 94 Conference, Koninklijke Vermande, Amsterdam, 1994, p. 85.

[48] LEITH P., *The Computerised Lawyer: A Guide to the Use of Computers in the Legal Profession,* Springer-Verlag, 1991, p. 213.

[49] BUCHANAN B. & HEADRICK TH., *Some Speculation About Artificial Intelligence and Legal Reasoning,* in STANFORD LAW REVIEW, Vol. 23, p. 40, November, 1970.

[50] MCCARTY'S TAXMAN projects and the Imperial College 'Formalisation of the British Nationality Act' are two of the best known examples. See in the bibliography for further details.

A major difficulty is how to transfer all the rules of Interpretation (see section 1.7) into the inference engine of an expert system and especially the problem of *subsumptive judgement* (see section 1.7.6) which has to be performed by the Lawyer. In some instances this judgement is more important than the subsequent judgement of the expert system, thus rendering the system almost useless (for a detailed example see *infra* in 2.4.5).

> **Link to the Model:**
> In such a system the *Interpretation* part of the Checklist must be followed in order to include all the rules

Apart from these considerations, a series of problems hamper the efforts of researchers. The first problem is inherited from the rule-based approach which restricts the applications to use only knowledge that can be transformed to rules.[51] There exists (1) a general obstacle as to whether every kind of knowledge (such as the empirical and social knowledge of the model) can be transformed into rules, but (2) more important is the fact that 'rules' contained in a legal system do not necessarily resemble the *if-then* approach of the rules in the knowledge base (see *supra* 2.2.3) of a typical expert system. At a minimum, legal rules which incorporate a subjective element do not always produce a definite 'yes or no' answer. The inquiry into the introduction of other techniques, such as reasoning by deduction, and analogy from previous cases (Case-Based-Reasoning), and Neural Nets, could find a fertile ground here.

The second problem is how to represent knowledge that falls within the margins of the model,[52] such as repercussions from the surrounding social environment, and which, if we abide by the rules of the model, must be included. The difficulty lies in the fact that this knowledge is changeable over short periods of time. What is considered 'just and fair' now may not be so within a few years, and the idea of 'justice' adopted by one society can be different for another. Consequently, the problem is not to find possible ways of representing this knowledge, but to identify its content. The problem becomes greater if this borderline knowledge crucially

---

[51] LEITH argues that "[t]he context is more important than the rule for the rule is only means of making sense of the context...the rules are only illustrative tools to make sense of the real law which lies elsewhere." LEITH P., *Legal Expert Systems: Misunderstanding the Legal Process*, in COMPUTERS & LAW, No. 49, September, 1986, p. 31.

[52] See SVENSSON J., *Enhancing the Applicability of Empirical Data using Legal Knowledge Based Systems*, in PROCEEDINGS OF THE 5ᵀᴴ INTERNATIONAL CONFERENCE ON ARTIFICIAL INTELLIGENCE AND LAW, University of Maryland, 21-24 May, 1995, ACM Press, 1995, p. 104.

affects the core of the model, i.e. in legal systems that permit external interventions, such as appeals to 'justice' or 'fairness' to override the apparent rules.[53]

> **Link to the Model:**
> The *Input* and *Output* parts of the Checklist must be studied here. More importantly, analysts must examine the *Social Knowledge Repercussions*.

The third problem, if the outline of the proposed model is followed, is that a consistent expert system must be able to support both courses of argumentation, from the side of the Judge and from the side of the Counsel, which entails that methods other than the restricted backward and forward chaining techniques must be invented. *Neural nets* techniques, which provide more than one input channels and use a number of weighting factors, could be of help in order to represent these two types of argument.

> **Link to the Model:**
> For this problem analysts must follow the *Rule of Oscillation*, select the *Course of Argument* and then perform the *Search of the legal sources*.

Last but not least, the peculiar character of everyday legal practice constitutes another barrier. Expert systems built up to now are capable of answering a reasonable level of questions for 'hard cases' based on rules or precedent. In the present situation, however, it is much easier for a Lawyer to find the expertise that the expert system is providing by other means. Mainly, a Lawyer may browse through his/her books,[54] which contain a far more detailed analysis of the legal problem in question, or through personal communication he/she may consult the best available expert in a certain area of law.

> **Link to the Model:**
> The considerations about the *Disqualifying Facts* and the *Background*

---

[53] A typical example would be English equity in the English legal system. Civil law codifications quite often include 'vague' clauses such as 'fair compensation' (Greek Civil Code arts. 225 and 918) which must be interpreted by the judge. Again the problem is transposed to the question of the freedom that the legal system appoints to the judge. (see *supra* section 1.3.7).

[54] See STAUDT defending that people prefer to read paper than computer screens, in STAUDT R., *An Essay on Electronic Casebooks: My Pursuit of the Paperless Chase*, in INTERNATIONAL YEARBOOK OF LAW COMPUTERS AND TECHNOLOGY, Vol. 8, 1994, p. 157. See also the recent speculations of SUSSKIND about the coming changes in the legal profession, SUSSKIND R., *The Future of Law*, Clarendon Press, Oxford, 1996.

Knowledge which affect the 'economics' of everyday legal practice must be invoked here.

A possible cause for this malfunction is that existing practical legal expert systems are built on the model of MYCIN,[55] which was a medical expert system. It is worth shedding light on the basic intention of MYCIN: It was intended to help non-highly-experienced doctors, being on call at a hospital, to identify bacterial diseases. Notwithstanding the differences in terms of goals between medicine and law (see *supra* section 1.3.7), it is important to realise that, in Law, the time pressure factor is valued differently. With the present dynamics of a legal practice - be it a law firm, an individual practitioner or the judiciary - the Lawyer normally has enough time to look for those other sources (books, other colleagues etc.) before formulating his/her decision.

From the technical point of view, as explained *supra* in section 2.2.5, the user interface must be enhanced because badly designed and cumbersome interfaces to expert systems (and generally to computer applications), provoke the mistrust of the Lawyers. Concerning the qualifications of the user of such applications, the so called 'open-textured' nature of law has been addressed as a problem for all Information Technology Applications in Law (see *supra* 1.7 Interpretation), but in the case of legal expert systems for legal reasoning, it has another consequence: It is obvious that trivial legal decisions (such as the subsumption of facts to rules) must be provided by the user and not by the system. Therefore, it must be repeated that for the coverage of the 'open-textured' cases, the user of legal expert systems must be legally educated.

2.3.3   For Information Retrieval

Since the time of JOHN HORTY'S 'let there be LITE',[56] great developments have seen the light in the area of legal information retrieval. Since the sixties, there has

---

[55] BUCHANAN B. & SHORTLIFFE E. (Eds.), *Rule Based Expert Systems: The MYCIN experiments of the Stanford Heuristic Programming Project,* Addison Weshley, Reading MA, 1984.

[56] In 1960 Professor John Horty of the University of Pittsburgh demonstrated successfully for the first time a legal text retrieval systems which was the basis for the US Air Force Legal Information Thru Electronics system. For details see also TAPPER C., *Lawyers and Machines,* in THE MODERN LAW REVIEW, Vol. 26, p. 121, March, 1963.

been a vast production of a large number of legal information retrieval systems, mainly in the form of legal data bases.

Although much can be said about the true amount of time that a practitioner spends in legal research (BING & HARVOLD[57] refer to "a relatively small part of the total time spent on a case" while MORISON & LEITH[58] refer to one hour per week!) Information Retrieval and Office Automation systems play a leading role in everyday practice. Complaints about the effectiveness[59] of these systems can be heard in every legal office, but from the subjective point of view you can never satisfy all customers. Difficulties concerning the access procedures and the query languages are often put forward as obstacles. From the technical point of view, many remedies have been proposed since the early nineties, changing according to the technical developments, but mainly focussing on the following points:[60]

1. The introduction of hypertext techniques, especially for statutes, and running on CD-Roms.

2. The introduction of multi-media applications including sound, video etc.

3. The introduction of Language Analysis techniques for conceptual retrieval i.e. the search based on concepts rather that keywords and traditional Boolean operators.

---

[57] BING J. & HARVOLD T., *Legal Decisions and Information Systems*, Universitetsforlaget, Oslo, 1977, p. 255.

[58] MORISON J. & LEITH P., *The Barrister's World and the Nature of Law*, Open University Press, Milton Keynes - Philadelphia, 1992, p. 52.

[59] The specific technical problems of Information retrieval fall outside the scope of this study. See however SALTON G. & MCGILL M., *Introduction to Modern Information Retrieval*, Mcgraw-Hill, New York, 1983, as well as the landmark research of BLAIR & MARON in the eighties concerning the particular problems of retrieving information in the legal domain BLAIR D. & MARON M.E., *An Evaluation of Retrieval Effectiveness for a Full-Text Document Retrieval System*, in COMMUNICATIONS OF THE ACM Vol. 28, No. 3, p. 289, March 1985. Researchers in the area of knowledge-based systems believe that many of these problems can be solved by using knowledge-based techniques.

[60] See for example SMEATON in NAGEL STUART (Ed.), *Law, Decision Making and Microcomputers*, Quorum Books, New York, 1991.

4. Expert systems techniques for front-ends i.e. programs that are added to databases and help the user formulate his/her query, and for conceptual retrieval.

Nowadays, this prospect of hypertext is a reality (see for example in the UK the Context Ltd. CD-Roms). The second proposal is gaining in popularity, also in view of the development of global networks, including a multitude of options. The rather fashionable **WWW** (World Wide Web) is nothing but a combination of hypertext with multimedia. Numerous legal applications use hypertext for linking.

The last two options are still in the research phase,[61] but current results are promising. Front-ends are important to a legal environment, since many of the complaints originate from the cumbersome user interface of existing information retrieval systems.

> **Link to the Model:**
> Apart from the considerations for expert systems performing legal reasoning already explained in the previous section, systems targeting Information Retrieval must be consistent with the notion of the *Legal Sub-System* in order to identify the totality of the legal sources. The same notion can be used in order to select the legal sources to be included in a possible Information Retrieval system.

Finally, it is important to emphasise that current legal databases do not represent knowledge, they just contain static information. In many aspects, they maintain Horty's initial design of keywords and thesauri, causing a lot of shortcomings. Since 1987, BING has pointed out that "a new generation of systems - more user friendly, with a different search logic, and incorporating elements from the AI field... have a future."[62] Indeed, such systems incorporating knowledge-based techniques (rule and case-based) combined with information retrieval techniques can help in improving the efficiency in retrieving those data. Last, but not least,

---

[61] See also HAFNER in the bibliography.

[62] BING J., *The Law of the Books and the Law of the Files, Possibilities and Problems of Legal Information Systems*, in VANDENBERGHE (Ed.), Kluwer, Computer/Law Series, 1989, p. 180 an article which also appeared earlier in COMPUTERS & LAW, 54, p. 31, December, 1987.

automatic document classification systems have been proposed as a possible domain for knowledge-based systems.[63]

2.3.4   For Legal Office Automation

As every legal practice is also a commercial office, it requires office automation as far as the known applications of word processing, local databases, communications, time billing etc. are concerned.

However, word processing, although representing a substantial improvement compared to the typewriter, offers minimal help to a Lawyer. In that sector of office automation, expert systems could be of use in the automatic assembly of legal documents, where fixed text is followed by text that varies.[64] The system provides support for choosing between different branches of the law, and a decision-tree solution (also described and followed in the Chapter 3 prototype) can be used. This technique will involve reference to a knowledge base in order to decide the text that will be included in the final version of a legal document. The explanatory character of expert systems could be exploited here in order to guide the user in drafting legal documents. Similarly, the justificatory function could be used to create checklists and memory tools that highlight the important elements in a document. Furthermore, automatic forms, which query the user about the input into their fields, can use the same technique and analogous systems can incorporate text from statute or from a library of precedents. Such systems may also include traditional algorithmic programming methods for calculating numerical values, amounts, dates and deadlines etc.

> **Link to the Model:**
> The restrictions and the formalities for documents that the legal system imposes (referred to in the *Input* and *Output* sections of the checklist) must be taken into account here.

---

[63] See GELBART D. & SMITH J.C., *The Application of Automated Text Processing Techniques to Legal Text Management*, in YEARBOOK OF LAW COMPUTERS AND TECHNOLOGY, Vol. 8, 1994, p. 208.

[64] See for example in the area of EDI (Electronic Data Interchange) the creation of automated interchange agreements from a repository of legal terms. The implementation is based on JURICAS, a legal advisory system shell. MITRAKAS A., *Open EDI and Law in Europe*, Kluwer Law International, The Hague, 1997, Chapters 7-8.

Finally, it has been postulated to combine all of the previously stated aspects into one integrated workstation that will permit the use[65] of all the different sources (knowledge based systems, information retrieval and office automation). Such a system would be able, for example, to connect the knowledge base of expert systems to existing databases; it could include a front-end 'intelligent' interface to the text retrieval systems; it could produce 'intelligent' decisions in automatic document assembly etc.

2.3.5   For Legal Education

The optimistic *Virtual Law School* of WIDDISON[66] may be a distant dream, but already expert systems are used for tutoring legal students.[67] The majority of legal curricula is based on the assumption that law is a system of rules and, therefore, students learn how to detect legal rules and concepts in different areas of law.

WAHLGREN argues that "[i]n this way, in the process of education law students become accustomed to identifying and relating the upcoming situations to the relevant legal sub-areas, the corresponding legal rules and concepts. There is therefore no doubt that one basic function of legal education in the positivist paradigm is to communicate and develop a conceptual structure that is ready to function as an effective fact recognition and classification tool."[68]

The process of developing and refining the knowledge base of possible expert systems is very similar to the process used for training young lawyers.

---

[65] See BING J., *Computer Assisted Working Environment for Lawyers. Part II: From Information Retrieval to Active Decision Support*, in 9TH SYMPOSIUM ON LEGAL DATA PROCESSING IN EUROPE, Bonn, 10-12 October 1989, Report to the Council of Europe, 22 May, 1989 and OSKAMP A. & VAN DEN BERG PETER H., *Legal Expert Systems and Legal Text Retrieval Systems :How About Integration,* in KASPERSEN & OSKAMP (Eds.), Kluwer, Deventer, 1990.

[66] WIDDISON R., *Virtual Law School*, in YEARBOOK OF LAW COMPUTERS AND TECHNOLOGY, Vol. 8, 1994, p. 185.

[67] See for example ALEVEN V. & ASHLEY K., *What law Students Need to Know to WIN*, in YEARBOOK OF LAW COMPUTERS AND TECHNOLOGY, Vol. 8, 1994, p. 115 and ASHLEY K. & ALEVEN T., *Towards an Intelligent Tutoring System for Teaching Law students to Argue with Cases,* in PROCEEDINGS OF THE THIRD INTERNATIONAL CONFERENCE ON ARTIFICIAL INTELLIGENCE AND LAW, Oxford, ACM Press, 1991.

[68] WAHLGREN P., *Automated Legal Reasoning: A Study on Artificial Intelligence and Law*, Kluwer, Computer/Law Series, 1992, p. 158.

Consequently, this explains why the inclusion of intuitive techniques that will improve the reliability of expert systems must be based on some of the assumptions of the legal curriculum. Matters in legal education, however, are much more complicated. SCOTT & WIDDISON, although supporting the same idea as a general model for research into law students learning,[69] point out the criticism for the first generation interactive computer-based learning software made in the UK by Law Courseware Consortium,[70] which used a number of AI techniques.

Hypothetical knowledge-based systems, for practice and exercise, can also find their place in clinical legal education[71] and a trainee user can always interact with the system on the grounds of a posed question, or for explanations etc. It has also been proposed to use an 'intelligent' tutoring system shell for legal education.[72]

2.3.6 The Information Crisis of Legal Decision Making

Before proceeding with actually inserting expert systems into the above points of the model, it is necessary to clarify a few details concerning the insertion of modern technology into legal practice.[73] It is generally perceived that we have an information crisis whenever someone searching for, or using, information has difficulties in managing the information he/she obtains. The problem is inherent to

---

[69] In the UK the Law Courseware Consortium is moving towards that direction SCOTT C. & WIDDISON R., *Law Courseware: The Next Generation*, in LAW TECHNOLOGY JOURNAL, Vol. 3, No. 2, May 1994, p. 9. HUNTER is more enthusiastic about the same issue HUNTER D., *Teaching Artificial Intelligence to Law Students*, in LAW TECHNOLOGY JOURNAL, Vol. 3, No. 3, October 1994, p. 36.

[70] See DALE J., *Law Courseware Consortium: towards an Integrated Model for Legal CBL*, in YEARBOOK OF LAW COMPUTERS AND TECHNOLOGY, Vol. 8, 1994, p. 167.

[71] See for example the BILETA efforts in the UK; for practical applications see LAURITSEN MARC, *Project Pericles in Retrospect*, in YEARBOOK OF LAW COMPUTERS & TECHNOLOGY, Vol. 5, p. 50, 1991 and GREGOR S.D., RIGNEY H.M. & SMITH J.D., *The Applicability of a KBS to Legal Education*, in THE AUSTRALIAN COMPUTER JOURNAL, Vol. 23, No. 1, p. 17, February, 1991., who, nevertheless, add that "the use of auxiliary material, such as printed example problems, would still seem appropriate and perhaps necessary".

[72] SPAN G., *LITES: an Intelligent Tutoring System Shell for Legal Education*, in YEARBOOK OF LAW COMPUTERS AND TECHNOLOGY, Vol. 8, 1994, p. 103.

[73] For recent speculations about things to come in the legal office see SUSSKIND R, *The Future of Law*, Clarendon Press, Oxford, 1996 and KATSH M. E., *Law in a Digital World*, Oxford University Press, New York, 1995. The analysis here, however, is of a more pragmatic nature examining the current situation.

law and legal practice for institutional reasons. The old Latin motto *ignorantia juris semper nocet* is prevailing in most legal systems. On the other hand, the theory of promulgating the laws also dominates in most democratic societies. The result is obvious: citizens must not be ignorant of a huge volume of laws.

It is also known that "[p]art of the difficulty of systems analysis is that bringing a computer system into an environment always changes that environment and causes clerical or computer problems further along the line."[74] The legal environment, however, presents a remarkable resistance to change. This is due to many reasons, but the shortcomings of many applications are also put forward.[75] The question, however, is not whether the said systems can practically be implemented, but whether they will finally be accepted by the users. Indeed, in the legal field, theoretical models have been implemented practically but have failed to reach the level of an every day *realistic* use.[76]

> **Link to the Model:**
> This discussion of realistic applications is reflected in the initial rules of the model (see sections 1.3.1-1.3.7). These rules must be used in order to connect the practicality of the foreseen applications to realistic levels of use in a working environment.

These two observations, brought together, increase the crisis of information in the legal world. However, two specific aspects will be highlighted here: (1) the specific relation of lawyers to textual material and (2) the culture of legal offices.

The first aspect entails that Lawyers are text and book bound.[77] The basic element for transfer of information is printed material, and the basic rival to electronic

---

[74] LEITH P., *The Computerised Lawyer: A Guide to the Use of Computers in the Legal Profession*, Springer-Verlag, 1991, p. 140.

[75] WIDDISON *et al.* argue for information retrieval that "[t]hese computer-based methods bear little resemblance to the traditional ways in which lawyers do their research. To respond that lawyers just have to learn new ways is not a satisfactory answer. There is no excuse for producing software whose workings are incomprehensible to users. Every effort should be made to produce, on screen, a close electronic analogy to traditional legal research tools and techniques." WIDDISON R., PRITCHARD F., & ROBINSON W., *Expert Systems meet Hypertext: The European Conflicts Guide*, in JOURNAL OF LAW AND INFORMATION SCIENCE, Vol. 3, No. 1, 1992, p. 86.

[76] E.g. sound on-line databases are under used, and sophisticated computer systems are used only for word processing.

[77] See however the diversified opinion of Leith that law in practice is much less text-based than academics imagine, LEITH PHILIP, *What Future for the Electronic Legal Text?* In YEARBOOK OF LAW COMPUTERS AND TECHNOLOGY, Vol. 8, 1994, p. 213 and also MORISON J. & LEITH P., *The*

information is the book. MITAL & JOHNSON postulate that "when making inferences, developers either take a restricted view of the domain or rely on the user to make what are, on occasions, complex legal decisions. This is fine if the user is a highly experienced specialist lawyer; but, if so, the question which has to be answered is whether *the system will quickly exhaust its utility down to the level of a much less expensive text book.*"[78]

On the second aspect, legal practice is a working environment where information is disseminated 'by word of mouth'. This is something intuitively acquired in the law school and at the time of apprenticeship (see also *infra* 2.4.2 Enigma II: Knowledge Acquisition). This attitude promotes the idea of consulting readily available experts rather than machines, and thus, creates a certain distrust for computers and modern technology. Furthermore, in legal problem solving, the time pressure is not as great compared with other disciplines (as for example in medicine). Therefore, cultural bias and time availability encourage the exhaustion of these other sources (text, books, other experts) before using the electronic ones. Finally, to understand the problem in its true dimensions, one has to be aware of the reluctance to change within the legal environment. Consequently, tradition-bound Lawyers, in most cases, are not ready to adopt advanced Information Technology applications.

2.4 IMPLEMENTING EXPERT SYSTEMS FOR LEGAL REASONING: SPECIFIC PROBLEMS

Apart from the general discussion about the insertion points and the usability of Expert Systems, the empirical investigation (described in detail in Chapter 3) shed light on some specific problems that arise while implementing legal expert systems for legal reasoning. These specific problems, in view of similar published results, led to the following general remarks:

Barrister's World and the Nature of Law, Open University Press, Milton Keynes - Philadelphia, 1992, p. 179.

[78] And they propose that a hypertext representation may be used for a more complex structure, with less effort than that required to build a knowledge base. MITAL V. & JOHNSON L., *Advanced Information Systems for Lawyers*, Chapman & Hall, London, 1992, p. 226 (emphasis added).

2.4.1   Enigma I: What Legal Knowledge for a Knowledge Base?

In itself, the representation of knowledge is one of the most difficult tasks in this field of research. Legal knowledge, moreover, is quite unmanageable because of the 'vagueness' and 'open texture' (already explained in Chapter 1).[79]

Various authors insist that "[h]ow to represent knowledge is one of the key questions in the construction of expert systems. It is often claimed that once this question has been decided, the remaining tasks are 'easy' to do."[80] The enigma, however, of defining what's in a Lawyer's mind, is an old one.[81] SUSSKIND submits that "expert systems in law [must] be designed today to perform this most fundamental operation of drawing legal conclusions based on the universe of legal discourse (as represented in the legal knowledge base), through the deployment of some rational reasoning mechanism (embodied in the legal inference engine, whose rationality may well be that of deductive logic)".[82]

If, nevertheless, the answer to the previous question of *how* to represent knowledge is found, the next question would be to identify, according to the methodology of a rule-based expert system, *what* knowledge will constitute the 'knowledge base'. Two examples can show, however, how diversified this task may be. MORISON & LEITH present a diverting view about legal knowledge:

> "[s]olicitors are viewed as small businessmen running an operation the main concern of which is negotiation and the resolution of various types of cases. These cases are in the widest sense legal; but they do not normally require any particularly full understanding of substantive law in order to be carried out. Most legal knowledge held by solicitors is fairly general or is of a procedural nature, i.e. knowing the correct forms and precedents to use in

---

[79] See also BING J., *Rules and Representation; Interaction between Legal Knowledge Based Systems and the General Theory of Legal Rules*, in BLUME (Ed.), Kluwer, Computer/Law Series, 1991 for the specific problems of representing legal rules.

[80] See for example GUENTHNER F., LEHMAN H., SCHÖNFELD W., *A Theory for the Representation of Knowledge*, IBM JOURNAL, Vol. 30, No. 1, Jan, 1986.

[81] See for example BING J. & HARVOLD T., *Legal Decisions and Information Systems*, Universitetsforlaget, Oslo, 1977, p. 21, on the semantics of legal norms.

[82] SUSSKIND R., *Expert Systems in Law*, Clarendon, Oxford 1987, p. 43.

various types of cases. This knowledge and business acumen is directed towards the sole goal of keeping the client happy." [83]

A view that BING & HARVOLD have already articulated by saying that

"other factors too may reduce objectivity. An example: tax law cases are often connected with considerable financial interests, and consequently clients who really have something to gain will be the ones seeking legal advice in this field. The conflicts will in turn generate legal sources (case law, administrative decisions etc.) which would reflect the problems of this clientele - and which might distract the attention of lawyers from more pressing and practical problems where less money is at stake, but where a greater number of people are involved."[84]

These views entail that, apart from the pragmatic considerations already included in the model, a number of other factors should alert potential analysts of an integrated system of practical legal decision making. As explained in the previous chapter, it is surprising that little attention has been paid to the notion of *what* to represent. It is, therefore, likely that the knowledge to be represented must be extended in order to include a much wider spectrum of sources.

Link to the Model:
The *Doctrine of the Valid Legal Sources* and their reduction to the notion of the *legal sub-system* must be applied now.

"[F]ormalization of legislation is necessary to be able to build a legal expert system, but *that method is only valid when it is combined with the formalization of other sources of the law*".[85] In deciding what to represent, the notion of the legal sub-system, or momentary system, must be brought forward and guide the whole process. To determine "how much of the matter contained in the whole system goes to make up one law"[86] a broad knowledge of the relevant legal material and sources is needed. RAZ suggests that "in deciding on a principle of individuation

---

[83] MORISON J. & LEITH P., *The Barrister's World and the Nature of Law*, Open University Press, Milton Keynes - Philadelphia, 1992, p. 50.

[84] BING J. & HARVOLD T., *Legal Decisions and Information Systems,* Universitetsforlaget, Oslo, 1977, p. 250.

[85] OSKAMP A., *Knowledge Representation and Legal Expert Systems*, in VANDENBERGHE (Ed.), Kluwer, Computer/Law Series, 1989, p. 208, her emphasis.

[86] RAZ J., *The Concept of a Legal System, An Introduction to the Theory of Legal System*, second edition, Clarendon, Oxford, 1980, p. 71.

two conflicting aims should be borne in mind and a proper balance be struck between them. The first is to define small and manageable units of law, units which could be discovered by reference to a small and easily identifiable portion of the legal material. The other aim is to define units which are relatively self-contained and self-explanatory so that each contains a significant part of law."[87] Consequently, it is essential for the developer to posses 'broad-minded' extensive legal experience.

Two peculiarities must be emphasised here: (1) The decision of what to represent must lead to accurate links pointing to the relevant legal material. All relevant parts of law must be interconnected (like hypertext systems) in order to represent the full picture that, normally, a lawyer has in his/her mind. Technically, apart from hypertext techniques, current matching techniques for texts in natural language are promising but not perfect.[88] Therefore, interference of a human decision is needed, in most cases, involving relevancy criteria. (2) Law is an evolving field, and a real life lawyer will change his/her mind to get the desired result. Therefore, potential expert systems must be flexible enough to permit easy adaptation and update[89] techniques. Without this learning facility, potential systems will not show any creativity and will not be used.

2.4.2   Enigma II: Knowledge Acquisition

Knowledge acquisition is the transfer and transformation of potential problem solving expertise from some knowledge source to a computer program.[90] The main stream methodology to acquire knowledge is for the *domain expert* to communicate with a *knowledge engineer*, i.e. the person who encodes knowledge directly into the representation chosen. Therefore, the dominant source of knowledge is the domain expert from whom the knowledge engineer elicits the knowledge through

---

[87] RAZ J., *The Concept of a Legal System, An Introduction to the Theory of Legal System*, second edition, Clarendon, Oxford, 1980, p. 115.

[88] SUSSKIND states that the lack of natural language processing is one of the known limitations of Information technology, SUSSKIND R., *The Future of Law*, Clarendon Oxford, 1996, p. 65.

[89] WIDDISON R., PRITCHARD F., & ROBINSON W., *The European Conflicts Guide,* ARTIFICIAL INTELLIGENCE AND LAW, Vol. 1 No. 4, 1993, p. 299.

[90] ZELEZNIKOW J. & HUNTER D., *Building Intelligent Legal Information Systems, Representation and Reasoning in Law,* Kluwer, Computer/Law Series, 1994, p. 172.

interviews and hypothetical problem situations. However, the research into the particular ways that lawyers acquire their knowledge and skills (to be transferred into an expert system) is a problematic one and the particular qualifications of the 'legal expert' have not been thoroughly investigated.[91]

The basic motto of the 'domain expert' approach was that *knowledge elicitation is the major bottleneck in the development of expert systems*. Few researchers, however, emphasised, that "[o]ne major difficulty in the area is that people have tended to think of knowledge as being a 'unitary thing',.. a 'substance' portions of which can be emitted and / or hewn off by the knowledge engineer. Such views of knowledge have led to the suggestion that what is needed is a large scale study to find good knowledge elicitation techniques... A more realistic and positive way to approach the problem, however, is to recognise that, even in a single domain, expert knowledge is of several different kinds. Moreover, the different kinds of knowledge require different knowledge elicitation techniques to capture them most effectively."[92]

BING explains that "[l]egal reasoning is probably in many ways *iterative*, homing in on a target through a number of approximations. Some of the less well-defined elements of the legal decision process may be the rarely formalised knowledge making a lawyer intuitively identify the correct relevant circumstances at the first pass, or the intuition of when the iterative process should be appropriately stopped. Perhaps such knowledge is 'tacit', difficult or impossible to formulate, and only communicated to others through an arrangement akin to apprenticeship, an arrangement with long traditions in the legal profession."[93]

It is true that the knowledge lawyers have is often characterised as *implicit knowledge* and as a major obstacle for those working in the area of knowledge elicitation. Implicit knowledge is difficult to articulate, but, nevertheless, it is required to understand the rest of the knowledge. It is true that, resulting from their education, lawyers learn to perform tasks in such a way that important aspects of

---

[91] Even in the late nineties SUSSKIND admits that more formal work should be undertaken on the profile and specification of the human legal specialist, SUSSKIND R., *The Future of Law*, Clarendon Press, Oxford, 1996, p. 284.

[92] BERRY D., *Implicit Knowledge and Expert Systems*, in SINDING-LARSEN (Ed.), COMPLEX 7/88, Oslo, 1988

[93] BING J., *Legal Decisions and Computerised Systems*, in SEIPEL (Ed.), Kluwer, Computer/Law Series, 1990, p. 228.

their knowledge are implicit in nature, but it is not impossible for knowledge engineers - if they acquire a legal background - to extract this knowledge and represent it in a meaningful way in a computer system. The conclusion is that, in the case of legal knowledge acquisition, the best solution would be to have the *expert* and the *knowledge engineer* represented by the same person.

Otherwise, opinion is divided as to what methodology to follow and who is supposed to have more responsibility in performing this task. SUSSKIND in his early writings[94] emphasises the role of the expert to tuning the system; recently he speculates whether "a new breed of law graduate, equipped more as a legal analyst who will start work as legal information engineer" will emerge;[95] GREENLEAF ET AL[96] do not use a knowledge engineer, while ZELEZNIKOW & HUNTER insist on the value of the interviews of the knowledge engineer with the domain expert.[97] This difference has been addressed by OSKAMP who concludes that "along with a knowledge engineer, a domain expert be involved with the development team of a legal expert system from the start. He must play a critical role in selecting the knowledge. Considering the complex issues of knowledge acquisition and selection in developing legal expert systems, a knowledge engineer cannot work without a domain expert."[98]

It is still not guaranteed that all the necessary expertise will be elicited. In the selection process one could distinguish two questions. Firstly, what knowledge *should* be part of the knowledge base? Secondly, what knowledge *could* be part of the knowledge base? The answers to these questions are related to the knowledge source.

---

[94] SUSSKIND R., *Expert Systems in Law: a Jurisprudential Inquiry*, Clarendon Press, Oxford, 1987, p. 59.

[95] In connecting generally the problem of 'legal expertise' with legal education and admitting that he has no 'pat' answers. SUSSKIND R., *The Future of Law*, Clarendon Press, Oxford, 1996, p. 282-3.

[96] GREENLEAF G., MOWBRAY A., & TYREE A., *Expert Systems in Law, The Datalex Project*, IN PROCEEDINGS OF THE FIRST INTERNATIONAL CONFERENCE ON ARTIFICIAL INTELLIGENCE AND LAW, BOSTON, ACM, 1987.

[97] ZELEZNIKOW J. & HUNTER D., *Building Intelligent Legal Information Systems, Representation and Reasoning in Law*, Kluwer, Computer/Law Series, 1994, p. 172.

[98] OSKAMP A., *Model for Knowledge and Legal Expert Systems*, in ARTIFICIAL INTELLIGENCE AND LAW, Vol. 1, No. 4, 1993, p. 269.

Referring to the knowledge source 'legislation' and given the considerations of the previous paragraph, one could argue persuasively that all relevant knowledge should be part of the knowledge base. Moreover, it is necessary to include the structure of the knowledge.

Link to the Model:
In law the structure of this knowledge is represented by the *Doctrine of Valid Legal Sources*, which is defined in the model.

The methodology to include all relevant knowledge brings up the problem of the size of a possible knowledge base. OSKAMP argues that "[m]ethods of limiting the size of this knowledge base source make this feasible. Limits of relevancy could be set by narrowing the domain and the task of the system. A more critical selection process is required for the knowledge sources 'case law' and 'legal literature'. Here the limits set by domain and task will not reduce the knowledge sufficiently. Thus the participation of the expert is even more important because the selection of knowledge is such a subjective matter. By selecting the knowledge the expert puts his personal mark on the system."[99] This view coincides with the above expressed (2.4.1) argument concerning the use of automatic matching methods. To summarise, all these precautions do not permit - at the current state of art - the use of automatic methods (see further in Chapter 3) to acquire legal knowledge, and, therefore, this task must remain a human activity.

2.4.3   Anathema I: The Scientist's Perception[100] of Law

The evolution of expert systems originates in science and, as explained, the first legal expert systems were based on scientific ones (in medicine and geology). This was the source of a multiple of misunderstandings about the true nature of law, its procedural and substantive issues, as well as legal methodology.

The scientist's dogmatic position, applied in many legal expert systems, is that "[t]here is only one language suitable for representing information - whether

---

[99] OSKAMP A., *Model for Knowledge and Legal Expert Systems*, in ARTIFICIAL INTELLIGENCE AND LAW, Vol. 1, No. 4, 1993, p. 269.

[100] LEITH ironically says "it is almost as though when God made computer scientists , he made them all think of law the same way - as a system of rules." LEITH P., *Legal Expert Systems: Misunderstanding the Legal Process*, in COMPUTERS & LAW, No. 49, September, 1986, p. 27.

declarative or procedural - and that is first-order predicate logic. There is only one intelligent way to process information and that is by applying deductive inference methods."[101] These, of course, are some of the solutions adopted by this study as well, but the previous quotation says nothing about manipulating judgmental knowledge, which is of vital importance to a legal knowledge environment.

The other deficiency is that the drafting and the implementation of legal expert systems is left to the hands of people having no legal education. GREENLEAF ET AL emphasise that "[y]et, people who would not dream of beginning construction of a medical expert system without the firm support of a medical physician will happily go to work on a legal system. The reason, of course, lies in the widespread misconception that law is a simple system of rules and that legal inference consists of a simple deductive application of these rules"[102]

> **Link to the Model:**
> This directly contradicts the definition of a *Lawyer* and the *Rule of Integration*.

The Imperial College experiment with the British Nationality Act followed a methodology in which "[m]ost of the Act was translated into Horn clause logic...by a student, without any expert legal assistance",[103] and produced, for this reason assertions like "[t]he knowledge elicitation problem is almost entirely absent in the formalisation of legislation. By its very nature, the law is well documented; its provisions are written down, and where they are not, decisions in previous cases are recorded for future reference".[104] Such conclusions, inconceivable even for first year law students, caused great embarrassment amongst lawyers. Any Lawyer could give a number of examples and arguments which would illustrate the extent to which these quotations miss the reality of the nature of law.

---

[101] KOWALSKI R. in BRACHMAN R.J. AND SMITH B.C. (Eds.), *SIGART Newsletter: Special Issue on Knowledge Representation*, Vol. 70, February, 1980.

[102] GREENLEAF G., MOWBRAY A., TYREE A., *Expert Systems in Law: The Datalex Project*, in PROCEEDINGS OF THE FIRST INTERNATIONAL CONFERENCE ON ARTIFICIAL INTELLIGENCE AND LAW, Boston, 1987.

[103] SERGOT M, CORY H.T., HAMMOND P., KOWALSKI R., KRIWACZEC F.& SADRI F., *Formalisation of the British Nationality Act*, in YEARBOOK OF LAW COMPUTERS AND TECHNOLOGY, Vol. 2, 1986, p. 41.

[104] SERGOT M, SADRI F.,KOWALSKI R., KRIWACZEC F., HAMMOND P.,.& CORY H.T., *The British Nationality Act as a Logic Program,* in COMMUNICATIONS OF THE ACM, Vol. 29, p. 370, 1986.

Link to the Model:
These views contradict the *Rule of the Legal System and the Rule of Content.*

Only after abandoning these appalling positions, do the Imperial College team admit, regarding their method:

> "[they] take some legislative text, typically a statute or a set of regulations, and represent its provisions in a formal logical language. (More precisely, given the nature of the language in which the original legislation is expressed, we represent particular interpretations or readings of these provisions.) we thus obtain a logical representation of what the legislation expresses (or again, more precisely, *of what we think it is that the legislation expresses*)."[105]

and furthermore that

> "[w]e are not suggesting that law as a normative system is the only abstraction of value, nor that the are no other aspects of law equally deserving of attention; nor are we suggesting that deontic logic is the only analytical and representational tool that can be brought to bear on the representation of law."[106]

As early as 1986, however, PHILIP LEITH, the main opponent[107] of the use of law as input for logic programming, has condemned their methodology and these hypotheses as "naïve, [because there is] much law which is not part of the legislation".[108] This initial reaction of LEITH has triggered a long term debate between critics of logic programming one side and the Imperial College Logic Programming team on the other.[109]

---

[105] KOWALSKI R. & SERGOT M., *The Use of Logical Models in Legal Problem Solving*, in RATIO JURIS, Vol. 3, No. 2, July, 1990, p. 201 (emphasis added).

[106] JONES A. & SERGOT M., *Deontic Logic in the Representation of Law: Towards a Methodology*, in ARTIFICIAL INTELLIGENCE AND LAW, Vol. 1, No. 1, 199p. 62.

[107] See also MOLES R. N, *Logic Programming - An Assessment of its Potential for Artificial Intelligence Applications in Law*, in JOURNAL OF LAW AND INFORMATION SCIENCE, Vol. 2, No. 2, 1991.

[108] See all his writings and LEITH P., *Fundamental Errors in Legal Logic Programming*, in THE COMPUTER JOURNAL, Vol. 29, No. 6, 1986, p. 545.

[109] See also ZELEZNIKOW J. & HUNTER D., *Rationales for the Continued Development of Legal Expert Systems*, in JOURNAL OF LAW AND INFORMATION SCIENCE, Vol. 3, No. 1, 1992, p. 102 and TYREE A., *The Logic Programming Debate*, in JOURNAL OF LAW AND INFORMATION SCIENCE, Vol. 3, No. 1, 1992, p. 111.

LEITH has tried to explain the reason for these false assumptions by arguing that "the problems of logic programmers are the result of a false epistemology: they see the world in terms of computational model and fail to stand outside that model. Thus whenever they attempt to apply their model to the real world, they will always fail. For the world is not a logical world"[110] ZELEZNIKOW & HUNTER are milder in their criticism by arguing that "[u]nfortunately much work in the area of Legal Expert Systems has involved non-lawyers developing systems which naively attempt to mechanistically interpret statutes. They fail to use current developments in Case Based Reasoning and Qualitative Reasoning. Whilst the aforementioned production rule systems are of great use in judicial decision making, they are inadequate as a litigation support tools."[111]

The personal testimony from the *Nomos* project (Chapter 3) is that the perception of scientists about the Law is completely distorted. Most think of law as a definite set of rules with n6 links to other parts of the social phenomenon. This attitude causes various shortcomings, especially when they try to build practical legal applications, i.e. targeting practising lawyers. Scientists should not be forced to "study real law",[112] but their method of treating law on the procrustean bed of their laboratories must be anathematised. Potential developers from science should be more careful and knowledgeable in studying the needs of the legal profession. *For law is the complicated means to solve social problems and dispense justice rather than a simple set of rules which can be mechanically manipulated.*

2.4.4 Anathema II: The Linguist's Perception of Law

Another sort of confusion comes from the side of linguists.[113] They treat law as a language puzzle to be solved, and not as a normative reality to be applied within a

---

[110] LEITH P., *Fundamental Errors in Legal Logic Programming*, in THE COMPUTER JOURNAL, Vol. 29, No. 6, 1986, p. 552.

[111] ZELEZNIKOW JOHN & HUNTER DANIEL, *Rationales for the Continued Development of Legal Expert Systems*, in JOURNAL OF LAW AND INFORMATION SCIENCE, Vol. 3, No. 1, 1992, p. 109

[112] "Professionals should send the AI researchers back to their keyboards, requesting them to study real law, rather than this pseudo-law which they present." LEITH P, *Legal Expert Systems: Misunderstanding the Legal Process*, in COMPUTERS & LAW, No. 49, September, 1986, p. 31.

[113] The main input for this paragraph comes from the *Nomos project* (see also Chapter 3).

social context. This is obvious when they miss the importance of Interpretation (emphasised in the model) by saying, for example, that:

> ALCOURRON AND BULYGIN[114] argue that "law is not a mere transcription of statutes and other legal norms, but it also involves interpretation". Our task should instead be to derive a representation of the law which can support this interpretation task, by using different tools for extracting the relevant concepts and relations, ***reducing at this stage the interpretation task to the minimum***. A 'legal rule' in its core is only a constrained set of objects (defined in the context of the current law system) and a set of relations between objects (defined in the same context).[115]

At other times, they misunderstand fundamental issues of legal methodology, for example, when they enumerate a possible methodology for legal problem solving in a natural language processing environment:

> In the legal domain to solve a problem means:
>
> - to be able to classify an instance as belonging to redefined concept;
> - to be able to 'alert' the final user, if an instance, which was supposed to have certain attributes, has not one;
> - to foresee 'consequences' for each class of entities;
> - to handle optional vs. mandatory attributes;
> - to handle exceptions to the concept;
> - to handle negations of attributes;[116]

> **Link to the Model:**
> These views contradict the definition of a *Lawyer*, the *Rule of Integration* and the *Rule of the Legal System*.

Furthermore, it is an established view amongst scientists and linguists that 'law' is only contained in the text of a certain law. Thus, they assume that they know everything about a legal domain (e.g. taxation law) if they only know the text of a

---

[114] The passage is taken from ALCHOURRÓN C. E. & BULYGIN E., *Normative Systems*, Springer Verlag, Wien, 1971.

[115] GIANNETTI A., (ESPRIT DOC SG-31-50-01), *Legal Knowledge Engineering: A Case Study*, 15-Sep-91, p. 4 (emphasis added).

[116] GIANNETTI A., (ESPRIT DOC SG-31-50-01), *Legal Knowledge Engineering: A Case Study*, 15-Sep-91, p. 4

statute (e.g. a Tax law) without any further linking to the rest of the legal order. This is clear when they say "this type of definition is very common at the beginning of the law texts when the legislator should provide the minimal requirements for an action or entity to belong to that class",[117] assuming that there are no other definitions outside the text of this law.

Likewise, in another example, they assert that "usually the definition by rule is contained in a numbered paragraph and the definition by roster is contained in a numbered paragraph, with sub-paragraphs signalled by numbers or letters."[118] This hypothesis, concerning a specific enumeration, may be valid for a particular law (or laws of a legal system), but cannot constitute a general rule for all legislation.

> **Link to the Model:**
> This directly contradicts the notion of *Valid Legal Sources* and the *Legal Sub-system.*

While, even from the linguistic point, it is accepted "that in natural language processing the system interprets word associations outside a context. This may give rise to several interpretations for a single syntactic collocate, even though the domain has very little lexical ambiguity",[119] in the case of the representation of legal concepts, linguists have anticipated that:

> "The main idea is to consider any potential legal concept as a set provided with:(1) a general rule which has to be used for a general definition; (2) enumeration of potential instances of the concept; (3) enumeration of 'positive and 'negative' instances which have to be included or excluded by derogation or exception"[120]

and then they have reached the extreme position that

> ...specific legal structures are expressed linguistically through *always the same schemes* and using specific words...The [program] tries to recognise

---

[117] GIANNETTI A., (ESPRIT DOC SG-31-50-01), *Legal Knowledge Engineering: A Case Study,* 15-Sep-91, p. 25.

[118] GIANNETTI A., (ESPRIT DOC SG-31-50-01), *Legal Knowledge Engineering: A Case Study,* 15-Sep-91, p. 25.

[119] ESPRIT DOC TE-31-40-01, *Design of ILAM module for NOMOS,* 16-Sep-91, p. 56

[120] ESPRIT DOC IL-31-50-01, *Annex II, Representational Issues Concerning Art. 7,* 20-Mar-92.

the occurrence of a schema of article containing the definition of a legal concept[121]

In other instances, they appear to understand some aspects of legal methodology, but they focus on the specific details and they fail to conceive the unity of a legal system. In the following example they elaborate the notion of 'open texture' but there is no mention about other parts of law, and they adhere to the narrow linguistic description of 'juridical style':

> Under a linguistic point of view, the legal domain is particularly interesting as it expresses a tacitly defined sublanguage, exhibiting that special kind of regular structures that implicitly defines a 'juridical style'...On the other hand, legal texts exhibit a high degree of complexity, both under a conceptual and linguistic point of view. The conceptual problems are often related to the fact that many concepts in law cannot be defined thoroughly and completely: These ill-defined concepts are known as open texture, since they are defined by using new concepts that are just as vague."[122]

Link to the Model:
This directly contradicts the *Rule of the Legal System* and basic elements of *Interpretation*.

They continue with another misconception about the use of procedural and empirical knowledge by the Lawyers:

> "This metalanguage does not seem to have been formalised, but it is used tacitly by legal experts. It is not suggested here that legal experts use a formal and rigid language. But, because of the very nature of the concepts that they are expressing in their prescriptive texts, and relying on their experience, they have settled on a language characterised by 'a juridical style'."[123]

but they confess, however, that "[t]he rules derived from the regulation statements prescribe constraints from the 'standard world'. We do not have to use these rules

---

[121] ESPRIT-DOC SG-61-50-01, *ILAM & FLAM Preliminary Evaluation,* 12-Oct-92, p. 8 (emphasis added).

[122] GIANNETTI *et al., Nomos: Knowledge Acquisition for Normative Reasoning Systems,* FINAL REPORT, P. 1(emphasis added).

[123] MOULIN B. & ROUSSEAU D., *Designing Deontic Knowledge Bases from Regulation Texts,* in KNOWLEDGE BASED SYSTEMS, Vol. 3, No. 2, June 1990, p. 110.

in a deductive mode, but we must determine if the properties describing the 'observation world' satisfy these constraints."[124]

Link to the Model:
This directly contradicts the *Rule of the Legal System* (concerning especially the *procedural* and *methodological* rules) and the notion of *Background Knowledge*.

All these findings indicate that linguists, too, have developed a completely distorted image of what the law is. It is true that linguistic research has much to offer to legal applications, where many of the problems lie in the ambiguity of natural language. *This fact, however, does not entitle linguists to treat law as another ordinary text rather than as the regulative instrument of an organised society.*

2.4.5   Exegesis: How to Create and Use Legal Expert Systems

The economically successful expert systems so far have each addressed a specialised task, such as finding mineral deposits.[125] It is worth observing that most human experts specialise, too, in many professions. However, each human expert also has common sense knowledge about the world in general, and knows how to consult experts in subjects other than his/her own. While it is easy to undertake common sense reasoning, no one so far has produced an account of *how* we do so (or even of the declarative knowledge we might be using) that would be sufficient to write a 'common sense expert system'. It can be speculated that, as in the case of specialised expert systems, good progress will only be made where there is an interplay between theory (influenced by logic) and specific empirical work in building prototype common sense systems.[126]

---

[124] MOULIN B. & ROUSSEAU D., *Designing Deontic Knowledge Bases from Regulation Texts*, in KNOWLEDGE BASED SYSTEMS, Vol. 3, No. 2, June 1990, p. 112.

[125] Like the PROSPECTOR system. See however LEITH denying this being true in LEITH P., *Legal Expert Systems: Misunderstanding the Legal Process*, in COMPUTERS & LAW, No. 49, September 1986, p. 27.

[126] See also the rules for creating legal expert systems proposed by GOEBEL J.W. & SCHMALZ R., *Problems of Applying Legal Expert Systems in Legal Practice*, in MARTINO & SOCCI-NATALI (Eds.), North Holland 1986, p. 620.

The next question is articulated by GREENLEAF ET AL: "Should we aim to automate legal decision-making or to provide support for legal decision-makers?"[127] A possible answer from the same research team, indicates that legal expert systems should allow access to as rich a collection of support materials as possible, so as to support intelligent choices by the user when interpretation of an open textured predicate is required (i.e. when the user has to make a choice which the system is incapable of making). The user needs to be given open-ended access to the relevant supporting materials, rather than for the system simply to direct the user to a few definitions which may assist interpretation ('closed ended' assistance)

VANDENBERGHE has, similarly, answered earlier "No! The computer can and may not be considered to be a system that is able to replace a judge or a lawyer; even in its most advanced construction it should be considered to be a decision-supporting system"[128] and he also stresses the task for transparency i.e. legal decision-supporting systems will have to reflect how and why they reached a solution, which will enable the testing of the justification.

STAMPER, in turn, argues that "[e]xpert systems are the creation of the artificial intelligence paradigm which presumes that an objective reality can be understood and controlled by an individual expert intelligence that can be replaced by machinery. The alternative paradigm assumes that reality is the subjective product of human beings striving to collaborate through shared norms and experiences, *a process that can be assisted by but never replaced by computers.*"[129] and he concludes the ideal expert system would be "a mechanical aid to essentially intuitive expert problem solving".

Last, but not least, ZELEZNIKOW & HUNTER clarify that a computer system can only aid the human user and is not independently expert. They emphasise that they

---

[127] GREENLEAF G., MOWBRAY A. & TYREE A., *The DataLex Legal Workstation, integrating Tools for Lawyers*, PROCEEDINGS OF THE 3RD INTERNATIONAL CONFERENCE ON ARTIFICIAL INTELLIGENCE AND LAW, Oxford, June 25-28 1991, ACM Press, 1991, p. 221.

[128] VANDENBERGHE G. P.V., *Software Oracles, in* KASPERSEN & OSKAMP (Eds.), Kluwer, Deventer, 1990, p. 19.

[129] STAMPER R., *Expert Systems, Lawyers Beware*, in NAGEL (Ed.), Quorum Books, New York, 1991, p. 37 (his emphasis).

use the expression 'legal decision support system' only synonymously with 'legal expert systems' and 'legal knowledge based systems'.[130]

Link to the Model:
The discussion here is mainly affected by the *Rule of Practicality*.

The current state of the art entails that natural language problems, and especially the problem of subsumption of real facts to legal rules (defined in the model see section 1.7.1) and knowledge acquisition (see section 2.4.2), cannot be fully automated. As a result, a number of decisions must be solved by the user.[131] Systems with this configuration are trying to solve 'hard' cases based on assumptions that the user is taking on a first level. However, if the user is taking these important decisions in the first place, what is the point of letting the system decide later about questions of a lesser importance?

Example:
In the hypothetical problem of the permanently fixed caravan[132] of the N-A prototype the really 'hard' question is if the caravan falls within the category of mobile or immobile property of the Italian VAT law. If the user, at a first stage, supplies the system with his/her decision about this important issue, then the next questions that the system would be capable of answering (i.e. whether the transaction is taxable, the percentage of VAT etc.) are not of much importance.

Therefore, instead of trying to produce decisions, it is advantageous and more productive to target the support to the formulation of a decision.[133] In the previous example the user would rather estimate, e.g. a list with all the cases involving caravans, or one with all the classifications of real property as mobile or immobile etc.

---

[130] ZELEZNIKOW J. & HUNTER D., *Deductive, Inductive and Analogical Reasoning Legal Decision Support Systems*, in PROCEEDINGS OF THE FOURTH NATIONAL CONFERENCE ON LAW, COMPUTERS & AI, University of Exeter, 1994, p. 177.

[131] For this reason I think that SUSSKIND is optimistic in saying that legal expert systems will be useful to the non-lawyer. SUSSKIND R. *The Future of Law*, Clarendon, Oxford, 1996, p. 121.

[132] See 1.10.1 and Chapter 3.

[133] See also *Decision Support v. Decision Making* in DAYAL S. & MOLES R., *The Open Texture of Language: Handling Semantic Analysis in Legal Decision Support Systems*, in JOURNAL OF LAW AND INFORMATION SCIENCE Vol.4, No. 2, 1993, p. 334.

SUSSKIND'S rather pessimistic conclusion that research should concentrate "on designing systems to solve clear and deductive cases"[134] might be overcome by making the improvement of the interpretative resources of users a central aim of legal expert systems research. A realistic approach may be to find the boundary between those elements of open texture problems that legal expert systems can handle (given existing technology) and those elements that users must provide. Research into non-deductive methods of inferencing may, over time, push back this boundary.[135]

GREENLEAF ET AL have proposed that "[a] useful way to view a legal expert system from the perspective of the user, may be as an interaction between a semi-expert inferencing system and a semi-expert user / interpreter, with control over the course of the problem's solution alternating between the two parties to the interaction. Each does what he/she does better, then hands back control to the other. Given existing technology, the program controls those steps in the solution process, that are capable of being embodied in a computerised inferencing agent. The user controls those steps of the solution process, involving abilities which cannot (at least as yet) be so embodied, including the lawyer's various interpretative skills."[136]

On a practical level, a promising proposal comes from ZELEZNIKOW & HUNTER, who articulate the idea that "neither rule-based reasoning nor case based reasoning will be of much benefit to lawyers undertaking litigation. What is required is a system that reasons with both statutes and cases...Initially the system would perform statutory interpretation. When the statutes become insufficient, ambiguous or contradictory, the system would revert to searching for precedent case which would help interpret the statutes. Such a systems would more accurately model the way legal practitioners reason."[137]

---

[134] SUSSKIND R., *Expert Systems in Law*, Clarendon, Oxford 1987, p. 192. A view, however, which now SUSSKIND has reconsidered, SUSSKIND R., *The Future of Law*, Clarendon Press, Oxford, 1996, p. 281.

[135] MOWBRAY, GREENLEAF & TYREE, *Legal Expert Systems: An Introduction*, in GORDON (Ed.) p. 471, 1992.

[136] GREENLEAF G., MOWBRAY A. & TYREE A., *The DataLex Legal Workstation, Integrating Tools for Lawyers*, in PROCEEDINGS OF THE 3RD INTERNATIONAL CONFERENCE ON ARTIFICIAL INTELLIGENCE AND LAW, Oxford, June 25-28 1991, ACM Press, 1991.

[137] ZELEZNIKOW J. & HUNTER D., *Rationales for the Continued Development of Legal Expert Systems*, in JOURNAL OF LAW AND INFORMATION SCIENCE, Vol. 3, No. 1, 1992, see also

The most important function, however, which may be the only - simultaneously - *practical* and *realistic* application of a legal expert system, at the present state of the art, is its use as a 'checklist'. In such a method, a number of criteria are listed in a predetermined order. This checklist acts as an aide-memoire which reminds the user of all the possible formal rules and their interrelations, helping him/her not to forget a criterion. LEITH is convinced that "the systems which are being called expert systems are no more than checklists, and the explanations they give, no more than reading off the ticks or crosses on the checklist." [138]

The attitude of the legal professions has been postulated as a possible cause for under-using information systems, and, especially legal expert systems (see *supra* 2.3.2 For Legal Reasoning). If, however, legal expert systems are simply presented as tools, like any other, to assist the Lawyer in presenting a case or advising a Client, they can be expected to gain their trust, the way other electronic means (like databases) have a long time ago. This corresponds to what STAMPER[139] has laconically put as "less need for cognitive legal machine than for a less sophisticated but more humble product to support intelligent human interaction".

Economic aspects should not be neglected (see also the conclusions of Chapter 3, about this aspect of the *Nomos* project) since, often, they may be overlooked in the search for the foreseen efficiency of an Expert System. WAHLGREN articulates that "[a]t the same time more or less stable organisational preconditions may be too expensive to be changed, which will seriously delimit the possibilities of introducing AI-systems in an effective way... in some cases it may be necessary to compare the prospective benefits following from the system development project with other kinds of options. For example, the operations of a commercial organisation (e.g. a law firm) may become constrained due to a demand for a fast return of investment".[140]

ALLEN *et al.* proposing a legal expert system that will constitute a synthesis of the multiple jurisdictions in the USA in ALLEN L., PAYTON S. & SAXON C., *Synthesizing Related Rules from Statutes and Cases for Legal Expert Systems,* in RATIO JURIS Vol. 3, No. 2, July 1990.

[138] LEITH P., *The Computerised Lawyer: A Guide to the Use of Computers in the Legal Profession,* Springer-Verlag, 1991, p. 190, see, however the comments for the 'checklists' in page 199.

[139] STAMPER R., *Expert Systems, Lawyers Beware,* in NAGEL (Ed.), Quorum Books, New York, p. 38.

[140] WAHLGREN P., *Automated Legal Reasoning: A Study on Artificial Intelligence and Law,* Kluwer, Computer/Law Series, 1992, p. 245.

From a more philosophical point of view on the use of expert systems, the *mainstream view* has stated that general methods of expert problem solving can be found, and that these can be made computational, and can be applied to many different problems. Implicit in this *position* is the concept that the declarative and procedural aspect of how to solve a problem is independent of the task in hand.

FEIGENBAUM'S *antithesis* is that "rather than looking for generality, we should set out empirically to capture human knowledge and procedures for specific tasks. Essentially, we should be willing to write a new program for each task. Actually, this technique led to the first practical expert systems. It is evident, however, that this approach is intellectually labour intensive, as far as the acquisition of knowledge is concerned. A *knowledge engineer* must study the task, specify appropriate inference engines, and then work with task experts and programmers to construct a system".[141] In the case of law, apart from following this object-oriented methodology, one also has to tackle the already exposed problems. If we then build a proper Legal Expert System, with a Knowledge Base created according to the previous thoughts, it may be able to solve real life legal problems and then it will overcome the stage of a simple 'checklist'.

2.5   LAWYER'S BASIC INSTINCT - CONCLUSIONS OF CHAPTER 2

From the early dawn of AI and Law, ALLEN has argued that "symbolic logic employed in legal thinking will *not* deny the role of intuition", and that, "exponents of symbolic juristic logic are not seeking to promote legal dogmatism by means of a 'super logic'; on the contrary, they suggest that it provides a logical means of penetration into the sociological substratum of law, and excels traditional logic in doing so".[142]   L ater on, SUSSKIND has added that "legal reasoning involves complex mental processes that are not susceptible to direct observation. All we can do is reflect on our own experiences and also draw inferences based on all external manifestations of legal reasoning processes."[143] And finally, WAHLGREN has

---

[141] See for information purposes FEIGENBAUM E. & MCCODRUCK P., *The Fifth Generation,* Addison Weshley, Reading, Ma., 1983.

[142] ALLEN L. E., *Symbolic Logic: A Razor-edged Tool for Drafting and Interpreting Legal Documents,* in YALE LAW JOURNAL, Vol. 66, 1957, p. 879.

[143] SUSSKIND R., *Expert Systems in Law,* Clarendon, Oxford 1987, p. 205.

asserted that "[a] well-trained lawyer, even a very experienced one will then often make use of external knowledge representation, e.g. by reading the description of the available representation of the rule in a statute or case, and mapping all the relevant prerequisites one by one onto the elements of the current situation. If everything fits, the lawyer will be ready to formulate a decision."[144]

For expert systems, specifically, MITAL & JOHNSON submit that "an extremely important point in legal applications is that in high risk domains, there is an onus on the expert system, to convince the user of its recommendation in order to avoid putting the user in a difficult situation, where he/she has to choose between his/her own instincts and the system's recommendation".[145] The problem with law is that lawyers are taught to both cultivate and widely use this 'instinct', at least as far as legal reasoning is concerned. This partiular problem is also brought forward from legal methodologists who have argued that the debate concerning the legal syllogism, and, generally, the connection of logic to law seems too scholastic to a practising Lawyer.[146] Normally, for him/her, the performance of legal reasoning is attached to such an *instinctive certainty*, that there is no need to think about logic while he/she is taking legal decisions, in order to justify this certainty about his/her decision. Modern legal methodology entails that input from other sources, such as jurisprudential and empirical knowledge, can find its place in the major premiss sentence of the legal syllogism.

The above scheme can be used to introduce the notion of *Lawyer's basic instinct* in order to justify the viability of legal expert / knowledge based systems. This term should cover the intuitive qualification of Lawyers, and of laymen occasionally, to perform reasoning with rules, and to justify their decisions within a normative context. It is not only a matter of legal education but of empirical knowledge of the outer world.[147]

---

[144] WAHLGREN P., *Automated Legal Reasoning: A Study on Artificial Intelligence and Law*, Kluwer, Computer/Law Series, 1992, p. 206.

[145] MITAL V. & JOHNSON L., *Advanced Information Systems for Lawyers*, Chapman & Hall, London, 1992, p. 103.

[146] See also SOURLAS P., *Themeliodi Zitimata tis Methodologias tou Dikeou, (Fundamental Issues of Legal Methodology,* in Greek), Athens 1986, p. 113.

[147] Notice however the objections of WRÓBLEWSKI that "[t]he intuitive search for a just decision could be combined with the proper *ex post* justification with arguments expected by the law and its ideology. The ideology of legal and rational decision does not tolerate the intuition argument but expects a justification by proper arguments concerning rules, facts and values if made explicit.

171

The following points summarise the conclusions of this Chapter:

1. It must be re-emphasised that this Chapter has examined the use of expert systems for legal applications and especially the use of expert systems to perform the central / core legal reasoning function of the model (described under the notions of *Interpretation* and the *Legal Syllogism* in Chapter 1).

2. This examination shows that an expert system can only perform that legal reasoning function properly if it takes account of the other parts of the model. Such a system should not be designed as a stand-alone application, which derives its knowledge base solely from the strictly expressed rules of a limited legal domain. It must incorporate the whole procedure, which takes place intuitively in the legal mind. If this fragment of legal knowledge (substantive, procedure and empirical) can be snapshot, translated and transformed to a knowledge base, under the analysed notion of the legal sub-system, then it can be expected to build expert systems that will exhibit the *'deep understanding'* that a lawyer possess.

3. An expert system which exhibits such a 'deep understanding', even if it only automates the core legal reasoning function and leaves the other parts of the model to be carried out by humans, will be of real practical value and sooner or later, will be trusted by practitioners. Otherwise, expert systems, in attempting to perform this central function, will not be able to provide complete and accurate solutions, although they could be of great help as 'assistants' in other parts of the legal decision making process.

The institutional mechanisms of controlling law-applying decisions concern proper arguments and not the psychology of decision-making." WRÓBLEWSKI J., *Legal Expert Systems and Legal Reasoning*, in MARTINO (Ed.), North Holland, 1992, p. 383.

3. EMPIRICAL INVESTIGATION

3.1   INTRODUCTION

Apart from the author's background (professional and academic) in Information Technology Applications in Law, the main empirical input for the Ph.D. research was his participation as the *domain expert* and *knowledge engineer* for the *Nomos-Advisor* prototype expert system of the *Nomos* project. The need to create the model of Chapter 1 became apparent at the early stages of the implementation of the *Nomos-Advisor* system. Furthermore, most of the theoretical considerations, the methodological limitations, the rules and the procedures of the model in Chapter 1 were inspired during the analysis and the implementation of the aforementioned system. As explained, these inspirations have motivated the author to create the model of Chapter 1. At the same time, the model was tested in parallel and refined in the course of implementation.

The purpose of this Chapter (3) is to describe this analysis and implementation in order to point out the reasons behind certain decisions and directions taken in the model. The entire description is a continuous effort to justify the need for the model itself (totally) and for its separate components. However, two clarifications are needed here: (1) At any step of the implementation of the *Nomos-Advisor* system, the particular details that crucially affected the drafting of the model and the solutions followed, will be explicitly referred to under the *Link to the Model* notion. It should be noted that, at the same time, the model has been tested and evaluated around these points. (2) Some of the decisions for the model are not justified by the implementational stages, but, rather, lie in the background of the whole *Nomos* project. To cover this aspect the next paragraphs attempt to outline the history of the project, its objectives, and its internal structure.

3.2   THE PROJECT'S HISTORICAL OVERVIEW

3.2.1   General Description

The European Strategic Programme for Research and Development in Information Technology (ESPRIT) is a well known European Community (and now European Union) project carried out under the auspices of Directorate General 12 (DG XII). The *Nomos* project, named after the Greek word for Law (*Νόμος*), was an Esprit phase II, twenty-four month research project in Information Systems, which started in 1990 and ended in December 1992. The project was numbered 5330 and its full title was: *Knowledge Acquisition for Normative Reasoning Systems.*[1]

The project was classified under the 'knowledge engineering' subset of applications concerning 'Information Processing Systems and Software' and the triumphant explanation in the Esprit 1992 Exhibition Guide announced that

> "Knowledge - Based Systems have been successfully implemented in numerous application areas and the strong demand for such systems now raises the necessity to apply state of the art good industrial practice in their development process. Consequently, the IT industry needs to be supplied with Knowledge Engineering methods and tools able to support the various activities involved in the Knowledge Engineering process and to broaden the range of potential applications".

According to the rules concerning Esprit projects, the constituting companies must create a consortium; in the case of *Nomos 5330* the Esprit consortium structure (in the final stage of the project) was:

1. Sogei (Italian company), coordinator,
2. Tecsiel S.A. (Italian company), associated partner of Sogei,
3. Orion S.A. (Greek company), partner,
4. Step Informatique, (French Company), partner
5. IRETIJ (the University of Montpellier), associated partner of Step Informatique and
6. Axon (Portugese company), partner

---

[1]   The full details on the intentions of the project can be found in the special Esprit Bibliography and especially in the Esprit Documentation.

Two distinct branches of the project were envisaged: (1) ILAM (Italian Linguistic Analysis Module) with Sogei, Tecsiel and Orion participating in and (2) FLAM (French Linguistic Analysis Module) with Step, Iretij and Axon. The total budget was 2,245,600 ECUs of which 1,165,300 was EEC funding.

3.2.2   The Project's Objectives

According to the project summary,[2] the project was devoted to the design and development of toolsets for knowledge acquisition in the normative field. The validity of the toolsets to be developed would be tested through demonstrative prototypes of specific applications. The project included the following environments:

1. an acquisition toolset called Normative Knowledge Acquisition Tools (NKAT) which comprised *ILAM (Italian Linguistic Analysis Module)* (hereinafter ILAM) and *FLAM (French Linguistic Analysis Module)*. The approach in developing this toolset would include linguistic analysis of law texts and topic identification, aiming at a text formalisation, and providing a usable NKB (Normative Knowledge Base) able to support different applications;

2. a Normative Knowledge Engineering Environment (NKEE) providing support to a normative knowledge engineer in the formalisation of the texts, and a standard user interface for the different tools and for the validation and refinement of the knowledge-base.

What it was called 'knowledge representation language' (KRL) would be tested against the specific requirements of the normative fields (French and Italian). In particular, the "latest generation approaches to KRL would be taken as a basis and augmented with normative elements resulting from the analysis of normative texts", which would be performed in the project.

The foreseen applications were Legal Advisory Systems for the French and Italian domains; those systems would produce legal advice and suggestions when specific 'cases' (legal problems) would be submitted to the system. Starting from the

---

[2] For these initial ambitions see the *Nomos* summary in ESPRIT-DOC II, Area 1,5,4, Technical Annex, amendment I, November 1991, p. 4.

175

specification of a 'case', they would be able to deduce the relevant legal consequences, based on the formalised norms, extracted from the normative texts. Furthermore a study on a Text Retrieval System (TRS) would be undertaken in order to demonstrate that the Normative Knowledge-Base was also suitable for applications other than advisory systems.

> **Link to the Model:**
> At this stage there was no consideration about the character and the goals of these applications. This deficiency has inspired the *Rule of Integration* and the *Rule of Practicality*.

The major aim of the system was to provide a tool which should significantly help the job of the knowledge engineer of normative texts. The basic assumption was that given the *high cost* of this task (and even though a certain amount of interaction with the domain expert was still required), the tool should represent a major advantage for the development of knowledge-based applications in the normative field. To this extent, it was anticipated that "the domain characterisation study and the legal ontology (for the French and Italian legal domains) as well as the acquisition and representation methodology developed in the project, should constitute fundamental building blocks for these kinds of tasks".[3]

> **Link to the Model:**
> The wrong assumption that the cost of 'legal knowledge' lies in quantity rather in quality led to the *Rule of Content*.

This aim is directly opposed to SUSSKIND'S view that "[i]t is not possible, as it is for database systems in law, simply to feed statute law into an expert system in the fixed form in which it is expressed in statute law-formulations, such as the Acts of Parliament; for...no inference engine could operate on knowledge represented in natural language and no program could currently be written to transform the text into an implementable format."[4]

The designers of the project, however, had already accepted that the demand for knowledge based applications in the normative field has been growing fast in the last few years, and most partners in the consortium would exploit the outcomes of the project in this direction. In more details they explain that "[t]he main obstacle to a wider use and exploitation of the knowledge based technology lies in the *cost*

---

3   ESPRIT-DOC II, Area 1,5,4, Technical Annex, amendment I, November 1991, p. 6.

4   SUSSKIND R., *Expert Systems in Law*, Clarendon, Oxford 1987, p. 80.

and complexity of the knowledge acquisition task."[5] The main industrial objective of the project was, therefore, the creation of a software development environment to help the construction of knowledge based applications, with a special focus on the features of normative reasoning. The industrial interest was motivated by the potential to commercialise knowledge based systems for final users or for internal purposes.

The choice of the normative domain depended on the following hypotheses (for a Criticism see *infra* section 3.2.4):

1. Normative language is by definition mainly coded in natural language texts,

2. Large corpora of which are available on machine-manageable devices,

3. The technical nature of normative texts makes their processing more feasible (sublanguage processing),

4. Law constitutes the oldest and most important form of explicit rules about normative structure ('meta-rules'),

5. Normative applications are *per se* commercially interesting and directly usable in a broad range of environments (e.g. public administration, services, companies...), in particular for the needs which were envisaged as emerging in view of the 1992 single market (the project's drafting started in 1990) .

Other major objectives of the project were the following:

- To test to what extent formal languages would be able to fully express the semantic content of the texts (to be analysed) according to their textual, pragmatic nature; such languages would focus on the features of the normative domain, but would possibly be suitable for other kinds of texts.

- To obtain practical prototypes to be converted into real products at the end of the project

The project had two specific objectives:

---

[5]   In the same document ESPRIT-DOC II, Area 1,5,4, Technical Annex, amendment I, November 1991, p. 10 (emphasis added).

1. To produce two versions (one for French and one for Italian) of an experimental prototype of the Knowledge Acquisition Toolset; enhancements to this toolset would be built on the prototypes to produce a demonstration version.

2. To produce two demonstration applications (one for the French and one for the Italian domain).

3.2.3   The Project's Workplan

To better understand the exact role of the author in the project, it is necessary to describe its workplan. The project finally consisted of 6 workpackages (WP in Esprit terminology) of which one (WP4) was abandoned and another (WP6) referred to the overall management of the project.

Workpackage 1, in the consortium's words, "was devoted to the deepening of general theoretical issues, providing a sound domain analysis to be used in the design and development of each software module. It should also provide details of the system's functionalities, a system architecture, a sketch of the system's external behaviour, hardware and software requirements and selection, the identification of common services, a sketch of the communications protocols and of the links among the components, a sketch of the Normative Knowledge Base contents and structure etc.. Other important goals of the Workpackage are the identification of the target texts, depending on some general criteria as specified below, and the definition of the guidelines of the applications" .[6]

At this stage, the global design of the system's architecture as well as detailed characteristics like the user qualifications, the user interface (Input / Output), the internal architecture etc. were decided. On choosing hardware and software it was assumed that "both linguistic analysis and knowledge representation are very complex tasks, involving algorithms and techniques that require a considerable amount of computing recourses, and these requirements have been matched with

---

6   ESPRIT-DOC II, Area 1,5,4, *Technical Annex, amendment I*, November 1991, p. 31.

cost considerations, aiming to maximise the performance / price ratio and the need for a standard operating environment has been kept an important decision factor".[7]

It was, therefore, decided to use a Sun Sparc-2 station, running at 40 MHz, 25 Mips, a Risc Central Processing Unit (CPU), with 16 MB of standard memory running a Unix-based Operating System. In the same vein, because "the history of Prolog and current Natural language Processing and Knowledge Representation Trends lead to the choice of this language as a 'natural' tool to map the linguistic and reasoning problems at hand".[8] *Bim Prolog* was selected as the programming language. It was further argued that Bim Prolog offered better benchmarks, an impressive set of tools, a bi-directional interface to the C programming language, it would cost less and, finally, Tecsiel S.A. and its consultants had developed significant pieces of software in this language.[9]

Finally, this Workpackage produced a draft classification of the normative documents, in terms of document types, content and subject, and a, so called, 'finer-grained' linguistic analysis of the legal texts, with a list of recurrent word and text patterns to be used by the ILAM and FLAM components.

Workpackage 2 has produced a preliminary version of the *'Normative Knowledge Representation Language' (NKRL)* and some of the associated reasoning tools. In the endless documentation of the project, it was clearly stated that "NKRL must be a basic knowledge representation language with a very precisely defined syntax and semantics entities of the modules with which it interfaces. The Normative Language documents to be translated can be roughly assigned to the following categories:

1. statutory laws and regulations

2. descriptive norms giving instructions and definitions about the concrete application of a statutory norm;

3. doctrine (case law, court decisions), relating to the application of the statutory norm to real cases;

---

[7] ESPRIT DOC AS-10-40-02, *Hardware and Software Choice,* p. 67.

[8] ESPRIT DOC AS-10-40-02, *Hardware and Software Choice,* p. 67.

[9] ESPRIT DOC AS-10-40-02, *Hardware and Software Choice,* p. 68.

4. event descriptions, e.g. Natural Language descriptions of particular events which must be examined (ruled, judged) according to the statutory norm, and of all the other input (witnesses etc.) related to the events under examination".[10]

At the same time it was emphasised that the knowledge to be represented should include:

1. *Normative knowledge,* which mainly takes the form of rules making use of logical and deontic operators, and having the form of an implication

2. *Descriptive knowledge,* which concerns the representation of detailed particular facts (mainly from the last two categories of texts)

3. *Definitional knowledge,* which provides the definition of the entities (legal and non-legal concepts, individual characters etc.) used in the two previous classes of knowledge.

Nevertheless, although these promises coincide with the concept of a legal subsystem, which has already been described in *Chapter 1*, the final outcome, was much less ambitious and the processed texts were only a very small subset of this proposal.

> **Link to the Model:**
> This deficiency confirms the *need to use a model as a checklist*, because although this specific knowledge is described in this initial analysis of the project, later it was forgotten.

Workpackage 3 has been dedicated to the development of the Normative Knowledge Acquisition Toolset (NKAT), which was concerned with the problem of semi-automatically capturing the normative knowledge from textual sources. Towards that direction, syntactic analysers, semantic parsers and juridical lexica were used. It was assumed that the textual sources were in machine readable form, and that text scanning facilities would not be a major problem.

This neglected factor, of the scanning time, could be of great importance. No matter how fast scanning techniques can be, a large proportion of legal

---

[10] ESPRIT-DOC II, Area 1,5,4, Technical Annex, amendment I, November 1991, p. 33.

documentation is not yet transformed or cannot be available[11] in machine-readable form. From the practical experience of the project, it was proved that scanning was significantly more time consuming, than originally thought it would be.

In this Workpackage it was stated that "the normative texts will be considered as written in a sort of sublanguage", that *"the degree of refinement of the target formal representation will be determined only with reference to the objectives of the practical applications* developed in Workpackage 5", and that "human intervention will be required".[12] Unfortunately, many of these promises were not kept, and decisions were already taken at this early stage without any consideration for the final applications.

It is perhaps ironic, in the light of the conclusions of this Chapter, that, even at the outset, the objectives of the project presented a contradiction in terms with the 'fully automatic' - without intervention - acquisition described in its title.

3.2.4   Criticism

A first critical reading of the initial objectives and endeavours of the project shows that it suffered fundamental defects right from the beginning. These defects have affected the whole course of the *Nomos-Advisor* implementation and a discussion, based on the author's experience of working on the project will follow at the end of this Chapter. However, some of these problems triggered the initial thoughts for the core hypothesis of the model of Chapter 1. For this reason, a number of the objections to the design and theoretical basis of the project is summarised here:

1. The basic hypothesis upon which the project was drafted was that the 'law' is mainly contained in huge collections of textual documents. This is not true; it was shown in *Chapter 1 (The Doctrine of Valid Legal Sources)* that much law can also be found in sources other than statute or cases. Especially, it can be found in free-form texts like doctrine etc. and not always in rule-form texts.

---

[11] Sometimes for legal reasons concerning promulgation or copyright.

[12] ESPRIT-DOC II, Area 1,5,4, Technical Annex, amendment I, November 1991, p. 35 (emphasis added).

Link to the Model:
This wrong hypothesis led to the development of the rule to search all Valid
Legal Sources and create the legal sub-system.

2. Furthermore, it was assumed that the EU is one of the biggest producers of
textual legal material. Therefore, if we can automatically process this volume of
knowledge we can save time and effort. Actually, it was known through
personal communication, that this assumption was put forward to the EU for
obtaining the project. Even though EU produces a lot of legal material, the truth
is that, in order to create the 'legal subsystem' (*supra* Chapter 1), the Lawyer,
and particularly the practitioner, is always reducing this 'huge volume' of
information to a much smaller set of 'relevant' legal material. The development
of Information Technology Applications that will help him/her in this specific
task of reduction is, of course, a completely different situation.

Link to the Model:
This assumption, based on a wrong perception about the use of legal
applications, led to the development of the Rule of Practicality.

3. On the same grounds, it is not self-evident that 'knowledge engineering of
normative texts' will be an expensive task. Experience from other practical
knowledge based applications shows that the detection of the 'expert', and the
acquisition of the 'knowledge' were the less 'expensive' tasks in terms of a
cost / benefit analysis.[13]

4. It is not certain whether the initial ambition to produce a general 'Normative
Knowledge Base', would be able to serve all three different kinds of
Information Technology Applications in Law, i.e. legal reasoning, information
retrieval, office automation.

Link to the Model:
In the model these parts are interrelated but distinct from each other. The
peculiarities of each part, described in Chapter 2, show that it is not yet
technically feasible to transfer components from one part to the other. For
example, a knowledge base for a rule-based expert system is not suitable for
a front-end expert system or for conceptual retrieval.

---

[13] See for example BREUKER J.A - DE MULDER R.V. - HAGE J.C., *Legal Knowledge Based Systems*,
Koninklijke Vermande BV, Lelystad, 1991 and CAPPER P. & SUSSKIND R., *Latent Damage Act,
The Expert System*, Butterworths, London, 1988.

5. The assumption that large corpora of law are available in machine-readable format did not prove true, since most of the input of the project was fed through scanners and OCR (optical character recognition) software. This led, irrespective of the sophisticated equipment, to further delays in processing the legal texts.

6. The enthusiasm to commercialise the results of the project was not justified by the 'trading' history of similar applications.

   Link to the Model:
   The *Rule of Practicality* and the economics of everyday legal practice were tested on this point.

7. The 'knowledge', endeavoured by the designers to be represented (described in Workpackage 2, *supra* at 3.2.3 The Project's Workplan), was not included in the final application. Instead, only a limited version of *'normative knowledge'*, namely the text of a single article (number 7) of the Italian VAT Law was processed.

   Link to the Model:
   This omission has inspired the *Rule of the Checklist* which helps to memorise all the necessary elements.

8. The final phase of the project openly contradicted the initial plans, by adopting a *semi-automatic processing and elaboration of legal texts*, and finally accepting the intervention of a human expert.

9. Many different teams were involved in the development of the different workpackages, and, therefore, the condition set in Workpackage 3 (*supra* 3.2.3 The Project's Workplan), to consider the objectives of the final application, was not consistently adhered to. Instead, all the workpackages were fragmentary approaches trying to coincide with the main aim of the project, that of *knowledge acquisition for normative reasoning systems*. This is mainly due to administrative reasons.

3.2.5 The Research Team

The author participated in a research team which had to fulfil two tasks of the Workpackage 5 of the project. It is, therefore, considered essential to list here the basic ambitions of this Workpackage which were

"To set the requirements for the construction of two demonstrators which will take into account significative subsets of the French and Italian Normative systems (originally expressed in natural language) and will show non-trivial reasoning capabilities on concrete case which refer to these subsets. The construction of the two demonstrators will be carried out with the ambition of establishing practical policies for dealing with the automated treatment of all the rules and regulations which are used to govern the running of institutions and organisations. We use the term regulation in a very wide sense, not only to refer to the particular regulations a given organisation might use in order to administer its activities, but also to include the general laws of a state. The domain of the potential applications of the demonstrators results is consequently enormous. It ranges from legal advisory and analysis systems which deal with aspects of law (tax law, corporate law, labour law, EEC law, etc.), to systems which advice on or administer the regulations of large organisations (internal regulations), to programs which perform simple and routine administrative tasks in the style of conventional data processing applications".[14]

Furthermore, the specific tasks of this Workpackage and the guidelines for the prototype were framed within the general aims of the project by adding that:

1. The prototype should "verify the flexibility of Normative Knowledge Representation Language (NKRL) used in the Normative Knowledge Acquisition Tool (NKAT) toolset and the soundness and adequacy of the acquisition process".[15] It was also stated that "a very interesting result of the Workpackage will be the practical experience on the integration of ILAM and FLAM Normative Knowledge Bases with other sources of knowledge. This means a real feedback on 'what is missing' in the acquisition tool, helping us to understand what can be improved in ILAM and FLAM and *what cannot be realistically done by any automatic tool*." (emphasis added)

2. The prototype should establish some preliminary criteria concerning the future industrial commercialisation of the tool developed in the project, namely "the evaluation of the cost saving of semi-automated procedure of knowledge extraction with respect to a completely manual one, the verification of the existence of cross-countries similarities in the automated treatment of legal

---

[14] ESPRIT-DOC II, Area 1,5,4, Technical Annex, amendment I, November 1991, p. 39.

[15] ESPRIT-DOC II, Area 1,5,4, Technical Annex, amendment I, November 1991, p. 39. It is characteristic that this methodology was never followed in reality.

norms and, therefore, of the possibility of developing European market for the results of the project, etc."[16]

These considerations were exposed to show the basis upon which the final details of the two tasks of the Workpackage were drafted. In the words of the official Esprit documentation, the two tasks were:

> *Task 5.1*: Definition of the Italian Application devoted to the detailed definition of the functionalities which the demonstrator must support. The system would deal with the problem of VAT applicability, introduced in WP1. This Task was contracted to Sogei and Orion together.

> *Task 5.3*: Development of the Italian Application, devoted to the development of the Italian demonstrator starting from the output of ILAM, i.e. the formalisation of the first 10 articles of the Italian VAT law.

Orion S.A., a Greek company specialising in Information Systems Development, had a contractual obligation, as an Esprit partner, to fulfil the above 'tasks'. In order to do so, Orion associated with the University of Westminster[17] Artificial Intelligence Research Group (hereinafter UW-AIRG), and employed the author as the legal expert and analyst. The author, together with the aforementioned group, formed the working team that implemented the project. The specific role of the author was twofold: first, I was the *domain expert* - in terms of AI methodology - providing the knowledge about the Italian VAT Law and second, due to my computer background, I was also the *knowledge engineer*, trying to amend and refine the knowledge base of the prototype (constructed by the rest of the team).

It must be confessed, however, that, during the project, the research team had to play another two roles, a kind of Dr Jekyll and Mr Hyde: On the one hand, the team was bound by a contractual obligation to create a working prototype demonstrator according to the above mentioned tasks 5.1 and 5.3. This prototype should be able to meet the requirements, and 'pass' the examination of the European Commission officials at the end of the project, so that the participating companies would be able to collect their remuneration. On the other hand, the team was challenged by the research interest that the *Nomos* project presented. These two different views are reflected in the two papers that have resulted from the

---

16 ESPRIT-DOC II, Area 1,5,4, Technical Annex, amendment I, November 1991, p. 39.

17 Former Polytechnic of Central London – PCL.

project: the first[18] is an attempt to describe the project as it was presented to the Commission's examiners, while the second[19] is a more critical scrutiny of the knowledge engineering problems encountered during the implementation of the prototype.

However, the analysis that will follow, exposing the course of development of the prototype, is mostly affected by a personal 'legal' observation and by the need to justify the use of the model. Therefore, both the details of the implementation and the specific problems that had to be solved, are perceived through the eyes of a lawyer seeking a practical legal application.

3.3   THE PROJECT'S INTERNAL ELEMENTS

3.3.1   The Theoretical System Architecture

In its theoretical dimension the whole project was seen as a composite computerised tool, with three distinct components:

1. The *Knowledge Acquisition* environment that would provide the tools for the textual analysis of the legal material and for the formalisation of the extracted knowledge. The input to this environment would be selected normative documents and the output would be a representation of the meaning of the text in Natural Knowledge Representation Language (NKRL).

    Link to the Model:
    This attitude has caused the introduction of the phase of *decoding the meaning of words* and especially the need to emphasise that subsumption can only be carried out by humans.

---

[18] KONSTANTINOU V., SYKES J. & YANNOPOULOS G. N., *Can Legal Knowledge be derived from Legal Texts?* in PROCEEDINGS OF THE 4TH INTERNATIONAL CONFERENCE ON ARTIFICIAL INTELLIGENCE AND LAW, Amsterdam, 1993, p. 218.

[19] KONSTANTINOU V., SYKES J. & YANNOPOULOS G. N., *Legal Reasoning Methodology: The Missing Link*, in PROCEEDINGS OF THE 4TH NATIONAL CONFERENCE ON LAW, COMPUTERS AND ARTIFICIAL INTELLIGENCE, University of Exeter, April, 1994, p. 29.

2. The *Knowledge Engineering* environment that would provide the necessary tools for representing and processing all the knowledge, together with reasoning techniques and

3. The *Final applications* that would evaluate and use practically the results of these two environments.

The Knowledge Acquisition process consisted of two phases: The phase of *Linguistic Acquisition* and the phase of *Deep Knowledge Processing*. The first would provide a first formalisation of the text of the law while the second would obtain a 'canonical' form of the semantics of the text. This would be able to present, under a unified form, the different conceptual contents used in the law. It was admitted, however, that even at the last stage of development "a certain degree of human intervention will be required",[20] and that is why, finally, the whole project was seen as *semi-automatic knowledge acquisition*.

It is interesting to quote the theoretical view on how this formalisation could both support a rule-based reasoner as well as a case-based one. It was enthusiastically endorsed that the above second phase output could allow:

1. A 'traditional deductive reasoning, [which] needs to find the pertinent specialisation of a universally quantified rule; then it needs only the identification of the path of a conceptual hierarchy that brings from the predicate(s) of the 'case' to the predicate(s) of the rule(s) in order to select the suitable rule (e.g. if the rule of a law regulates the real estates and the case concerns an apartment, in order to select and apply such a rule the system needs to recognise that an apartment is a type of building and a building is a type of real estate); in short a simple mechanism for the bottom-up traversal of a [decision] tree is needed.

2. On the contrary a case-based reasoning [which] needs the identification of a possible common conceptual root (or intermediate node) among the case under examination and all the other available cases, so that if the cases are formalised in terms of the concepts expressed in the text the system should analyse all the cases in order to find such a common point of contact. It should be evident the advantage of having just available a formalisation in terms of pre-defined semantic primitives

---

[20] ESPRIT DOC TE-31-40-01, *Design of ILAM module for NOMOS*, 16-Sep-91.

that would allow an easy identification of the cases that are relevant for the case under examination.[21]

Link to the Model:
This notion inspired the *openness* of the model to any valid automated reasoning technique, i.e. rule-based, case-based, neural nets or any other technological development. (see also Chapter 2)

A large part of the project's documentation was devoted to the description of the *Natural Knowledge Representation Language* (NKRL). The important decision here, which affected the whole project, was that on the implementation level, the 'structured objects principle' and the '*is_a* inheritance principle' entailed the use of a *'frame'* or an *'object oriented'* representation. Moreover, NKRL provided a *descriptive component* for the expression of stable concepts and a *definitional component* for the description of concepts in need of definition by means of a 'frame' structure composed of a name, a set of slots and a set of procedures. Although this 'Language' was not fully developed and implemented (see *infra* 3.3.3 The ILAM Module Architecture), it has crucially affected certain aspects of the project, especially the selection of 'frames' for knowledge representation.

Link to the Model:
This *'frame'* and *'is_a'* structure, which entailed the use of known rule-base expert systems techniques was the initial motive for choosing *rule-based deduction* for the model.

3.3.2   SOWA'S[22] Conceptual Graphs

Following SERGOT'S[23] effort to classify all the projects concerning the representation of law in computer programs, it is believed that the distinctive factor of Nomos is its *computational formalism,* i.e. the method used to represent natural language (and hence law) to an entity 'understandable' by a computer. In this case, the core theory and the method chosen by the Esprit consortium to 'formalise' the Italian VAT Law was SOWA'S *Conceptual Graphs,* a brief analysis of which will

---

[21] See ESPRIT DOC AS-10-40-02, *Normative Field Selection, Part II: System Architecture*, 1-Mar-91, p. 21.

[22] SOWA J. F., *Conceptual Structures, Information Processing in Mind and Machine*, Addison Weshley, 1984.

[23] SERGOT M, *The Representation of Law in Computer Programs*, in BENCH-CAPON(ED.) p. 10.

follow[24] (for additional examples see *infra* 3.3.5 The ILAM Knowledge Representation).

In an effort to represent natural language, SOWA accepts, from the linguistic point of view, that "a sentence is derived from six different kinds of information:

1. *Conceptual graphs* are the logical forms that state relationships between persons, things, attributes and events

2. *Tense and modality* describe how conceptual graphs relate to the real world. They state whether something has happened, can happen, will happen, or should happen.

3. *Presupposition* is the background information that the speaker and listener tacitly assume.

4. *Focus* is the new point that the speaker is trying to make

5. *Conference links* show which concepts refer to the same entities. In a sentence, these links are expressed as pronouns and other *anaphoric references*.

6. *Emotional connotations* are determined by associations in the minds of the speaker and the listener.[25]

From the empirical point of view, SOWA defines that "[a] Conceptual Graph is a diagram that represents the literal meaning of a sentence. It shows the concepts (represented by boxes) and the relations between them (represented by circles)."[26] The sentence *John is going to Boston by Bus*,[27] is depicted in *Figure 3-1 as* a graph.

As SOWA explains, this example has two individual concepts [PERSON: John] and [CITY: Boston] that refer to a specific person and a specific city; [GO] is a generic concept that refers to some unspecified instance of going; and [BUS] is also a generic concept that refers to an unspecified bus. The AGNT relation shows that John

---

[24] Mainly this analysis will explain the terminology which is used later. For more information see all the writings of SOWA and the special Bibliography for the N-A prototype.

[25] SOWA J. F., *Conceptual Structures, Information Processing in Mind and Machine*, Addison Weshley, 1984, p. 10.

[26] Sowa J. F., *Special Notation*, 27-Aug-1987.

[27] Example and graph by Sowa.

is the agent of going. DEST shows that Boston is the Destination, and INST shows that Bus is the instrument.

Moreover, a linear representation is proposed, in order to save space, by using square brackets for the boxes and rounded parentheses for the circles. The graph for the previous sentence can be written as:

[PERSON: John]←(AGNT) ←(GO)→(DEST) →[CITY:Boston]

When a concept has more than two relations attached to it, like, in this case, the concept [GO], the graph can be mapped into the linear form by putting a hyphen after [GO] to show that its relations are listed on subsequent lines:

[GO] -
    →(AGNT) [PERSON: John]
    →(DEST) [CITY: Boston]
    →(INST) [BUS]

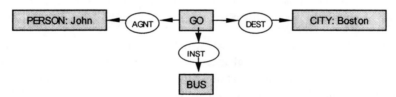

Figure 3-1: A Conceptual Graph

Normally, the starting point is the most highly connected concept, but any node could be chosen as a start. Concepts are considered as symbols that represent the meanings of words. They may refer to actions, properties or events in the world.

To distinguish, the type of object a concept refers to, from the specific individual, the concept box is divided in two parts: a *type field* on the left and a *referent field* on the right. In the basic notation for conceptual graphs only three kinds of referents are permitted:

1. *Existential*: The symbol * indicates the existence of some individual of the appropriate type. A generic concept like [BUS] is actually an abbreviation for

190

the full notation [BUS:*], where the asterisk indicates an unspecified referent of type BUS. It corresponds to an existential qualifier ∃ in symbolic logic.

2. *Individual marker*: The symbol # followed by an integer, such as #3776, identifies a unique individual. It corresponds to a constant in logic.

3. *Literal*: A quoted string like "abc" or a number like 123 identifies an individual by its form. It also corresponds to a constant in logic.

In conclusion, after the practical definition, the theoretical assumption is that "*[c]onceptual graphs* are a system of logic for representing natural language semantics. They form a knowledge representation language based on linguistics, psychology and philosophy. In the graphs, concept nodes represent entities, attributes, states and events, and relation nodes show how the concepts are interconnected".[28] It is, furthermore, conjectured that "[c]onceptual graphs are a universal, language independent deep structure. In AI the term *concept* is used for the nodes that encode information in networks or graphs: a concept is a basic unit for representing knowledge."[29]

Canonical graphs are those that enforce selectional constraints. They correspond to the case frames in linguistics and the category restrictions in philosophy.

Schema, is a Kantian term, initially used for a rule that organises perceptions into unitary wholes and then, at the next level of complexity, *incorporates domain-specific* knowledge about the typical constellations of entities, attributes, and events in the real world.

Type hierarchy is a partial ordering, defined over a set of concepts, arranged in a supertype-subtype order (like for example vehicle > car > cabriolet). For AI purposes, the important factor is the inheritance of properties from supertypes to subtypes of concepts.[30]

---

[28] SOWA J. F., *Conceptual Structures, Information Processing in Mind and Machine*, Addison Weshley, 1984, p. 69.

[29] SOWA J. F., *Conceptual Structures, Information Processing in Mind and Machine*, Addison Weshley, 1984, p. 39.

[30] SOWA J. F., *Conceptual Structures, Information Processing in Mind and Machine*, Addison Weshley, 1984, p. 81.

For the purposes of this study, it is interesting to focus on SOWA'S confession that an "Aristotelian[31] type hierarchy is possible only for the artificially constructed types of a programming language. In the fields of science, accounting, or *law*, the practitioners strive to develop complete definitions for all concepts. But as long as those fields are growing, *that goal can never be achieved*. In ordinary language very few concepts have complete definitions. Some types may be specified by definitions, but most are simply used without definitions. One reason for not defining everything is that present knowledge may be incomplete."[32]

> **Link to the Model:**
> This notion confirms the considerations of the model about *Decoding the Meaning of Words and Legal Linguistics* as well as *Linguistic Interpretation*.

However, it is known from personal communication, that the following passage, where SOWA refers to the Taxman project,[33] was the main reason behind the use of Conceptual graphs for the ILAM system and the Italian VAT law:

> "Definitions can specify a type in two different ways: by stating necessary and sufficient conditions for the type, or by giving a few examples and saying that everything similar to these belongs to the type. The first method derives from Aristotle's method of definition by *genus* and *differentiae,* and the second is closer to Wittgenstein. AI systems have supported both methods ...definitions by examples or prototypes are essential for dealing with natural language and its applications to the real world, but their logical status is unclear. Some systems that support prototypes are...and Taxman. Taxman is designed for legal reasoning in corporate tax law. Since most legal disputes arise when the issues are vague, ill-defined, or otherwise difficult to classify, definitions by necessary and sufficient conditions are not possible. For greater flexibility Taxman uses prototypes that represent the standard cases and deformations that adapt the prototypes to changing conditions. Conceptual graphs support type definitions by genus and differentiae as well as *schemata* and *prototypes*, which specify sets of family

---

[31] I.e. a type hierarchy where the subtypes are determined by explicit type definitions. Only primitive types (nine: Substance, Quantity, Quality, Relation, Time, Position, State, Activity, and Passivity) had no definitions. When all types other than the primitives are introduced by definitions the partial ordering is complete. see SOWA JOHN F., *Conceptual Structures, Information Processing in Mind and Machine*, Addison Weshley, 1984, p. 112.

[32] SOWA J. F., *Conceptual Structures, Information Processing in Mind and Machine*, Addison Weshley, 1984. P.113 (emphasis added).

[33] MCCARTY L.T. & SRIDHARAN N. S., *The representation of an evolving system of legal concepts: II. Prototypes and Deformations,* in PROCEEDINGS of the INTERNATIONAL JOINT CONFERENCE ON ARTIFICIAL INTELLIGENCE, 1981.

resemblances. Both methods are based on *abstractions*, which are canonical graphs with one or more concepts designated as formal parameters."[34]

It should be added that SOWA proposes the use of all Boolean operators as ordinary conceptual relations[35] and also the performance of deduction in a graph.[36] It is interesting that, in order to illustrate his rules of inference, he uses a legal example about citizenship.[37]

To complete the picture, SOWA defends the suitability of Conceptual Graphs for use in a conceptual processor based on *production rules*. *Production rules* is a model of human thinking, consisting of two parts: a *pattern* that matches something in current working storage, and an *action* part that specifies something to be done. He proposes the following method:

1. The first step in reasoning or computation is the selection of a conceptual graph that anticipates the form of the desired goal

2. Certain concepts in the graph are flagged with control marks. Each control mark triggers a search for schemata that match all or part of the goal

3. When the associative comparator finds a matching schema, the assembler joins it to the working graph. If the resulting graph satisfies the control marks, it attains a state of closure where all the control marks are erased.

4. The result of joining a schema to the working graph may cause control marks to be propagated to new nodes in the graph. When control marks can be neither propagated nor satisfied by the actor currently bound to a conceptual graph, the associative comparator searches for schemata containing other actors.

5. The limited number of working registers limits the number of control marks that can be active at the same time. If there are more than three

---

34 SOWA J. F., *Conceptual Structures, Information Processing in Mind and Machine*, Addison Weshley, 1984, p. 104.

35 SOWA J. F., *Conceptual Structures, Information Processing in Mind and Machine*, Addison Weshley, 1984, p. 147.

36 See also SOWA J. F., *Conceptual Structures, Information Processing in Mind and Machine*, Addison Weshley, p. 150.

37 SOWA J. F., *Conceptual Structures, Information Processing in Mind and Machine*, Addison Weshley, 1984, p. 155.

unsatisfied control marks, earlier ones are suspended until the more recent ones are satisfied.

6. When the control marks for recent subgoals attain closure, earlier control marks are reactivated until the original goal is satisfied.[38]

SOWA accepts many shortcomings for the completion of his method, but he admits that Conceptual Graphs can serve as data structures for a conceptual processor. He emphasises, however, the need for further research in the area of heuristics i.e. background knowledge about the application and in the area of the logical basis of the application.

3.3.3 The ILAM Module Architecture

The ILAM module of the *Nomos* system is responsible for the semi-automatic acquisition of knowledge from normative texts (see *Figure 3-2*).[39] In the beginning the system is completely blank concerning the domain, but it has some 'primitive' knowledge in the form of role slots, attributes, rule frames etc., which must be filled during the acquisition process. Although the texts are not pre-processed, ILAM was set to 'exploit' certain features of the restricted domain, such as segmentation (of a law in paragraphs, sections etc.), legal semantic information (e.g. definitions), and standard text markup symbols.

In addition, it should be noted again that the system is *semi*-automatic: There is a need for a degree of human intervention (such as additional syntactic information and the provision of a type hierarchy) within the module, to ensure correct results. Under the 'semi-automatic' considerations, the ILAM Module envisaged three persons: (1) An *Administrator*, in charge of developing and maintaining the system, (2) a *Knowledge Engineer* who would insert the legal text into the system, would answer questions posed by the system and would integrate the 'extracted' knowledge with other sources of knowledge in order to build the Knowledge Base, and (3) the *Final User* who uses the application.

---

[38] SOWA J. F., *Conceptual Structures, Information Processing in Mind and Machine*, Addison Weshley, 1984, p. 197.

[39] Courtesy of Orion S.A., Athens (Esprit Consortium).

Link to the Model:

This interference of humans confirms that, if *integrated* and *practical* (according to the model) legal applications are to be built, it would be better if the *domain expert* and the *knowledge engineer* are the same person.

Thus, two basic types of input are necessary: The full text of an article of the law, and a certain amount of validation and interpretation of the resulting representations, by a human knowledge engineer / expert.

The ILAM module itself can be decomposed[40] into a main module, the *text formaliser,* and other sub-systems. The *text formaliser* is, in turn, subdivided into three *major* processing units that process the legal text at different levels of

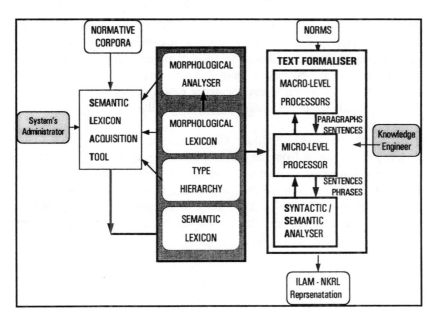

Figure 3-2: The ILAM System Architecture

aggregation and abstraction. These units are strongly interactive in operation, co-operating with each other as necessary, to achieve the best results. Their operation can briefly be described individually, as follows :

---

[40] see especially, ESPRIT DOC TE-31-40-01, *Design of ILAM module for NOMOS,* 16-Sep-91, p. 5. *Figure 3-2* courtesy of Orion S.A., Athens (Esprit Consortium).

1. The *'Macro-Level Processors'*. These act at the article level, segmenting the text into logical substructures: articles, paragraphs, sub-paragraph (letters) etc. The input is the result of morphological analysis on the article and the output is the *'structural view'* of the text, i.e. an indexed set of sentences describing its overall organisation, which is ready to proceed to the next stage (micro-level). The second 'macro-processor' (logical view analyser) accepts the output of the next stage (micro-level) on the whole article, in order to define the inter-relations of its substructures: For example, the fact that a certain paragraph is a definition, and that some later paragraph is an exception to it. It produces the *'logical view'*, of the legal text.

2. The *'Micro-Level Processors'*. These work at the sentence level, discovering the functional roles of phrases, via semantic processing, legal markup symbols in the text and a certain amount of contextual information. According to its creators, the knowledge about the special markup language and the typical expressions of the normative domain were included in this module. The functional roles assigned to each sentence describe its function as a definition, property, argument to a conditional 'or', and similar.

3. The *'Syntactic/Semantic Analyser (SSA)'*. This is the unit which produces the majority of the output from the ILAM module. Using a chart parsing technique, it accepts sentences, or logical sentences and phrases, with their functional roles, from the micro-level processors, and produces a *'Conceptual Graph'* representation (see *supra* 3.3.2) of the text. It makes use of a syntactic Italian grammar, and the applicability of its rules was subordinated to semantic constraints contained in a *lexicon*.

Other important sub-systems were:

4. The *Semantic Lexicon*, which, based on the Conceptual graphs framework, represented, for each word, all the possible conceptual relations.

5. This *Morphological Analyser* which processed each word of a sentence in order to retrieve the *lemma,* its syntactic (such as noun, verb etc.) and morphological (such as plural-singular, indicative etc.) features. Its main components were: (1) a context free grammar that described the rules of word derivation, (2) a specific context grammar for idioms, compounds, data, numbers, superlative forms and adjectives, and (3) the *Morphological Lexicon*, which contained a set of *lemmata* (each one having a stem, an ending class and a syntactic category).

196

6. The *Type Hierarchy*, which was a taxonomy of concepts. The lowest level included concepts directly tied to the lemmata. Each term in the text was classified in the hierarchy. It was used by the text formaliser and the lexicon acquisition tool.

7. The *Semantic Lexicon Acquisition Tool(SLAT)*, which semi-automatically produced the semantic lexicon.

Concerning *lexica,* in connection with the general line of this book, it can be quoted here that even the theoretical designers[41] of the ILAM *lexicon* have admitted that "[w]hen implementing computational lexicons it is important to keep in mind the texts that a Natural Language Processor must deal with. Words relate to each other in many different, often queer, ways: this information is rarely found in dictionaries, and it is quite hard to be invented *a priori, despite the imagination that linguists exhibit at inventing esoteric examples"*.

The three main units, however, in conjunction with *lexica* and the other sub-systems, produce an output which, following possible validation and refinement by the human knowledge engineer or expert, should represent the knowledge embodied within the text.

In the ILAM designers' words[42] the steps taken for this process are:

1. Morphological analysis of the normative text

2. For each article the structural *Macro Level Processor* produces an indexed segmentation of the text in suitable parts (typically at single sentence level) following the typical structural form of normative texts

3. For each segment of step 2, the *Micro Level Processor* assigns the functional role to the chunks of the segment (e.g. for a definition sentence: definiens and definiendum). The process can be affected by the 'story' of previous sentences.

4. The chunks of step 3 are analysed by SSA (Syntactic/Semantic Analyser). A *Conceptual Graph* for each one is provided.

---

[41] BASILI R,. PAZIENZA M.T. & VELARDI P., *Computational Lexicons: the Neat examples and the Odd Exemplars,* in 3RD CONFERENCE ON 'APPLIED NATURAL LANGUAGE PROCESSING', Trento, Italy, 1-3 April, 1992, (emphasis added).

[42] ESPRIT DOC TE-31-40-01, *Design of ILAM module for NOMOS,* 16-Sep-91, p. 6.

5. The *Conceptual Graphs* representations of step 4 are composed by the Macro-Level processor in special frames corresponding to the functional roles found in step 3

6. The results of the *Micro-Level Processing* are examined by the *Macro-Level logical view analyser* in order to find out the macro logical role of paragraphs and letters (e.g. a paragraph could represent an exception to a general definition)

7. The formal representation of the article is stored in some permanent structure.

3.3.4   The Law Chosen for Processing

In view of its wide range of potential users, the statute chosen for processing was the Italian VAT Law i.e. *Decreto del Presidente della Republica (DPR) no.633, 26/10/1972,* including subsequent amendments and modifications.

Many arguments[43] have supported the justification of that decision. First, historically, tax laws have always been at the centre of research on Legal Expert Systems,[44] second, they affect a greater circle of people (other than Lawyers, such as accountants, public servants and, finally, every citizen), third, they are – in theory - more precisely defined, fourth they concern a narrow domain and fifth, they are relatively more carefully drafted than other laws.[45] On the substantive value of the project it could be argued that VAT is a tax applied in all EEC[46] countries, affecting the every day life of millions of citizens and, therefore, a possible fruitful outcome could signify the future commercial exploitation of the project.[47]

---

[43] See also *infra* 3.6.1 Feasibility Analysis and Scoping.

[44] See the general bibliography and especially McCARTY'S *Taxman* projects and SUSSKIND R., *Expert Systems in Law*, Oxford,1987, p. 52.

[45] Although this latter point was not confirmed in our case, since even the single article 7, presented inconsistencies.

[46] See also SUSSKIND R. & TINDALL C., *VATIA: Ernst & Whinney's VAT Expert System*, offprint, p. 97, 1989 and FLESHER T., *What the IRS Knows About Artificial Intelligence That You Should Know*, in the TAX MAGAZINE, Vol. 65, No. 11, p. 707, November, 1987.

[47] The futuristic idea of having systems installed in public places, giving on-line expert advice on VAT law is described in ESPRIT-DOC SG51-40-01: *Requirements Capture and Architectural*

It was envisaged that the final 'Italian Application' - as opposed to the French one, which presented more the characteristics of an intelligent assistant in search of legislation - would be an *'Intelligent Advisor'* which should incorporate:

1. an adequate knowledge of the VAT domain;

2. a set of reasoning procedures which are able to derive conclusions from the knowledge;

3. a user interface which serves the purpose of taking information from the user and giving guidance to him/her.

It was assumed that the system would be also able to answer whether an activity falls within the scope of the Law and, particularly, it could verify the three main presumptions of the VAT law (see *infra* 3.6.3 The General Organisation of the Italian VAT Law), i.e. *subjectivity*, *objectivity* and the question of *territoriality*. The system would be based on the knowledge representation of the first ten articles of the Law (DPR. 633).

3.3.5   The ILAM Knowledge Representation

In contrast to the initial predictions, the ILAM Module has processed, for the purposes of the project, *only one* article of the Law (DPR. 633), i.e. article 7. This article referred to 'territoriality' and constituted the input of the ILAM system.

The representation, used by the SSA (Syntactic/Semantic Analyser), is based upon the *Conceptual Graph* formalism, developed by SOWA, and has been shown to be effective for knowledge representation in both the linguistic[48] and retrieval domains.[49]

Briefly, the data structure (Block) associated to a text segment would be composed of two components: the Conceptual_Representation and the Textual_Representation:

Details for Nomos. See also the ILAM and FLAM preliminary evaluation, Esprit-Doc AS62-50-01, 28-Oct-92.

[48]   See in the bibliography SOWA in all his writings.

[49]   See in the bibliography VELARDI ET AL. and FARGUES ET AL.

BLOCK(Phrase(< Source Text)
   Conceptual_Representation
      (< Conceptual Roles' Schemata filled with Conceptual Graphs >)
   Textual_Representation
      (< list of context (view) descriptors >)

The *contextual representation* for a block was completed through a list of 'context descriptors' each pointing to a possible point of view. This included the 'structural context' pointing to the physical location of a text segment (in terms of the enumeration of the text):

   Structural_view (Law(DPR.633)
        article (7)
        paragraph(4)
        letter (c)

and the 'definitional context' pointing to the general definition block and indicating the logical role of a statement. The following example

   logical_def_view(context(possitive_exception)
        general_definition(paragraph(3))

indicates that the Block should be interpreted as belonging to the set of positive exceptions in relation to the general definition of paragraph 3. For a different 'local meaning' of a concept (other than the one proposed by the general definition), a 'local_information' slot pointing to the amended version was provided.

> **Link to the Model:**
> It is clear from this analysis that such a representation could not contain contextual information from other parts of the legal system. Furthermore, this analysis shows a distorted view about the law: it is believed that legal texts always present a certain linguistic structure.

The *conceptual representation* was achieved through frame structures (the Conceptual Role Schemata) filled by conceptual representations expressed in terms of Conceptual Graphs.

   Conceptual_Role_Schema(< schema type >)
      CRS_slot(CR1(< CR1 filler >),

The slot filler is then represented by a Conceptual Graph which can be augmented with Boolean operators:

|**focus_entity**| (**Conceptual Graph** ([cessioni (transfer)] -- > (OBJ) -- > [beni (goods)]

200

This representation provided, especially in the case of definitions, an easy translation into an IF-THEN production rule format. In that format, the Left Hand Side (LHS) of the rule is a Conceptual Role Schema expressed in Conceptual Graphs formalism; the Right Hand Side (RHS) rule is asserting that the given situation matches the definition if the conditions of the LHS are satisfied. This specific ability was very important for the particular type of Conceptual Graphs that the ILAM Module was using.

3.4   THE PUZZLE OF THE N-A PROTOTYPE

3.4.1 Justifying the Creation of an Expert System

The Orion Research Team was assigned eleven man-months for the drafting and the implementation of the final prototype of the project. The final goal was to construct a prototype that would prove the original intentions of the project which, as said, was *Knowledge Acquisition for Normative Reasoning Systems*, by using the ILAM output created by the Italian company Sogei, during the previous workpackages of the project.

> **Link to the Model:**
> This problem of participating in an on-going project came to support the need of an integrated model. This may seem a general problem of Information Technology applications, but in the case of legal applications it is more important because such a model will define the legal accuracy and hence the viability of possible applications. Furthermore, such a model could show the full course of action so that researchers intervening at a later stage will be able to identify their tasks.

At a first investigation, the above described ILAM output (see also Appendix I) presented most of the characteristics, namely the 'frame-like' structures and 'conceptual hierarchies', of a *Knowledge Base*; the Knowledge Base is conceived here as one of the three essential parts of an Expert System[50] in its classical

---

[50] See *supra* Chapter 2. The discussion here will be limited to the specific problems arisen during the analysis and the implementation of the N-A Legal Expert System.

configuration (the other two parts being the *Inference Engine* and the *User Interface*).

On the other hand, the shortage of time forced the use of existing and well elaborated methodologies. Therefore, the initial proposal of the research team, which was drafted in two weeks, concluded that the most feasible way to implement a prototype would be to develop a *Knowledge Based Expert System* in its traditional form. This Legal Expert System should exploit the ILAM output as a Knowledge Base.

In the technical part, the notation used for the representation was reminiscent of *Prolog* structures, and, furthermore, the designers of the ILAM system (Sogei and Tecsiel) had guaranteed that at the implementational level these structures could also be interpreted as retrievable and easy to manipulate *Prolog objects*. This was also confirmed by FARGUES ET AL,[51] who have already described the representational and algorithmic power of the Conceptual Graphs formalism for natural language semantics and knowledge representation, as well as a transformation to Prolog-like structures, which allows deduction to be performed. Therefore, it was decided to use *ADVISOR*, an Expert System shell,[52] using Prolog structures, developed by the UW-AIRG, running on a Sun Sparc-2 station under SunOS or interactive Unix/386. The prototype was named *Nomos-Advisor* (hereinafter *N-A*).

3.4.2 Methodologies for Building a Legal Expert System

Although, at this initial stage the long debate and criticism (see *supra* 2.4.3) concerning the applicability of Legal Expert Systems was known, it did not negatively affect the project, in creating an expert system. However, the known

---

[51] FARGUES J., LANDAU M., DUGOURD A., CATACH L., *Conceptual Graphs for Semantics and Knowledge Processing*, IBM Journal, Vol. 30, No. 1, Jan, 1986.

[52] A solution supported also by SUSSKIND R., *Expert Systems in Law: A Jurisprudential Inquiry*, Clarendon Press, Oxford, 1987, p. 53, where he explains that it would be better to use also a shell for all Legal Expert Systems since the Lawyers will deal only with the jurisprudential problems and not with the technical ones.

developments in the relevant field,[53] and as many opinions as possible were always taken into account.

The presence of obstacles and contradictions, as in any large scale project, was obvious from the beginning (see *supra* 3.1) and highlighted that the whole task was more cumbersome than was initially thought. The only methodological guideline, deriving from contractual obligations, was that the construction of the prototype should be considered within the framework of the whole project, and not as an integrated self-existing part of it. Thus, although the N-A demonstrator was one of the peaks of the project, this analysis must, in addition, deal with the work on which it was based.

As exposed in the *Prolegomenon* interdisciplinary research usually lacks a well-defined methodology. Each discipline has its own methods, and it is, therefore, difficult to combine them into the new field of research. *Information Technology and the Law*, being, moreover, the combination of two completely different disciplines, could not make an exception to the rule. History[54] shows that the branch of AI and Law, since its birth in the mid-70s, and particularly the research in Legal Expert Systems (see *supra* Chapter 2) has not developed a concrete methodology. Each time, researchers followed different ways of solving the problems that the two conflicting disciplines (jurisprudence and computer science) posed.

Although certain tensions exist within the scientific debate, none of the above authors follow a certain methodology, or apply any kind of standards. It is, for this reason, not considered useful to present all these different solutions. It should be noted, however, that SUSSKIND'S *Expert Systems in Law*[55] provided some very useful and stable guidelines that, although not strictly, have been implemented

---

53 See for example the recent (those days) articles in the 1992 AUSTRALIAN JOURNAL OF LAW AND INFORMATION SCIENCE and especially TYREE A., *The Logic Programming Debate* in JLIS Vol. 3, 1992, No. 1.

54 For a detailed analysis on AI and Law see Chapter 2 and the general bibliography. For previous legal expert systems see especially SUSSKIND, *Expert Systems in Law*, Oxford 1987, SERGOT, *A Survey and Comparison* in BENCH-CAPON (Ed.) *Knowledge Based Systems and Legal Applications*, Academic Press 1991 including a detailed analysis and classification of all the recent projects with extensive commentaries, and ZELEZNIKOW J. & HUNTER D., *Building Intelligent Legal Information Systems, Representation and Reasoning in Law*, Kluwer, Computer/Law Series, 1994.

55 SUSSKIND R., *Expert Systems in Law: A Jurisprudential Inquiry*, Clarendon Press, Oxford, 1987.

during this work. Furthermore, a (then recent) article by SMITH, GELBART AND GRAHAM[56] provided, for the first time, enumerated methodological steps for creating a legal expert system and helped to streamline the process of the undertaken task, especially for the non-legally orientated members of the team. During the whole implementation, but especially at the last stages, the model developed in Chapter 1 was also used as a stable methodological guideline.

3.4.3 Three Inherent Difficulties

Constructing a prototype may already sound an unmanageable task, but, additionally, three specific difficulties were inherent in this project:

First, the prototype was not developed from scratch but was a continuation of the efforts of the ILAM group. This of course contradicted the rules of *Integrity* and *Practicality* of the model. However, it was required that the prototype:

- Would validate the usability of the ILAM output, as it is obtained through the knowledge acquisition tool;

- Would help in understanding what could be automatically done in order to refine the ILAM output;

- Would constitute the basis for an evaluation of the amount of the knowledge re-engineering, required for the development of an application;

- Would foresee re-use of the software components developed in the acquisition environment or auxiliary repositories, i.e. the type hierarchy, the lexica etc.;

- Would provide sound and clear grounds for the design and implementation of reasoning capabilities on the 'acquired' texts, i.e. the expertise;[57]

It is obvious that this lack of flexibility allowed little space for improvisations and experiments.

---

[56] SMITH, GELBART, GRAHAM, *A Procedure for Creating Expert Systems in Law* in COMPUTERS AND LAW, Vol. 3, Issue 3, July 1992, p. 23.

[57] ESPRIT DOC SG-51-40-01, *Requirements Capture and Architectural Details for Nomos Italian Application*, 2-Jun-92, p. 3.

Second, there was a continuous pressure to comply with the basic intention of the project i.e. *[semi-automatic] Knowledge Acquisition for Normative Reasoning Systems:* "The principal aim of the Nomos project should be that of showing the feasibility of a mapping from a legal text to a knowledge base able to support different kinds of applications."[58] Therefore, a continuity of the chain from Knowledge Acquisition (input of a legal text) to the actual Legal Advice should be shown.

In this respect, (a) the ILAM output should stay in Conceptual Graphs formalism, and (b) it was dictated that "[b]ecause of the multi-purpose character of the final application, which could span from Information and Text Retrieval to Knowledge Based Systems, the more appropriate choice seems that of maintaining an almost complete isomorphism between text and representation, and between textual strategies and manipulation of the representation. *That is to say that the level of complexity of the mapping from text to knowledge, should be the lowest. It is of paramount importance to maintain a hybrid representation, where analysed role structure and possible fillers, together with structural and cross-referencing pointers to other normative corpora, are handled much in the same way.*"[59] Therefore, observing this 'line' entailed that it was not 'allowed' to refine the knowledge base, e.g. add more *knowledge, heuristics* and *rules of thumb* derived from sources beyond the text of the Italian Law, as normally happens in the majority of knowledge based systems.

Link to the Model:
It should be obvious that these considerations inspired the *Rule of Content* and the *Steps* of the *Search* section of the model.

To this point it should be added, that in contrast to most other known systems that admit human intervention by eliciting expert knowledge at a later stage, the N-A prototype stays closer to the project's main line, arguing that the latter sort of information *should* be acquired before the ILAM processing.

---

[58] ESPRIT DOC SG-31-50-01, *Legal Knowledge Engineering: A Case Study*, 15-Sep-91, p. 2.

[59] ESPRIT DOC SG-31-50-01, *Legal Knowledge Engineering: A Case Study*, 15-Sep-91, p. 2 (emphasis added).

Third, it is obvious that the linguistic aspects of the ILAM module exhibit rather the characteristics of an 'automated analysis of legal texts' system,[60] open to many applications, than those of an *ad hoc* knowledge base dedicated to support a certain legal reasoner, such as the N-A prototype. It is evident that the contribution of the *domain expert*, i.e. the legal expert, described as standard methodology[61] during the stage of development of the ILAM system, was underestimated, if not ignored.

> **Link to the Model:**
> That is why the model insists on using a *Lawyer* for the analysis and that the legal decision process must be seen through his/her eyes.

As a result, some crucial components of the legal reasoning process were not included in the initial output, and had to be decided and added later. It, therefore, follows that further investigation, especially on the *legal concepts*[62] *process*, is needed if future applications are to involve a broader legal domain.

3.5 SOLVING THE PUZZLE I: THE TECHNICAL ASPECTS

From the technical point of view, the ILAM output was handed to the research team in plain ASCII format (see Appendix I and II) containing two lists with the `MICRO_STRUCTURE` and `MICRO_SEGMENT_OUTPUT` of the ILAM system. The main technical difficulty was encountered in transferring this representation to a form understandable by ADVISOR, the expert system shell of the University of Westminster.

In this technical domain, the author was assigned two tasks: (1) in the role of the *domain expert*, to verify that the various results, which were produced by the N-A system, were legally acceptable and correct, and (2) in the role of the *knowledge engineer*, - if these results were not valid - to scan the final knowledge base and

---

[60] See on that point MARTINO in MARTINO-SOCCI NATALI (Eds.) in p. 289 underlining that automated analysis of law *is not* creating an expert system.

[61] See ZELEZNIKOW-HUNTER and the relevant citations, in ZELEZNIKOW-HUNTER, *Rationales for the Continued Development of Legal Expert Systems*, in JLIS, Vol. 3, 1992, No. 1, p. 107.

[62] See for example the difficulties in connecting common sense knowledge and legal concepts which may prove insurmountable in very big corpora of normative texts, described by LEHMAN H., *Legal Concepts in a Natural Language Based Expert System* in RATIO JURIS Vol. 3, No. 2, July 1990.

refine its content, as far as the technical capabilities of the ADVISOR system permitted. Therefore, the discussion concerning the technical problems will be confined to those areas which required intervention by the author acting in the above roles (see especially sections 3.5.2, 3.6 and 3.7.3). However, to clarify these roles, this analysis will be preceded by a few remarks about the content of the ILAM output.

3.5.1   Peculiarities of the ILAM Output

The first crucial observation was that the ILAM system does not employ full, complex conceptual graphs, but a simplified form of the Concept-Relation-Concept (CRC), in which a graph consists only of two concepts connected by a single relation.[63] Related graphs, forming a clause or (logical) sentence, are linked by cross-referencing variables:[64]

```
crc( conc(effected : [1])
        rel(loc : in)
                conc(territory : [#,3]) )

crc(  conc(territory : [#,3])
        rel(poss : of)
                conc(state_nation : [#,5]) )
```

(Two CRCs representing the logical sentence of 'effected within state territory', in Italian: *'effettuare in territorio di stato nazione'*).

Link to the Model:
This representation corresponds to the *rule-based deduction* of the model.

Additionally, in contrast to SOWA'S conceptual graph notation, the CRC carries value fields on *relations*, as well as concepts. This enables the orthography of both concepts and relations to be retrieved, as well as their semantic roles, ensuring that the representation conserves the information accurately (i.e. The original text of the document can be reconstructed from the CRC notation).

---

[63] See in the special bibliography for the N-A prototype FARGUES *et al.*

[64] All of the following examples were unofficially translated into English from the original Italian text for the purposes of the N-A implementation and the Ph.D. Thesis.

207

Also, in some cases *anaphora* is explicitly flagged in the value field of the relations. For example: paragraph 4.e. of Article 7, "...or to subjects resided *therein*" translates into the CRC form :

```
crc( conc(resided : [13])
        rel(loc : (\therein))
                conc([general_place...] : [_102311]) )
```

Here, the backslash (\) in the value field of the relation indicates that an anaphoric pronoun has been identified. Unfortunately, the referent is not resolved, as indicated by the uninformed variable on the following concept. Nevertheless, it was decided to identify the anaphors in this way, even though the resolution had to be performed manually.

In the next layer of structure, (the *micro-level*) several of these CRCs are grouped together within the scope of a logical operator (AND/OR) to form a representation of a logical sentence of the source text. Within each such block, parentheses indicate precedence ordering of the operators.

The output also contains the *macro-level* logical and structural views, and the complete text of the logical paragraph (or 'block') under consideration. For informational purposes, the complete structure of an ILAM block, looks as in the *Table 3-1*, p. 209.

3.5.2   Mapping Conceptual Graphs to Production Rules

From the first moment, the main concern was to ensure that, given the aims of the project, a practical implementation of the system was feasible. Therefore, the start was slightly controversial: firstly, the disposed technical tools were examined; a series of experiments took place using a 'draft' theory; subsequently the full theory

BLOCK· **-- STRUCTURAL VIEW** [art([[7,-]]),num(633), tipo(dpr), comma(4), letter(d), stru_comma(item), item_period(1)] **--- SOURCE TEXT** [the supply of services deriving from hiring out, chartering and similar contracts concerning mobile material goods other than means of transport is considered to be effected within the state territory if it is the object of the above services] **--- MICRO_STRUCTURE** micro_crs def_prop_1 def_prop_focus [the supply derives from hiring out, chartering and similar contracts concerning mobile goods other than means of transport] def_property [effected within the state territory] condition cond [the goods constitute the object of the above services, and are used within the state territory]	**SSA_OUTPUT** **MICRO_SEGMENT_OUTPUT** [micro_crs,def_prop)1,def_prop_focus]. **SSA_INTERPRETATION · gn** [crc(conc(deriving : [3]) rel(subj : subj) conc(supply of services: [#,{*},2])) crc(conc(deriving : [3]) rel(fsrc : from) conc(contract : [{*},5])) AND . . . Other CRC blocks...

Table 3-1: The Complete Structure of an ILAM Block

was developed in detail, in order to support the prototype, including crucial conclusions that were derived during the implementation time.[65]

It was attempted to manually map the structures, in detail, onto a more 'conventional' knowledge representation notation. This notation was a hybrid of frames and production rules supported by the modified version of the ADVISOR shell. The major issue was how to extract production rules from Conceptual Graphs.

As exposed (see supra 3.3.5 The ILAM Knowledge Representation), the ILAM Schemata (CRSs) are frame-like structures, containing slots describing the main conceptual roles of the domain (in this case, a paragraph, or logical sentence of the article).

In the following example, there are three possible slots (although more are necessary for other domain structures); focus_entity (describing the entity for which a property is to be defined), definiendum_prop (describing the entity of the focus to be defined), and def_condition (containing the actual definition of the property):

```
CRS (CRS_type(CRS_DEF_PROPERTY)
    CRS_slots (| focus_entity | (X)
              | definiendum_prop | (Y),
              | def_condition | (Z)),
```

The variables X, Y, Z represent blocks of Concept-Relation-Concept representation of the paragraph text. These are identified for this purpose by the SSA (Syntactic/Semantic Analyser) processor of the ILAM system. Subsequently, this CRS becomes the left hand side (LHS) of a rewriting rule, indicating the reorganisation necessary to produce a production rule. The right hand side (RHS) of the rewritten rule then defines the order of elements within the production rule:

If X and Z then Y

---

[65] This methodology is also described by SUSSKIND as "Popperian in nature, essentially a feedback process, theory being propounded in conjunction with practice, tentative solutions and procedures being refined through elimination of errors and shortcomings" and seems inevitable while building legal expert systems. See also SUSSKIND R., *Expert Systems in Law*, Clarendon, Oxford 1987, p. 33.

In other words, if a paragraph (of the law) has the structure identified in the CRS, it can be transformed into a production rule which requires that the focus (focus_entity · X) and condition (def_condition· Z) parts are proved, in order to assert that the definition (definiendum_prop · Y) is true.

Using this technique, the resulting rules were coded into a nested Prolog list used by N-A. This input to the N-A prototype, despite the manual conversion, is designed to be close to the actual coding of the ILAM system. Further to this 'manual' technique, an experimental mechanism for automatically converting the ILAM output into ADVISOR rule format was proposed[66] (see *Figure 3-3:* Mapping the ILAM Output to ADVISOR Rules. Note, however, that the automatic mapper stayed in experimental phase)

For the numerous issues not covered by the Conceptual Graphs Formalism, it was decided to add a hypertext facility that would 'guide' the user during a consultation session (see *infra* 3.7.2 The Hypertext Link).

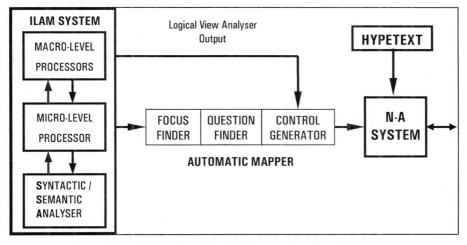

Figure 3-3: Mapping the ILAM Output to ADVISOR Rules

---

[66] See KONSTANTINOU V., SYKES J. & YANNOPOULOS G., *Can Legal Knowledge be derived from Legal Texts?* in PROCEEDINGS OF THE 4TH INTERNATIONAL CONFERENCE ON ARTIFICIAL INTELLIGENCE AND LAW, Amsterdam, 1993.

Apart from these general technical considerations further technical problems and especially that of 'missing information', were solved during the implementation. (see further *infra* 3.7.1)

3.6 SOLVING THE PUZZLE II: THE ANALYSIS

3.6.1 Feasibility Analysis and Scoping

The area of the law was set in advance (Italian VAT law), therefore, questions may arise only on *why* it was chosen and on *how narrow* the domain should be. The first question has been answered earlier (see *supra* 3.3.4 The Law Chosen for Processing); on the latter question the ILAM module had formalised Article 7 of the Law which refers to the 'Territoriality of the Tax' and which seems manageable enough in terms of size, but at the first instance, does not look complex enough to justify the need for formalisation. However, it was submitted that the Italian Ministry of Finance (*Ministero delle Finanze*) keeps a whole Department devoted to the interpretation and the application of the Law (*Direzione Generale delle Tasse e delle Imposte Indirette sugli Affari*). Furthermore it was emphasised that a whole division of that Department (*Divisione XIV - IVA*) deals with the 'territoriality of the tax', that is with the specific interpretation and application of Article 7 of the Law.

Under these circumstances, it is possible to conclude that Article 7 of the Italian VAT Law satisfies all five criteria, defined by SUSSKIND,[67] for assessing the suitability of any legal domain for formalisation:

1. It is relatively autonomous, since there is only one basic source (DPR 633), constituting a self-contained branch of law (even within the general taxation laws).

2. It requires true expertise, since a whole administrative division is dealing with it and the problems cannot be solved by brief research.

---

[67] SUSSKIND R., *Expert Systems in Law: A Jurisprudential Inquiry*, Clarendon Press, Oxford, 1987, p. 53.

3. It covers, intensively, a narrow legal domain, allowing an exhaustive, in depth manipulation.

4. There appears to exist consensus amongst experts over the jurisprudential problems of the scope and the content involved.

5. It does not require 'common-sense' knowledge for problem solving.

3.6.2 Data Collection

There has been a long debate concerning the underlying legal theory, upon which legal reasoning is based in Legal Expert Systems. In the case of *Nomos*, such decisions on the legal theory were taken in previous stages, and their explanation would add nothing to the present discussion.

Given also the statutory character of the law, there was no *prima facie* need to gather all the previous relevant cases in a case-based common law manner. Nevertheless, during the knowledge acquisition phase of the project, information from the director of the relevant division (*Tax Management*) of the Italian Ministry of Finance (taken through interviews by the Italian company Sogei), indicated that previous solved cases, though not binding, show the path subsequent interpretations must follow.

> **Link to the Model**
> This move corresponds to the guideline of the model to search for *Valid Legal Sources*

The author had information that petitions (*instanza* or *quesito*) are very frequently forwarded to the authorities (to the Ministry), in order to obtain a resolution from the Ministry concerning the application - or not - of the law. These petitions are then sent to the local offices, depending on the territorial competence, such as the Regional Tax Inspectorate (*Ispettorato Compartimentale Tasse*) which are obliged to collect all the relevant documentation, and they can give their opinion or proposal. The complete material is back-routed to the Ministry, and is used for the final resolution. In terms of harmonisation, once issued, the resolution is taken into account in all other analogous cases.

In most cases, this petition takes the simple form of the question "I have carried out an action, do I have to pay VAT?", but sometimes the application is misleading.

Examples:

A company claimed that it was a 'non-profit organisation', which is irrelevant to the VAT applicability; or, an agricultural entrepreneur who owned an estate of 40 acres and had built a stable was asking whether he should pay the rate of 4% or 19%; again the question is irrelevant because the tax relief for building a stable can be found in other parts of Italian legislation.[68]

Link to the Model

These examples have generated the considerations about bias and misunderstandings in the *Input* section of the model. Furthermore, they inspired the definitions of *Legal Problem* and *Legal Decision* as well as the notion of *'Easy Cases'*.

For the purposes of the N-A prototype, the so called 'Swiss Case' was often used as a test case for the system.

A Swiss company[69] through the Italian Embassy in Bern and the Italian Ministry for Foreign Affairs, was asking the Italian Ministry of Finance whether they should pay VAT for the fee paid to an Italian magazine for an advertisement, given that such a payment is not required for advertisement in a British or German magazine.

The Regional Inspectorate gave the following resolution:

The advertising services supplied to a subject non-resident in the EEC, specifically Switzerland, are considered to be effected in the State territory, when they are used in the same territory (article 7§4 under g). Because the *usage* of the advertisements in Italian magazines can only be done, at least for the most part, and because it is linked to the *location* of diffusion of magazines, in the Italian territory, those services are liable to VAT.

It is important to notice that, in order to explain the assimilation of the case, the resolutions refer to clauses outside the VAT Law: The 'open textured' terms of 'usage' and 'location' (defined in the legal context outside the VAT Law) were

---

[68] See also ESPRIT DOC SG-51-40-01, *Requirements Capture and Architectural Details for Nomos Italian Application*, 2-Jun-92, p. 8.

[69] This is a real petition (instanza) No.405390/83 : *"Instanza della ditta Elvetica"*.

214

used in order to interpret the law. Furthermore, the EEC Directive[70] on VAT Law was taken into consideration, since the Italian VAT Law is based on it.[71] Also examined were Article 3§2 (referring to the Italian *'tax exempted territories'*) and Articles 8 and 9 (referring to definitions of *supply of goods* and *services* respectively). The terminology used in the directive was partly used for the draft translation of the Italian law.

> **Link to the Model**
> It is evident that the *Interpretation* and *Search* functions of the model were used and tested here in order to identify the sources outside the VAT Law.

Concerning this 'data collection' phase, the following points should be added: First, all these precautions, form the side of our research team, were taken in order to ensure a broader coverage of the domain. This could extend the system's capabilities beyond the contents of the ILAM output and, finally, persuade the user that it is sufficiently integrated to represent a *'legal subsystem'*, according to the theoretical demands[72] of the model of Chapter 1. Second, this particular effort should not be mistaken for Case-Based-Reasoning systems, which reason from previous cases and examples. In the N-A prototype, previous cases, and the other material not provided by ILAM, are presented for information purposes only, to support the decision of the user. Third, this latter procedure to supply more information could finally increase the system's transparency, which is always desirable.

3.6.3   The General Organisation of the Italian VAT Law

Although the original text of the Law, as well as the ILAM output, is in Italian, this work (knowledge structuring) was based on a draft translation in English of the Law (see Appendix III. The terminology used was based on the Directive 77/6 of 17 May 1977 on the harmonisation of VAT Laws.). DPR 633 has 7 chapters:

---

[70] DIRECTIVE 77/6 EC (6th of 17 May 1977), *On the harmonisation of VAT Law*, OJ L145, 13/06/77.

[71] Article 1 of the Directive states that "member states shall modify their present value added tax systems in accordance with the following articles. They shall adopt the necessary laws, regulations and administrative provisions so that the systems as modified enter into force at the earliest opportunity and by 1 January 1978 at the latest".

[72] SUSSKIND R., *Expert Systems in Law: A Jurisprudential Inquiry*, Clarendon Press, Oxford, 1987, p. 53.

1. General provisions,

2. Obligations of the tax payers, (norms for the parties involved in transactions)

3. Sanctions and penalties (for not respecting the law),

4. Collection and control conditions, (norms by which the State can check the respect of the obligations)

5. Imports,

6. & 7.Transient provisions and tax allowances.

In our case, in addition to the Article 7 (formalised by ILAM), some definitions from the general provisions were included in the hypertext facility.

The general structure of every article consists of the provision of a general definition, a list of positive cases and a list of exceptions (negative cases). The focus (in linguistic terms) of the judgement is on the object-role (type of 'service') of the main activity and on the actual performance of the activity. The *territoriality* presumption, being the core of the N-A prototype, concerned the question whether an activity is carried on within the State borders. Territoriality has to be verified on each of the other two general presumptions: *objectivity* (on whether a transaction is *transfer of goods* or *supply of services*) and *subjectivity* (two categories depending on who is carrying out an activity: a *person* or a *company*). Analytically, Article 1 of the Law states that a transaction becomes subject to VAT if:

1. It definitely belongs to one of the two categories: *supply of services* or *transfer of goods*

2. It is carried out by an agent definitely belonging to one of the two categories: a *person* (*artist* or *professional*) or a *company*

3. It is actually carried out within the State borders.

    Link to the Model
    This question, of characterising a transaction, has tested the *Disqualifying Rule* of the Pre-process and revealed the necessity of a human intervention when a *subsumptive judgement* is involved.

However, the last paragraph (§5) of Article 7 reveals a third category, which expands the *subjectivity* presumption: *goods for exportation*. Consequently, the initial trichotomy which provided the starting point for the user interaction with the system, had to be extended accordingly.

216

Definitions for the above categories can be found in Articles 3, 4, 8, 8bis & 9 of the Law. They normally embody a general definition, with positive and negative parts, and they also include a list of 'borderline cases'.

3.6.4   Legal Knowledge Structuring for the *Nomos-Advisor* Environment

Nomos-Advisor handles a very narrow legal domain, and, furthermore, all the legal expertise was derived from an authoritative source: the *Advice Bureau*, of the Italian Ministry of Finance, which solves ambiguities and, through previous, cases has the power to harmonise the interpretation of the law.

Despite the theoretical demand of the *Rule of Integration* and the *Rule of the Legal System* (see Chapter 1) little attention had been paid to legal reasoning from the *Nomos* researchers. In Italy, legal experts believe that a general consensus on the concept of VAT law exists, without ambiguities and conflicting opinions. In practice, the above mentioned Division of the Ministry of Finance solves ambiguities and through previous cases it has the power to harmonise the interpretation of the law. This Division is also the editor of a periodical on the modifications and the interpretation of the VAT Law, (*Codice Imposta Valore Aggiunto*), which is usually followed by the 'front-end' civil servants at Tax Regional Offices (*Ispettorato Compartimentale Tasse*) and other public services.

Link to the Model
This analysis provides some of the authoritative sources which one can search in order to identify the *Valid Legal Sources* proposed by the model

Nevertheless, contradictions are still present and there is no sign of a strong theoretical background acting as a basis for resolving them. Therefore, N-A's *predictive function*,[73] i.e. assisting the lawyer's task to predict judicial and official behaviour, could never reach a high standard. Overruling a case is, through the rules of interpretation (which differ from the Common Law system), also a privilege of Civil Law, and since the heuristic predictive knowledge on this matter is not incorporated in the knowledge base, this function is not guaranteed. In its other two fundamental functions, N-A will react as follows: In its *justificatory function*, i.e. in its capability to give apparent reasons for its decisions, it exhibits

---

[73] Described by SUSSKIND R., *Expert Systems in Law: A Jurisprudential Inquiry*, Clarendon Press, Oxford, 1987, p. 42.

217

adequate performance through the backward-chaining mechanism and the hypertext explanations. In its *persuasive function*, i.e. the lawyer's task to convince the decision maker of the argument he/she is presenting, it exhibits satisfactory transparency through the juxtaposition of the rules and the conclusions, reinforced by the hypertext facility.

From the legal point of view, it must be stressed that much attention has been given by the ILAM group to the knowledge contained within the text of the Law, as if this was the only source of Law or, even worse, as if this was the only Law dealing with VAT. This result shows the underestimation of legal analysis during the design of the system, and indicates the cause for future shortcomings.

3.6.5   Goal Definition for the N-A Prototype

The system should be able to support a decision on the applicability of the VAT on a certain activity. It should also be able to justify the partial and final conclusions and to advise the users about their obligations, rights and duties in connection with their activity.

The basic goal of the N-A system is to answer whether a legal entity (*person* or *company*) is liable to pay VAT in connection with the place where its economic activity (usually *transfer of goods* or *supply of services*) has taken place.

> **Example:**
> The system should be capable of answering such questions as: A Swiss company is advertising in Italian magazines distributed in Italy and elsewhere. Is the company liable to pay VAT?

Because the real facts of the problem are entered by the user in response to questions posed by the system, two basic assumptions (which will also be referred to later when discussing the interface) were made: First, that in accordance to the definition of the model, the user is - if not a *Lawyer* - at least capable of answering the 'trivial' legal questions generated during the phase of data input to the system, e.g. whether a certain transaction falls within the *transfer of goods* or the *supply of services* category etc. The target is for an 'expert user' to be supported in the discovery of the relevant points of the law, and also to be provided with an explanation for each step. This policy is rather narrower than the one envisaged by the designers of the project, according to which laymen (in public booths), or a novice clerk, could exploit the system for hypothetical cases. Achieving this targets, however, would result in the knowledge base being enormously expanded.

Link to the Model
These considerations inspired the use of definitions in the beginning of the model. The definition of the *Lawyer* in connection with the *Rule of Integration* were used here to identify the qualifications of the user of the system

Second, in accordance with considerations about the *User Interface* (see section 2.2.5) the user should not be left free to input his/her question, but should always be guided with menus and restricted answers in order (a) to avoid his/her intervention in the knowledge base and (b) to diminish his/her ability to actually interpret the Law.

The *deep structure rule*[74] in the case of Article 7 of the Italian VAT Law should be: *All transfers of goods and services carried out on Italian territory are liable to VAT*. Exceptions arise for certain goods and services (named in the law) or due to special attributes assigned to the subject making the transfer (e.g. domicile, legal seat etc.) or the object of the transfer (e.g. real estate situated within a certain territory). Furthermore, the article provides the basic concept of what constitutes Italian Territory and assimilates certain transactions as if they have taken place within that territory.

3.6.6 Graphical Representation

Both SMITH ET AL[75] and SUSSKIND[76] propose the use of AND/OR decision trees,[77] i.e. of a graphical representation with *nodes* and *branches*. In the N-A analysis, trees were also introduced (see *Figure 3-4*) since ADVISOR (the expert system

---

[74] According to the model proposed by SMITH, GELBART AND GRAHAM, *A Procedure for Creating Expert Systems in Law* in COMPUTERS AND LAW, Vol. 3, issue 3, p. 23, July 1992.

[75] SMITH, GELBART AND GRAHAM, *A Procedure for Creating Expert Systems in Law* in COMPUTERS AND LAW, Vol. 3, Issue 3, July 1992, p. 23.

[76] SUSSKIND R., *Expert Systems in Law: A Jurisprudential Inquiry*, Clarendon Press, Oxford, 1987, p. 144.

[77] See however the objections OSKAMP for the use of trees, OSKAMP A., *Model for Knowledge and Legal Expert Systems*, in ARTIFICIAL INTELLIGENCE AND LAW, Vol. 1, No. 4, 1993, p. 252.

shell used) permits and simulates such a structure. Briefly, the top node depicts the ultimate goal of the system (to decide on the application of VAT) while the three main branches concern the three main presumptions (*objectivity*, *subjectivity*, *territoriality*). These structures[78] helped to build the first sample sessions of the prototype, as a journey through their branches (see Appendix IV). The knowledge, represented by the trees (or the Conceptual Graphs structure), was mapped to rules of inference in ADVISOR. Multiple choice questions were generated at the leaves

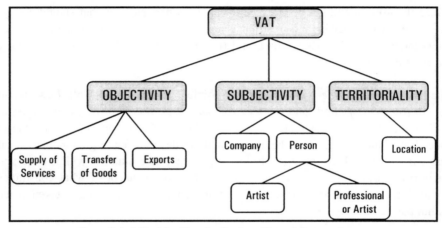

Figure 3-4: A Decision Tree for the three General Presumptions

of the trees. The user's responses to these questions would provide the facts upon which the rules of inference operate. The presentation of conclusions is enhanced by means of IDEAs (an hypertext facility made by the AI Research Group of the University of Westminster).

Analytically, the steps following the branches of the trees were:

---

[78] The 'trees' concept was also proposed by the ILAM designers who have also drafted some initial sketches. However, further adaptations and modifications were made for the ADVISOR environment, see also ESPRIT DOC SG-51-40-01, *Requirements Capture and Architectural Details for Nomos Italian Application*, 2-Jun-92.

1. A case is in the scope of the VAT Law if the three general presumptions of (1) *Objectivity*, (2) *Subjectivity* and (3) *Territoriality*, are verified, or if the case deals with *exports*.

2. To verify *subjectivity*, the list of positive and negative cases of both article 4 (*Esercizio di Imresa* - Exercise of enterprise) and 5 (*Esercizio di arti e professioni* - Exercise of arts and professions) must be evaluated; only if a suitable case for the current problem is not found, then the general definitions of these articles must be evaluated (Articles 4§1 and 5§1).

3. To verify *objectivity*, the list of positive and negative cases of both Article 2 (*Cessioni di beni* - Transfer of goods) and 3 (*Prestazioni di servizio* - Supply of services); again only if a suitable case for the current problem is not found, the general definitions of these articles must be evaluated (Articles 2§1 and 3§1).

4. To verify *territoriality*, the list of positive cases of article 7 and the list of negative cases of articles 8 and 8bis must be evaluated; only if a suitable case for the current problem is not found, must the general definitions of '*Effettuazione nel Territorio dello Stato delle Operazioni*' (actual operation in the territory of the state) in Article 2§7 for *transfer of goods* and in Article 3§7 for *supply of services* be evaluated.

5. If every presumption is verified, then the negative list (tax-free operations) of Article 10 must be evaluated.

6. It should be noted that, when a particular rule matches the current case, this is the last step of the procedure; otherwise, if the rule does not succeed, then the law is not applicable to the case

   Link to the Model
   The *Pre-Process* and especially the identification of *relevant* and *sufficient* as well as *disqualifying* facts were tested at this stage.

This procedure was tested by our Team with the 'Swiss case', and a graphical representation of the *Territoriality* presumption has been drawn. Part of the whole tree is depicted in *Figure 3-5*. [79]

---

[79] Courtesy of Vassilis Konstantinou, UW-AIRG.

As explained (see *supra* note 78*)*, the concept of trees was introduced and supported by the ILAM Team, but further adaptations were made by our Team in

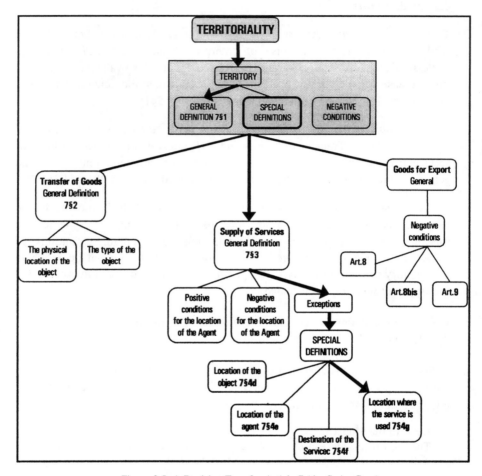

Figure 3-5: A Decision Tree for Article 7 (the Swiss Case)

order to adjust the trees to the ADVISOR environment. In *Figure 3-5* the bold arrows denote the route of the 'journey' through the tree, ending with the selection of Article 7§4g.

3.7 SOLVING THE PUZZLE III: LINKING TO THE 'MISSING KNOWLEDGE'

At this stage of the implementation, after the examination of the ILAM 'raw material', and after the information from the interviews with the officials and the legal analysis, it was obvious that essential elements, affecting the legal reasoning process were missing. Furthermore, parts of information affecting the technical integrity of the system were also missing. Actually, this material helped to identify and expand theoretically many of the directives of *the model of Chapter 1, which was built from a negative result i.e. trying to identify what was missing and to avoid future omissions*. The following paragraphs will examine these deficiencies, and the solutions followed.

3.7.1 *'Missing'* Information

First Article 7 itself pointed for definitions to other parts of the law and explicitly or tacitly to other parts of Italian legislation.

Example:
The definition for what constitutes *transfer of goods* was to be found in Article 2 of the Law
The definition for what constitutes *supply of services* was to be found in Article 3 of the Law and
The definition for what constitutes *mobile* or *immobile* property was to be found in the Italian Civil Code (art 842).

Link to the Model
This was the main reason for defining the *Search for Legal Sources* and the *Doctrine of Valid Legal Sources* functions in the model.

Second, previous cases, either from the administrative authority (Internal Revenue Authorities across the country of various ranks, comprising the hierarchy from 'front-end' clerks up to the Ministry of Finance) or from the courts, interpret the Law as well as the applicability of definitions.

Example:
Previous cases could decide whether a permanently fixed caravan (a transaction not included in the definitions of the law) constitutes *mobile* or *immobile* property. Or whether the supply of atomic energy (also not included) constitutes *supply of services* or *transfer of goods* etc.

Link to the Model

If case-law is a *Valid Legal Source* then cases can also be included for the creation of the *Legal Sub-system*. The use of *analogy* and *similarities* of the *Interpretation* function is being tested in the above example.

Third, there was no reference at all to the methodological and procedural rule, to the general legal theory and to the legal doctrines that predominate every legal reasoning process.

Example:

The following questions could not be answered by the ILAM output:

What is the relevance of the Law to Constitutional restrictions?

Is there a formal procedure that has to be followed (e.g. written forms etc.)?

Who is competent to decide about a certain case?

Is the general attitude of the law in favour of paying, or not paying tax in dubious cases?

Is reasoning by analogy allowed?

Link to the Model

These considerations created the need for the *Rule of the Legal System* especially in order to identify the procedural and methodological rules of the legal system.

Fourth, empirical knowledge, heuristics and rules of thumb, all essential to everyday legal practice, were also omitted.

Example:

A qualified practitioner could advise that it is not feasible to examine transactions under a certain amount because of huge administrative and legal costs,

or, (hypothetically) that all transactions for books are tax exempted

or, (hypothetically) that all disabled persons are tax exempted

or, (hypothetically) that tax for medicines is always x%

Link to the Model

The necessity of that information created the need for the *Search* function to include *heuristic* and *empirical* legal knowledge.

Fifth, from the technical point of view the text does not contain any control information

Example:

The precedence of the exceptions

The order of applying various general clauses etc.

This type of information, however, is not explicitly stated in any legal text and falls in the third and fourth category above.

A major drawback, at this stage, was that the non-legally-educated members of the team were not able to understand why that 'missing' information was so important for legal reasoning. Another difficulty was to find a method for showing where this information could be found. In order to cover these difficulties, the author organised a series of informal seminars during which basic legal principles (known to first-year-law-students) were taught to the other members. In these lectures, it was attempted to make them conceive and understand law as an integrated whole, as a system where all the parts are interconnected, opposing the false fragmentary approach of the *Nomos* environment. The importance of *Interpretation* and of the *Doctrine of Valid Legal Sources* for the system that we were implementing were also emphasised.

The most difficult part was how to memorise all this information. It was at this stage that the author prepared draft lists with all the necessary legal sources, based on the *Doctrine of Valid Legal Sources,* which included the whole hierarchy of the Italian legal system, ranging from Constitutional Law and the Civil Code to administrative regulations, case-law, procedural law etc. Subsequently a 'checklist' showing the other necessary components of the legal decision process was created, mainly in order to emphasise the importance of the methodology that the legal system imposes. Furthermore, draft sketches and arrows were used to show all the possible connections of the elaborated text (of the ILAM output) with other parts of the VAT Law, as well as with the rest of the Italian legal system.

It was this series of seminars and these draft 'checklists' and sketches that produced the idea of creating the full scale theoretical model of the legal decision process which is presented in Chapter 1.

3.7.2   The Hypertext Link

On the technical front, the crucial question was how rules extracted from definitions, cases, and other parts of the *'missing knowledge'* of the relevant legal

225

domain, could be added to the system, while leaving the Conceptual Graphs ILAM knowledge base intact. The effective, although not perfect, solution was to link in this knowledge with a *hypertext facility*, which seems to be a useful tool to overcome the problems of interconnections among different sources of information. Hypertext systems have been designed as management tools for creating and linking the document contents. The fundamental concept upon which such systems are based is that of providing the user with the possibility to manage documents in a non-linear, non-sequential order. The documents are, in fact, placed within a network of connections permitting an associative approach for their consultation. The users gain access to the information contained within the documents simply by following these connections and, furthermore, have the possibility to create new connections or remove those which no longer have any significance (see also *supra* 2.2.6).

WIDDISON ET AL, who had already used hypertext for a legal application,[80] assert their support of this decision[81], by explaining that "[w]ith hypertext, a document is presented to the user in a traditional form as a series of consecutive 'pages'. The document can be read in the normal way, by moving forward or backwards through the document one page at a time, or jump straight to the first or last page. In addition however the user can move sideways. Every time he or she comes across a referenced item in a document, the user can select that item by clicking onto the relevant 'button' in the document. He or she is then taken to the full text of the referenced item. If the user finds an interesting reference in this second document, he or she can select the new item, and then be taken to the full text of this document, and so on. When the user finds the sought-for information, or decides that a particular line of enquiry is fruitless, he or she can 'collapse' the search and return to the starting point." [82]

---

[80] See also ALLEN T. & ROBINSON W.F., *The Defamation Tutor: Integrating CAL and Hypertext*, in LAW TECHNOLOGY JOURNAL, Vol. 2, No. 1, October, 1992 and AGOSTI *et al.*, *A Hypertext Prototype as a Tool for Retrieving Environmental Legal Information*, in CONGRES INTERNATIONAL INFORMATIQUE & DROIT, Buenos Ayres, 16-19 October, 1990.

[81] See also the same proposal by SAVOY J., *Searching Information in Legal Hypertext Systems*, in ARTIFICIAL INTELLIGENCE AND LAW, Vol. 2, No. 3, 1994, p. 205 and by SOPER P. & BENCH-CAPON T., *Coupling Hypertext and Knowledge Based System*, in ARTIFICIAL INTELLIGENCE AND LAW, Vol. 2, No. 4, 1994, p. 293.

[82] Definition of hypertext by WIDDISON R., PRITCHARD F., & ROBINSON W., *Expert Systems meet Hypertext: The European Conflicts Guide*, in JOURNAL OF LAW AND INFORMATION SCIENCE, Vol. 3, No. 1, 1992, p. 87.

In the N-A prototype, a 'pop-up' window[83] would advise the user on items not covered by the ILAM output, but referred to instead in questions and answers. The question of what to add, and the structure of the links, were decided in relation to the current situation, by identifying the nature of the specific problem. Again, the basic conceptions about valid legal sources in the model, and the notion of the *legal sub-system* were used.

Examples:

1. *During the input phase*: A window telling the user that, according to case 'C', already solved by the Ministry, or the Courts, an uncharacterised transaction 'T' has been characterised as *transfer of goods*, thus giving arguments to support his/her characterisation of a transaction while he/she inputs the relevant facts to the system. (to reach these conclusions *analogy* and the *legal arguments of Interpretation* are applied)

2. *During the input phase:* An explanation of the definitions that can be found in articles 2, 3, 4 & 8 of the Law (the concept of *relevant, sufficient* and *disqualifying facts* and generally the steps of the *Pre-Process* of the model have found ground here)

3. *During the Consultation:* An explanation of the Definitions in the Italian Civil Code. (by applying the *Doctrine of Valid Legal Sources*)

4. *During the Consultation:* A reminder of rules of thumb, i.e. VAT special categories (e.g. books), or heuristics, i.e. a better ordering in the triggering of the rules, when a case is directly addressed by a rule.

5. *During the consultation:* A window explaining terms and supporting arguments with cases, e.g. saying that transfer of goods 'T' [*action described in the Italian Civil Code as such*] which according to the rules...is liable to VAT [*solution also followed in case 'C', arguing that...*]

Technically, this was achieved by using other parts of the law (mainly Articles 2 and 3) in order to acquire the definitions manually. To prepare the hypertext links, for all texts appearing on any screen at any one time, an automated cross-referencing program (developed by the AI Research Group of the University of

---

[83] See also the solution chosen by ALLEN *et al.* in order to tackle the problems of the user interface and definitions in an expert system that could combine related rules ALLEN L., PAYTON S. & SAXON C., *Synthesizing Related Rules from Statutes and Cases for Legal Expert Systems,* in RATIO JURIS V.3, No.2, July 1990, p. 296.

Westminster),[84] which creates and maintains the links, was used, without affecting the knowledge base. This cross-referencing was based on the draft sketches and 'checklists' of the previous paragraph. Furthermore, knowledge from previously resolved cases provided by the Italian Ministry of Finance was also included, as explained in the previous example.

For the N-A prototype, a few terms were defined as hypertext definitions and they were automatically cross-referenced and linked to different legal texts. At the time of experimentation definitions have included all of the FOCUS values and some sample key phrases. Ideally, all occurrences of the same term in either questions or advice could be linked to the relevant definitions and made available to the user. In real terms, the implementation has included a significant number of definitions and links for experimentation. The end result was welcomed by both the developers and the users of the system especially for the ability to expand and for its transparency,

3.7.3   'Missing' Inference Control Information[85]

Two types of rules were envisaged by the ILAM system: *Goal-driven*, i.e. rules asserting that some conclusion holds, provided that some preconditions are satisfied; and Data-driven, i.e. rules asserting that a fact concerning a particular entity is true. All of the rules conformed the known scheme:

$$\text{antecedent} \rightarrow \text{(condition)} \rightarrow \text{consequent}$$

The choice of the rule to activate was supposed to take place when the syntactic trigger, which tags them, pointed them out. However, the most serious problem was the lack of inference control information, which became obvious during the design of the N-A knowledge base, because the general structure of the ILAM Module :

---

[84] See KONSTANTINOU V. & MORSE P., *Electronic Documentation System: Using Automated Hypertext Techniques for Technical Support Services,* ACM SIGDOC '92, August 1992 Ottawa, Canada.

[85] An attempt is made here to shed light to the purely technical problems that the AI Research Group had to solve. This analysis completes the preceding legal analysis. Again, in every technical step, the author had to intervene in order to verify that the followed solution was 'legally correct' or at least 'within the purposes' of the Italian law.

BLOCK
‑‑> STRUCTURAL VIEW
> (which contains pointers to the exact text location in the article)

‑‑> SOURCE TEXT
> (the full text of the paragraph/rule/case)

‑‑> MICRO_STRUCTURE
> (the general overview of the paragraph/rule/case including a focus field)

‑‑> SSA OUTPUT
> (Concept‑Relation‑Concept (CRC) representation of the knowledge contained in the paragraph/rule/case in question)

1. Succeeded in representing the knowledge of the different sentences of the text of the law as well as the right relations between concepts in one sentence (i.e. logical sentence), but failed to correctly represent the relationships between sentences as the dependencies between rules or even the order of evaluation of the rules.

2. Did not contain enough information for generating the question texts needed by the inference engine.

However, this was expected, as it was wrongly perceived that there is no need for 'human inference control' information in legal texts, and, consequently, the ILAM modules could not 'find' it. Therefore, several heuristics were used in order to create a usable knowledge base.

The obvious control structure that could be used for an automatic mapping, was the information in the *focus fields* (def_prop_focus). As explained (see *supra* 3.6.6 Graphical Representation), three possible top level values were identified for the focus*: transfer of goods (cessioni di beni), supply of services (prestazioni di servizi)* and transfer of goods *for export (cessioni all' esportazione)*.

From the technical point of view, the notion of 'top level values' entails that the above focus information exists in all of the ILAM structures, and effectively, categorises the rules. In the ILAM output, there are also several other values for the focus field which attempt to categorise the rules in even narrower groups, but for the purposes of the N‑A prototype (as it included only Article 7), the top level focus was adequate.

The steps to solve the problem were the following:

1. An ADVISOR category that includes all rules defined for Article 7. This category is used to find values for two attributes: FOCUS and ADVICE.

2. FOCUS is defined as a *frame variable* that has one of the three top level values as described above. There is no default value for this variable, but the system will force the user to select one of the above values (see also the sample session in Appendix IV). The value of FOCUS is determined by a direct question, rather than the invocation of any production rules.

3. The search strategy employed by N-A in order to scrutinise this category is to look for the FOCUS first. Once the FOCUS has been determined, then the category rules are searched to find the ADVICE for the given problem.

4. ADVICE is defined as a *text variable* without any default values. To trace a value for it, N-A uses a series of production rules that have a close relationship with the ILAM structures.

5. In the case where no rule can succeed, N-A asks the user to suggest a solution (see Appendix IV). This question will accept any answer and can be used to trace cases that are not covered by the Knowledge Base, as N-A keeps track of all previous solutions.

6. All CRC (Concept-Relation-Concept) conditions (based on the ILAM structures) were translated into straight-forward (Boolean type) questions. Only those conditions that were defined by other rules were characterised as *frames*; the inference engine was triggered by a similar function.

3.7.4   The Problem of 'exceptions' to Article 7

Article 7 (see Appendix III) defined *exceptions* to the rules by preceding the paragraphs referring to exceptions with the phrase *"with exception to the previous paragraph"*. For example, paragraph 4 of Article 7 defines all the exceptions for paragraph 3. Although the phrase *"with exception to the previous paragraph"* (*in deroga...*) is included in the STRUCTURAL_VIEW of all of the affected structures generated by ILAM for paragraph 4, there is no explicit information about its meaning or relationship to paragraph 3.

The main problem that arises here is again that of inference control. If it is assumed that the inference engine of the application evaluates the rules for paragraph 3 first (this is the most likely scenario), the following possible control strategies are envisaged:

1. None of the rules of paragraph 3 succeeds and the inference engine continues with the evaluation of paragraph 4.

2. One of rules for paragraph 3 succeeds and the inference engine continues with the evaluation of paragraph 4.

3. One of the rules for paragraph 3 succeeds and the inference engine stops the search and reports its conclusion.

4. None of the rules in paragraph 3 succeeds and the inference engine does not continue with paragraph 4.

Strategy 3 above seems to be the logical (not legal) course of action, but it may apply just in this particular example (Article 7). In any other case, the two paragraphs are not connected with any control information which will explain the meaning of the phrase *"with exception to"* (*in deroga de*) (see the link to the model *infra*).

Strategy 2 on the other hand, could reinforce the validity of the conclusion, as the rules in paragraph 4 appear to deal with specialised cases. The problem with this strategy is that the meaning of the phrase *"with exception"* is effectively ignored as the inference engine is forced to try all rules. However, the inference engine could be forced to try all of the *related* rules only. 'Related' could be – for knowledge engineering purposes - defined as those connected with that phrase; It has been proposed, as matter of further study, to examine the uses of that phrase in other articles in order to determine whether this control strategy can be fixed.

Link to the model:

It is not clear – even if we find an appropriate 'control strategy'- how this could produce legally acceptable results. To this point a key issue was to explain to the research team that parts of the law (relevant to a problem) may lie in other parts of the text (of the particular law) or in other pieces of legislation. Additionally, the research team was oriented to knowledge engineering techniques where the 'control information' had to be searched within the knowledge base. Again, it was necessary to emphasise that in law the methodological rules lie outside substantive legislation.

Strategy 1 is the one that will be used by any of the conventional shells that use the *frame / production rule* knowledge representation and a conventional *backward chaining* search technique. This may be the correct strategy if the phrase *"with exception to the previous paragraph"* is interpreted as meaning that *"if the rules for 3 fail then try the following"*. Technically this is not the correct solution because it contradicts the exhaustive interpretation for Strategy 2.

Link to the model
This interpretation cannot be accepted legally. An average lawyer would have immediately examined the exceptions first (see 1.6.2 Disqualifying Facts).

Strategy 4 is clearly wrong as it will not result in any values for ADVICE. The reason is that the FOCUS 'supply of services' applies only to rules for paragraphs 3 and 4. Therefore, if the inference engine stops after paragraph 3, it is definite that there will be no more solutions.

Link to the Model:
The model and especially the *Interpretation* function was tested in this technical issue in order to make the other members of the team understand which strategy was producing legally correct results. It was important to emphasise that the technical solution of this problem was crucially affecting the legal integrity of the system. Furthermore the need for *Interpretation* before the intervention of the system has shown once more the deficiencies of the linguistic treatment of law.

During the experimentation period, the N-A knowledge base has used strategy 2 or 1, if it applied (i.e. all rules for paragraph 3 fail). This implementation is achieved through a manual 'mapping' for the search among the rules for paragraphs 3 and 4. An automated solution for this problem, however, could be found by utilising the output of the Logical View Analyser module of the ILAM system. The output of the Logical View Analyser could guide the N-A system by using a modified agenda mechanism that would be triggered directly by collecting the different Logical Block Structures, and not through the 'mapping' used (see *Figure 3-3*, p. 211).

3.7.5 User Interface

It has been emphatically argued that "usually little attention is paid to the 'Cinderella' of expert system design: the user interface. A legal practitioner, used to assuming a heavy responsibility for any advice given, reacts badly to the sense of disorientation and powerlessness engendered by many legal expert systems. Systems should not only be made more 'user friendly', they should acquire a look-and-feel which more closely reflects that of traditional legal research tools. Success in system development depends on more than the production of systems that embody domains of law and legal procedure accurately and efficiently. Developers need to ensure that their software has a familiar and reassuring feel. Failure to pay attention to this third dimension of system development will result in systems that are unused".[86]

> **Link to the Model:**
> These considerations helped to identify some of the issues for the *Input* and *Output* functions of the model, as well as some of the qualifications of the user of legal applications.

Using these considerations as guidelines the N-A prototype has tried:

1. to reflect very closely the structure of the Italian VAT Law; additionally, the Conceptual Graphs formalism - being a natural language transformation - ensures a result which abides by the theory of an 'isomorphic'[87] knowledge base.

2. to draft, accordingly, the structure, the difficulty and the length of the questions posed to the user

3. to ensure compatibility between the environment of ADVISOR and of IDEAs (the hypertext facility of UW-AIRG)

---

[86] WIDDISON R., PRITCHARD F., & ROBINSON W., *Expert Systems meet Hypertext: The European Conflicts Guide*, in JOURNAL OF LAW AND INFORMATION SCIENCE, Vol. 3, No. 1, 1992, p. 89.

[87] See BENCH-CAPON T. & CONEN F., *Exploiting Isomorphism: Development of a KBS to Support British Coal Insurance Claims* in PROCEEDINGS OF THE 3RD INTERNATIONAL CONFERENCE ON ARTIFICIAL INTELLIGENCE AND LAW, Oxford, June 25-28 1991, ACM Press, 1991 and earlier ALLEN L. E. & ENGHOLM C.R., *Normalized Legal Drafting and the Query Method*, in JOURNAL OF LEGAL EDUCATION, Vol. 29, 1978, p. 380.

The ADVISOR environment supports the query-the-user interface,[88] a method also supported by SUSSKIND, who defends the *interactive user interface*.[89] This is explained as a 'step-by-step' incremental process with plain menu-driven questionnaires. It was decided that questions should make sense, both in wording and order. The logical structure of the law (three general presumptions) provides the starting point for a session with the system (see also Appendix IV).

The UW-AIRG hypertext facility (IDEAs) is simultaneously providing *on screen help* to the user during the input procedure. Further explanations are shown using the same method (IDEAs) during the consultation session, and all conclusions are explained. A full history of the session can be traced back and forth, allowing the user freedom to browse through his/her findings. Additionally, a bilingual (English and/or Italian) version of the user interface was introduced.

3.7.6   Generating the Question Texts

As mentioned above, the N-A system has followed the query-the-user interface paradigm, that is, the user is prompted with a question and he/she is expected to answer. Whenever possible, his/her options are delimited by presenting a menu with multiple choices.

Using this approach, a complex problem in the design of the knowledge base was the generation of the question texts. This was a serious consideration for the user interface, as the questions should be unambiguous and correctly phrased. One solution would be to use the Conceptual Graphs themselves to create the text, but because they were not related to each other (ILAM had produced a separate Conceptual Graphs structure for every logical sentence) it was not possible to produce the correct texts.

In the N-A prototype knowledge base, the texts were constructed manually from the original text but with reference to the ILAM Conceptual Graphs (see also Appendix IV with two sample sessions: one with questions generated by the Conceptual Graphs and one created manually). The main problem, however, was

---

[88] Menu-driven and graphic user interface environment is also available for future implementation.

[89] SUSSKIND R., *Expert Systems in Law*, Clarendon, Oxford 1987, p. 66.

encountered when the system tried to generate texts for *exceptions*, or add *alternative cases* to questions.

Question texts for exceptions must include the text of the original question. This is needed because it is impossible to guarantee the order of evaluation of questions in a *production rule* system (some of the questions may have been evaluated by another rule etc.). Therefore, if the text for an 'exception question' does not include the original question (case), the question is not clearly understood.

To illustrate the problem for the case of *alternative cases* above, consider the following extract from Article 7§1 of the law:

> "...with exception to the Districts of Livigno, Campio d' Italia and of the national waters of the lake Lugano..."

This exception is described in a separate Conceptual Graph structure in the ILAM output. If this Conceptual Graph is used to generate the text, one similar to the following will be generated:

> "Is the activity carried out in one of the following territories (Please select by number):
> 1.   District of Livigno
> 2.   Campio d' Italia
> 3.   National Waters of lake Lugano"

This may seem to be correct but there is a need for an 'escape case', i.e.

> 4.   None of the above

If this case is not there, the inference engine will force the user to answer one of the three choices. It is obvious that the case, 'none of the above', must be included for the system to function properly. But again, this, at the time of experimentation was only done manually.

Link to the Model:
Methodological rules concerning the *sufficiency of Interpretation* were used in order to identify the correctness of this technical solution. Again the problem was that this Interpretational phase had to take place (manually) before the intervention of the system.

3.7.7 Testing and Evaluation

Although the N-A prototype was not tested for full coverage of VAT Law, but only for one article, it can be argued that, on the territoriality domain, it was precise and reliable. (Sample sessions can be found in Appendix IV). In theory, Conceptual Graphs present an extensive power of formalism, but up to now this has only been implemented in *natural language* applications, not *legal applications*. Additionally, numerous researchers[90] have argued the following positions for the knowledge acquisition and representation phase of Legal Expert Systems:

1. That representing legal knowledge is a human activity and

2. That the use of conceptual models supporting rule-based expert systems is impossible

Apart from the general considerations of this book, the N-A implementation, in order to comply with the project's intentions, also had to challenge these two *a priori* arguments. For the *stricto sensu* implementation of the *Nomos* project, the first argument was denying the very core of the project. This could be weakened in view of the results of the N-A prototype. The second argument was mainly provoked by some older methods of conceptualisation. It could be answered, in turn, by the end result. The N-A implementation, even under the difficulties described here, has used a conceptual formalism (Conceptual Graphs) for a rule-based expert system (N-A).

In terms of performance, during the final presentation of the prototypes, the following statistics were revealed[91] for the complete - up to the level of the delivered ILAM output - analysis of the 697 words of article 7 by the ILAM system:

---

[90] For example SUSSKIND, WAHLGREN, ZELEZNIKOW & HUNTER, see also Chapter 2.

[91] See ESPRIT-DOC SG-61-50-01, *ILAM & FLAM Preliminary Evaluation,* 12-Oct-92, p. 7.

Reference specialist	28	seconds
Macro Processor	16	seconds
Micro Processor	55	seconds
Syntactic/Semantic Analyser	410	seconds
Complete Processing	509	seconds (8 min 29 sec)

These numbers may seem impressive, but they lose a lot their value because they do not include the time spent for input of the text into the system. This procedure may take a significant amount of time, especially in the case of legal texts, available only in printed form and in different formats, which have to be scanned. Additionally, the time spent by the knowledge engineers to refine the knowledge base is not calculated; and all this effort was needed for a single article of only one law.

> **Link to the Model:**
> These results again raise the issue of the *economics of everyday legal practice*, and the *economics of creating legal expert systems* (see also section 2.4.5)

In terms of evaluation, this neglected cost/benefit analysis undermines the general theoretical assumption of the *Nomos* project (see *supra* 3.2.4 Criticism, points 1, 2 & 3) i.e. to automatically process a huge volume of legal material, in order to reduce the cost and the complexity of the knowledge acquisition task. First, because this process was achieved neither automatically nor quickly. Second, it is not indisputable that acquiring legal knowledge is either costly or complex, at least to the degree the designers of the project have proposed.

Finally, with these measurements in mind, the whole ILAM system proved to be inflexible to update,[92] which signifies a particular drawback in relation to the taxation law, which is evolving day by day.[93]

---

[92] See also the considerations of Widdison *et al.* in Widdison R., Pritchard F., & Robinson W., *Expert Systems meet Hypertext: The European Conflicts Guide*, in Journal of Law and Information Science, Vol. 3, No. 1, 1992, p. 89.

[93] Sometimes only by regional taxation authorities decisions.

3.8   CONCLUSIONS - CHAPTER 3

After the end of the *Nomos* project, a careful examination reveals that the attempted 'applied' research presented many of the classic characteristics of 'basic' research. With the exception of DICK'S[94] project, which was a Case Law conceptual retrieval system,[95] this is, to the best of the available knowledge, the first time that Conceptual Graphs have been used for legal reasoning. The conclusions drawn and the experience gained can be divided in two categories: first, in results concerning the effort to comply with the project's intentions and deliver the N-A prototype, and second, in thoughts concerning the whole *Nomos* project. The latter, in most cases, confirm the criticism already exposed at the initial stage of the N-A implementation (see *supra* 3.2.4). The following two paragraphs outline these views.

3.8.1   Conclusions from the N-A Implementation

1. From the erroneous hypothesis[96] that "...in the normative domain, knowledge is mainly contained in natural language texts such as *laws*, *decrees* and *regulations*..." the approach of *Nomos* finds a suitable theoretical basis to justify a correct representation of *normative texts*.[97] Within this framework, the N-A prototype has proved that Conceptual Graphs can be used, with limitations, for

---

[94] DICK J., *Conceptual Retrieval and Case Law*, PROCEEDINGS OF THE 1ST INTERNATIONAL CONFERENCE ON ARTIFICIAL INTELLIGENCE AND LAW, Boston, 1987, and DICK J., *Representation of Legal Text for Conceptual Retrieval*, in PROCEEDINGS OF THE 3RD INTERNATIONAL CONFERENCE ON ARTIFICIAL INTELLIGENCE AND LAW, Oxford, June 25-28 1991, ACM Press, 1991, p. 244, where she concludes that "[a]t present the representation used describes the meaning of the text adequately for inference at a suitable level. It is not adequate to make possible a full translation from English, nor the generation of a full text response in English. *We are attempting to model conceptual content in order to facilitate the retrieval of information rather than to reason to definitive conclusions.* It has been demonstrated that retrieval based on semantics and inference can be perceptive and powerful."(emphasis added).

[95] SERGOT believes that Information Retrieval falls outside the scope of AI and Law. SERGOT M, *The Representation of Law in Computer Programs*, in BENCH-CAPON(ED.).

[96] See also section 2.4.4 Anathema II: the Linguist's Perception of Law.

[97] GIANNETTI *et al.*, *Nomos: Knowledge Acquisition for Normative Reasoning Systems*, Final Report, p. 1 (emphasis added).

the representation of *stricto sensu* normative texts, and hence can be applied to a rule-based expert system.

2. The N-A system mainly tried to fulfil the tasks set in the beginning, as a purely research prototype. It did not try to answer the *interim* contradictions or deviations from the 'main stream' methodology, nor to develop *a priori* arguments. To paraphrase TYREE,[98] the important question was whether the Conceptual Graphs approach could build systems at an affordable price. Since TURING'S[99] approach to building an intelligent machine has not proved productive, *a priori* arguments should not prevent *research* work in the search for improvements of information systems. This is, of course, something quite distinct[100] from practical legal applications. The facts that an application operates, and proves some parts of the theory do not appear to work in the legal domain, where further adaptations are needed in order to create *realistic* applications (see *supra* 2.4.5 and the Epilogue) acceptable by the legal world. Many of these deficiencies led to the identification of the definitions and the rules exposed in the model of Chapter 1.

3. Notwithstanding the best efforts of linguists, the ILAM system was perfected only as far as it concerns linguistics: the ILAM output was, according to the opinion of other experts, a perfected linguistic transformation of natural language to SOWA'S Conceptual Graphs. It did not, however, contain crucial legal reasoning information, not only in terms of *procedural,* but also in terms of *substantive* knowledge about the law. The model of Chapter 1, and especially the notion of the *Doctrine of Valid Legal Sources,* was used in order to complete this knowledge. Consequently, although it can be argued that in theory Conceptual Graphs is a suitable method to represent legal (in the sense of normative) texts, it is not yet clear how they could represent *legal knowledge as a whole,* i.e. not only the text of a certain law, but empirical and procedural knowledge as well (in the sense of a legal subsystem) and provide applications of true practical value.

---

[98] TYREE A., *The Logic Programming Debate* in JOURNAL OF LAW AND INFORMATION SCIENCE, Vol. 3, 1992, No. 1, p. 115.

[99] In his known paper of the fifties *Computing Machinery and Intelligence* (1950) 59 MIND 433 and in TURING A. M., *Computing Machinery and Intelligence*, in FEIGENBAUM-FELDMAN (Eds.), p. 11, 1963.

[100] See the objections of MOLES R., *Expert Systems - The Need for Theory*, in GRÜTTERS *et al.* (EDS.), JURIX PROCEEDINGS 1992, Koninklijke Vermande, Lelystad, 1992.

4. The N-A system has shown that the additional sources of knowledge are equally vital for the creation of a useful and legally acceptable system. The hypertext links were used, in this case, in order to support other sources of knowledge, especially definitions and previous cases. It is not, therefore, clear how an automatic acquisition system could extract legal knowledge as a *legal subsystem* (see the section 1.8.4 in Chapter 1), i.e. by eliciting it from other sources of law, empirical background and social knowledge.

3.8.2 Overall estimations for the *Nomos* project

1. The basic hypothesis of the *Nomos* project is not correct. 'Law' is not only contained in huge collections of texts (see also *supra* Chapter 1). In the N-A prototype, the most important parts of procedural knowledge, heuristics and rules of thumb, were derived from the legal experts, minimising the value of the information displayed by the Conceptual Graphs representation. Without pin-pointing these parts by using the model the whole project would be useless.

2. The second hypothesis that

> "[t]he knowledge extracted from a human expert remains a fundamental component of a Knowledge Based System; nonetheless, large amounts of knowledge are usually stored in various textual forms (e.g. manuals, textbooks, specifications and regulations). These texts can often be considered a *primary source of expertise for knowledge-based systems*. An important example is in the field of normative knowledge that is by definition mainly coded in natural language texts" [101]

is also false. The knowledge acquisition task in the legal domain, lies sometimes more in the interrelation of these sources, and seems, in practice, less cumbersome than originally thought by the *Nomos* designers (see also the evaluation measurements *supra* 3.7.7 Testing and Evaluation). It is much easier to find and consult the 'best expert' in any chosen area of law (see also *supra* 2.4.2), than to process, at length, legal texts which ultimately do not contain the full information.

---

[101] GIANNETTI *et al. Nomos: Knowledge Acquisition for Normative Reasoning Systems*, FINAL REPORT, p. 2 (emphasis added).

3. The third hypothesis that knowledge acquisition would be performed automatically was never confirmed. Human intervention was anticipated at various stages, either at the knowledge acquisition or at the knowledge engineering phases of the project, thus leading to its characterisation as 'semi-automatic'.

4. As was shown in Chapter 2, *Information Technology Applications in Law*, adapted to the proposed model, present three different aspects: Legal Reasoning, Information Retrieval and Office Automation. 'Knowledge based' applications for each of these aspects need a specific 'knowledge base', respectively. Therefore, the Conceptual Graphs 'knowledge base', which proved defective even for the narrow domain of the N-A prototype, could not serve, as such, a much wider spectrum of applications.

On a final note, it should be highlighted that formalising Legal Knowledge definitely involves legal skills and legal interpretation. ATIYAH clarifies that "very few statutes are self-contained instruments even when they deal with a remote or esoteric branch of the law"[102].

OSKAMP furthermore postulates that "[u]sing only statutory rules is not sufficient for law application. Other types of knowledge are needed as well as common sense knowledge... Without further means of interpretation, a legal expert system may only be able to give a schematic overview of the legal rules in the domain chosen. In certain cases it could mechanically follow the applicable rules and by mere deduction come to a conclusion. This might solve easy cases when the circumstances of the case strictly match the condition of the rules. Even then, most choices and interpretations will have to be made by the user of the system. She will have to decide whether the facts match the conditions of the rules. These systems by setting forth a narrow framework to be filled in by the user often provide a rather clear overview of the rules within a certain domain. *But they only offer the user very restricted paths within which those rules can be applied*"[103]. And finally, to coincide precisely with the intentions of the modelling attempted in this book, MAHALINGAM-CARR articulates that:

---

[102] ATIYAH P.S., *Common Law and Statute Law*, in THE MODERN LAW REVIEW, Vol. 48, No. 1, p. 2.

[103] OSKAMP A., *Model for Knowledge and Legal Expert Systems*, in ARTIFICIAL INTELLIGENCE AND LAW, Vol. 1, No. 4, 1993, p. 246 (emphasis added).

"[I]t can be said that legal rules based on a statute, even where definitions are provided, cannot be formulated without some amount of interpretation. The task of interpretation, however, may prove to be a formidable one since it may not always be possible to discern one underlying principle determining the decisions drawn by the courts and even where an underlying principle is formulated somehow it may go against other well-established principles that are regarded as sacrosanct. The job of the expert system builder then becomes a highly individualistic one based on his perception of what is law, what is aiming to achieve in a given social context and the nature of legal principle... a great deal of interpretation on part of the expert system builder is required even where the statute is the source of the legal rule. The underlying reason for this is because *law uses language which derives its sense from use in a social context*. As a consequence, however well formulated the rules may be in a statute, they need to be interpreted. *No rule carries its own interpretation and each awaits further unfolding to derive its content.*"[104]

A term borrowed from the school of thought of *American Legal Realism* and not any enthusiasm to adopt its basic argument, summarises these conclusions: Out of the empirical investigation of the *Nomos* project and the implementation of the N-A prototype, it is more than ever clear that *automated legal reasoning cannot be guided only by 'paper rules'*.

---

[104] MAHALINGAM CARR I., *Statute Law as a Source for Expert Systems*, in COMPUTERS & LAW, Vol. 1, Issue 2, April 1990, p. 16 (emphasis added).

4. SYNTHESIS – GENERAL CONCLUSIONS

4.1   THE EMPIRICAL INPUT

The empirical testbench for the Ph.D. Thesis, before this book, was the implementation of the *Nomos-Advisor* (N-A) expert system (Chapter 3). The objectives of the project immediately revealed a series of defects[1] that would not have occurred if a basic legal methodology would have been used. The detailed examination of the whole architecture of the project's system demonstrated that the choice of a method for representation, in this case SOWA'S[2] Conceptual Graphs, is not the main problem in legal applications and especially expert systems.

In a working, practical, and real-life legal application the problem lies in *what* to represent not *how* to represent it.[3] It is a fundamental legal skill in performing legal reasoning to include those procedural and substantive rules which are not included in the text of a certain law, and to relate them to other parts of the legal decision process. For these reasons, the Italian Linguistic Analysis Module (ILAM) knowledge representation not only proved inadequate to represent legal knowledge for use in an expert system, but, furthermore, the scientific[4] and linguistic[5] view of law adopted for the knowledge engineering methodology resulted in a system which

---

[1]   See 3.2.4 Criticism.

[2]   See SOWA in all his writings and the special bibliography for the N-A prototype.

[3]   See sections 1.3.4 and 2.4.1 above.

[4]   See section 2.4.3.

[5]   See section 2.4.4.

contained a distorted representation of the law and which did not fulfil its intended function, i.e. the accurate representation of normative legal texts.[6]

The main conclusion from this phase was that *legal expert systems, adopting as their knowledge base only parts of legislation, are condemned to produce wrong and unacceptable results.* Therefore they must use a representation of the legal knowledge in a certain area of law which should remain coherent with the idea of the *Legal Subsystem.*[7]

To rectify the situation, during the early stages of the implementation of the *Nomos-Advisor* prototype a draft method of sketches with interconnections and 'checklists' with basic legal principles was applied. This method helped to extend the participants' understanding of the law and to present all the interconnected parts of a particular legal domain. Without this method it was impossible for the researchers (especially the non-lawyers) to remember and correctly represent all the necessary elements of the legal decision process. Therefore, it was apparent that in order to achieve the desired kind of 'full representation', such a method *should* always be used.

The author's experience with other legal applications, such as on-line databases and office automation programs, as well as the results from field research[8] into the everyday practice of typical law firms, indicated that a number of problems encountered in the *Nomos* project were also apparent in an identical form in other applications. In particular, the fragmentation of the legal phenomenon was apparent both in legal databases and office automation programs. Each application, in turn, concentrated on the narrow field of law of its own interest, without any reference to other parts of the legal decision process. This observation led to the conclusion *that the proposed method for building legal expert systems is also a necessary condition in all attempts to produce automated legal decision-making tools.*

In order to solve this problem, the integrated model of Chapter 1 was developed so as to describe theoretically this method and to interconnect all the parts of the legal decision process. It was also envisaged that the model will be used in constructing applications other than expert systems. The conclusions of this enterprise will be

---

[6] See section 3.4 The Puzzle of the N-A Prototype.

[7] See section 1.8.

[8] See section 1.1.2.

described in the next section. However, still in the empirical field, the model, after having been developed, was partly tested for the *Nomos-Advisor* system. It was especially followed in covering the gaps[9] of the knowledge base and in the completion of the hypertext facility nodes.

4.2   THE THEORETICAL CONSTRUCTION OF THE MODEL

4.2.1   Methodological Tools

The initial findings of the Ph.D. research showed that much confusion and misunderstanding were dominant in the area. Therefore, an attempt in this book is made to define a concrete terminology and some basic methodological tools, in order to proceed. It was asserted that through the formation of a *paradigm*,[10] the new discipline of *Information Technology and the Law* had been created. This discipline presents a diptych including: (1) *Information Technology Law* regarding the issues of legal usage of Information Technology as well as the legal regulation of Information Technology usage, and (2) *Information Technology Applications in Law* regarding the technological developments targeting law as a field of usage. It was, subsequently, made clear that the object of this study belongs to the second leg of Information Technology Applications in Law, as opposed to issues of substantive Information Technology Law, which is something completely different (*Prolegomenon*). It was concluded that a stable methodology for the new discipline has to be developed.

4.2.2   Methodological Limitations

Proceeding with the development of the model, it was clear that few writings dealt with the issue in question. Therefore, given the lack of bibliographical resources in the field, the model tried to combine the old information retrieval model of BING &

---

[9]   See section 3.7 Solving the Puzzle III: Linking to the 'Missing Knowledge.

[10]   Under the notion of *paradigm* described by KUHN T., *The Structure of Scientific Revolutions*, The University of Chicago Press, Chicago, 1962.

HARVOLD[11] with the newer ones proposed by SUSSKIND,[12] WAHLGREN[13] and ZELEZNIKOW & HUNTER,[14] in order to expand the model beyond AI applications.

The first methodological limitation of the model was a set of definitions concerning the terms to be used. It was defined that *Clients* are persons experiencing a *Legal Problem*, that is problems that need *Legal Reasoning*, i.e. a mental process encapsulating legal interpretation and the legal syllogism as a solution. *Lawyers* are persons entitled to solve legal problems (called *Judges*), or to advise on the solution of legal problems (called *Counsel*). These two categories also define the difference in the course of argument: the first category (Judges) is trying to solve the problem abiding by the rules of the legal system, while the second (Counsel) is trying to find or predict the 'optimum' solution for the Client according to the rules and professional ethics. *Legal Decision* was defined as the target to reach a conclusive and integrated piece of advice for the Client. These limitations enable researchers to identify the potential users of *Information Technology Applications in Law*, therefore, they should not design applications for   persons who do not fall in the above categories.

A second methodological limitation was a set of rules to be followed when creating *Information Technology Applications in Law*. The input for these rules was mainly defined by the character of the   foreseen applications and by the empirical experience of the *Nomos* project. Furthermore some findings of *sociological jurisprudence* as exposed in a number of writings of LEITH and STAMPER[15] have affected the final formulation of these rules.

---

[11] BING J. & HARVOLD T., *Legal Decisions and Information Systems*, Universitetsforlaget, Oslo, 1977.

[12] SUSSKIND RICHARD, *Expert Systems in Law: a Jurisprudential Inquiry*, Clarendon Press, Oxford, 1987.

[13] WAHLGREN P., *Automation of Legal Reasoning, A Study on Artificial Intelligence and Law*, Kluwer, Deventer, 1992.

[14] ZELEZNIKOW J. & HUNTER D., *Building Intelligent Legal Information Systems, Representation and Reasoning in Law*, Kluwer, Computer/Law Series, 1994.

[15] LEITH P., *The Computerised Lawyer: A Guide to the Use of Computers in the Legal Profession*, Springer-Verlag, 1991 and MORISON J. & LEITH P., *The Barrister's World and the Nature of Law*, Open University Press, Milton Keynes - Philadelphia, 1992 and STAMPER R., *Expert Systems, Lawyers Beware*, in NAGEL (Ed.), New York, 1991.

The distorted view of the law adopted by scientists and linguists dictated the first rule: the Legal Decision Process must be treated as an integrated whole defined by active legal practitioners, not by theorists or non-legally educated persons.[16]

Second, Information Technology Applications in Law are part of the legal system and must abide by its theory as well as by its substantive, procedural and methodological rules.[17] Infringing this rule produces technically correct but legally erroneous results and leads Lawyers to mistrust modern technology.

The third rule emerged from the *pragmatist*[18] line of this book, i.e. having as its final target the production of applications with practically exploitable results.[19] If this rule is not followed, Information Technology will become another theoretical self-goal and not a productive tool in the hands of lawyers.

Fourth, more attention must be paid to the problem of *what* and *which* parts of the law must be represented in Information Technology Applications, rather than *how* to formalise law.[20]

Fifth, if the previous problem is solved, the results and, consequently, the whole model can be used as a memory tool, a 'checklist', that can depict a compact picture of the Legal decision Process.[21] This method is also useful for representing the methodological rules, the interconnections with other parts of the law, and the interventions of the surrounding environment.

Sixth, the model was based on the assumption that law is a system of rules[22] but other forms of information as well as feedback from the surrounding environment may be included.[23]

---

[16] 1.3.1 The Rule of Integration.

[17] 1.3.2 The Rule of the Legal System.

[18] See on that SUSSKIND R., *Pragmatism and Purism in AI and Legal Reasoning*, in AI & SOCIETY, Vol. 3, p. 28, 1989.

[19] 1.3.3 The Rule of Practicality.

[20] 1.3.4 The Rule of Content.

[21] 1.3.5 The Rule of Checklist.

[22] The debate about this issue is a long one starting from the known dispute between HART (especially in his *Concept of Law*) and DWORKIN (especially in his *Matter of Principle*) and extending to the opinions of the American Legal Realism school of thought.

Finally, seventh, it is stressed that legal problem solving is not a static linear input-output process leading from 'facts' to the 'decision', but rather a dynamic representation of the lawyers' course of argument in search of justice.[24]

This set of limitations enables researchers to determine what type of automated decision-making systems can be developed, ruling out applications that do not fall within the above criteria, or modifying them in order to meet these rules.

4.2.3   The Role of the *Input / Output Endings* of the Model

However, for practical reasons a traditional input - process - output model is used as a skeleton for the whole model. The 'input' is represented by real facts exposed to the lawyer. It is emphasised that these 'facts' are the product of human behaviour and, therefore, in most cases are biased and mixed with irrelevant facts. It is the Lawyer's task to overcome the language barriers and interpret them accordingly. Furthermore, this 'input' of the process, and the whole model, stays open to the surrounding environment. Therefore, law cannot be considered outside the surrounding social, economical and political framework, and, hence, the 'input facts' are in most cases affected by this environment.

These considerations crucially affect the user profile: *the users must possess certain qualifications (legal or para-legal)*. Subsequently, the user interface must be designed to accommodate these special needs.

At this stage, the general attitude of 'data handling' is also affected: in most applications, and especially in expert systems, it is here that the subsequent *course of argumentation* is formulated. Additionally, the same considerations apply for applications using electronic forms as their input. On a more general level, this part of the model enables researchers to determine the 'inputs' and 'outputs' for an automated system; how they should be discovered; and, thus, what the limitations of the system are.

For the output of the process, it should be repeated that it remains susceptible to feedback from the surrounding environment, depending, however, on the freedom

---

[23]   1.3.6 The Rule of Rule-based Deduction.

[24]   1.3.7 The Rule of Oscillation and legal Problem Solving.

that the legal system gives to the Judge.[25] The most important conclusion is that *researchers in the area of office automation must be aware of the formalities that the law defines for the issuing and the formal appearance of a legal decision.*

4.2.4   The Role of the *Pre-Process* of the Model

The next stage, after the Initial Thoughts, is the Pre-Process where the lawyer must in five steps (1) reduce the input facts to those relevant and sufficient to the legal problem in question, (2) check possible disqualifying facts, (3) select the branch of law out of the totality of legal sources and the possible course of argument, (4) estimate pragmatic considerations and, finally, (5) decide whether this case is a 'hard' one and shall enter interpretation, or it is an 'easy' one and a decision shall be formulated.

For *Information Technology Applications in Law* steps (1) and (2) must be elaborated while designing the user interface: they will provide the choices for the user (through menus or other methods) and they will restrict his/her options. Of extreme importance is step (3) in defining the direction towards which (in favour or against a rule) the application will 'move'. The 'matching' functions of the systems must be very thoroughly examined at this stage. The *costs indemnity rule* of step (4) is usually neglected in computerised applications, but it is a true fact of everyday legal practice and in view of practical applications must be addressed. Finally, the Hartian 'easy' cases (5) are used in a broader sense, to disqualify those cases that will not enter the Interpretation process and will immediately produce a decision.

4.2.5   The Role of *Interpretation*

Interpretation is the next stage of the model. Provided that the sources are sufficient, the Lawyer must abide by the methodological rules of the legal system, to try and interpret the input facts to relevant legal formulations, resolve vagueness, conflicts and gaps by using the general rules of Interpretation, and perform the legal syllogism in order to reach sufficient Interpretation.

---

[25] See again the writings of HART and DWORKIN.

The important conclusion here was that this subsumption, as emphasised by SUSSKIND[26] in the case of expert systems, *needs an initial human subsumptive judgement based on knowledge of linguistic usage and, therefore, cannot be computerised.* This view, however can be extended to other applications where it must be stressed that legal linguistics should be carefully examined in both their syntactic, semantic and pragmatic nature. Otherwise, reliable results cannot be expected and, furthermore, the spectrum of the possible users of the system will be restricted. Secondly, it should be noted that legal methodologies are very strict as to what constitutes valid interpretation, and, therefore, *researchers must follow these general rules almost dogmatically, without, however, forgetting that Interpretation is a means to apply law,* and does not represent an end in itself. Finally, the performance of the legal syllogism opens the discussion on whether an informal logic[27] is needed to represent law.

4.2.6   The Role of the *Search for Legal Sources*

If the sources are considered insufficient, the Lawyer must search for more legal sources. *The course of argument,* defined in the Pre-Process, and not any restrictive Boolean techniques will guide this search. The Lawyer, based on *the doctrine of valid legal sources* which is a system of clearly defined rules following an established hierarchy, will try to reduce the total volume of legal sources to those relevant to the problem in question in order to create a *Legal Subsystem.*[28] In order to abide by the methodological rules and the steps of the pre-process, a practical model must also include, apart from the traditional sources, *heuristic* and *empirical legal knowledge* and *social knowledge repercussions*[29] (only to the

---

[26] SUSSKIND R., *Expert Systems in Law: a Jurisprudential Inquiry*, Clarendon Press, Oxford, 1987, p. 184.

[27] Amongst the supporters see WEINBERGER O., *Philosophische Studien zur Logic*, Prague, 1964 and WEINBERGER O., *Rechstlogic*, Vienna-New York, 1970.

[28] See section 1.8; this notion is also supported by SUSSKIND R., *Expert Systems in Law: a Jurisprudential Inquiry*, Clarendon Press, Oxford, 1987 and WAHLGREN P., *Automation of Legal Reasoning, A Study on Artificial Intelligence and Law*, Kluwer, Deventer, 1992. See, however, SUSSKIND'S recent considerations about hyperregulation and the Technology Lag i.e. the problem of accumulating and searching vast amounts of information. SUSSKIND R., *The Future of Law*, Clarendon Press, Oxford, 1996, p. 59.

[29] This is theoretically supported by ALEXY R., *A Theory of Legal Argumentation, The Theory of Rational Discourse as Theory of Legal Justification,* (English Translation), Clarendon Press, Oxford, 1989 and by PECZENIK A., *On Law and Reason*, Kluwer, 1989 see also the institutional

extent, however, that the legal methodology permits them). *Designers of Information Technology Applications in law must be careful in determining the scope of the legal system and, consequently, the method of reducing it to the legal sub-system.*

4.3   FROM THE GENERAL MODEL TO SPECIFIC APPLICATIONS

In order to transpose, test and apply the general theoretical model of Chapter 1 to the specific expert system of Chapter 3, it was necessary to add more information about expert systems and their particular problems. This information was included in Chapter 2 which tries to highlight these issues and act as a 'bridge' between Chapters 1 and 3. First, certain technical characteristics of expert systems were exposed so as to inform the reader about basic terminology and procedures. The selection of the method used to represent law[30] is of great importance, since, in most cases, it determines the whole course of implementation. The conclusion here was that *researchers should be careful not to chose representations that in the past proved cumbersome and difficult to handle for legal applications.* The model can help in that direction, because representations tested against it are likely to work.

Of additional importance is the neglected problem[31] of the *User Interface.* To accommodate the generally computer-phobic lawyers, a user-friendly interface is needed. The model can be used[32] to define the structure of such an interface which would attract the user's interest and convince him/her about the system's reliability. Allied to the User Interface is the notion of Hypertext, which can be used as an enhancement tool for expert systems. Designers must follow the model and be very careful in drafting the hypertext links in legal documents in order to avoid interpreting the law in an unacceptable manner.

---

theory of MACORMICK N. & WEINBERGER O., *An Institutional Theory of Law, New Approaches to Legal Positivism,* D. Reidel Publishing Company, Dordrecht, 1986.

[30] See section 2.2.2 Knowledge Representation.

[31] Analytically exposed by WIDDISON R., PRITCHARD F., & ROBINSON W., *Expert Systems meet Hypertext: The European Conflicts Guide,* in JOURNAL OF LAW AND INFORMATION SCIENCE, Vol.3, No.1, 1992, p. 89.

[32] Mainly by the restrictions of the *Input* and *Output* functions. See also section 3.7.5.

It is concluded that with the present level of technology, expert systems could be inserted in all three distinct parts of the model: (a) In the core of legal reasoning as 'intelligent' advisors to solve 'hard cases' or checklists for methodological and procedural rules, (b) in the area of legal search as conceptual retrieval tools or 'intelligent' front-ends and (c) in the area of input-output as 'intelligent' fill-in forms, or for document assembly. Systems inserted in the first part (Legal Reasoning) must be capable of sound legal reasoning techniques in order to produce reliable and trustworthy results, while systems in the subsequent parts can act as delimited assistants to legal decision making, where the final decision stays with the user. Finally, another possible use of expert systems lies in Legal Education for exercises and teaching of hypothetical situations.

Four specific problems originating from the *Nomos* project must be considered when applying the model to the creation of expert systems: (1) The problem of defining what is in a Lawyer's mind,[33] and, consequently, the contents of a knowledge base, could be tackled by adopting the pragmatic considerations of the model. (2) The problem of knowledge acquisition[34] is also dominating, since much of legal knowledge is intuitively acquired in the law school, and after many years of practice it cannot be elicited. A possible solution could be for the domain expert and the knowledge engineer to be the same person. The last two problems (3) and (4)[35] could be solved by strictly applying the *Rule of Integration* that future applications will only be drafted by lawyers.

The conclusion[36] that, even if these guidelines are followed, in practice very few expert systems will be used by lawyers, is inevitably disappointing. The use of integrated workstations providing access to different kinds of information and, amongst others, to expert systems and 'intelligent' assistants[37] has been, however, proposed as a solution. It must also be stressed that these problems may also arise

---

[33] 2.4.1 Enigma I: What Legal Knowledge for a Knowledge Base.

[34] 2.4.2 Enigma II: How to Elicit Knowledge.

[35] 2.4.3 Anathema I: The Scientist's Perception of Law and 2.4.4 Anathema II: the Linguist's Perception of Law the conclusion.

[36] 2.4.5 Exegesis: How to Create and use Legal Expert Systems.

[37] For possible solutions see GREENLEAF G., MOWBRAY A. & TYREE A., *The DataLex Legal Workstation, Integrating Tools for Lawyers*, in PROCEEDINGS OF THE 3RD INTERNATIONAL CONFERENCE ON ARTIFICIAL INTELLIGENCE AND LAW, Oxford, June 25-28 1991, ACM Press, 1991, p. 221.

when the model is applied to other kinds of applications, e.g. information retrieval. In each particular case researchers must be aware that further investigation into the specific problems of each application is needed in order to develop a similar methodology, which will act as a 'bridge' between theory and practice.

4.4   GENERAL CONCLUSIONS

4.4.1   On the Micro Level of the N-A Prototype

On the micro-level, the N-A implementation has shown that the theoretical description of any application in law should be carefully designed by people having legal education. Scientists and linguists are always keen to undertake research in Artificial Intelligence and Law, without knowing the complexities and the peculiarities of law. Furthermore, the transposition from the theoretical concepts to the practical implementation must be performed in very careful steps. The *Nomos* designers rushed to prove that "legal knowledge is mainly contained in natural language texts" which in turn could be "automatically acquired and processed" and finally be used in "expert legal advisors".[38] The N-A system proved that this was an oversimplification: *additional sources of knowledge are not only of equal importance, but sometimes they constitute the core knowledge that an acceptable application must use.* Therefore, the idea of the 'unity' of the whole legal system and the accurate bordering of the 'legal sub-system', which also includes procedural and empirical knowledge, must prevail in this process.

4.4.2   On the Level of Expert Systems

On the level of expert systems implementation, it was shown that such systems can be theoretically designed and practically implemented, but they are still under-used because their design follows a *non-realistic* approach, i.e. they neglect the actual needs of the user. The picture of the lawyer as a user of information systems has not been fully examined. The problem of creating expert systems for the non-expert

---

[38]   In the words of the ILAM designers.

has been tackled[39] but the problem of *expert systems for the expert* has not yet been fully addressed. In the case of law, expert systems (as currently being built) do not contain knowledge outside their boundaries which is essential to understanding the law. Additionally, it is not clear whether the knowledge they purport to convey is exceptionally scarce or not.

Recently SUSSKIND seems more optimistic about the use of expert systems by non-experts (non-lawyers in our case) and the quality of their 'expertise'.[40] However, the findings of this study coincide with what SUSSKIND & CAPPER have demonstrated earlier: that "[first generation systems] are not able to apply non-rule standards, such as principles, policy and purpose. Conclusions of these systems, therefore, are necessarily 'conditional' in nature, always being subject to implied exceptions - on grounds of principle, policy or purpose - to any rules used in the reasoning process."[41]

This was verified, if we accept the theoretical notion of the legal sub-system, by the 'missing knowledge' of the *Nomos* project, and the final conclusion is that such systems cannot simply make the decision for the user. This, however, opens the discussion about the general character of *Information Technology Applications in Law* which will follow in the Epilogue.

4.4.3   On the Level of Information Technology Applications in Law

On the macro-level of *Information Technology Applications in Law* the conclusions are similar. It is beyond doubt that Information Technology presents advantages and benefits. However, these changes have been observed in typical commercial

---

39 SUSSKIND concludes that "the Latent Damage System is intended for use by legal practitioners or legally aware persons as an intelligent assistant for solving problems of latent damage law that would present few difficulties for latent damage experts but would pose problems for non-experts precisely because they are not familiar with the complex web of interrelated rules that constitute this branch of law." SUSSKIND R., *The Latent Damage System: A Jurisprudential Analysis*, in PROCEEDINGS OF THE SECOND INTERNATIONAL CONFERENCE ON ARTIFICIAL INTELLIGENCE AND LAW, Vancouver, 1989.

40 SUSSKIND R., *The Future of Law*, Clarendon Press, Oxford, 1996, pp. 121 & 212.

41 SUSSKIND R. & CAPPER P., *The Latent Damage System, A First Generation Expert System in Law*, in MARTINO (Ed.), North Holland, 1992, p. 317.

environments where automation has brought visible – and sometimes overvalued – results.[42]

The dogma of Information Technology conforms with the general and unquestionable improvements in the field of office / business automation within the legal system, especially in big organisations such as the law firms and the administration of justice. It cannot not explain, however, why sound theoretical and practical applications in the core area of the legal environment have fallen short of their optimistic early predictions and people are simply ignoring them.

In the light of the analysis on the micro-level of the previous section, the answer lies in (1) cultural reasons, i.e. the prejudice of the user against modern informational systems, which is particularly strong in the case of lawyers and (2) from the side of creators, the underestimation of a *realistic analysis*. Such an analysis should examine the identity and the true needs of the user;[43] without such an examination, an analysis cannot support the implementation of practical applications. Furthermore, it should also connect these applications with the surrounding social processes and needs, because the legal process itself is of a social nature. The end result should be for these applications to be trusted and used by the user in real life conditions. To do so, however, for the legal decision process, one must enter the risky area of legal philosophy, and, finally, must define what is law, a matter about which legal philosophers have disagreed for the past twenty-five centuries.[44]

---

[42] See the analysis of SUSSKIND, where the analysis of Information Technology advantages is based on the changes conferred upon traditional manual systems and enterprises, he also makes the distinction between office automation and automation of some *lawyering* activities. SUSSKIND R., *The Future of Law*, Clarendon Press, Oxford, 1996, pp. 47 & 77.

[43] An additional consideration is that the notion of the user should target the lawyers themselves (as end-users) and not intermediate persons.

[44] On a more abstract level LEITH argues that the transfer of techniques from science to law is errant because law is of a qualitatively different nature and he emphasises the need to solve the problem of computing in the social sciences. He further on compares legal ideology to a minefield into which researchers in artificial intelligence must enter if they wish *to build practical systems for practical purposes.* LEITH P, *The Computerised Lawyer: A Guide to the Use of Computers in the Legal Profession*, Springer-Verlag, 1991, pp. 202-207 (emphasis added).

4.5   THE STATUS OF THE MODEL

A final clarification is necessary here. The main argument of this book is that when an Information Technology Application in Law is attempted, *some* model of the legal decision process must be used. In order to propound that thesis, the model of Chapter 1 was developed. However, it would be unrealistic to claim that that model is absolutely accurate or complete, or even that it should be favoured over any other model which might be developed. The status of the model of Chapter 1 is therefore two-fold:

1. It is *a* model of the legal decision process, used in the elaboration of the Ph.D. thesis; and

2. it is *one possible* model of the legal decision process, which might be adopted by future builders of *Information Technology Applications in Law*, with or without modifications.

One claim which is made, however, is that *some* model is necessary for the construction of realistic Information Technology Applications in Law. This model must present the legal phenomenon in all its extent in the same way lawyers are taught and understand the practice of law in the law schools. The target should be to create an integrated legal sub-system that can support practical problem solving. The role of the model is to assist creators in understanding *where* automated systems can be used, of what *type* and with what *limitations*. It will further facilitate the identification of the limitations concerning the potential *users* and the *results*.

Applications developed without a model may be perfected in terms of computer science, but they will be far from perfect in terms of law. These applications, as the examples in this book show, will never produce legally acceptable and correct results.

EPILOGUE

One of the arguments of this book was that Information Technology can improve the legal informational system and finally, as a distant goal, can eliminate the 'crisis of information' for lawyers. Additionally, it could bring about an increase in productivity, as has already happened for many other professions. However, in order to achieve these targets, further research into *Information Technology Applications in Law* is needed, from the *theoretical*, the *practical*, but mainly the *realistic* point of view.

The *theoretical analysis* refers to the considerations as to whether such applications can be build, and to the specific theoretical hypotheses that permit such an implementation. This analysis predominated in the seventies[1] after the writings of the pioneers[2] in the field, BUCHANAN & HEADRICK.[3] MCCARTY'S TAXMAN projects[4] belong to this era. The *practical analysis* is reflected in the majority[5] of the projects of the eighties which tried to actually build such applications and

---

[1] For a detailed history of all expert systems projects see SUSSKIND R., *Expert Systems in Law: A Jurisprudential Approach to Artificial Intelligence and Legal Reasoning*, in ESSAYS ON LAW AND AI, COMPLEX 7/93, NRCCL, Oslo, 1993.

[2] See also note 2 in the *Prolegomenon*.

[3] BUCHANAN B. & HEADRICK TH., *Some Speculation About Artificial Intelligence and Legal Reasoning*, in STANFORD LAW REVIEW, Vol. 23, p. 40, November, 1970.

[4] See for example MCCARTY'S early writings for the TAXMAN I & II projects since MCCARTY L.T., *Reflections on TAXMAN: An Experiment in Artificial Intelligence and Legal Reasoning*, Harvard Law Review, 90, p. 837, 1977. In more recent article he leans toward more *practical* applications see MCCARTY L.T., *An Implementation of Eisner v Macomber*, in PROCEEDINGS OF THE 5ᵀᴴ INTERNATIONAL CONFERENCE ON ARTIFICIAL INTELLIGENCE AND LAW, University of Maryland, 21-24 May 1995, ACM Press, 1995, p. 276.

[5] Such as the Imperial College project. see SERGOT, CORY, HAMMOND, KOWALSKI, KRIWACZEC & SADRI, *Formalisation of the British Nationality Act*, in YEARBOOK OF LAW COMPUTERS AND TECHNOLOGY, Vol. 2, 1986, p.40.

evaluate their results. Finally, the *realistic analysis* examines whether these applications can be actually used in a working environment, which is what in SUSSKIND'S words was endeavoured with the expert system for the Latent Damage Act[6] "out of the research laboratory and into the marketplace". The final problem, however, is how to make the users *profit* from what they have bought in the marketplace. No matter how theoretically valid those practically implemented applications are, they will have no appeal to the legal practice if they are not *realistic*.

One of the reasons that such systems are not used is the very fact that they are not able to take decisions because much of the applicable law is 'missing'.[7] In the rare cases that they produce decisions, their value is minimal compared to the decisions that the user must make. In both cases all they do - and that was, for example, the job for the hypertext link in the N-A prototype - is to direct the user to texts, and ask him/her to make a decision based on those texts. This resembles the old motto, that the basic rival of electronic systems is the book, though it won't structure the presentation of texts so precisely toward the actual problem as an expert system will. Books, in the case of Lawyers, attain a high degree of authority. BING has emphasised that "[k]nowledge represented as texts written in natural language still has no alternative among the more recent methods of knowledge based systems. For the foreseeable future, people - and most certainly lawyers - will be working with text."[8] *As long as such applications cannot offer anything more than books, traditional professions - like lawyers - will not use them.*

ALLEN & SAXON similarly suggest that only "[w]hen expert systems come to be viewed as just another secondary source in the legal literature - ones that can be contradicted and qualified by primary sources and other secondary sources, ones that are given credence and weight by virtue of the quality of the ideas they express rather than the impressiveness of the computer that stores and processes them - then lawyers - users will, hopefully be less inclined to accept the results from such

---

6 SUSSKIND R., *The Latent Damage System: A Jurisprudential Analysis*, in PROCEEDINGS OF THE SECOND INTERNATIONAL CONFERENCE ON ARTIFICIAL INTELLIGENCE AND LAW, Vancouver, 1989.

7 See section 3.7.

8 BING J., *The Law of the Books and the Law of the Files, Possibilities and Problems of Legal Information Systems*, in VANDENBERGHE(Ed.), Kluwer, Computer/Law Series, 1989, p. 180.

systems uncritically."[9] And for the specific case of the Internet, WIDDISON argues that "[t]here are still generations of individuals who have grown up communicating and researching by means of the medium of paper...[s]uch people are disinclined to develop enthusiasm for the jump into 'cyberspace'. At this moment, however, a new generation is growing up for whom the screen is as natural a medium as the page".[10] The same argument can be adopted here: The *realistic analysis* on this level should attempt to identify in detail *who* should be the user of such systems and what should be expected from them. In that perspective, *Lawyer's Basic Instinct*, i.e. the intuitive qualification of lawyers to perform legal reasoning and justify their decisions, must be taken into account.

However, even if the question of the user profile is studied in depth, and users' attitudes change, *it will also be necessary to change the culture and working practice of law offices* (both of Lawyers and Judges). This practice is characterised, for what concerns this point, by two attitudes: (1) the most common behaviour, towards a given problem, is to consult experts who are readily available; and (2) law, unlike medicine, does not proceed so fast and decisions are not taken instantly. The plethora of experts in the legal professions, and the administration of justice in modern societies, can respectively be put forward as the reasons. Therefore, there is 'enough' time for the lawyers to consult books and experts, thus rejecting *Information Technology Applications in Law*, because, simply, there exist easily accessible alternative sources of expertise.

Therefore, the general attitude of *Information Technology Applications in Law* must be changed. ZELEZNIKOW ET AL., also trying to build an integrated system, state in their preamble that "our fundamental philosophy is that existing computer systems should not try to replace lawyers, but rather seek to improve their productivity. We believe it is at present unrealistic to build general purpose legal reasoning systems: we do not intend to create legal reasoning systems which take as input a given fact situation and, without reference to a human, generate the 'answer'. We prefer to restrict ourselves to building legal support tools in specific domains. Such an approach is consistent with modern Artificial Intelligence philosophy, which rejects the notion of constructing General Purpose Solvers in favour of building systems

---

[9] ALLEN L. & SAXON C., *Relationship of Expert Systems to the Operation of a Legal System*, in MARTINO (Ed.), North Holland, 1992, p. 55.

[10] WIDDISON R., *Lawyering in the Internet*, in WEB JOURNAL OF CURRENT LEGAL ISSUES, 1995.

that solve specific problems."[11]   A similar approach can be followed for this *realistic analysis*: *Applications should not attempt to replace skilled persons but should instead try to increase the productivity of skilled persons or to replace the relatively unskilled.* Reliable 'intelligent' assistants for specific tasks and domains will gradually gain the confidence of lawyers, as, for example, has been the case for computerised databases over manual library catalogues. This may be the profit[12] from *Information Technology Applications in Law*.

The proposed model is based on strict methodological rules in order to support this *realistic analysis*. However, further difficulties lie in the fact that in law many of the elements of the legal decision process, as was already mentioned for expert systems, can be found outside the text of the law or even outside the *stricto sensu* legal system. Even if these elements are identified, it is not possible to represent the subsumption of facts described in natural language under the descriptions of the law.[13]

It is evident that such problems will be augmented without the protective framework of the methodological rules as well as in the peripheral parts of the model, where the 'knowledge acquisition'[14] from the surrounding environment entails natural language communication. This is necessary because law is expressed in natural language and it does not lend itself to be translated exactly into a form which can be used directly in Information Technology Applications in Law. Thus, the user needs to be prepared to answer a number of legal decisions which derive from natural language and the nature of law. As long as research in natural language processing is not able to solve these problems, such applications cannot be fully automated. *Therefore, in the area of law, such applications will rely heavily on the decisions of the user and, it is much more realistic to try to support these decisions than try to produce them.* Or, in other words it may be concluded that

---

[11]   ZELEZNIKOW J., VOSSOS G. & HUNTER D., *The IKBALS project: Multi Modal Reasoning in Legal Knowledge Based Systems*, in ARTIFICIAL INTELLIGENCE AND LAW, vol. 2, No. 2, 1994, p. 170.

[12]   It should be noted that the notion of profit may differ for the *economics of law firms*. In that case there are two profitability levers: (1) attracting clients by reducing fees charged (=spending less time on a matter) and (2) increasing profitability (=spending less time but charging the same), which requires abandonment of charging fees primarily on a time spent basis. However, these factors are often calculated by law firms when a new automated system is to be introduced.

[13]   See 1.7.6 Reasoning with Rules and the Legal Syllogism and in 3.7.5 the decisions about the User Interface, and the whole N-A implementation, where this task was performed manually.

[14]   Here, in a broader sense, covering all applications - not only knowledge-based systems.

these *realistic applications* will be delimited to offer "intelligent assistance" to already "knowledgeable users".[15]

In contrast, focus to date has been on applications - especially expert systems - that take decisions. This book has shown that, although it is possible to build such applications in practical terms, this does not necessarily lead to *realistic* applications. Therefore, with the present tools, the best that can be achieved in the legal field is *decision support systems*. If the model described here is used as a 'checklist' for the 'minimum requirements', it can succeed in implementing these 'supportive' applications because: (1) It represents the full course of legal decision making; (2) it depicts the interconnections with other parts of the law as well as with other parts of the surrounding social environment; (3) it stays neutral to the prevailing legal theories; and (4) it follows a practical jurisprudential point of view.

Computers cannot, in the current state of art, replace Lawyers but they provide substantial support for Lawyers, and therefore, Lawyers must familiarise themselves with modern technology, and develop confidence in the computer applications they use. The model presented in this book shows clearly how such applications, including expert systems, should be created if they are to be functional, useful and widely adopted, in other words *Realistic Information Technology Applications in Law*.

---

[15] SUSSKIND R. & CAPPER P., *The Latent Damage System, A First Generation Expert System in Law*, in MARTINO (Ed.), North Holland, 1992, p. 317. See, however, the recent views of Susskind on the development of the 'latent legal market', in SUSSKIND R., *The Future of Law*, Clarendon Press, Oxford, 1996; see also the speculation of expanding the spectrum of the users *supra* Chapter 1, note 189.

APPENDIX I:
THE ILAM OUTPUT[1] IN ASCII FORMAT[2]

BLOCK
···· STRUCTURAL_VIEW
      [art([[7,-]]),num(633),tipo(dpr)]
···· SOURCE_TEXT
    [
law_ref(tipo(dpr),data(26,10,72),vigenza([_91719
| _91720],[_91721 | _91722],[_91723 |
_91724]),num(633),art([[7,-]]),comma([_91737 |
_91738]),lettera([_91741 | _91742]))
law_ref(tipo(dpr),data(26,10,1972),vigenza(1,1,1
982),num(633),art([[7,-]]),comma([_91775 |
_91776]),lettera([_91779 | _91780]))
title(phrase([istituzione,e,disciplina,dell',imposta,su
l,valore,aggiunto,.]))
art_object(phrase([territorialita',dell',imposta,.]))]

BLOCK
···· STRUCTURAL_VIEW
      [art([[7,-
]]),num(633),tipo(dpr),comma(1),period(1)]
···· SOURCE_TEXT

[si considera territorio dello stato quello
soggetto alla sua sovranita' , fatta eccezione dei
comuni di livigno , campione e delle acque nazionali
del lago di lugano delimitate dall'
law_ref(tipo(dpr),data(23,1,1973),vigenza(_9205
3,_92054,_92055),num(43),art([[2,-
]]),comma([4]),lettera(_92071))
.]
···· MICRO_STRUCTURE
   micro_crs
     def_ent_1
       def
         def_dum
           ssa
             [territorio dello stato]
         def_ens
           ssa
             [quello   soggetto   alla   sua
sovranita']
         exception

---

[1]   Courtesy of Orion S.A., Athens (Esprit Consortium).

[2]   This is the exact output that was handed to the research team in a 3½" diskette, formatted as
ASCII text.

[dei comuni di livigno , campione
e delle acque nazionali del lago di lugano delimitate
dall'
law_ref(tipo(dpr),data(23,1,1973),vigenza(_9219
1,_92192,_92193),num(43),art([[2,-
]]),comma([4]),lettera(_92209))
]
---- SSA_OUTPUT

   MICRO_SEGMENT_OUTPUT
   [micro_crs,def_ent_1,def,def_dum,ssa].
   SSA_INTERPRETATION · gn
     crc(conc(territorio : [1])
      rel(poss : di)
      conc(stato_nazione : [#,3]))
   MICRO_SEGMENT_OUTPUT
   [micro_crs,def_ent_1,def,def_ens,ssa].
   SSA_INTERPRETATION · gn
     crc(conc(soggetto_a : [2])
      rel(attr : (\ nil))
      conc([entita] : [quello,1]))
     crc(conc(soggetto_a : [2])
      rel(fsrc : a)
      conc(sovranita' : [#,{*},5]))
     crc(conc(sovranita' : [#,{*},5])
      rel(spec : (\ suo))
      conc([organo_stato] : [_92419]))

MICRO_SEGMENT_OUTPUT

[micro_crs,def_ent_1,def,def_ens,exception].
   SSA_INTERPRETATION · l_attr
[crc(conc(comune : [{*},2])
      rel(spec : di)
      conc(citta : [livigno,4]))
    OR
    crc(conc(comune : [{*},2])
      rel(spec : di)
      conc(citta : [campione,6]))]
OR
crc(conc(acqua_luogo : [#,{*},9])
      rel(attr : nil)
      conc(nazionale : [{*},10]))
   crc(conc(lago : [#,12])
      rel(part : di)
      conc(acqua_luogo : [#,{*},9]))

crc(conc(lago : [#,12])
   rel(spec : di)
   conc(citta : [lugano,14]))
crc(conc(delimitare : [15])
   rel(ptnt : ogg)
   conc(acqua_luogo : [#,{*},9]))
crc(conc(delimitare : [15])
   rel(agnt : da)
   conc(law_ref(...) : [#,{*},17]))

BLOCK
---- STRUCTURAL_VIEW
   [art([[7,-
]]),num(633),tipo(dpr),comma(2),period(1)]
---- SOURCE_TEXT
   [le cessioni di beni si considerano effettuate
nel territorio dello stato se hanno per oggetto beni
immobili ovvero beni mobili nazionali , nazionalizzati
o   vincolati   al
regime_della_temporanea_importazione esistenti
nel territorio stesso .]
---- MICRO_STRUCTURE
   micro_crs
     def_prop_1
      def_prop_focus
       [le cessioni di beni]
      def_property
       [effettuate nel territorio dello stato]
      condition
      cond
       [hanno per oggetto beni immobili
ovvero beni mobili nazionali , nazionalizzati o
vincolati   al
regime_della_temporanea_importazione esistenti
nel territorio stesso]
---- SSA_OUTPUT
MICRO_SEGMENT_OUTPUT
   [micro_crs,def_prop_1,def_prop_focus].
   SSA_INTERPRETATION · gn
     crc(conc(cessione : [#,{*},2])
      rel(obj : di)
      conc(bene : [{*},4]))
   MICRO_SEGMENT_OUTPUT
   [micro_crs,def_prop_1,def_property].
   SSA_INTERPRETATION · gv
     crc(conc(effettuare : [1])

```
              rel(loc : in)
              conc(territorio : [#,3]) )
         crc( conc(territorio : [#,3])
              rel(poss : di)
              conc(stato_nazione : [#,5]) )
MICRO_SEGMENT_OUTPUT
     [micro_crs,def_prop_1,condition,cond].

     SSA_INTERPRETATION - gv
[ crc( conc(graph:    crc( conc(avere : [1])
                          rel(obj : per)
                          conc(oggetto : [3]) )
          )
          rel(obj : ogg)
          conc(graph:        crc( conc(bene :
[{*},4])
                          rel(attr : nil)
                          conc(immobile_a      :
[{*},5]) )
          ) )
          OR
[ crc( conc(graph:    crc( conc(avere : [1])
                          rel(obj : per)
                          conc(oggetto : [3]) )
          )
          rel(obj : ogg)
          conc(graph:        crc( conc(bene :
[{*},7])
                          rel(attr : nil)
                          conc(mobile : [{*},8]) )
)
          ) )
          crc( conc(esistere : [16])
          rel(subj : sogg)
          conc(graph:        crc( conc(bene :
[{*},7])
                          rel(attr : nil)
                          conc(mobile : [{*},8]) )
)
          ) )
          crc( conc(esistere : [16])
          rel(loc : in)
          conc(territorio : [#,?,18]) )
AND
[ crc( conc(graph:    crc( conc(bene : [{*},7])
                          rel(attr : nil)
```

```
                          conc(mobile         :
[{*},8]) )
          )
          rel(attr : nil)
          conc(nazionale : [{*},9]) )
OR
crc( conc(graph:     crc( conc(bene : [{*},7])
                          rel(attr : nil)
                          conc(mobile         :
[{*},8]) )
          )
          rel(attr : nil)
          conc(nazionalizzato : [{*},11]) )
OR
crc( conc(vincolare : [13])
          rel(ptnt : ogg)
          conc(graph:        crc( conc(bene :
[{*},7])
                          rel(attr : nil)
                          conc(mobile         :
[{*},8]) )
          ) )
          crc( conc(vincolare : [13])
          rel(fdst : a)

conc(regime_di_temporanea_importazione     :
[#,15]) )
     ] ] ]

BLOCK
---- STRUCTURAL_VIEW
          [art([[7,-
]]),num(633),tipo(dpr),comma(3),period(1)]
---- SOURCE_TEXT
     [le prestazioni di servizi si considerano
effettuate nel territorio dello stato quando sono
rese da soggetti che hanno il domicilio nel territorio
stesso o da soggetti ivi residenti che non abbiano
stabilito il domicilio all' estero , nonche' quando
sono rese da stabili organizzazioni in italia di
soggetti domiciliati e residenti all' estero ; non si
considerano effettuate nel territorio dello stato
quando sono rese da stabili organizzazioni all'
estero di soggetti domiciliati o residenti in italia . ]
---- MICRO_STRUCTURE
     micro_crs
```

265

```
            def_prop_1
              def_prop_focus
              [le prestazioni di servizi ]

              def_property
              [effettuate nel territorio dello stato ]
              condition
                cond_or
                  cond
                      [sono rese da soggetti che hanno
il domicilio nel territorio stesso o da soggetti ivi
residenti che non abbiano stabilito il domicilio all'
estero , ]
                  cond
                      [sono      rese      da     stabili
organizzazioni in italia di soggetti domiciliati e
residenti all' estero ]
              extension_def
                def_prop_focus
                neg
                          [effettuate  nel  territorio
dello stato ]
                condition
                  cond
                      [sono     rese     da     stabili
organizzazioni all' estero di soggetti domiciliati o
residenti in italia ]
---- SSA_OUTPUT
MICRO_SEGMENT_OUTPUT
    [micro_crs,def_prop_1,def_prop_focus].
      SSA_INTERPRETATION · gn
       crc( conc(prestazione : [#,{*},2])
          rel(obj : di)
          conc(servizio : [{*},4]) )
    MICRO_SEGMENT_OUTPUT
    [micro_crs,def_prop_1,def_property].
      SSA_INTERPRETATION · gv
       crc( conc(effettuare : [1])
          rel(loc : in)
          conc(territorio : [#,3]) )
       crc( conc(territorio : [#,3])
          rel(poss : di)
          conc(stato_nazione : [#,5]) )
MICRO_SEGMENT_OUTPUT

[micro_crs,def_prop_1,condition,cond_or,cond].
```

```
      SSA_INTERPRETATION · gv
[
      [ crc( conc(rendere_fornire : [2])
          rel(agnt : da)
          conc(soggetto_n : [{*},4]) )
AND
crc( conc(avere : [6])
          rel(subj : sogg)
          conc(soggetto_n : [{*},4]) )
       crc( conc(avere : [6])
          rel(obj : ogg)
          conc(domicilio : [#,8]) )
       crc( conc(domicilio : [#,8])
          rel(loc : in)
          conc(territorio : [#,?,10]) )
]
       OR
[ crc( conc(rendere_fornire : [2])
          rel(agnt : da)
          conc(soggetto_n : [{*},14]) )
       crc( conc(risiedere : [16])
          rel(subj : sogg)
          conc(soggetto_n : [{*},14]) )
       crc( conc(risiedere : [16])
          rel(loc : ( \ ivi))

conc([luoghi_generici,luoghi_giuridici_di_diritto_pu
bblico,organo_stato] : [_94608]) )
AND
crc( conc(graph:neg( crc( conc(stabilire : [20])
                      rel(obj : ogg)
                      conc(domicilio : [#,22])
)
                              crc(    conc(domicilio  :
[#,22])
                      rel(loc : a)
                      conc(estero : [#,24]) )
))
          rel(subj : sogg)
          conc(soggetto_n : [{*},14]) ) ] ]
    MICRO_SEGMENT_OUTPUT

[micro_crs,def_prop_1,condition,cond_or,cond].
      SSA_INTERPRETATION · gv
[ crc( conc(rendere_fornire : [2])
          rel(agnt : da)
```

```
                conc(organizzazione : [{*},5]) )
        crc( conc(organizzazione : [{*},5])
            rel(attr : nil)
            conc(stabile_a : [{*},4]) )
        crc( conc(organizzazione : [{*},5])
            rel(loc : in)
            conc(italia : [7]) )
        crc( conc(organizzazione : [{*},5])
            rel(part : di)
            conc(soggetto_n : [{*},9]) )
AND
[ crc( conc(domiciliare : [10])
            rel(subj : sogg)
            conc(soggetto_n : [{*},9]) )
        crc( conc(domiciliare : [10])
            rel(loc : a)
            conc(estero : [#,14]) )
OR
crc( conc(risiedere : [12])
            rel(subj : sogg)
            conc(soggetto_n : [{*},9]) )
        crc( conc(risiedere : [12])
            rel(loc : a)
            conc(estero : [#,14]) )
  ] ]
     MICRO_SEGMENT_OUTPUT
     [micro_crs,def_prop_1,extension_def,neg].
     SSA_INTERPRETATION · gv
        crc( conc(effettuare : [1])
            rel(loc : in)
            conc(territorio : [#,3]) )
        crc( conc(territorio : [#,3])
            rel(poss : di)
            conc(stato_nazione : [#,5]) )
MICRO_SEGMENT_OUTPUT

[micro_crs,def_prop_1,extension_def,condition,co
nd].
     SSA_INTERPRETATION · gv
[ crc( conc(rendere_fornire : [2])
            rel(agnt : da)
            conc(organizzazione : [{*},5]) )
        crc( conc(organizzazione : [{*},5])
            rel(attr : nil)
            conc(stabile_a : [{*},4]) )
        crc( conc(organizzazione : [{*},5])
```

```
            rel(loc : a)
            conc(estero : [#,7]) )
        crc( conc(organizzazione : [{*},5])
            rel(part : di)
            conc(soggetto_n : [{*},9]) )
AND
[ crc( conc(domiciliare : [10])
            rel(subj : sogg)
            conc(soggetto_n : [{*},9]) )
        crc( conc(domiciliare : [10])
            rel(loc : in)
            conc(italia : [14]) )
OR
crc( conc(risiedere : [12])
            rel(subj : sogg)
            conc(soggetto_n : [{*},9]) )
        crc( conc(risiedere : [12])
            rel(loc : in)
            conc(italia : [14]) )
  ] ]


BLOCK
---- STRUCTURAL_VIEW
        [art([[7,-
]]),num(633),tipo(dpr),comma(3),period(2)]
---- SOURCE_TEXT
        [per i soggetti diversi_dalle persone fisiche ,
agli effetti del
law_ref(tipo(dpr),data(_95489,_95490,_95491),
vigenza(_95493,_95494,_95495),num(633),art([[
7,-]]),comma(_95507),lettera(_95509))
, si considera domicilio il luogo in cui si trova la
sede legale e residenza quello in cui si trova la sede
effettiva . ]
---- MICRO_STRUCTURE
        micro_crs
            def_ent_1
                def_scope
                    scope_focus
                        [per i soggetti diversi_dalle persone
fisiche ]
                    scope_range
                        [
law_ref(tipo(dpr),data(_95631,_95632,_95633),
vigenza(_95635,_95636,_95637),num(633),art([[
7,-]]),comma(_95649),lettera(_95651))
```

267

```
]
        def
          def_dum
            ssa
              [domicilio ]
          def_ens
            ssa
              [il luogo in cui si trova la sede
legale ]
          def
            def_dum
              ssa
                [residenza ]
            def_ens
              ssa
                [quello in cui si trova la sede
effettiva ]
···· SSA_OUTPUT
MICRO_SEGMENT_OUTPUT

[micro_crs,def_ent_1,def_scope,scope_focus].
      SSA_INTERPRETATION - gn
          crc( conc(soggetto_n : [#,{*},3])
            rel(-eq : diverso_da)
            conc(persona : [#,{*},5]) )
          crc( conc(persona : [#,{*},5])
            rel(attr : nil)
            conc(fisico : [{*},6]) )
      MICRO_SEGMENT_OUTPUT

[micro_crs,def_ent_1,def_scope,scope_range].
      SSA_INTERPRETATION - gn
          conc(law_ref(...) : [{*},1])
      MICRO_SEGMENT_OUTPUT
        [micro_crs,def_ent_1,def,def_dum,ssa].
      SSA_INTERPRETATION - gn
          conc(domicilio : [1])
      MICRO_SEGMENT_OUTPUT
        [micro_crs,def_ent_1,def,def_ens,ssa].
      SSA_INTERPRETATION - gn
[ conc(luogo : [#,2])
AND
crc( conc(trovarsi : [6])
            rel(loc : in)
            conc(luogo : [#,2]) )
          crc( conc(trovarsi : [6])
```

```
            rel(subj : sogg)
            conc(sede : [#,8]) )
          crc( conc(sede : [#,8])
            rel(attr : nil)
            conc(legale_a : [9]) )
]
      MICRO_SEGMENT_OUTPUT

[micro_crs,def_ent_1,def,def,def_dum,ssa].
      SSA_INTERPRETATION - gn
          conc(residenza : [1])
      MICRO_SEGMENT_OUTPUT
        [micro_crs,def_ent_1,def,def,def_ens,ssa].
      SSA_INTERPRETATION - gn
[ conc(quello : [1])
AND
crc( conc([luoghi] : [quello,1])
            rel(loc : ( \ in))
            conc(trovarsi : [5]) )
          crc( conc(trovarsi : [5])
            rel(subj : sogg)
            conc(sede : [#,7]) )
          crc( conc(sede : [#,7])
            rel(attr : nil)
            conc(effettivo : [8]) )
]

BLOCK
···· STRUCTURAL_VIEW
          [art([[7,·
]]),num(633),tipo(dpr),comma(4),stru_comma(head)
]
···· SOURCE_TEXT
          [in deroga al
law_ref(tipo(dpr),data(_96323,_96324,_96325),
vigenza(_96327,_96328,_96329),num(633),art([[
7,·]]),comma([3]),lettera(_96345))
]

BLOCK
···· STRUCTURAL_VIEW
          [art([[7,·
]]),num(633),tipo(dpr),comma(4),letter(a),stru_com
ma(item),item_period(1)]
···· SOURCE_TEXT_HEAD
          [in deroga al
```

268

law_ref(tipo(dpr),data(_96639,_96640,_96641),
vigenza(_96643,_96644,_96645),num(633),art([[
7,-]]),comma([3]),lettera(_96661)))]
---- SOURCE_TEXT
  [le prestazioni di servizi relativi a beni immobili , comprese le perizie , le prestazioni di agenzia e le prestazioni inerenti alla preparazione e al coordinamento dell' esecuzione dei lavori immobiliari , si considerano effettuate nel territorio dello stato quando l' immobile e' situato nel territorio stesso]
---- MICRO_STRUCTURE
  micro_crs
   def_prop_1
    def_prop_focus
     [le prestazioni di servizi relativi a beni immobili , comprese le perizie , le prestazioni di agenzia e le prestazioni inerenti alla preparazione e al coordinamento dell' esecuzione dei lavori immobiliari ,]
    def_property
     [effettuate nel territorio dello stato]
    condition
     cond
      [l' immobile e' situato nel territorio stesso]
---- SSA_OUTPUT
  MICRO_SEGMENT_OUTPUT
  [micro_crs,def_prop_1,def_prop_focus].
  SSA_INTERPRETATION - gn
   [crc(conc(prestazione : [#,{*},2])
    rel(obj : di)
    conc(servizio : [{*},4]))
   crc(conc(servizio : [{*},4])
    rel(attr : nil)
    conc(relativo : [{*},5]))
   crc(conc(relativo : [{*},5])
    rel(fsrc : a)
    conc(graph: crc(conc(bene :
[{*},7])
      rel(attr : nil)
      conc(immobile_a :
[{*},8]))
))
   crc(conc(prestazione : [#,{*},2])

rel(psxt : compreso)
conc(perizia : [#,{*},12]))
OR
  crc(conc(prestazione : [#,{*},2])
   rel(obj : di)
   conc(servizio : [{*},4]))
  crc(conc(servizio : [{*},4])
   rel(attr : nil)
   conc(relativo : [{*},5]))
  crc(conc(relativo : [{*},5])
   rel(fsrc : a)
   conc(graph: crc(conc(bene :
[{*},7])
     rel(attr : nil)
     conc(immobile_a :
[{*},8]))
))
  crc(conc(prestazione : [#,{*},2])
   rel(psxt : compreso)
   conc(prestazione : [#,{*},15]))
  crc(conc(prestazione : [#,{*},15])
   rel(obj : di)
   conc(agenzia : [17]))
OR
[crc(conc(prestazione : [#,{*},2])
   rel(obj : di)
   conc(servizio : [{*},4]))
  crc(conc(servizio : [{*},4])
   rel(attr : nil)
   conc(relativo : [{*},5]))
  crc(conc(relativo : [{*},5])
   rel(fsrc : a)
   conc(graph: crc(conc(bene :
[{*},7])
     rel(attr : nil)
     conc(immobile_a :
[{*},8]))
))
  crc(conc(prestazione : [#,{*},2])
   rel(psxt : compreso)
   conc(prestazione : [#,{*},20]))
  crc(conc(prestazione : [#,{*},20])
   rel(attr : nil)
   conc(inerente : [{*},21]))
AND
[crc(conc(inerente : [{*},21])

269

```
            rel(fsrc : a)
            conc(preparazione : [#,23]) )
        crc( conc(preparazione : [#,23])
            rel(obj : di)
            conc(esecuzione : [#,28]) )
        crc( conc(esecuzione : [#,28])
            rel(obj : di)
            conc(lavoro : [#,{*},30]) )
        crc( conc(lavoro : [#,{*},30])
            rel(attr : nil)
            conc(immobiliare : [{*},31]) )
OR
crc( conc(inerente : [{*},21])
            rel(fsrc : a)
            conc(coordinamento : [#,26]) )
        crc( conc(coordinamento : [#,26])
            rel(obj : di)
            conc(esecuzione : [#,28]) )
        crc( conc(esecuzione : [#,28])
            rel(obj : di)
            conc(lavoro : [#,{*},30]) )
        crc( conc(lavoro : [#,{*},30])
            rel(attr : nil)
            conc(immobiliare : [{*},31]) )
] ] ]
    MICRO_SEGMENT_OUTPUT
    [micro_crs,def_prop_1,def_property].
    SSA_INTERPRETATION - gv
        crc( conc(effettuare : [1])
            rel(loc : in)
            conc(territorio : [#,3]) )
        crc( conc(territorio : [#,3])
            rel(poss : di)
            conc(stato_nazione : [#,5]) )
MICRO_SEGMENT_OUTPUT
[micro_crs,def_prop_1,condition,cond].
SSA_INTERPRETATION - frase
    crc( conc(situare : [4])
        rel(subj : sogg)
        conc(immobile_n : [#,2]) )
    crc( conc(situare : [4])
        rel(loc : in)
        conc(territorio : [#,?,6]) )

BLOCK
···· STRUCTURAL_VIEW
```

```
            [art([[7,·
]]),num(633),tipo(dpr),comma(4),letter(b),stru_com
ma(item),item_period(1)]
···· SOURCE_TEXT_HEAD
    [in deroga al
law_ref(tipo(dpr),data(_98091,_98092,_98093),
vigenza(_98095,_98096,_98097),num(633),art([[
7,·]]),comma([3]),lettera(_98113))
]
···· SOURCE_TEXT
    [le prestazioni di servizi , comprese le perizie ,
relative a beni mobili materiali e le prestazioni di
servizi culturali , scientifici , artistici , didattici ,
sportivi , ricreativi e simili , nonche' le operazioni di
carico , scarico , manutenzione e simili , accessorie
ai trasporti di beni , si considerano effettuate nel
territorio dello stato quando sono eseguite nel
territorio stesso ]
···· MICRO_STRUCTURE
    micro_crs
        def_prop_1
            def_prop_focus
                [le prestazioni di servizi , comprese le
perizie , relative a beni mobili materiali e le
prestazioni di servizi culturali , scientifici , artistici
, didattici , sportivi , ricreativi e simili , nonche' le
operazioni di carico , scarico , manutenzione e
simili , accessorie ai trasporti di beni , ]
            def_property
                [effettuate nel territorio dello stato ]
            condition
                cond
                    [sono eseguite nel territorio stesso ]
···· SSA_OUTPUT
MICRO_SEGMENT_OUTPUT
    [micro_crs,def_prop_1,def_prop_focus].
    SSA_INTERPRETATION - gn
        crc( conc(prestazione : [#,{*},2])
            rel(obj : di)
            conc(servizio : [{*},4]) )
        crc( conc(prestazione : [#,{*},2])
            rel(psxt : compreso)
            conc(perizia : [#,{*},8]) )
        crc( conc(prestazione : [#,{*},2])
            rel(attr : nil)
            conc(relativo : [{*},10]) )
```

```
         crc( conc(relativo : [{*},10])
              rel(fsrc : a)
              conc(graph:        crc( conc(bene :
[{*},12])
                              rel(attr : nil)
                              conc(mobile : [{*},13]) )
                    ) )
         crc( conc(graph:        crc( conc(bene :
[{*},12])
                              rel(attr : nil)
                              conc(mobile : [{*},13]) )
                    )
              rel(attr : nil)
              conc(materiale_a : [{*},14]) )
OR
[ crc( conc(prestazione : [#,{*},17])
            rel(obj : di)
            conc(servizio : [{*},19]) )
AND
[ crc( conc(servizio : [{*},19])
            rel(attr : nil)
            conc(culturale : [{*},20]) )
OR
crc( conc(servizio : [{*},19])
            rel(attr : nil)
            conc(scientifico : [{*},22]) )
OR
crc( conc(servizio : [{*},19])
            rel(attr : nil)
            conc(artistico : [{*},24]) )
OR
crc( conc(servizio : [{*},19])
            rel(attr : nil)
            conc(didattico : [{*},26]) )
OR

            crc( conc(servizio : [{*},19])
            rel(attr : nil)
            conc(sportivo : [{*},28]) )
OR
crc( conc(servizio : [{*},19])
            rel(attr : nil)
            conc(ricreativo : [{*},30]) )
OR
SIMILE ] ]
OR
```

```
[ crc( conc(operazione : [#,{*},36])
            rel(attr : nil)
            conc(accessorio : [{*},46]) )
    crc( conc(accessorio : [{*},46])
            rel(fsrc : a)
            conc(trasporto : [#,{*},48]) )
    crc( conc(trasporto : [#,{*},48])
            rel(obj : di)
            conc(bene : [{*},50]) )
AND
[ crc( conc(operazione : [#,{*},36])
            rel(obj : di)
            conc(carico_caricare : [38]) )
        OR
crc( conc(operazione : [#,{*},36])
            rel(obj : di)
            conc(scarico : [40]) )
OR
crc( conc(operazione : [#,{*},36])
            rel(obj : di)
            conc(manutenzione : [42]) )
OR
SIMILE ] ]
    MICRO_SEGMENT_OUTPUT
    [micro_crs,def_prop_1,def_property].
    SSA_INTERPRETATION - gv
        crc( conc(effettuare : [1])
            rel(loc : in)
            conc(territorio : [#,3]) )
        crc( conc(territorio : [#,3])
            rel(poss : di)
            conc(stato_nazione : [#,5]) )
MICRO_SEGMENT_OUTPUT
    [micro_crs,def_prop_1,condition,cond].
    SSA_INTERPRETATION - gv
        crc( conc(eseguire : [2])
            rel(loc : in)
            conc(territorio : [#,?,4]) )

BLOCK
---- STRUCTURAL_VIEW
        [art([[7,-
]]),num(633),tipo(dpr),comma(4),letter©,stru_com
ma(item),item_period(1)]
---- SOURCE_TEXT_HEAD
        [in deroga al
```

271

law_ref(tipo(dpr),data(_99359,_99360,_99361),
vigenza(_99363,_99364,_99365),num(633),art([[
7,-]]),comma([3]),lettera(_99381))
]
---- SOURCE_TEXT
[le prestazioni di trasporto si considerano
effettuate nel territorio dello stato in proporzione
alla distanza ivi percorsa]
---- MICRO_STRUCTURE
    micro_crs
        def_prop_2
            def_prop_focus
                [le prestazioni di trasporto]
            def_prop
                history
                    [effettuate nel territorio dello stato]
                condition
                    [distanza ivi percorsa]
---- SSA_OUTPUT
MICRO_SEGMENT_OUTPUT
    [micro_crs,def_prop_2,def_prop_focus].
    SSA_INTERPRETATION - gn
        crc(conc(prestazione : [#,{*},2])
            rel(obj : di)
            conc(trasporto : [4]))
    MICRO_SEGMENT_OUTPUT
    [micro_crs,def_prop_2,def_prop,history].
    SSA_INTERPRETATION - gv
        crc(conc(effettuare : [1])
            rel(loc : in)
            conc(territorio : [#,3]))
        crc(conc(territorio : [#,3])
            rel(poss : di)
            conc(stato_nazione : [#,5]))
    MICRO_SEGMENT_OUTPUT
    [micro_crs,def_prop_2,condition].
    SSA_INTERPRETATION - gn
        crc(conc(percorrere : [3])
            rel(obj : ogg)
            conc(distanza : [1]))
        crc(conc(percorrere : [3])
            rel(loc : ivi)
            conc([luoghi] : [_2CBC]))

BLOCK
---- STRUCTURAL_VIEW

272

[art([[7,-
]]),num(633),tipo(dpr),comma(4),letter(d),stru_com
ma(item),item_period(1)]
---- SOURCE_TEXT_HEAD
    [in deroga al
law_ref(tipo(dpr),data(_99871,_99872,_99873),
vigenza(_99875,_99876,_99877),num(633),art([[
7,-]]),comma([3]),lettera(_99893))
]
---- SOURCE_TEXT
    [le prestazioni derivanti da contratti di
locazione , noleggio e simili di beni mobili materiali
diversi dai mezzi di trasporto si considerano
effettuate nel territorio dello stato quando il bene
che ne forma oggetto e' utilizzato nel territorio
stesso]
---- MICRO_STRUCTURE
    micro_crs
        def_prop_1
            def_prop_focus
                [le prestazioni derivanti da contratti di
locazione , noleggio e simili di beni mobili materiali
diversi_dai mezzi di trasporto]

        def_property
            [effettuate nel territorio dello stato]
            condition
                cond
                    [il bene che ne forma oggetto e'
utilizzato nel territorio stesso]
---- SSA_OUTPUT
    MICRO_SEGMENT_OUTPUT
    [micro_crs,def_prop_1,def_prop_focus].
    SSA_INTERPRETATION - gn
        [crc(conc(derivare : [3])
            rel(subj : sogg)
            conc(prestazione : [#,{*},2]))
        crc(conc(derivare : [3])
            rel(fsrc : da)
            conc(contratto : [{*},5]))
        AND
        [crc(conc(contratto : [{*},5])
            rel(obj : di)
            conc(locazione : [7]))
        crc(conc(locazione : [7])

```
                    rel(obj : di)
                  conc(bene_n : [{*},13]) )
            crc( conc(bene_n : [{*},13])
                  rel(attr : nil)
                  conc(mobile : [{*},14]) )
            crc( conc(bene_n : [{*},13])
                  rel(attr : nil)
                  conc(materiale_a : [{*},15]) )
            crc( conc(bene_n : [{*},13])
                  rel(-eq : diverso_da)
                  conc(mezzo : [#,{*},17]) )
            crc( conc(mezzo : [#,{*},17])
                  rel(use : di)
                  conc(trasporto : [19]) )
                        OR
                        crc(  conc(contratto  :
[{*},5])
                  rel(obj : di)
                  conc(noleggio : [9]) )
            crc( conc(noleggio : [9])
                  rel(obj : di)
                  conc(bene_n : [{*},13]) )
            crc( conc(bene_n : [{*},13])
                  rel(attr : nil)
                  conc(mobile : [{*},14]) )
            crc( conc(bene_n : [{*},13])
                  rel(attr : nil)
                  conc(materiale_a : [{*},15]) )
            crc( conc(bene_n : [{*},13])
                  rel(-eq : diverso_da)
                  conc(mezzo : [#,{*},17]) )
            crc( conc(mezzo : [#,{*},17])
                  rel(use : di)
                  conc(trasporto : [19]) )
                        OR
                        SIMILE ] ]


MICRO_SEGMENT_OUTPUT
  [micro_crs,def_prop_1,def_property].
  SSA_INTERPRETATION - gv
    crc( conc(effettuare : [1])
          rel(loc : in)
          conc(territorio : [#,3]) )
    crc( conc(territorio : [#,3])
          rel(poss : di)
          conc(stato_nazione : [#,5]) )
```

```
MICRO_SEGMENT_OUTPUT
  [micro_crs,def_prop_1,condition,cond].
    SSA_INTERPRETATION - frase
[ crc( conc(utilizzare : [8])
          rel(obj : ogg)
          conc(bene : [#,2]) )
    crc( conc(utilizzare : [8])
          rel(loc : in)
          conc(territorio : [#,?,10]) )
AND
    crc( conc(formare : [5])
          rel(subj : sogg)
          conc(bene : [#,2]) )
    crc( conc(formare : [5])
          rel(fsrc : ( \ ne))
          conc([attivita_servizi] : [_100258]) )
    crc( conc(formare : [5])
          rel(obj : ogg)
          conc(oggetto : [6]) )

]
BLOCK
---- STRUCTURAL_VIEW
      [art([[7,-
]]),num(633),tipo(dpr),comma(4),letter(e),stru_com
ma(item),item_period(1)]
---- SOURCE_TEXT_HEAD
      [in deroga al
law_ref(tipo(dpr),data(_100729,_100730,_1007
31),vigenza(_100733,_100734,_100735),num(6
33),art([[7,-]]),comma([3]),lettera(_100751))]
---- SOURCE_TEXT
      [le prestazioni di servizi indicate_al
law_ref(tipo(dpr),data(_100452,_100453,_1004
54),vigenza(_100456,_100457,_100458),num(6
33),art([[3,-]]),comma(_100470),lettera([2,sing]))
```

, le prestazioni pubblicitarie , di consulenza tecnica o legale , di elaborazione e fornitura di dati e simili , le prestazioni relative ad operazioni bancarie , finanziarie e assicurative e quelle relative a prestiti di personale , nonche' le prestazioni di intermediazione inerenti alle suddette prestazioni e quelle inerenti all' obbligo di non esercitarle , si considerano effettuate nel territorio dello stato quando sono rese a soggetti domiciliati nel territorio stesso o a soggetti ivi residenti che non abbiano stabilito il domicilio all' estero e quando

273

sono rese a stabili organizzazioni in italia di soggetti domiciliati e residenti all' estero , a meno che non siano utilizzate fuori_della c_e_e]
---- MICRO_STRUCTURE
    micro_crs
        def_prop_1
            def_prop_focus
                [le prestazioni di servizi indicate_al law_ref(tipo(dpr),data(_100798,_100799,_1008 00),vigenza(_100802,_100803,_100804),num(6 33),art([[3,-]]),comma(_100816),lettera([2,sing])) , le prestazioni pubblicitarie , di consulenza tecnica o legale , di elaborazione e fornitura di dati e simili , le prestazioni relative ad operazioni bancarie , finanziarie e assicurative e quelle relative a prestiti di personale , nonche' le prestazioni di intermediazione inerenti alle suddette prestazioni e quelle inerenti all' obbligo di non esercitarle ,]
            def_property
                [effettuate nel territorio dello stato]
            condition
                cond_or
                    cond
                        [sono rese a soggetti domiciliati nel territorio stesso o a soggetti ivi residenti che non abbiano stabilito il domicilio all' estero]
                    cond
                        [sono rese a stabili organizzazioni in italia di soggetti domiciliati e residenti all' estero]
                cond_exception
                    [non siano utilizzate fuori_della c_e_e]
---- SSA_OUTPUT
MICRO_SEGMENT_OUTPUT
    [micro_crs,def_prop_1,def_prop_focus].
    SSA_INTERPRETATION · gn
        crc(conc(prestazione : [#,{*},2])
            rel(obj : di)
            conc(servizio : [{*},4]))
        crc(conc(prestazione : [#,{*},2])
            rel(spec : indicato_a)
            conc(law_ref(...) : [#,{*},6]))
OR
[crc(conc(prestazione : [#,{*},9])
        rel(attr : nil)

conc(pubblicitario : [{*},10]))
    OR
[crc(conc(prestazione : [#,{*},9])
        rel(obj : di)
        conc(consulenza : [13]))
AND
[crc(conc(consulenza : [13])
        rel(attr : nil)
        conc(tecnico : [14]))
OR
crc(conc(consulenza : [13])
        rel(attr : nil)
        conc(legale_a : [16]))]]
OR
crc(conc(prestazione : [#,{*},9])
        rel(obj : di)
        conc(elaborazione : [19]))
crc(conc(elaborazione : [19])
        rel(obj : di)
        conc(dato : [{*},23]))
OR
crc(conc(prestazione : [#,{*},9])
        rel(obj : di)
        conc(fornitura : [21]))
crc(conc(fornitura : [21])
        rel(obj : di)
        conc(dato : [{*},23]))
OR
SIMILE]
OR
[crc(conc(prestazione : [#,{*},28])
        rel(attr : nil)
        conc(relativo : [{*},29]))
crc(conc(relativo : [{*},29])
        rel(fsrc : a)
        conc(operazione : [{*},31]))
AND
[crc(conc(operazione : [{*},31])
        rel(attr : nil)
        conc(bancario : [{*},32]))
OR
crc(conc(operazione : [{*},31])
        rel(attr : nil)
        conc(finanziario : [{*},34]))
OR
crc(conc(operazione : [{*},31])

```
                    rel(attr : nil)
                    conc(assicurativo : [{*},36]) ) ] ]
OR
crc( conc(prestazione : [#,{*},38])
            rel(attr : nil)
            conc(relativo : [{*},39]) )
        crc( conc(relativo : [{*},39])
            rel(fsrc : a)
            conc(prestito : [{*},41]) )
        crc( conc(prestito : [{*},41])
            rel(rcpt : di)
            conc(personale : [43]) )
OR
crc( conc(prestazione : [#,{*},47])
            rel(obj : di)
            conc(intermediazione : [49]) )
        crc( conc(prestazione : [#,{*},47])
            rel(attr : nil)
            conc(inerente : [{*},50]) )
        crc( conc(inerente : [{*},50])
            rel(fsrc : a)
            conc(prestazione : [#,?,{*},53]) )
OR
crc( conc(prestazione : [#,{*},55])
            rel(attr : nil)
            conc(inerente : [{*},56]) )
        crc( conc(inerente : [{*},56])
            rel(fsrc : a)
            conc(prescrizione : [#,obbligo,58]) )
        crc( conc(prescrizione : [#,obbligo,58])
            rel(obj : di)
            conc(graph:neg( crc( conc(esercitare :
[61])
                        rel(obj : ( \ lo))
                        conc(\([attivita_servizi]  :
[_101992],[f])) )
                    )) )
MICRO_SEGMENT_OUTPUT
    [micro_crs,def_prop_1,def_property].
    SSA_INTERPRETATION · gv
        crc( conc(effettuare : [1])
            rel(loc : in)
            conc(territorio : [#,3]) )
        crc( conc(territorio : [#,3])
            rel(poss : di)
            conc(stato_nazione : [#,5]) )
```

```
MICRO_SEGMENT_OUTPUT

[micro_crs,def_prop_1,condition,cond_or,cond].
    SSA_INTERPRETATION · gv
[ crc( conc(rendere_fornire : [2])
            rel(rcpt : a)
            conc(soggetto_n : [{*},4]) )
        crc( conc(domiciliare : [5])
            rel(subj : sogg)
            conc(soggetto_n : [{*},4]) )
        crc( conc(domiciliare : [5])
            rel(loc : in)
            conc(territorio : [#,?,7]) )
OR
[ crc( conc(rendere_fornire : [2])
            rel(rcpt : a)
            conc(soggetto_n : [{*},11]) )
        crc( conc(risiedere : [13])
            rel(subj : sogg)
            conc(soggetto_n : [{*},11]) )
        crc( conc(risiedere : [13])
            rel(loc : ( \ ivi))

conc([luoghi_generici,luoghi_giuridici_di_diritto_pu
bblico,organo_stato] : [_102311]) )
AND
crc( conc(graph:neg( crc( conc(stabilire : [17])
            rel(obj : ogg)
            conc(domicilio : [#,19])
)
                            crc(    conc(domicilio  :
[#,19])
                        rel(loc : a)
                        conc(estero : [#,21]) )
))
                    rel(subj : sogg)
                    conc(soggetto_n : [{*},11]) ) ] ]
    MICRO_SEGMENT_OUTPUT

[micro_crs,def_prop_1,condition,cond_or,cond].
    SSA_INTERPRETATION · gv
[ crc( conc(rendere_fornire : [2])
            rel(rcpt : a)
            conc(organizzazione : [{*},5]) )
        crc( conc(organizzazione : [{*},5])
            rel(attr : nil)
```

275

```
            conc(stabile_a : [{*},4]) )
crc( conc(organizzazione : [{*},5])
        rel(loc : in)
        conc(italia : [7]) )


crc( conc(organizzazione : [{*},5])
        rel(part : di)
        conc(soggetto_n : [{*},9]) )
AND
[ crc( conc(domiciliare : [10])
        rel(subj : sogg)
            conc(soggetto_n : [{*},9]) )
    crc( conc(domiciliare : [10])
        rel(loc : a)
        conc(estero : [#,14]) )
OR
crc( conc(risiedere : [12])
        rel(subj : sogg)
        conc(soggetto_n : [{*},9]) )
    crc( conc(risiedere : [12])
        rel(loc : a)
        conc(estero : [#,14]) )
] ]
    MICRO_SEGMENT_OUTPUT

[micro_crs,def_prop_1,condition,cond_exception].
    SSA_INTERPRETATION · gv
    neg(        crc( conc(utilizzare : [3])
            rel(loc : fuori_di)
            conc(c_e_e : [#,{*},5]) )

BLOCK
---- STRUCTURAL_VIEW
        [art([[7,-
]]),num(633),tipo(dpr),comma(4),letter(f),stru_com
ma(item),item_period(1)]
---- SOURCE_TEXT_HEAD
        [in deroga al
law_ref(tipo(dpr),data(_103036,_103037,_1030
38),vigenza(_103040,_103041,_103042),num(6
33),art([[7,-]]),comma([3]),lettera(_103058))
]
---- SOURCE_TEXT
        [le prestazioni di servizi di_cui_alla
```

```
law_ref(tipo(dpr),data(_102903,_102904,_1029
05),vigenza(_102907,_102908,_102909),num(6
33),art([[7,-]]),comma(4),lettera([e]))
rese a soggetti domiciliati o residenti in altri stati
membri della c_e_e , si considerano effettuate nel
territorio dello stato quando il destinatario non e'
soggetto passivo dell' imposta nello stato in cui ha
il domicilio o la residenza ]
---- MICRO_STRUCTURE
    micro_crs
        def_prop_1
            def_prop_focus
                [le prestazioni di servizi di_cui_alla
law_ref(tipo(dpr),data(_103105,_103106,_1031
07),vigenza(_103109,_103110,_103111),num(6
33),art([[7,-]]),comma(4),lettera([e]))
rese a soggetti domiciliati o residenti in altri stati
membri della c_e_e , ]
            def_property
                [effettuate nel territorio dello stato ]
            condition
                cond
                    [il destinatario non e' soggetto
passivo dell' imposta nello stato in cui ha il
domicilio o la residenza ]
---- SSA_OUTPUT
MICRO_SEGMENT_OUTPUT
    [micro_crs,def_prop_1,def_prop_focus].
    SSA_INTERPRETATION · gn
[ crc( conc(prestazione : [#,{*},2])
        rel(obj : di)
        conc(servizio : [{*},4]) )
    crc( conc(prestazione : [#,{*},2])
        rel(spec : di_cui_a)
        conc(law_ref(...) : [#,{*},6]) )
    crc( conc(rendere_fornire : [7])
        rel(obj : ogg)
        conc(prestazione : [#,{*},2]) )
    crc( conc(rendere_fornire : [7])
        rel(rcpt : a)
        conc(soggetto_n : [{*},9]) )
AND
[ crc( conc(domiciliare : [10])
        rel(subj : sogg)
        conc(soggetto_n : [{*},9]) )
    crc( conc(domiciliare : [10])
```

```
              rel(loc : in)
              conc(stato_nazione : [\=,{*},15]) )
     crc( conc(stato_nazione : [\=,{*},15])
              rel(chrc : nil)
              conc(graph:     crc( conc(membro :
[{*},16])
                         rel(spec : di)
                         conc(c_e_e       :
[#,{*},18]) )
              ) )
OR
crc( conc(risiedere : [12])
              rel(subj : sogg)
              conc(soggetto_n : [{*},9]) )
     crc( conc(risiedere : [12])
              rel(loc : in)
              conc(stato_nazione : [\=,{*},15]) )
     crc( conc(stato_nazione : [\=,{*},15])
              rel(chrc : nil)
              conc(graph:     crc( conc(membro :
[{*},16])
                         rel(spec : di)
                         conc(c_e_e       :
[#,{*},18]) )
              ) )
] ]
     MICRO_SEGMENT_OUTPUT
     [micro_crs,def_prop_1,def_property].
     SSA_INTERPRETATION - gv
        crc( conc(effettuare : [1])
              rel(loc : in)
              conc(territorio : [#,3]) )
        crc( conc(territorio : [#,3])
              rel(poss : di)
              conc(stato_nazione : [#,5]) )
MICRO_SEGMENT_OUTPUT
     [micro_crs,def_prop_1,condition,cond].
     SSA_INTERPRETATION - gn
[ crc( conc(destinatario : [#,2])
              rel(chrc : nil)
              conc(graph:neg( crc( conc(soggetto_n
: [5])
                         rel(attr : nil)
                         conc(passivo : [6]) )
              crc( conc(soggetto_n : [5])
                    rel(spec : di)
```

```
              conc(imposta : [#,8]) )
        crc( conc(soggetto_n : [5])
              rel(loc : in)
              conc(stato_nazione       :
[#,10]) )
)) )
AND
[ crc( conc(avere : [13])
              rel(subj : sogg)
              conc(destinatario : [#,2]) )
        crc( conc(avere : [13])
              rel(loc : in)
              conc(stato_nazione : [#,10]) )
AND
[ crc( conc(avere : [13])
              rel(obj : ogg)
              conc(domicilio : [#,15]) )
OR
crc( conc(avere : [13])
              rel(obj : ogg)
              conc(residenza : [#,18]) ) ] ] ] ]

BLOCK
---- STRUCTURAL_VIEW
       [art([[7,-
]]),num(633),tipo(dpr),comma(4),letter(g),stru_com
ma(item),item_period(1)]
---- SOURCE_TEXT_HEAD
       [in deroga al
law_ref(tipo(dpr),data(_104740,_104741,_1047
42),vigenza(_104744,_104745,_104746),num(6
33),art([[7,-]]),comma([3]),lettera(_104762))
]
---- SOURCE_TEXT
       [le prestazioni di servizi di_cui_alla
law_ref(tipo(dpr),data(_104401,_104402,_1044
03),vigenza(_104405,_104406,_104407),num(6
33),art([[7,-]]),comma(4),lettera([e,sing]))
, escluse quelle di consulenza tecnica e legale , di
elaborazione e fornitura di dati e simili , rese a
soggetti domiciliati e residenti fuori_della c_e_e
nonche' quelle derivanti da contratti di locazione ,
anche finanziaria , noleggio e simili di mezzi di
trasporto rese da soggetti domiciliati o residenti
fuori_della comunita' stessa ovvero domiciliati o
residenti nei territori esclusi a_norma_del
```

277

law_ref(tipo(dpr),data(_104561,_104562,_1045
63),vigenza(_104565,_104566,_104567),num(6
33),art([[7,-]]),comma([1]),lettera(_104583))
ovvero da stabili organizzazioni operanti in detti
territori , si considerano effettuate nel territorio
dello stato quando sono ivi utilizzate ; queste
ultime prestazioni , se rese da soggetti domiciliati o
residenti in italia a soggetti domiciliati o residenti
fuori_della c_e_e , si considerano effettuate nel
territorio dello stato quando sono utilizzate in italia
o in altro stato membro della comunita' stessa]
···· MICRO_STRUCTURE
    micro_crs
      def_prop_1
        def_prop_focus
          [le prestazioni di servizi di_cui_alla
law_ref(tipo(dpr),data(_104810,_104811,_1048
12),vigenza(_104814,_104815,_104816),num(6
33),art([[7,-]]),comma(4),lettera([e,sing)))
, escluse quelle di consulenza tecnica e legale , di
elaborazione e fornitura di dati e simili , rese a
soggetti domiciliati e residenti fuori_della c_e_e
nonche' quelle derivanti da contratti di locazione ,
anche finanziaria , noleggio e simili di mezzi di
trasporto rese da soggetti domiciliati o residenti
fuori_della comunita' stessa ovvero domiciliati o
residenti nei territori esclusi a_norma_del
law_ref(tipo(dpr),data(_104970,_104971,_1049
72),vigenza(_104974,_104975,_104976),num(6
33),art([[7,-]]),comma([1]),lettera(_104992))
ovvero da stabili organizzazioni operanti in detti
territori ,]
        def_property
          [effettuate nel territorio dello stato]
        condition
          cond
            [sono ivi utilizzate]
        extension_def
          def_prop_focus
            [queste ultime prestazioni , se rese
da soggetti domiciliati o residenti in italia a
soggetti domiciliati o residenti fuori_della c_e_e ,]
          def_prop
            [effettuate nel territorio dello stato]
          condition
            cond

[sono utilizzate in italia o in altro
stato membro della comunita' stessa]
···· SSA_OUTPUT
MICRO_SEGMENT_OUTPUT
    [micro_crs,def_prop_1,def_prop_focus].
    SSA_INTERPRETATION - gn
[
        [crc(conc(prestazione : [#,{*},2])
          rel(obj : di)
          conc(servizio : [{*},4]))
        crc(conc(prestazione : [#,{*},2])
          rel(spec : di_cui_a)
          conc(law_ref(...) : [#,{*},6]))
        crc(conc(prestazione : [#,{*},2])
          rel(psxt : escluso)

        conc(prestazione : [#,{*},9]))
        crc(conc(rendere_fornire : [25])
          rel(obj : ogg)
          conc(prestazione : [#,{*},2]))
        crc(conc(rendere_fornire : [25])
          rel(rcpt : a)
          conc(soggetto_n : [{*},27]))
AND
[crc(conc(domiciliare : [28])
        rel(subj : sogg)
        conc(soggetto_n : [{*},27]))
        crc(conc(domiciliare : [28])
        rel(loc : fuori_di)
        conc(c_e_e : [#,{*},32]))
OR
crc(conc(risiedere : [30])
        rel(subj : sogg)
        conc(soggetto_n : [{*},27]))
        crc(conc(risiedere : [30])
        rel(loc : fuori_di)
        conc(c_e_e : [#,{*},32]))
  ]]
AND
[
        [crc(conc(prestazione : [#,{*},9])
          rel(obj : di)
          conc(consulenza : [11]))
AND
[crc(conc(consulenza : [11])
        rel(attr : nil)

conc(tecnico : [12]))
OR
crc(conc(consulenza : [11])
　　　　　　rel(attr : nil)
　　　　　　conc(legale_a : [14]))]]
OR
crc(conc(prestazione : [#,{*},9])
　　　　　rel(obj : di)
　　　　　conc(elaborazione : [17]))
　　　crc(conc(elaborazione : [17])
　　　　　rel(obj : di)
　　　　　conc(dato : [{*},21]))
OR
crc(conc(prestazione : [#,{*},9])
　　　　　rel(obj : di)
　　　　　conc(fornitura : [19]))
　　　crc(conc(fornitura : [19])
　　　　　rel(obj : di)
　　　　　conc(dato : [{*},21]))
OR
SIMILE]]
OR
[conc(prestazione : [#,{*},34])
AND
[
　　　[crc(conc(derivare : [35])
　　　　　rel(subj : sogg)
　　　　　conc(prestazione : [#,{*},34]))
　　　crc(conc(derivare : [35])
　　　　　rel(fsrc : da)
　　　　　conc(contratto : [{*},37]))
　　　　　AND
[
　　　　　[crc(conc(contratto : [{*},37])
　　　　　　rel(obj : di)
　　　　　　conc(locazione : [39]))
　　　　　crc(conc(locazione : [39])
　　　　　　rel(obj : di)
　　　　　　conc(mezzo : [{*},48]))
　　　　　crc(conc(mezzo : [{*},48])
　　　　　　rel(use : di)

conc(trasporto : [50]))
AND
psbl(crc(conc(locazione : [39])
　　　　　　rel(attr : nil)

conc(finanziario : [42])))))
　]
OR
crc(conc(contratto : [{*},37])
　　　　　rel(obj : di)
　　　　　conc(noleggio : [44]))
　　　crc(conc(noleggio : [44])
　　　　　rel(obj : di)
　　　　　conc(mezzo : [{*},48]))
　　　crc(conc(mezzo : [{*},48])
　　　　　rel(use : di)
　　　　　conc(trasporto : [50]))
OR
SIMILE]]
　　　AND
[crc(conc(rendere_fornire : [51])
　　　　　rel(obj : ogg)
　　　　　conc(prestazione : [#,{*},34]))
AND
[
　　　　　[crc(conc(rendere_fornire : [51])
　　　　　　rel(agnt : da)
　　　　　　conc(soggetto_n : [{*},53]))
AND
[crc(conc(domiciliare : [54])
　　　　　rel(subj : sogg)
　　　　　conc(soggetto_n : [{*},53]))
　　　crc(conc(domiciliare : [54])
　　　　　rel(loc : fuori_di)
　　　　　conc(comunita_cee　　　　　:
[#,?,{*},58]))
OR
crc(conc(risiedere : [56])
　　　　　rel(subj : sogg)
　　　　　conc(soggetto_n : [{*},53]))
　　　crc(conc(risiedere : [56])
　　　　　rel(loc : fuori_di)
　　　　　conc(comunita_cee　　　　　:
[#,?,{*},58]))
OR
crc(conc(domiciliare : [61])
　　　　　rel(subj : sogg)
　　　　　conc(soggetto_n : [{*},53]))
　　　crc(conc(domiciliare : [61])
　　　　　rel(loc : in)
　　　　　conc(territorio : [#,{*},65]))

279

```
                    crc( conc(escludere : [66])
                        rel(ptnt : ogg)
                        conc(territorio : [#,{*},65]) )
                    crc( conc(escludere : [66])
                        rel(fsrc : a_norma_di)
                        conc(law_ref(...) : [#,{*},68]) )
OR
crc( conc(risiedere : [63])
                        rel(subj : sogg)
                        conc(soggetto_n : [{*},53]) )
                    crc( conc(risiedere : [63])
                        rel(loc : in)
                        conc(territorio : [#,{*},65]) )
                    crc( conc(escludere : [66])
                        rel(ptnt : ogg)
                        conc(territorio : [#,{*},65]) )
                    crc( conc(escludere : [66])
                        rel(fsrc : a_norma_di)
                        conc(law_ref(...) : [#,{*},68]) )
] ]
OR
crc( conc(rendere_fornire : [51])
                        rel(agnt : da)
                        conc(organizzazione : [{*},72]) )
                    crc( conc(organizzazione : [{*},72])
                        rel(attr : nil)
                        conc(stabile_a : [{*},71]) )
                    crc( conc(operare : [73])
                        rel(agnt : sogg)
                        conc(organizzazione : [{*},72]) )
                    crc( conc(operare : [73])
                        rel(loc : in)
                        conc(territorio : [?,{*},76]) )
] ] ] ]
    MICRO_SEGMENT_OUTPUT
        [micro_crs,def_prop_1,def_property].
        SSA_INTERPRETATION · gv
            crc( conc(effettuare : [1])
                rel(loc : in)
                conc(territorio : [#,3]) )
            crc( conc(territorio : [#,3])
                rel(poss : di)
                conc(stato_nazione : [#,5]) )
MICRO_SEGMENT_OUTPUT
        [micro_crs,def_prop_1,condition,cond].
        SSA_INTERPRETATION · gv
```

```
                    crc( conc(utilizzare : [3])
                        rel(loc : ( \ ivi))
                        conc([luoghi,organo_stato]        :
[_106714]) )
MICRO_SEGMENT_OUTPUT

[micro_crs,def_prop_1,extension_def,def_prop_f
ocus].
        SSA_INTERPRETATION · gn
        [conc(prestazione : [last,#,{*},3])
            AND
            necs(
                [crc( conc(rendere_fornire : [6])
                rel(obj : ogg)
                conc(prestazione : [last,#,{*},3]) )
                            crc( conc(rendere_fornire :
[6])
                rel(agnt : da)
                conc(soggetto_n : [{*},8]) )
                            crc( conc(rendere_fornire :
[6])
                rel(rcpt : a)
                conc(soggetto_n : [{*},15]) )
                    AND
[ crc( conc(domiciliare : [16])
                rel(subj : sogg)
                conc(soggetto_n : [{*},15]) )
            crc( conc(domiciliare : [16])
                rel(loc : fuori_di)
                conc(c_e_e : [#,{*},20]) )
                            OR
crc( conc(risiedere : [18])
                rel(subj : sogg)
                conc(soggetto_n : [{*},15]) )
            crc( conc(risiedere : [18])
                rel(loc : fuori_di)
                conc(c_e_e : [#,{*},20]) )
            ]
                    AND

[ crc( conc(domiciliare : [9])
                rel(subj : sogg)
                conc(soggetto_n : [{*},8]) )
            crc( conc(domiciliare : [9])
                rel(loc : in)
                conc(italia : [13]) )
```

OR
crc(conc(risiedere : [11])
   rel(subj : sogg)
   conc(soggetto_n : [{*},8]))
   crc(conc(risiedere : [11])
   rel(loc : in)
   conc(italia : [13]))
 ]])))
 ]

MICRO_SEGMENT_OUTPUT

[micro_crs,def_prop_1,extension_def,def_prop].
  SSA_INTERPRETATION - gv
   crc(conc(effettuare : [1])
   rel(loc : in)
   conc(territorio : [#,3]))
   crc(conc(territorio : [#,3])
   rel(poss : di)
   conc(stato_nazione : [#,5]))
MICRO_SEGMENT_OUTPUT

[micro_crs,def_prop_1,extension_def,condition,cond].
  SSA_INTERPRETATION - gv
[crc(conc(utilizzare : [2])
   rel(loc : in)
   conc(italia : [4]))
  OR
   crc(conc(utilizzare : [2])
   rel(loc : in)
   conc(stato_nazione : [\=,8]))
   crc(conc(stato_nazione : [\=,8])
   rel(chrc : nil)
   conc(graph: crc(conc(membro : [9])
     rel(spec : di)
     conc(comunita_cee :
[#,?,{*},11]))
))
 ]

BLOCK
···· STRUCTURAL_VIEW
 [art([[7,-
]]),num(633),tipo(dpr),comma(5),period(1)]
···· SOURCE_TEXT

[non si considerano effettuate nel territorio dello stato le cessioni all' esportazione , le operazioni assimilate a cessioni all' esportazione e i servizi internazionali o connessi agli scambi internazionali di_cui_ai successivi law_ref(tipo(dpr),data(_107179,_107180,_107181),vigenza(_107183,_107184,_107185),num(633),art([[8,-],[8,bis],[9,-]]),comma(_107209),lettera(_107211))
.]
···· MICRO_STRUCTURE
 micro_crs
  def_prop_3
   neg
   def_prop
    history
     [effettuate nel territorio dello stato]
    def_prop_focus
     [le cessioni all' esportazione , le operazioni assimilate a cessioni all' esportazione e i servizi internazionali o connessi agli scambi internazionali di_cui_ai successivi law_ref(tipo(dpr),data(_107331,_107332,_107333),vigenza(_107335,_107336,_107337),num(633),art([[8,-],[8,bis],[9,-]]),comma(_107361),lettera(_107363))
]
···· SSA_OUTPUT
MICRO_SEGMENT_OUTPUT
 [micro_crs,def_prop_3,def_prop,history].
  SSA_INTERPRETATION - gv
   crc(conc(effettuare : [1])
   rel(loc : in)
   conc(territorio : [#,3]))
   crc(conc(territorio : [#,3])
   rel(poss : di)
   conc(stato_nazione : [#,5]))
MICRO_SEGMENT_OUTPUT
 [micro_crs,def_prop_3,def_prop_focus].
  SSA_INTERPRETATION - gn
   crc(conc(cessione : [#,{*},2])

rel(prps : a)
   conc(esportazione : [#,4]))
OR

```
crc( conc(assimilare_paragonare : [8])
          rel(ptnt : ogg)
          conc(operazione : [#,{*},7]) )
        crc( conc(assimilare_paragonare : [8])
          rel(subj : a)
          conc(graph:        crc( conc(cessione :
[{*},10])
                          rel(prps : a)
                          conc(esportazione        :
[#,12]) )
          ) )
OR
[ crc( conc(servizio : [#,{*},15])
          rel(attr : nil)
          conc(internazionale : [{*},16]) )
      OR
      crc( conc(servizio : [#,{*},15])
          rel(attr : nil)
          conc(connesso : [{*},18]) )
      crc( conc(connesso : [{*},18])
          rel(fsrc : a)
          conc(scambio : [#,{*},20]) )
      crc( conc(scambio : [#,{*},20])
          rel(attr : nil)
          conc(internazionale : [{*},21]) )
      crc( conc(scambio : [#,{*},20])
          rel(spec : di_cui_a)
          conc(law_ref(...) : [#,subs,{*},24]) )
```

282

APPENDIX II:
THE N-A KNOWLEDGE BASE[1]

```
*Knowledge Base for Article Number 7
Revision: $Revision: 1.2 $
*/
single_solution.
No_CF.
Header :: "
".
name_of_system :: 'Nomos $Revision: 1.2 $'.
End_message :: "Fine della Consultazione".

Category(1,problem,[focus,advice]).

Parameter(advice,advice,_).
Parameter(integer,state_territory_exception,1..4).
parameter(integer,object,1..2).
% parameter(boolean,transfer_of_goods,_).
% parameter(boolean,supply_of_services,_).
Parameter(boolean,state_territory,_).
Parameter(word,organisation_permanent_location,
[italy,abroad]).
Parameter(word,focus,[ transfer_of_goods,

        supply_of_services,

        transfer_of_goods_for_export]).
```

```
Category_message(1) ::
"Questa e` il primo lancio della categoria per
art.7".

gen_mess(1)::
"l'interrogazione sull' IVA prossima sara` nominata
come:".
Describe is_state_territory as "attivita` effettuta
nel territorio dello stato"

describe transfer_of_goods as "cessioni di beni".

%%%% Find the the top focus (transfer or supply
of goods) of the question

parameter(integer,focus_type,1..3).

ask_text
"
Questa interrogazione e' relativa a:

1) prestazione di servizio
2) cessioni di beni
3) cessioni di beni all' esportazione
```

---

[1] Courtesy of Vassilis Konstantinou, University of Westminster, Artificial Intelligence Resaerch Group. This is the exact Knowledge Base used by the N-A prototype.

" for focus_type of Ent.

Rule (1,0.1) for focus of Ent ::
if
      same(Ent,focus_type,[1],_)
then supply_of_services with 1.0.

rule (1,0.2) for focus of Ent ::
if
      same(Ent,focus_type,[2],_)
then transfer_of_goods with 1.0.

rule (1,0.3) for focus of Ent ::
if
      same(Ent,focus_type,[3],_)
then transfer_of_goods_for_export with 1.0.

ask_text
"
E` l'attivita` effettuata nel un dei territori successivi:
(Scegliete un dei numeri):

1) Commune di Livigno
2) Campio di Italia
3) L' aque nazionali di lago di Lugano

4) Niente dall' alto"

for state_territory_exception of Ent.

Ask_text
"
Sono i beni:
1) mobili o
2) immobili
"
for object of Ent.

Question(is_state_territory,_,
"E`questo terrotorio soggetto alla sovranita` dello Stato?
").

/* Needs better question text */

question(existing_goods,_,
"Sono i beni esistenti nel territorio dello Stato?
").

Question(national_goods,_,
"Hanno le cessioni (di beni) per oggetto beni mobili nazionali?
").

Question(national_goods_2,_,
"Hanno le cessioni (di beni) per oggetto beni mobili nazionalizzatii?
").

Question(bonded_goods,_,
"Hanno le cessioni (di beni) per oggetto beni vincolati al regime della temporanea importazione?
").

%%%% Paragraph 1

rule (1,1) for state_territory of Ent ::
if
      questions([is_state_territory],_) and
      not(same(Ent,state_territory_exceptio
n,1,_)) and
      not(same(Ent,state_territory_exceptio
n,2,_)) and
      not(same(Ent,state_territory_exceptio
n,3,_)) and
      advice(test_advice)
then yes with 1.0.

rule (1,1.1) for state_territory of Ent ::
if
      mlt_same(Ent,state_territory_exceptio
n,[1,2,3],or,_)
%   advice(outside_territory) and
%   conclude(Ent,advice,[outside_territory],1.0)
then no with 1.0.

%%%% Paragraph 2

rule (1,2) for advice of Ent ::
if

```
              same(Ent,focus,transfer_of_goods,_)
and
              same(Ent,state_territory,        [yes],_)
and

              (
              same(Ent, object,2,_) or
              (
              questions([national_goods],_) or
              questions([national_goods_2],_) or
              questions([bonded_goods],_) ) and
              questions([existing_goods],_) ) and
              advice(transfer_of_goods_1)
then [transfer_of_goods_1] with 1.0.

rule (1,5) for advice of Ent ::
if
              same(Ent,state_territory,        [no],_)
and
              advice(outside_territory)
then [outside_territory] with 1.0.
```

%%%% Paragraph 3

/* The next question should probably be converted into a rule
because again it depends on the territory definition
*/

```
question(has_subject_domicile,_,
").

Question(residence_and_not_foreign_domicile,_,
```
"Sono le prestazioni (di servizi) rese da soggetti che sono
residenti nel territorio dello stato che non abbiano stabilito
il domicilio al' estero?
").

```
Rule (1,3) for advice of Ent ::
if
              same(Ent,focus,supply_of_services,_)
and
              same(Ent, state_territory,[yes],_) and
              (questions([has_subject_domicile],_) or
```

```
              questions([residence_and_not_foreign_domicile],_
              ) or

              same(Ent,organisation_permanent_location,[italy],
              _)) and
                          advice(supply_of_services)
then [supply_of_services] with 1.0.

question(permanent_domicile_in_italy,_,
```
"Is the organisation located in Italy, but owned by subjects domiciled and resided abroad?").

```
question(permanent_domicile_abroad,_,
```
"E` questa organizzazione stabile all'estero di soggetti domiciliati o
residenti in Italia?").

```
rule (1,3.1) for organisation_permanent_location
of Ent ::
if
              questions([permanent_domicile_in_ital
y],_)
              then italy with 1.0.

rule (1,3.2) for organisation_permanent_location
of Ent ::
if
              questions([permanent_domicile_abroad
],_)
              then abroad with 1.0.

rule (1,3.3) for organisation_permanent_location
of Ent ::
if
              questions([
permanent_domicile_abroad,

permanent_domicile_in_italy],_) and
                          advice(assume_abroad)
then abroad with 1.0.
```

%%%% Paragraph 4.1
/*The state territory rules must be treated as inherited

by several attributes. As in this rule we neen not
just "activity"
in the question but we must mention the "real
estate"
*/
 question(real_estate_expert_evidence,_,
"E`questa prestazione (di servizio) relativa a beni
immobili,
comprese le perizie?
").

Question(real_estate_agencies,_,
"E`questa prestazione (di servizio) relativa alle
prestazioni di agenzia
e alle prestazioni inerenti alla preparazione e al
coordimento dell' esecuzione
dei lavori immobiliari?").

rule (1,4.1) for advice of Ent ::
if
          same(Ent,focus,supply_of_services,_)
and
          same(Ent, object,[2],_) and
          (questions([real_estate_expert_eviden
ce],_) or
          questions([real_estate_agencies],_))
and
          same(Ent,state_territory,   [yes],_)
and
          advice(supply_of_services_4_1)
then [supply_of_services_4_1] with 1.0.

parameter(integer,services_2,1..8).

ask_text
"
Sono le prestazione (di servizi) rese relative a:
 (Scegliete un dei numeri)

1) servizi culturali
2) servizi scientifici
3) servizi artistici
4) servizi didattici
5) servizi sportivi
6) servizi ricreativi

7) simili dall' alto

8) niente dall' alto

" for services_2 of Ent.

 Parameter(integer,services_3,1..5).

ask_text
"
Sono le prestazione (di servizi) rese relative alle
operazioni di:
 (Scegliete un dei numeri)

1) carico
2) scarico
3) manutenzione

4) simile accessorie ai transporti di beni

5) niente dall' alto

" for services_3 of Ent.

Question(tangible_goods,_,
"E' questa prestazione relativa ai beni materiali").

 Rule (1,4.2) for advice of Ent ::
if
          same(Ent,focus,supply_of_services,_)
and
          same(Ent, object,[1],_) and
          questions([real_estate_expert_evidenc
e,tangible_goods],_) and
          (
          mlt_same(Ent,services_2,[1,2,3,4,5,6,
7],or,_) or
          mlt_same(Ent,services_3,[1,2,3,4],or,
_)
) and
          same(Ent,state_territory,   [yes],_)
and
          advice(supply_of_services_4_2)
then [supply_of_services_4_2] with 1.0.

 parameter(integer,distance,0..100).

parameter(boolean,transport_service,_).

Ask_text
"

E` questa prestazione una prestazione di transporto?
"
for transport_service of Ent.

Ask_text
"Date la proporzione della distanza percorsa nel territorio dello Stato:

(Rispondete con numeri entro 0 e 100
)"
for distance of Ent.

Rule (1,4.3) for advice of Ent ::
if
        same(Ent,focus,supply_of_services,_)
and
        same(Ent,state_territory, [yes],_) and
        same(Ent,transport_service,[yes],_)
and
        more_than((Ent,distance),50,_) and
        advice(supply_of_services_4_3)
then [supply_of_services_4_3] with 1.0.

question(means_of_transport,_,"Sono questi beni mezzi di transporto?")
%%% question(good_is_not_object,_,"Forma il bene oggetto?").
question(good_is_used,_,"E` il bene utilizzato nel territorio dello Stato?").

question(leasing_service1,_,
" E` questo servizio derivanto da contrati di locazione? ").
Question(leasing_service2,_,
" E` questo servizio derivanto da contrati di nolegio e simili?").
question(object_goods,_,
"Forma il bene oggetto?").

rule (1,4.4) for advice of Ent ::
if
        same(Ent,focus,supply_of_services,_)
and
        same(Ent,state_territory, [yes],_) and
        same(Ent, object,[1],_) and
        (
        questions([leasing_service1],_) or
        questions([leasing_service2],_)
) and
        questions([tangible_goods],_) and
        not(questions([means_of_transport],_)
) and
%%   not(questions([good_is_not_object],_)) and
        questions([object_goods],_) and
        questions([good_is_used],_) and
        advice(supply_of_services_4_4)
then [supply_of_services_4_4] with 1.0.

parameter(boolean,services_in_art3_2,_).

Ask_text
"

E` questo servizio indicato al n.2 dell'art.3?
" for services_in_art3_2 of Ent.

Question(advertising_services,_, "Is advertising the supplied service?").
question(consultancy,_,
        "E` questo servizio consulenza legale?").
    question(technical,_,
        "E` questo servizio consulenza tecnica?").
        question(processing_of_data,_,
        "E` questo servizio relativo ad elaborazione di dati?").
        question(supply_of_data,_,
        "E` questo servizio relativo a fornitura di dati?").
        question(similar_services2,_,
        "E` questo servizio simile ai questi dalle suddette i.e:
        - consulenza legale
        - consulenza tecnica

- elaborazione di dati
- fornitura di dati").
Question(banking_operation,_,
       "Sono queste servizi relative ad
operazioni bancarie")
       question(finance_operation,_,
       "Sono queste servizi relative ad
operazioni finanziarie")
       question(insurance_operation,_,
       "Sono queste servizi relative ad
operazioni assicurative")
   question(personnel_agencies,_,
       "Sono queste servizi relative a prestiti
di personale")
   question(services_of_intermediation,_,
       "Sono queste servizi relative ad
prestazione di intermediazione
       inerenti alle suddette prestazioni ie:

       - le prestazioni pubblicitarie
       - consulenza legale
       - consulenza tecnica
       - elaborazione e fornitura di dati
       - operazione bancarie
       - operazioni finanziarie
       - operazioni assicurative
       - prestiti di personale").

Question(obligation_to_refrain,_,
       "Sono queste servizi inerenti all' obbigo
di non esercitarle
       le suddette prestazioni ie:

       - le prestazioni pubblicitarie
       - consulenza legale
       - consulenza tecnica
       - elaborazione e fornitura di dati
       - operazione bancarie
       - operazioni finanziarie
       - operazioni assicurative
       - prestiti di personale").

%% question(services_of_obligation,_,
%%   "Sono queste servizi relative all' obligo di
non esercitarle?").
question(for_domiciled_subject,_,

       "Sono queste servizi rese a soggetti
domiciliati
       nel terrtorio dell Stato?")

question(for_resided_subject,_,
       "Sono queste servizi rese a soggetti
residenti
       nel terrtorio dell Stato che non abbiano
stabilito
       il domicilio all' estero?")

question(used_in_eec,_,
       "Sono queste servizi utilizzate all'
interno della CEE?")

rule (1,4.5) for advice of Ent ::
if
       same(Ent,focus,supply_of_services,_)
and
       same(Ent,state_territory, [yes],_) and
       (
       same(Ent,services_in_art3_2,[yes],_)
or
              (
       questions([advertising_services],_) or
                     (
       questions([consultancy],_) or

       questions([technical],_)
) or
       questions([processing_of_data],_) or

       questions([supply_of_data],_) or

       questions([similar_services2],_)
) or
              (
       questions([banking_operation],_) or

       questions([finance_operation],_) or

questions([insurance_operation],_)
) or

questions([personnel_agencies],_) or

questions([services_of_intermediation]
,_) or

questions([obligation_to_refrain],_)
) and
(

questions([for_domiciled_subject],_) or

questions([for_resided_subject],_) or

same(Ent,organisation_permanent_loc
ation,[italy],_)
) and

not(questions([used_in_eec],_))
and
advice(supply_of_services_4_5)

then [supply_of_services_4_5] with 1.0.

question(services_of_letter_e,_,
"Sono queste servizi:

* quelchecose di suddette servizi;
* Servizi di intermediazione inerenti
alle suddette
prestazioni
* Inerenti all' obligo di non esercitarle
le suddette prstazioni ie:

- le prestazioni pubblicitarie
- consulenza legale
- consulenza tecnica
- elborazione e fornitura di dati
- operazione bancarie
- operazioni finanziarie
- operazioni assicurative
- prestiti di personale").

Question(domiciled_eec,_,
"E`questo servizio reso a soggetto
domiciliato in altri Stati membri
della CEE?").
question(resided_eec,_,
"E`questo servizio reso a soggetto
residento in altri Stati membri
della CEE?").
question(beneficiary_taxed,_,
"E`il destinatario di servizio soggetto
passivo dell' imposta
nello Stato in cui ha il domicilio?").
question(beneficiary_taxed_2,_,
"E`il destinatario di servizio soggetto
passivo dell' imposta
nello Stato in cui ha la residenza?").

rule (1,4.6) for advice of Ent ::
if
same(Ent,focus,supply_of_services,_)
and
same(Ent,state_territory, [yes],_) and
questions([services_of_letter_e],_)
and
(
questions([domiciled_eec],_) or
questions([resided_eec],_)
) and
(
not(questions([beneficiary_taxed],_))
or
not(questions([beneficiary_taxed_2],_)
)
) and
advice(supply_of_services_4_6)

then [supply_of_services_4_6] with 1.0.

question(supplied_to_outside_eec_1,_,
"E`questo servizio reso a soggetti
domiciliati fuori dell CEE?").
question(supplied_to_outside_eec_2,_,
"E`questo servizio reso a soggetti
residenti fuori dell CEE?")
question(excluded_services_1,_,

"E` questo servizio uno delle essezione succecive:

- Consulenza tecnica o legale
- Elaborazione di dati
- Fornitura di dati").

Question(derived_from_contract_hiring_out,_,
"E` questo servizio derivanto da contratto di locazione
anche finanziaria di mezzi di transporto?").

question(derived_from_contract_chartering,_,
"E` questo servizio derivanto da contratto di noleggio
di mezzi di transporto?").

question(derived_from_contract_similar,_,
"E` questo servizio derivanto da contratto simile alle suddette ie:
- locazione di mezzi di transporto
- finanziaria locazione di mezzi di transporto
- noleggio di mezzi di transporto ").

Question(supplied_by_outside_eec_1,_,
"E` questo servizio reso da un oggetto domiciliato fuori della CCE?").

question(supplied_by_outside_eec_2,_,
"E` questo servizio reso da un soggetto residento fuori della CCE?")

question(domiciled_excluded_territory,_,
"E` questo servizio reso da un soggetto domiciliato
nei terriori esclusi a norma del primo comma ie:
- Commune di Livigno
- Campio d'Italia
- L'aquue nazionali di lago di Lugano").

Question(resides_excluded_territory,_,
"E` questo servizio reso da un soggetto residento
nei terriori esclusi a norma del primo comma ie:
- Commune di Livigno
- Campio d'Italia

- L'aquue nazionali di lago di Lugano").

Question(organisation_acting_in_territories,_,
"E` questo servizio reso da organizzazioni stabili operanti
nei terriori esclusi a norma del primo comma ie:
- Commune di Livigno
- Campio d'Italia
- L'aquue nazionali di lago di Lugano").

Question(supplied_by_Italy,_,
"E` questo servizio reso da soggetti domiciliati in Italia?").

question(supplied_by_Italy,_,
"E` questo servizio reso da soggetti residenti in Italia?").

question(used_in_eec,_,
"E`questo servizio utilizzato in Italia o in altro
Stato membro della CEE?").

rule (1,4.7) for advice of Ent ::
if
        same(Ent,focus,supply_of_services,_)
and
        same(Ent,state_territory,[yes],_) and
        questions([services_of_letter_e],_)
and
        (
        questions([supplied_to_outside_eec_1
],_) or
        questions([supplied_to_outside_eec_2
],_) and
        not(questions([excluded_services],_))
) or
        (
        questions([derived_from_contract_hiri
ng_out],_) or
        questions([derived_from_contract_cha
rtering],_) or

290

```
                questions([derived_from_contract_sim
ilar],_) and

                    (

                questions([supplied_by_outside_eec_1
],_) or

                questions([supplied_by_outside_eec_2
],_) or

                questions([domiciled_excluded_territor
y],_) or

                questions([resides_excluded_territory],
_) or

                questions([organisation_acting_in_terr
itories],_)
                    ) or
                    (

                questions([supplied_by_Italy_1],_) or

                questions([supplied_by_Italy_2],_) and

                (questions([supplied_to_outside_eec_
1],_) or

questions([supplied_to_outside_eec_2],_))
                    ) and
                    questions([used_in_eec],_)
                ) and
                advice(supply_of_services_4_7)

then [supply_of_services_4_7] with 1.0.

question(transfer_for_export,_,
            "Sono cessioni all' esprotazione ?").
question(operations_classed_as_transfer_for_exp
ort,_,
            "Sono operazioni assimilate a cessioni
all' esportazione ?").
question(international_services,_,
            "Sono servizi internazionali ?").
ask_text
```

```
"Sono servizi connessi agli scambi internazionali
di cui ai successivi art.8, 8_bis e 9?").
" for services_in_art_8 of Ent.

Rule (1,5) for advice of Ent ::
if
        same(Ent,focus,transfer_of_goods_for
_export,_) and
        same(Ent,state_territory,[yes],_) and
        questions([transfer_for_export],_) or
        questions([operations_classed_as_tran
sfer_for_export],_) or
            (

        questions([international_services],_) or

        same(Ent,services_in_art_8,[yes],_)
            ) and
        advice(transfer_of_goods_for_export
_5)
then [transfer_of_goods_for_export_5] with 1.0.


/*
Texts for the advices
*/

test_advice :: "Questa e` la consultazione
esperimentale"

transfer_of_goods_1 :: " Consultazione per
cessioni di beni".

Supply_of_services :: "Consultazione per
prestazioni di servizi".

Outside_territory :: "Consultazione per oggetti
fuori del territorio dello Stato"

supply_of_services_4_1 ::
"Queste prestazioni di servizi si cosiderano
effetuate nel territorio dello Stato
Art. 7 Comma 4.a".

supply_of_services_4_2 ::
"Queste prestazioni di servizi si cosiderano
```

291

effetuate nel territorio dello Stato

Art. 7 Comma 4.b".

supply_of_services_4_3 ::
"Queste prestazioni di servizi si cosiderano
effetuate nel territorio dello Stato
Art. 7 Comma 4.c".

supply_of_services_4_4 ::
"Queste prestazioni di servizi si cosiderano
effetuate nel territorio dello Stato
Art. 7 Comma 4.d".

supply_of_services_4_5 ::
"Queste prestazioni di servizi si cosiderano
effetuate nel territorio dello Stato
Art. 7 Comma 4.e".

supply_of_services_4_6 ::
"Queste prestazioni di servizi si cosiderano
effetuate nel territorio dello Stato
Art. 7 Comma 4.f".

supply_of_services_4_7 ::
"Queste prestazioni di servizi si cosiderano
effetuate nel territorio dello Stato

Art. 7 Comma 4.g".

transfer_of_goods_for_export_5 ::
"Queste prestazioni di servizi NON si cosiderano
effetuate nel territorio dello Stato
Art. 7 Comma 5".

Assume_abroad ::
"Assumiamo che l' organizzazione e` domiciliato
all' estero'".
End_of_database.

APPENDIX III:
ARTICLE 7 OF THE ITALIAN VAT LAW

DPR 26.10.72 N.633 Article 7
Decree of the President of the Republic of the 26th October 1972,
Number 633, Article 7 (in force from 1.1.82)
Institution and Regulation of Value Added Tax.
(unofficial English translation)[1]

Object: *Territoriality of the Tax*

§1. State Territory is considered to be the one subjected to Its sovereignty, with the exception of the Districts of Livigno, Campio d' Italia and of the national waters of the lake of Lugano as they were bordered by the fourth paragraph of Art.2 of D.P.R. 23 January 1973, n.43.

§2. The transfer of goods is considered to be effected within the State Territory if its object is real estate or national or nationalised mobile goods [existing within that territory] or goods bonded under the temporary import regime existing within that territory :

§3. The supply of services is considered to be effected within the State Territory when services are supplied by subjects having their domicile within that territory or from subjects having therein their residence and not having a permanent domicile abroad, as well as when services are supplied by permanent organisations in Italy owned by subjects domiciled and resided abroad. When services are supplied from

---

[1] This translation (unofficial) is the actual text in use by the non-Italian speaking members of our Team. However, the official Italian text was continuously guiding the entire implementation, as the input to the ILAM system was the original Italian text of the law.

owned by subjects domiciled and resided abroad. When services are supplied from permanent organisations abroad, owned by subjects domiciled and resided in Italy, they are not considered to be effected within the State Territory. For subjects other than natural persons and for the purposes of this article, domicile is considered to be the place where the registered seat is located and residence is considered to be the place of the actual seat.

§4. With exception to the previous paragraph:

a. The supply of services connected with immobile property [relating to real estate], including expert evidence [evaluation], agency and services relative to the preparation and coordination of the execution of construction [real estate] works is considered to be effected within the State Territory if the real estate is situated within that territory.

b. The supply of services, including expert evidence, relative to mobile tangible property and the supply of cultural, scientific, artistic, educational, sporting, entertainment and similar services, as well as the operations of loading, unloading, maintaining and similar, as supplementary to the transport of goods, are considered to be effected within the State Territory when they are performed within that territory.

c. The supply of transport service is considered to be effected within the State Territory in proportion to the distance covered therein.

d. The supply of services deriving from hiring out [leasing], chartering and similar contracts concerning mobile material goods other than means of transport is considered to be effected within the State territory if the good, which does not constitute an object, is used within that territory.

e. The supply of the aforementioned services indicated in art.3§2, the supply of advertising services, of legal and technical consultancy, of processing and supply of data and similar, the supply of services relative to banking operations, finance, insurance, and personnel agencies, as well as the supply of services of intermediation relative to the above mentioned services and those relative to the obligation to refrain from carrying out the above mentioned services, are considered to be effected within the State territory when they are performed to subjects domiciled in that territory, or to subjects resided therein that have no permanent domicile abroad, as well as when they are performed to permanent organisations in Italy, owned by subjects domiciled and resided abroad, unless the services are used outside the European Economic Community.

f. The services of the previous letter (e) supplied to subjects domiciled or resided in other States members of the EEC is considered to be effected within the State Territory if the beneficiary is not passive subject to the tax in the State where he is domiciled or resided.

g. The supply of services of letter (e), with the exception of legal and technical consultancy and of elaboration and supply of data and similar, supplied to subjects domiciled and resided outside the EEC as well as those derived from hiring out, even financialy [financial leasing], chartering and similar contracts concerning transport means supplied by subjects domiciled or resided outside the EEC, or domiciled or resided within the territories excluded from the rule of the first paragraph, or from permanent organisations acting in the above mentioned territories are considered to be effected within the State territory if they are used within that territory; these last services, supplied by subjects domiciled or resided in Italy to subjects domiciled or resided outside the EEC are considered to be effected within the State Territory if they are used in Italy or in other State member of the EEC.

§5. Transfers for exportation and operations assimilated to exports, as well as international services and services connected to international transactions such as those described in the following Articles 8, 8-bis and 9 are not considered to be effected within State Territory.

APPENDIX IV:
SAMPLE SESSIONS WITH THE N-A PROTOTYPE

1. **SAMPLE SESSION WITH QUESTIONS GENERATED AUTOMATICALLY FROM CONCEPTUAL GRAPHS:**

   Q1:   Does the service derive from a contract?
   Q2:   Is the contract one of hiring out tangible mobile goods?
   Q3:   Is the contract one of chartering tangible mobile goods?
   Q4:   Is the contract similar to the above?
   Q5:   Are the goods a means of transport?

CONDITION

   Q6:   Are the goods used within the territory?
   Q7:   Are the goos the object of the above mentioned services?

The conclusion is triggered by the combination:

   Question (1) **AND** (2) **OR** (3) **OR** (4) **AND NOT** (5) **AND** (6) **AND** (7)

2. SAMPLE SESSION FOR THE FULL-VERSION OF THE PROTOTYPE[1]

	Question	Answer
1	**Describe transaction (T) as:** a. Supply of Services, b. Transfer of Goods, c. Exports	**A**
2	**If it is supply of services, who is the subject of (T):** a. A Company, b. A Professional, c. Other (describe)	**A**
3	**Describe in details (T)➔** Supply of Advertising Services [the choice is actually reduced with a menu] EXPLANATION: *If it is Advertising this falls within the case of 7§4 letter (e) of the Law*	
4	**If it is a Company where is the legal or actual seat of the company**[2] a: Within Italian territory b: Outside Italian Territory but within EEC c: Outside Italy and EEC d: Other describe [or further questions in order to find out more[	**C**
5	**If it is a company and it is supply of advertising services who is the receiver of the adverising sevices: (according to the rules of 7§4 letter (e))** a. A subject domiciled in Italy b. A subject resided in Italy that has no permanent domicile abroad c. An organisation in Italy owned by subjects domiciled or resided outside Italy. d: The place of the supply is outside EEC e: None (specify)	**E** [Answer leading to Article 7§3 letter (g) and thus to the following question (6)]
6	**Where is the advertising service used?** a. In Italy or within EEC, b. Outside EEC	**A**
RESULT: If the case is supply of services (7§3) and especially an advertising service (7§4-letter-e) supplied to a company having its legal seat ouside Italy or EEC (7§4-letter-g) and the service is used within Italian Territory (7§4-letter-g) then the above service shall be deemed to be effected within the State Territory and therefore liable to tax.		

---

1   This is a hypothetical session. It is based on the decision trees and it was used as a guideline in the implementation phase of the N-A prototype. It has not been tested on real cases.

2   Note: this particular question can be analysed to two sub-questions concerning domicile and residence of the subject according to the decision tree.

BIBLIOGRAPHY

I. MONOGRAPHS & COLLECTIONS

ABA COMMITTEE ON LAW & TECHNOLOGY, *Automated Law Research*, ABA Committee on Law & Technology, 1973.

ALBERICO R. – MICCO M., *Expert Systems for Reference and Information Retrieval*, Meckler, London, 1990.

ALCHOURRÓN C. E. & BULYGIN E., *Normative Systems*, Springer Verlag, Wien, 1971.

ALEXY ROBERT, *A Theory of Legal Argumentation, The Theory of Rational Discourse as Theory of Legal Justification, (English Transalation)*, Clarendon press, Oxford, 1989.

ARAVANTINOS VASSILIOS, *Isagogi sti Nomopliroforiki kai ti Dikeokivernitiki (Introduction to Legal Informatics and Law-cybernetics*, in Greek), Vol. 1, Sakkoulas, Athens, 1994.

ARAVANTINOS IOANNIS, *Isagogi stin Epistimi tou Dikeou, (Introduction to the Law*, in Greek), Sakkoulas, Athens, 1983.

ASHLEY KEVIN, *Case-Based Reasoning, Tutorial Notes* Presented at the 3RD INTERNATIONAL CONFERENCE ON ARTIFICIAL INTELLIGENCE AND LAW, Oxford 1991.

ASHLEY KEVIN, *Modeling Legal Argument*, MIT Press, Cambridge Mass., 1990.

BAADE HANS W. (Ed.), *Jurimetrics*, Basic Books, New York, 1963.

BENCH – CAPON TREVOR (Ed.), *Knowledge Based Systems and Legal Applications*, Academic Press, London, 1991.

BENNUN MERVIN (Ed.), *Computers, Artificial Intelligence and the Law*, Ellis Horwood, 1991.

BERWICK ROBERT, *The Acquisition of Syntactic Knowledge*, MIT Press, 1985.

BIBENT MICHEL, *L'Informatique Appliquée à la Jurisprudence*, Librairies Techniques, Paris, 1976.

BING JON & HARVOLD TRYGVE, *Legal Decisions and Information Systems,* Universitetsforlaget, Oslo, 1977.

BING JON & SELMER KNUT (Eds.), *A Decade of Computers and Law*, Universitetsforlaget, Oslo, 1980.

BING JON, *Handbook of Legal Information Retrieval,* North Holland, Amsterdam, 1984.

BLUME PETER (Ed.), *Nordic Studies in Information Technology and Law*, Kluwer, Deventer, 1991.

BREUKER J.A, DE MULDER R.V. & HAGE J.C., *Legal Knowledge Based Systems*, Koninklijke Vermande BV, Lelystad, 1991.

BRITISH COMPUTER SOCIETY IRG, *Abstracts and Notebook*: 11th Information Retrieval Research Colloquium, BCSIRSG, Huddersfield Polytechnic, 5-6 July, 1989.

BUCHANAN B. & SHORTLIFFE E. (Eds.), *Rule Based Expert Systems: The MYCIN experiments of the Stanford Heuristic Programming Project,* Addison Weshley, Reading MA, 1984.

CAMBELL COLLIN, *Data Processing and the Law*, Sweet & Maxwell, London, 1984.

CAPPER P. & SUSSKIND R., *Latent Damage Act, The Expert System*, Butterworths, London, 1988.

CARIDI GIANFRANCO, *Metodologia e Techniche dell' Informatica Giuridica*, Giuffrè, Milano, 1989.

CIAMPI CONSTANTINO (Ed.), *Artificial Intelligence and Legal Information Systems*, North-Holland Publisher, Amsterdam, 1982.

COUNCIL OF EUROPE, Recommendation No. R(80)3 *Teaching, Research and Training in the Field of "Computers & Law",* Council Of Europe, 30 April, 1980.

COUNCIL OF EUROPE, Recommendation No. R(83)3 *Concerning the Protection of Users of Computerised Legal Information Services*, Council Of Europe, 22 February, 1983.

COUNCIL OF EUROPE, *Systems Based on Artificial Intelligence in the Legal Field*, PROCEEDINGS OF THE 9TH SYMPOSIUM ON LEGAL DATA PROCESSING IN EUROPE, BONN, 10-12 OCTOBER 1989.

DAVIES ROY (Ed.), *Intelligent Information Systems*, Ellis Horwood, 1986.

DWORKIN RONALD, *A Matter of Principle*, Clarendon Press, Oxford, 1986.

300

DWORKIN RONALD, *Law's Empire*, Fontana Press, London, 1986.

DWORKIN RONALD, *Taking Rights Seriously*,(6th impression) Duckworth & Co., London, 1991.

ELMI GIANCARLO TADDEI-, *Dimensioni dell' Informatica Giuridica*, Liguori editore, Napoli, 1990.

FEIGENBAUM E. & FELDMAN J., *Computers and Thought*, McGraw-Hill, New York, 1963.

FEIGENBAUM E. & MCCODRUCK P., *The Fifth Generation*, Addison Weshley, Reading, Ma., 1983.

FIEDLER H. - HAFT F. - TRAUNMÜLLER R. (Eds.), *Expert Systems in Law, Impacts on Legal Theory and Computer Law*, Attempto Verlag, Tübingen, 1988.

FORSYTH RICHARD, *Expert Systems: Principles and Case Studies*, Chapman And Hall Computing, London, 1984.

GARDNER ANNE VON DER LIETH, *An Artificial Intelligence Approach to Legal Reasoning*, MIT Press, Cambridge Mass, 1987.

GINSBERG ALLEN, *Automatic Refinement of Expert Systems Knowledge Bases*, Pitman, London, 1988.

GRÜTTERS, BREUKER, VAN DEN HERIK, SHMIDT & DE VEY MESTDAGH (Eds.), *Legal Knowledge Based Systems: Information Technology & Law*, PROCEEDINGS OF THE JURIX 92 CONFERNECE, Koninklijke Vermande, Lelystad, 1992.

GORDON THOMAS, *The Pleadings Game: An Artificial Intelligence Model of Procedural Justice,* unpublished PhD Thesis, Fachbereich Informatik, Technische Hochschule, Darmastadt, 1993.

GUIDOTTI P., PRAKKEN H., SARTOR G., ELMI G. T., TISCORNIA D. & TURCHI F., *Rappresentazione della Conoscenza e Ragionamento Giuridico*, CLUEB, Bologna, 1995.

HART H.L.A., *The Concept of Law*, Clarendon Press, Oxford, 1961.

HASSETT PATRICIA, *Using Expert Systems Technology to Improve Bail Decisions*, Institute of Advanced Legal Studies Research Working Papers, London, 1992.

HOHFELD, WESLEY & NEWCOMB, *Fundamental Legal Conceptions as Applied in Judicial Reasoning*, Edited by Walter Wheeler Cook from the 1913, 23 YALE LAW JOURNAL article, Yale University Press, New Haven, 1963.

HOROVITZ JOSEPH, *Law and Logic*, Springer Verlag, New York, 1972.

INFORMATION TECHNOLOGY AND THE LAW, *An International Bibliography*, Vol. 1, No. 1, Martinus Nijhoff Publishers, 1992.

INTZESSILOGLOU NIKOLAOS, *Ilektroniki Epexergasia toy Dikeou*, (*Electronic Processing of the Law*, in Greek), Paratiritis, Thessaloniki, 1988.

KASPERSEN H.W.K. & OSKAMP A. (Eds.), *Amongst Friends in Computers and Law, A Collection of Essays in Remembrance of Guy Vandenberghe*, Kluwer, Deventer, 1990.

KATSH M. ETHAN, *Law in a Digital World*, Oxford University Press, New York, 1995.

KOERS A.W, KRACHT D., SMITH M., SMITS J.M. & WEUSTEN M.C.M., *Knowledge based Systems in Law, In search of Methodologies and Tools*, Kluwer, Deventer, 1991.

KRACHT D., DE VEY MESTDAGH C.N.J, SVENSSON J.S. (Eds.), *Legal Knowledge Based Systems: An Overview of Criteria for Validation and Practical Use*, Koninklijke Vermande BV, Lelystad, 1990.

KUHN THOMAS S., *The Structure of Scientific Revolutions*, The University of Chicago Press, Chicago, 1962.

LEITH PHILIP, *The Computerised Lawyer:A Guide to the Use of Computers in the Legal Profession*, Springer-Verlag, 1991.

LEITH PHILIP & INGRAM PETER (Eds.), *The Jurisprudence of Orthodoxy, Queen's University Essays on H.L.A. Hart*, Routledge London, 1988.

LARENZ KARL, *Methodenlehre der Rechtswissenschaft*, (5th edition), Berlin, 1983.

LEVI EDWARD H., *An Introduction to Legal Reasoning*, University of Chicago Press, Chicago, 1949.

LLOYD MICHAEL, *Legal Databases in Europe*, North Holland, 1985.

MACCORMICK NEIL, *Legal Reasoning and Legal Theory*, Clarendon Press, Oxford, 1978.

MACORMICK NEIL & WEINBERGER OTA, *An Institutional Theory of Law, New Approaches to Legal Positivism*, D. REIDEL PUBLISHING COMAPANY, Dordrecht, 1986.

MARIANI PAOLA & TISCORNIA DANIELA (Eds.), *Sistemi Esperti Giuridici*, Franco Angeli, Milano, 1989.

MARTINO A.A (Ed.), *Deontic Logic, Computanional Linguistics and Legal Information Systems*, North-Holland Publisher, 1982.

MARTINO A.A. (Ed.), *Expert Systems in Law*, NORTH HOLLAND, 1992.

MARTINO A.A. & SOCCI-NATALI F. (Eds.), *Automated Analysis of Legal Texts*, North Holland, Edited versions of Selected Papers from the INTERNATIONAL CONFERENCE ON LOGIC, INFORMATICS, LAW, FLORENCE SEPTEMBER 1985, North Holland, 1986.

MCTEAR M. & ANDERSON T., *Understanding Knowledge Engineering*, Ellis Horwood in IT, Chisester, 1990.

MITAL V. & JOHNSON L., *Advanced Information Systems for Lawyers*, Chapman & Hall, London, 1992.

MITRAKAS ANDREAS, *A Legal Advisory System Concerning Electronic Data Interchange within the European Community*, COMPLEX 6/96, Tano, Oslo, 1996.

MITRAKAS ANDREAS, *Open EDI and Law in Europe*, Kluwer Law International, The Hague, 1997.

MORISON JOHN & LEITH PHILIP, *The Barrister's World and the Nature of Law*, Open University Press, Milton Keynes - Philadelphia, 1992.

NAGEL STUART (Ed.), *Law, Decision Making and Microcomputers*, Quorum Books, New York, 1991.

NAGEL S.S. & NEEF, *The Legal Process, Modelling the System*, London , 1977.

NATHANSON STEPHEN, *What Lawyers Do: A Problem-Solving Approach to Legal Practice*, Sweet & Maxwell, London, 1997.

NIBLETT BRYAN, *Computer Science and the Law: an Advanced Course*, Cambridge University Press, 1980.

PASSIAS ANASTASIOS, *Pliroforiki ke Dikeo* (*Informatics and the Law*, in Greek), EENP, Thessaloniki, 1987.

PASSIAS ANASTASIOS, *Nomiki Pliroforiki, I Dikeiki Praxi sti Dynamiki ton Megalon Systimaton Ilektronikis Ipostirixis*, (*Legal Informatics, the Legal Practice under the Dynamics of Electronic Support Systems*, in Greek), Sakkoulas, Thessaloniki, 1995

PECZENIK ALEXANDER, *On Law and Reason*, Kluwer, 1989.

PRAKKEN H., MUNTJEWERFF A.J. & SOETEMAN A. (Eds.), *Legal Knowledge Based Systems the Relation with Legal Theory*, PROCEEDINGS OF THE JURIX 94 CONFERENCE, Koninklijke Vermande, Amsterdam, 1994.

PROCEEDINGS OF THE 1ST INTERNATIONAL CONFERENCE ON ARTIFICIAL INTELLIGENCE AND LAW, Boston, ACM Press, 1987.

PROCEEDINGS OF THE 2ND INTERNATIONAL CONFERENCE ON ARTIFICIAL INTELLIGENCE AND LAW, Vancouver, ACM Press, 1989.

PROCEEDINGS OF THE 3RD INTERNATIONAL CONFERENCE ON ARTIFICIAL INTELLIGENCE AND LAW, Oxford, 25-28 June 1991, ACM Press, 1991.

PROCEEDINGS OF THE 4TH INTERNATIONAL CONFERENCE ON ARTIFICIAL INTELLIGENCE AND LAW, Amsterdam, 15-18 June 1993, ACM Press, 1993.

PROCEEDINGS OF THE 5TH INTERNATIONAL CONFERENCE ON ARTIFICIAL INTELLIGENCE AND LAW, University of Maryland, 21-24 May 1995, ACM Press, 1995.

PROCEEDINGS OF THE FOURTH NATIONAL CONFERENCE ON LAW, COMPUTERS AND ARTIFICIAL INTELLIGENCE, University of Exeter, 21-21 April 1994.

RAZ JOSEPH, *The Concept of a Legal System, An Introduction to the Theory of Legal System*, second edition, Clarendon, Oxford, 1980.

REED CHRIS (Ed.), *Computer Law*, Blackstone Press, London, 1990.

SALTON GERARD & MCGILL MICHAEL, *Introduction to Modern Information Retrieval*, Mcgraw-Hill, New York, 1983.

SARTOR GIOVANNI, *Le Applicazioni Giuridiche dell' Intelligenza Artificiale*, Giuffrè, Milano, 1990.

SARTOR GIOVANNI, *Artificial Intelligence and Law, Legal Philosophy and Legal Theory*, COMPLEX 1/93, TANO, OSLO, 1993.

SAVIGNY FRIEDRICH CARL VON, *System des heutigen romischen Rechts*, I, 1840.

SCHILD URI JACOB, *Open-Textured Law, Expert Systems and Logic Programming*, unpublished PhD Thesis, University of London, 1989.

SEIPEL PETER, *Computing Law*, Liberfoerlag, Stockholm, 1977.

SEIPEL PETER (Ed.), *From Data Protection to Knowledge Machines*, Kluwer, Deventer, 1990.

SIMITIS SPIROS, *Informationskrise des Rechts und Datenverarbeitung*, Karlsruhe, 1970.

SINDING-LARSEN HENRIK (Ed.), *Artificial Intelligence and Language, Old Questions in a New key*, COMPLEX 7/88, Tano, Oslo, 1988.

SOCIETY FOR COMPUTERS & LAW, *Tomorrow's Lawyers: Computers and Legal Training*, SCL March, 1981.

SOETEMAN AREND, *Logic in Law*, Kluwer, 1989.

SOURLAS PAVLOS, *Themeliodi Zitimata tis Methodologias tou Dikeou*, *(Fundamental Issues of Legal Methodology*, in Greek), Athens 1986.

SOWA JOHN F., *Conceptual Structures, Information Processing in Mind and Machine*, Addison Weshley, 1984.

STAMATIS K., *Isagogi sti Methodologia tou Dikeou*, *(Introduction to Legal Methodolgy*, in Greek), Thessaloniki, 1991.

SUSSKIND RICHARD, *Expert Systems in Law: a Jurisprudential Inquiry*, Clarendon Press, Oxford, 1987.

SUSSKIND RICHARD, *Essays on Law and Artificial Intelligence*, COMPLEX 7/93, NRCCL, Oslo, 1993.

SUSSKIND RICHARD, *The Future of Law*, Clarendon Press, Oxford, 1996

SVENSSON J.S., WASSINK J.G.J. & VAN BUGGENHOUT B., *Legal Knowledge Based Systems, Intelligent Tools for Drafting Legislation, Computer - Supported Comparison of Law*, Proceedings of the JURIX 93 Conference, Koninklijke Vermande, 1993

TAPPER COLIN, *Computers and the Law*, Weidenfeld & Nicolson, London, 1973.

TISCORNIA DANIELA, *Il Diritto Nei Modelli dell' Intelligenza Artificiale*, CLUEB, Bologna, 1996.

VALENTE A., *Legal Knowledge Engineering, A Modelling Approach*, IOS Press, Amsterdam, 1995.

VANDENBERGHE GUY P.V. (Ed.), *Advanced Topics of Law and Information Technology*, Kluwer-Computer/Law, Deventer, 1989.

WAHLGREN PETER, *Automation of Legal Reasoning, A Study on Artificial Intelligence and Law*, Kluwer, Deventer, 1992.

WATERMAN D.A., *A Guide to Expert Systems*, Addison-Weshley, Reading MA., 1986.

WEINBERGER OTA, *Philosophische Studien zur Logic*, Prague, 1964 .

WEINBERGER OTA, *Rechstlogic*, Vienna - New York, 1970.

WIENER NORBERT, *Cybernetics: or Control and Communication in the Animal and the Machine*, MIT Press (2nd Edition), 1961.

ZELEZNIKOW J. & HUNTER D., *Building Intelligent Legal Information Systems, Representation and Reasoning in Law,* Kluwer, Computer/Law Series, 1994.

II. ARTICLES

AGOSTI M, ARCHI A., COLOTTI R., DI GIORGI R.M., GRADENIGO G., INGHIRAMI B, MATTIELLO P., NANNUCCI R. & RAGONA M., *A Hypertext Prototype as a Tool for Retrieving Environmental Legal Information*, in CONGRES INTERNATIONAL INFORMATIQUE & DROIT, Buenos Ayres, 16-19 October, 1990.

AIKENHEAD MICHAEL, *Legal Knowledge Based Systems: some Observations on the Future*, in WEB JOURNAL OF CUREENT LEGAL ISSUES, 1995.

ALCHOURRÓN C. & MARTINO A., *A Sketch of Logic without Truth*, in PROCEEDINGS OF THE SECOND INTERNATIONAL CONFERENCE ON ARTIFICIAL INTELLIGENCE AND LAW, Vancouver, 1989.

ALCHOURRÓN C. & BULYGIN E., *Limits of Logic and Legal Reasoning*, in MARTINO (Ed.), 1992, p. 9.

ALEXY ROBERT, *Legal Expert Systems and Legal Theory*, in FIEDLER et al. (Eds.), Attempto Verlag, Tübingen, 1988.

ALEXY ROBERT, *Justification and Application of Norms*, in RATIO JURIS Vol. 6, No. 2, p. 158, July, 1993.

ALLEN LAYMAN, *Symbolic Logic: A Razor-edged Tool for Drafting and Interpreting Legal Documents*, in YALE LAW JOURNAL, Vol. 66, 1957, p.833.

ALLEN LAYMAN, *Language, Law and Logic: Plain Legal Drafting for the Electronic Age*, in NIBLETT (Ed.), Cambridge University Press, 1980.

ALLEN LAYMAN, *Towards a Normalized Language to Clarify the Structure of Legal Discourse*, in MARTIN (Ed.), North Holland 1981.

ALLEN L.E. & CALDWELL M. E., *Modern Logic and Judicial Decision Making: A Sketch of One View*, IN BAADE (Ed.), Basic Books, New York, 1963.

ALLEN L., PAYTON S. & SAXON C., *Synthesizing Related Rules from Statutes and Cases for Legal Expert Systems*, in RATIO JURIS Vol. 3, No. 2, July 1990.

ALLEN LAYMAN & SAXON CHARLES, *Analysis of the Logical Structure of Legal Rules by a Modernised and Formalised Version of Hohfeld Fundamental LegalConceptions*, in MARTINO & SOCCI-NATALI (Eds.), North Holland 1986.

307

ALLEN LAYMAN & SAXON CHARLES, *Some Problems in Designing Expert Systems to Aid Legal Reasoning,* in PROCEEDINGS OF THE FIRST INTERNATIONAL CONFERENCE ON ARTIFICIAL INTELLIGENCE AND LAW, Boston, ACM, 1987.

ALLEN LAYMAN & SAXON CHARLES, *Automatic Generation of a Legal Expert System*, in NAGEL (Ed.), Quorum Books, New York, 1991, p. 243.

ALLEN LAYMAN & SAXON CHARLES, *Relationship of Expert Systems to the Operation of a Legal System*, in MARTINO (Ed.), North Holland, 1992.

ALLEN L. & RUDY E., *Normalized Legal Drafting and the Query Method*, in JOURNAL OF LEGAL EDUCATION 29, 1978. P. 381.

ALLEN T. & ROBINSON W.F., *The Defamation Tutor: Integrating CAL and Hypertext*, in LAW TECHNOLOGY JOURNAL, Vol. 2, No. 1, October, 1992.

ALLEN THOMAS & ROBINSON WILLIAM, *Improving Linear Computer Assisted Learning*, in YEARBOOK OF LAW COMPUTERS AND TECHNOLOGY, Vol. 8, 1994, p. 93.

ALEVEN VINCENT & ASHLEY KEVIN, *What law Students Need to Know to WIN*, in YEARBOOK OF LAW COMPUTERS AND TECHNOLOGY, Vol. 8, 1994, p. 115.

ARMER PAUL, *Attitudes Toward Intelligent Machines*, in FEIGENBAUM & FELDMAN (Eds.), 1963, p. 387.

ASHLEY K.D. & RISSLAND E., *Toward Modelling Legal Argument*, in MARTINO & SOCCI-NATALI (Eds.), North Holland, 1986.

ASHLEY K. & ALEVEN T., *Towards an Intelligent Tutoring System for Teaching Law Students to Argue with Cases,* in PROCEEDINGS OF THE THIRD INTERNATIONAL CONFERENCE ON ARTIFICIAL INTELLIGENCE AND LAW, Oxford, ACM Press, 1991.

ASHLEY K., *Case-Based Reasoning and its Implications in Legal Expert Systems*, in ARTIFICIAL INTELLIGENCE AND LAW, Vol. 1, No. 2, 1992, p. 113.

ATIYAH P.S., *Common Law and Statute Law*, in THE MODERN LAW REVIEW, Vol. 48, No. 1, p. 2.

BAINBRIDGE DAVID, *Computers in Legal Decision-Making*, in NAGEL (Ed.), Quorum Books, New York, 1991, p. 309.

BANNERMAN KEITH, *Expert Systems: Can we Expect to Witness Them?,* in COMPUTERS AND LAW, Vol. 53, p. 25, September, 1987.

BAUER-BERNET HÉLÈNE, *Effect of Information Science on the Formation and Drafting of Law*, in JURIMETRICS JOURNAL, p. 235, Summer, 1974.

BENCH-CAPON T. & COENEN F., *Exploiting Isomorphism: Development of a KBS to Support British Coal Insurance Claims* in PROCEEDINGS OF THE 3RD INTERNATIONAL CONFERENCE ON ARTIFICIAL INTELLIGENCE AND LAW, Oxford, June 25-28 1991.

BENCH-CAPON T. & COENEN F., *Isomorphism and Legal Knowledge Based Systems*, in ARTIFICIAL INTELLIGENCE AND LAW, Vol. 1, No. 1, 1992, p. 65.

BERMAN DONALD, *Developer's Choice in the Legal Domain: The Sisyphean Journey with CBR or Down Hill with Rules*, in PROCEEDINGS OF THE THIRD INTERNATIONAL CONFERENCE ON ARTIFICIAL INTELLIGENCE AND LAW, OXFORD, ACM, 1991.

BERMAN D. & HAFNER C., *Indeterminacy: A Challenge to Logic-based models of Legal Reasoning*, in YEARBOOK OF LAW COMPUTERS & TECHNOLOGY, Vol. 3, p. 1, 1987.

BERRY DIANE, *Implicit Knowldge and Expert Systems*, in SINDING-LARSEN (Ed.), COMPLEX 7/88, Oslo, 1988.

BIGELOW ROBERT, *LITE Legal Infromation thru Electronics*, in JURIMETRICS JOURNAL, December 1966, p. 83.

BING JON, *A Model of Legal Information Retrieval as Part of the Decision Process*, in INFORMATICA E DIRITTO, Vol. 2, No. 3, p. 259, 1976.

BING JON, *Legal Sources Availability and Access by Information System*, in BING & SELMER (Eds.) Universitetsforlaget, Oslo, 1980.

BING JON, *Deontic Systems a Sketchy Introduction,* in BING & SELMER (Eds.) Universitetsforlaget, Oslo, 1980.

BING JON, *Legal Norms, Discretionary Rules and Computer Programs,* in NIBLETT (Ed.), Cambridge University Press, 1980.

BING JON, *Uncertainty, Decisions and Informations Systems. Elements in the legal decision Process Introducing Uncertainty and their Relation to Legal Information Systems,* in CIAMPI (Ed.), North Holland, 1982.

BING JON, *Third Generation Text Retrieval Systems*, in JOURNAL OF LAW AND INFORMATION SCIENCE, Vol. 1, No. 3, 1983.

BING JON, *Legal Text Retrieval Systems: The Unsatisfactory State of the Art*, in JOURNAL OF LAW AND INFORMATION SCIENCE, Vol. 2, No. 1, 1986.

BING JON, *The Text Retrieval System as a Conversion Partner,* in YEARBOOK OF LAW COMPUTERS & TECHNOLOGY. Vol. 2, p. 25, 1986.

BING JON, *Designing Text Retrieval systems for 'Conceptual Searching*, in PROCEEDINGS OF THE FIRST INTERNATIONAL CONFERENCE ON ARTIFICIAL INTELLIGENCE AND LAW, Boston, 1987.

BING JON, *The Law of the Books and the Law of the Files: Possibilites and Problems of Legal Information Systems*, in COMPUTERS AND LAW, 54, p. 31, December, 1987.

BING JON, *Developing Knowledge Based Legal Systems for the Public Administration*, in LAW-TECHNOLOGY, Vol. 20, No. 1, 1st Quarter, 1987, p. 1.

BING JON, *Computer Assisted Working Environment for Lawyers. Part I: The Concept and Design of Integrated Workstations for Lawyers*, in 7th COLLOQUY ON THE USE OF COMPUTERS IN THE ADMINISTRATION OF JUSTICE, Lisbon 11-13 October 1988, Report to the Council of Europe, 12 February, 1988.

BING JON, *Computer Assisted Working Environment for Lawyers. Part II: From Information Retrieval to Active Decision Support*, in 9TH SYMPOSIUM ON LEGAL DATA PROCESSING IN EUROPE, Bonn, 10-12 October 1989, Report to the Council of Europe, 22 May, 1989.

BING JON, *The Law of the Books and the Law of the Files, Possibilities and Problems of Legal Information Systems*, in VANDENBERGHE (Ed.), Kluwer, Computer/Law Series, 1989.

BING JON, *ARCTIS Technical Description*. Report to the Norwegian Research Centre for Computers and Law, 1990.

BING JON, *Information law ?,* in MEDIA LAW AND PRACTICE, p. 210, 1990.

BING JON, *Legal Decisions and Computerized Systems*, in SEIPEL (Ed.), Kluwer, Computer/Law Series, 1990.

BING JON, *The Problem of Finding a Precedent*, in NAGEL (Ed.), Quorum Books, New York, 1991, p. 223.

BING JON, *Rules and Representation; Interaction between Legal Knowledeg Based Systems and the General Theory of Legal Rules*, in BLUME (Ed.), Kluwer, Computer/Law Series, 1991.

BING JON, *Three Generations of Computerized Systems for Public Administration and Some Implications for Legal Decision-Making*, in RATIO JURIS, Vol. 3, No. 2, July, 1990, p. 219.

BING JON, *Information Systems and Regulatory Management*, in LAW/TECHNOLOGY JOURNAL, Vol. 2, No. 1, p. 13, October, 1992.

BING JON, *Breaking New Ground: the Work of the Norwegian Research Centre for Computers and Law*, in YEARBOOK OF LAW COMPUTERS AND TECHNOLOGY, Vol. 8, 1994, p. 193.

BLAIR D. & MARON M.E., *An Evaluation of Retrieval Effectiveness for a Full-Text Document Retrieval System*, in COMMUNICATIONS OF THE ACM Vol. 28, No. 3, p. 289, March 1985.

BLAIR D. & MARON M.E., *Full-Text Information Retrieval: Further Analysis and Clarification*, in INFORMATION PROCESSING AND MANAGEMENT Vol. 26, No. 3, p. 437, 1990.

BLAKE H. & WESSEL M., *Where is the Computer T aking us?*, in YEARBOOK OF LAW COMPUTERS & TECHNOLOGY. Vol. 1, p. 141, 1984.

BLUME PETER, *Data retrieval and the Legal System*, in YEARBOOK OF LAW COMPUTERS & TECHNOLOGY. Vol. 2, p. 64, 1986.

BLUME PETER, *From Speech to Data*, Institute of Legal Science, University of Copenhagen, Akademisk Forlag, 1989.

BLUME PETER, *The Changing Shape of Legal sources and Communication*, in SEIPEL (Ed.), Kluwer, Computer/Law Series, 1990.

BRANTING K., *A Reduction-Graph Model of Ratio Decidendi*, in PROCEEDINGS OF THE 4TH INTERNATIONAL CONFERENCE ON ARTIFICIAL INTELLIGENCE AND LAW, Amsterdam, 15-18 June1993, ACM Press, 1993.

BRANTING KARL, *A Computational Model of Ratio Descidendi*, IN ARTIFICIAL INTELLIGENCE AND LAW, Vol. 2, No. 1, 1994, p. 1.

BROUWER P. W., *Legal Knowledge Representation in the Perspective of Legal Theory*, in PRAKKEN, MUNTJEWERFF & SOETEMAN (Eds.), Proceedings of the Jurix 94 Conference, Koninklijke Vermande, Amsterdam, 1994.

BOURCIER DANIÈLE, *The Judge's Discourse: Research on the Modelization of Reasoning in Law*, in CIAMPI (Ed.), North Holland 1982.

BOURCIER DANIÈLE, *Expert Systems and Reasoning Aids for Decision-Makers*, in MARTINO (Ed.), North Holland, 1992.

BOSWORTH KYLE, *Talking Up Computer Expectations*, in YEARBOOK OF LAW COMPUTERS & TECHNOLOGY, Vol. 5, p. 58, 1991.

BUCHANAN B. & HEADRICK TH., *Some Speculation About Artificial Intelligence and Legal Reasoning*, in STANFORD LAW REVIEW, Vol. 23, p. 40, November, 1970.

CALDWELL MARY ELLEN, *Jurisprudence in Interdisciplinary Environments*, in JURIMETRICS JOURNAL, p. 1, March, 1968.

CAMERON NEIL, *Computers: Myths about Integration Blues*, in LAW SOCIETY'S GAZETTE, Vol. 87, No. 6, p. 16, 14 February, 1990.

CAMMELLI A. & SOCCI F., *LEXIS: A Legal Expert System for Improving Legislative Drafting*, in PROCEEDINGS OF THE INTERNATIONAL CONFERENCE: DATABASE AND EXPERT SYSTEMS APPLICATIONS, Vienna, 1990.

CHALTON SIMON, *Small Law Firms: Technology to the Rescue*, in NEW LAW JOURNAL, Vol. 139, No. 6428, p. 1409, 20 October 1989.

CIAMPI CONSTANTINO, *Artificial Intelligence and Legal Information Systems*, in CIAMPI (Ed.), North Holland, 1981.

CLARK A. & ECONOMIDES K., *Technics and Praxis. Technological Innovation and Legal Practice in Modern Society*, in YEARBOOK OF LAW COMPUTERS & TECHNOLOGY, Vol. 4, p16, 1989.

CLARK ANDREW, *Information Technology in Legal Services*, in JOURNAL OF LAW AND SOCIETY, Vol. 19, No. 1, Blackwell, London, 1992.

COHEN MORRIS L., *Reserach Habbits of Lawyers*, in JURIMETRICS JOURNAL, p. 183, June, 1969.

COLLINS HUGH, *The Place of Computers in Legal Education*, in BIRKS (Ed.) *Reviewing legal education*, OXFORD, 1994.

CREMONA MARISE, *Expert Systems in Law – Workshop Seminar*, in COMPUTERS AND LAW No. 55, p. 10 March, 1988.

311

DALE JOHN, *Law Courseware Consortium: towards an Integrated Model For Legal CBL*, in YEARBOOK OF LAW COMPUTERS AND TECHNOLOGY, Vol. 8, 1994, p. 167.

DAVIS DAVID, *Word Statistics and the Law: Information Retrieval as an Indexing Process*, in YEARBOOK OF LAW COMPUTERS & TECHNOLOGY, Vol. 3, p. 168, 1987.

DAYAL SURENDRA & MOLES ROBERT, *The Open Texture of Language: Handling Semantic Analysis in Legal Decision Support Systems*, in JOURNAL OF LAW AND INFORMATION SCIENCE Vol. 4, No. 2, 1993, p. 330.

DE MULDER R. V., *A Model for Legal Decision –Making by Computer*, in MARTINO & SOCCI-NATALI (Eds.), North Holland 1986.

DE MULDER R. V. & COMBRINK-KUITERS C.J.M., *Is a Computer Capable of Interpreting Case Law?* In JOURNAL OF INFORMATION LAW & TECHNOLOGY, Issue 2, 1996.

DE MULDER R. V. & VAN NOORTWIJK C., *Dealing with Conceptual Diversity in Legal Information Systems*, in PROCEEDINGS OF THE FOURTH NATIONAL CONFERENCE ON LAW, COMPUTERS & AI, University of Exeter, 1994.

DE MULDER R.V., VAN NOORTWIJK C., KERKMEESTER H.O. AND VAN DER WEES, *Knowledge Systems and the Law: The Juricas project*, in EXPERT SYSTEMS WITH APPLICATIONS, Vol. 4, p. 415, 1992.

DE SCHUTTER BART, *A Human Scientist's Approach to Information Technology*, in YEARBOOK OF LAW COMPUTERS & TECHNOLOGY, Vol. 3, p. 136, 1987.

DICK JUDITH, *Representation of Legal Text for Conceptual Retrieval*, in PROCEEDINGS OF THE THIRD INTERNATIONAL CONFERENCE ON ARTIFICIAL INTELLIGENCE AND LAW, OXFORD, ACM, 1991.

DI GIORGI R., FAMELI E. & NANNUCCI R., *Expert System and Database Interaction in the Legal Domain*, in PROCEEDINGS OF THE INTERNATIONAL CONFERENCE: DATABASE AND EXPERT SYSTEMS APPLICATIONS, Vienna, 1990.

DUFFIN PAUL, *Expert Systems in Law and UK Government*, in COMPUTERS AND LAW, No. 61, p. 9, September, 1989.

EDWARDS LILIAN, *Building an Interstate Succession Adviser: Compartmentalisation and Creativity in Decision Support Systems*, in JOURNAL OF LAW AND INFORMATION SCIENCE, Vol. 3, No. 1, p116, 1992.

ELMI GIANCARLO TADDEI-, *L' Informatique Juridique entre la Philosophie et la Science: "Autonomie et Interdisciplinarité"*, in LES ANNALES DE L' IRETIJ, No. 1, Montpellier, 1989.

ELMI GIANCARLO TADDEI-, *L' Insegnamento dell' Informatica Giuridica in Italia*, in INFORMATICA E DIRITTO, Vol. 1, p. 188, 1989.

ERDELEZ S. & HILLMAN P, *Courses on Computers and Law in American Law Schools*, in YEARBOOK OF LAW COMPUTERS & TECHNOLOGY, Vol. 4, p. 38, 1989.

FAMELI E. & MERCATALI R., *Expert Systems and Legal Decision-Making Models*, in MARTINO & SOCCI-NATALI (Eds.), North Holland 1986.

FAMELI, NANNUCCI & DI GIORGI, *Expert Systems and Databases: a Prototype in Environmental Law*, in INFORMATICA & DIRITTO, XVII, January-December, 1991.

FEIGENBAUM E. & FELDMAN J., *Preface* in FEIGENBAUM-FELDMAN (Eds.), p. v, 1963.

FEIGENBAUM E. & FELDMAN J., *Simulation of Cognitive Process*, in FEIGENBAUM-FELDMAN (Eds.), p. 269, 1963.

FEIGENBAUM EDWARD, *The Simulation of Verbal Learning Behavior*, in FEIGENBAUM-FELDMAN (Eds.), p. 297, 1963.

FELSKY MARTIN, *The Canadian Experience in Teaching Computers and Law*, in YEARBOOK OF LAW COMPUTERS & TECHNOLOGY, Vol. 3, p. 97, 1987.

FIEDLER HERBERT, *Grundprobleme der Juristishen Informatik*, in DATENVERARBEITUNG IM RECHT, Vol. 3, p. 199, 1974.

FIEDLER HERBERT, *Expert Systems as a Tool for Drafting Legal Decisions*, in MARTINO & SOCCI-NATALI (Eds.), North Holland 1986.

FIEDLER HERBERT, *Grundlagen und Anwendungsmöglichkeiten von Expertensystemen für die Justiz*, in INFORMATIK UND RECHT, Vol. 3, p. 101, 1987.

FIEDLER HERBRET, *Introduction – Legal Expert Systems and the General Theory of Law*, in FIEDLER *et al.* (Eds.), Attempto Verlag, Tübingen, 1988.

FINKELSTEIN A. & FISCHER M., *Arranging Marriages in Pakistan and Legal Expert Systems*, in COMPUTERS AND LAW, No. 61, p. 11, September, 1989.

FLESHER TONYA, *What the IRS Knows About Artificial Intelligence That You Should Know*, in the TAX MAGAZINE, Vol. 65, No. 11, p. 707, November, 1987.

FREED ROY N., *Teaching and Practicing Computer Law Effectively: An Introductory Discussion*, in YEARBOOK OF LAW COMPUTERS & TECHNOLOGY, Vol. 5, p. 116, 1991.

FREEMAN PAUL, *Expert Systems and the Law*, in COMPUTERS AND LAW, No. 47, p9, March, 1986.

FROSINI VITTORIO, *Computer Law in the 80s*, in COMPUTER LAW & PRACTICE, July/August, 1986.

FROSINI VITTORIO, *Social Implications of the Computer Revolution Advantages and Disadvantages*, in INFORMATICA & DIRITTO, p. 7, September – December, 1987.

FROSINI VITTORIO, *Law Making and Legal Interpretation*, in RATIO JURIS, Vol. 6, No. 2, p. 118, July, 1993.

GALTUNG ANDREAS & MÆSEL DAG SYVERT, *XCITE, an Expert System for Naturalisation Cases*, in COMPLEX, 1, 1990, p. 234.

GARDNER ANNE VON DER LIETH, *Law Applications*, no further reference, .

GELBART DAPHNE & SMITH J.C., *Knowledge Based Information Retrieval Systems*, in COMPUTERS AND LAW, Vol. 1, No. 5, October 1990.

313

GELBART DAPHNE & SMITH J.C., *The Application of Automated Text Processing Techniques to Legal Text Management*, in YEARBOOK OF LAW COMPUTERS AND TECHNOLOGY, Vol. 8, 1994, p. 203.

GOEBEL J.W. & SCHMALZ R., *Problems of Applying Legal Expert Systems in Legal Practice*, in MARTINO & SOCCI-NATALI (Eds.), North Holland 1986.

GOLD D.I. & SUSSKIND R., EXPERT SYSTEMS IN LAW. *A Jurisprudential and Formal Specification Approach*, in MARTINO & SOCCI-NATALI (Eds.), North Holland 1986.

GONSER T., SOMA J., & WILHELM E., *The Computer as a Tool for Legal Decision Making*, in THE PRACTICAL LAWYER, Vol. 27, p. 11, 11 September, 1981.

GORDON THOMAS, *A Theory Construction Approach to Legal Document Assembly*, in MARTINO (Ed.), North Holland, 1992.

GORDON THOMAS, *From Jhering to Alexy – Using Artificail Intelligence Models in Jurisprudence*, in PRAKKEN, MUNTJEWERFF & SOETEMAN (Eds.), PROCEEDINGS OF THE JURIX 94 Conference, Koninklijke Vermande, Amsterdam, 1994.

GRAY G., MACLENNAN B., NOLT J. & PLOCH D., *Legal Expert System Building: A semi-Intelliegent Computer Program Makes it Easier*, in JOURNAL OF COMPUTER & INFORMATION LAW, Vol. XII,1994, p. 555.

GRAY PAMELA N., *Scaling Up to a Three Dimensional Graphic Trace*, not-published, Jurix 93 paper, 1993.

GREGOR S.D., RIGNEY H.M. & SMITH J.D., *The Applicability of a KBS to Legal Education*, in THE AUSTRALIAN COMPUTER JOURNAL, Vol. 23, No. 1, p. 17, February, 1991.

GREENLEAF G., MOWBRAY A., & TYREE A., *Legal Expert Systems: Words, Words, Words*, in YEARBOOK OF LAW COMPUTERS & TECHNOLOGY, Vol. 3, p. 119, 1987.

GREENLEAF G., MOWBRAY A., & TYREE A., *Expert Systems in Law, The Datalex Project*, IN PROCEEDINGS OF THE FIRST INTERNATIONAL CONFERENCE ON ARTIFICIAL INTELLIGENCE AND LAW, BOSTON, ACM, 1987.

GREENLEAF G. & MOWBRAY A., *The Privacy Workstation*, in PRIVACY LAWS & BUSINESS CONFERENCE, Cambridge, 2-4 July, 1991.

GREENLEAF G., MOWBRAY A. & TYREE A., *The DataLex Legal Workstation, Integrating Tools for Lawyers*, in PROCEEDINGS OF THE 3RD INTERNATIONAL CONFERENCE ON ARTIFICIAL INTELLIGENCE AND LAW, Oxford, June 25-28 1991, ACM Press, 1991, p. 221,.

GREINKE ANDREW: *Legal Expert Systems: A Humanistic Critique of Mechanical Legal Inference*, in E LAW, 1994,
ftp://infolib.murdoch.edu.au/pu/subj/law/jnl/elaw/referred/greinke.txt.

GUIDOTTI, LUCCHESI, MARIANI, RAGONA & TISCORNIA, *An Intelligent Interface to Data Bases on Environmental Law*, in PROCEEDINGS OF THE INTERNATIONAL CONFERENCE: DATABASE AND EXPERT SYSTEMS APPLICATIONS, Vienna, 1990.

GÜNTER KLAUS, *Critical Remarks on Rebert Alexy's "Special-Case Thesis"*, in RATIO JURIS, Vol. 6, No. 2, p. 144, July, 1993.

HAFNER CAROL, *Conceptual Organisation of Case Law Knowledge Bases*, in PROCEEDINGS OF THE FIRST INTERNATIONAL CONFERENCE ON ARTIFICIAL INTELLIGENCE AND LAW, Boston, ACM, 1987.

HAGE J., SPAN G.P.J., LODDER A.R., *A Dialogical Model of Legal Reasoning*, in PROCEEDINGS JURIX 92, Koninklijke Vermande, 1992.

HAGE J., LEENES R. & LODDER A., *Hard Cases: A Procedural Approach*, in ARTIFICIAL INTELLIGENCE AND LAW, Vol. 2, No. 2, 1994, p. 113.

HAGE J., *Teleological Reasoning in Reason-Based Logic*, in PROCEEDINGS OF THE 5TH INTERNATIONAL CONFERENCE ON ARTIFICIAL INTELLIGENCE AND LAW, University of Maryland, 21-24 May 1995, ACM Press, 1995, p. 11.

HART H.L.A., *Positivism and the Separation of Law and Morals*, in HARVARD LAW REVIEW, Vol. 71, 1958.

HARDY TROTTER I., *A Hypertext System for Teaching Legal Research*, in NAGEL (Ed.), Quorum Books, New York, 1991, p. 51.

HASSELTVEDT BEATE & HERRESTAD HENNING, *Modelling Assesment Rules and Case law Reasoning*, in COMPLEX 1, 1990, p. 248.

HOLLANDER ABRAHAM & MACKAAY EJAN, *Are Judges Economists at heart?*, in CIAMPI (Ed.), North Holland 1982.

HUNT E. & HOVLAND C., *Programming a Model of Human Concept Formulation*, in FEIGENBAUM-FELDMAN (Eds.), p. 310, 1963.

HUNT KENNETH, *A Computer in Practice*, in COMPUTER LAW & PRACTICE, p. 188, July/August, 1988.

HUNTER DAN, *Teaching Artificial Intelligence to Law students*, in LAW TECHNOLOGY JOURNAL, Vol. 3, No. 3, October 1994, p. 36.

JACKSON REPORT, Report on the BILETA inquiry into the provision of Information Technology in UK Law Schools, 1991.

JONES ANDREW J.I, *Deontic Logic and Legal Knowledge Representation*, in RATIO JURIS, Vol. 3, No. 2, July, 1990, p. 237.

JONES A. & SERGOT M., *Deontic Logic in the Representation of Law: Towards a Methodology*, in ARTIFICIAL INTELLIGENCE AND LAW, Vol. 1, No. 1, 1992, p. 45.

JONES R.P., *Expert Systems*, Technical Section, in YEARBOOK OF LAW COMPUTERS & TECHNOLOGY, Vol. 2, p. 142, 1986.

JONES RICHARD, *Computer-managed Teaching and Learning in Law*, in YEARBOOK OF LAW COMPUTERS AND TECHNOLOGY, Vol. 8, 1994, p. 173.

JONES R.P., *Using Artificilal Intelligence in Legal Computer Assisted Instruction*, in LAW TECHNOLOGY JOURNAL, Vol. 2, No. 1, p. 6, October, 1992.

315

KAYTON IRVING, *Can Jurimetrics be of Value to Jurisprudence*, in THE GEORGE WASHINGTON LAW REVIEW, Vol. 33, p. 287, 1964.

KLEMENS JON E., *The Future of Technology in Law Firms*, in ABA JOURNAL, July, 1989.

KOLASA SUSAN, *Systems Design and Research Techniques*, in ABA AUTOMATED LAW RESEARCH, p165, 1973.

KOWALSKI ANDREJ, *Leading Law Students to Unchartered Waters and Making them Think: Teaching Artificial Intelligence and Law*, in JOURNAL OF LAW AND INFORMATION SCIENCE, Vol. 2, No. 2, 1991.

KOWALSKI R. & SERGOT MAREK, *The Use of Logical Models in Legal Problem Solving*, in RATIO JURIS, Vol. 3, No. 2, July, 1990, p. 201.

KREVER RICK, *Computers and Legal Education in Australia*, in GORDON (Ed.), p. 494, 1992.

LASHBROOKE E.C., *Legal Reasoning and Artificial Intelligence*, in LOYOLA LAW REVIEW, Vol. 34, p. 287, 1988.

LAURITSEN MARC, *Project Pericles in Retrospect*, in YEARBOOK OF LAW COMPUTERS & TECHNOLOGY, Vol. 5, p. 50, 1991.

LAURITSEN MARC, *Technology Report: Building Legal Practice Systems with Today's Commercial Authoring Tools*, in ARTIFICIAL INTELLIGENCE AND LAW, Vol. 1, No. 1, p. 87.

LEHMAN HUBERT, *Legal Concepts in a Natural Language Based Expert System,* in RATIO JURIS Vol. 3, No. 2, July 1990, p. 245.

LEICHT A. & SIEBELINK V., *TWAICE – eine Expertensystem-Shell*, in INFORMATIK UND RECHT, Vol. 5, p. 208, 1988.

LEINDELNNER-RUPERTSBERGER ELISABETH. *Linguistics, Wittgensteinian Linguistic Philosophy and Artificial Intelligence*, in SINDING-LARSEN (Ed.), COMPLEX 7/88, OSLO, 1988.

LEITH PHILIP, *Formal Models and Legal Reasoning*, in JURIMETRICS, Vol. 24, p. 334, 1984.

LEITH PHILIP, *Cautionary Notes on Legal Expert Systems*, in COMPUTERS & LAW, No. 40, p. 14, May, 1984.

LEITH PHILIP, *Clear Rules and Legal Expert Systems*, in MARTINO & SOCCI-NATALI (Eds.), North Holland 1986.

LEITH PHILIP, *Fundamental Errors in Legal Logic Programming*, in THE COMPUTER JOURNAL, Vol. 29, No. 6, 1986, p. 545.

LEITH PHILIP, *Legal Expert Systems: Misunderstanding the Legal Process*, in COMPUTERS & LAW, No. 49, p. 26, September, 1986.

LEITH PHILIP, *Legal Expertise and Legal Expert Systems*, in YEARBOOK OF LAW COMPUTERS & TECHNOLOGY, vol 2, p. 1, 1986.

LEITH PHILIP, *The Emperor's New Expert System*, in THE MODERN LAW REVIEW, Vol. 50, p. 128, January, 1987.

LEITH PHILIP, *Common Usage, Certainty and Computing*, IN LEITH & INGRAM (Eds.), Routledge London, 1988.

LEITH PHILIP, *The LEXICAL System for Computer-Aided Legal Instruction*, in NAGEL (Ed.), Quorum Books, New York, 1991, p. 181.

LEITH PHILIP, *The Problem with Law in Books and Law in Computers: The Oral Nature of Law*, in ARTIFICIAL INTELLIGENCE REVIEW, Vol. 6, 1991, p. 227.

LEITH PHILIP, *What Future for the Electronic Legal Text?* In YEARBOOK OF LAW COMPUTERS AND TECHNOLOGY, Vol. 8, 1994, p. 212.

LEWIS DAVID P, *Case Law Databases: the Marginal Utility of Additional Historic Material*, in COMPUTERS LAW & PRACTICE, p. 150, May/June, 1987.

LEWIS DAVID P, *Computerised Legal Information in Australia*, in GORDON (Ed.) p. 457, 1992.

LINDSAY ROBERT K., *Inferential Memory as the Basis of Machines which understand Natural Language*, in FEIGENBAUM-FELDMAN (Eds.), p. 217, 1963.

LINK DAVID, *Law Searching by Computer*, in ABA AUTOMATED LAW RESEARCH, p. 3, 1973.

LINK DAVID, *Looking to the Future & Bibliography*, in ABA AUTOMATED LAW RESEARCH, p. 169, 1973.

LOESCHMANN DIANA, *Computers and the Management of a Law Practice: Russell & Dumoulin, a Case Study*, in YEARBOOK OF LAW COMPUTERS & TECHNOLOGY, Vol. 3, p. 68, 1987.

LOEVINGER LEE, *Jurimetrics: The Next Step Forward*, in MINNESOTA LAW REVIEW, Vol. 33, p. 455, April, 1949.

LOEVINGER LEE, *Jurimetrics, The Methodology of Legal Inquiry*, in BAADE (Ed.), Basic Books, New York, 1963.

LOEVINGER LEE, *Law and Science as Rival Systems*, in JURIMETRICS JOURNAL, p. 63, December, 1966.

LOEVINGER LEE, *Science, Technology and Law in Modern Society*, in JURIMETRICS JOURNAL, p. 1, Fall, 1985.

LOEVINGER LEE, Book Review of *The Emperor's New Mind*, by ROGER PENROSE, in JURIMETRICS JOURNAL, Vol. 30, p. 393, Spring, 1990.

LOUI P.R., *Hart's Critics on Defeasible Concepts and Ascriptivism*, in PROCEEDINGS OF THE 5TH INTERNATIONAL CONFERENCE ON ARTIFICIAL INTELLIGENCE AND LAW, University of Maryland, 21-24 May 1995, ACM Press, 1995, p. 21.

MACCORMICK NEIL, *Argumentatiion and Interpretation in Law*, in RATIO JURIS, Vol. 6, No. 2, p. 16, July, 1993.

MACAULAY MARK, *Mapping Legal Hypertext Systems*, in CONFERENCE PRE-PROCEEDINGS, 7TH BILETA CONFERENCE, 1992.

MAHALINGAM-CARR INDIRA, *Expert Systems: Ease at Law?*, in COMPUTERS AND LAW, No. 59, p. 19, March, 1989.

MAHALINGAM-CARR INDIRA, *Statute Law as a Source for Expert Systems*, in COMPUTERS AND LAW, No. 64, p. 15, March, 1990.

MAHONEY DENNIS, *Computerasiation of the Court System in Australia*, in GORDON (Ed.), p. 437, 1992.

MARTINO A., *Legal Models, Rationality and Informatics*, in MARTINO & SOCCI-NATALI (Eds.), North Holland 1986.

MARTINO A., *Legal Expert Systems*, in VANDENBERGHE (Ed.), Kluwer, Computer/Law Series, 1989.

MARTINO A., *Implementation of Expert Systems as an Aid to Legal Decision-Making*, in NAGEL (Ed.), Quorum Books, New York, 1991, p. 223.

MARTINO A. & GRU O., *International Sale: An Expert System Prototype*, in MARTINO (Ed.)., 1992.

MARBLE JOHN, *Computer Technology and in-office Systems*, in ABA AUTOMATED LAW RESEARCH, p. 11, 1973.

MARSHALL DAVID, Book Review: *Latent Damage Law, The Expert System*, by CAPPER P. & SUSSKIND R., in COMPUTERS AND LAW, No. 59, MARCH 1989.

MAWHOOD JOHN, *Information, Equity and Entropy*, in COMPUTER LAW & PRACTICE, p. 186, July/August, 1987.

MAY RONALD, *Preface & The Importance of Professional Involvment*, in ABA AUTOMATED LAW RESEARCH, p1, 1973.

MCCARTY L.T., *Reflections on TAXMAN: An Experiment in Artificial Intelligence and Legal Reasoning*, in HARVARD LAW REVIEW, Vol. 90, p. 837, 1977.

MCCARTY L.T., *The TAXMAN Project:Towards a Cognitive Theory of Legal Argument*, in NIBLETT (Ed.), Cambridge, 1980.

MCCARTY L.T., *A Computational Theory of Eisner v. Macomber*, in CIAMPI (Ed.), North Holland, 1982.

MCCARTY L.T., *Intelligent Legal Information Systems*, in RUTGERS COMPUTER AND TECHNOLOGY LAW JOURNAL, Vol. 9, 1983, p. 265.

MCCARTY L.T., *Permissions and Obligations, An Informal Inroduction*, in MARTINO & SOCCI-NATALI (Eds.), North Holland, 1986.

MCCARTY L.T., *Intelligent Legal Information Systems: An Update*, in FIEDLER *et al.* (Eds.), Tübingen, Attempto Verlag, 1988.

McCarty L.T., *A Language for Legal Discourse:Basic Features,* in Proceedings of the 2nd International Conference on Artificial Intelligence and Law, Vancouver, ACM Press, 1989,.

McCarty L.T., *Artificial Intelligence and Law: How to Get There from Here,* in Ratio Juris, Vol. 3, No. 2, July, 1990, p. 189.

McCarty L.T., *On the Role of Prototypes in Appellate Legal Argument,* in Proceedings of the 3rd International Conference on Artificial Intelligence and Law, Oxford, June 25-28, 1991, ACM Press, 1991.

McCarty L.T., *An Implementation of Eisner v Macomber,* in Proceedings of the 5th International Conference on Artificial Intelligence and Law, University of Maryland, 21-24 May 1995, ACM Press, 1995, p. 276.

Meldman Jeffrey, *Law Students Attitudes toward Computers and Legal Research,* in Jurimetrics Journal, p. 207, June, 1969.

Mehl L., *Automation in the Legal World: From the Machine Processing of Legal Information to the "Law Machine",* Symposium on the Mechanisation of the Thought Process, National Physical Laboratory, U.K., 1958.

Miller John, *Expert Systems – The End of Legal Profession?,* in New Zealand Law Journal, p. 85, March, 1984.

Mills A. & Jones R., *Expert Systems – Technical Section – Various Reports,* in Yearbook of Law Computers & Technology, Vol. 2, p. 142, 1986.

Minsky Marvin, *Steps Towards Artificial Intelligence,* in Feigenbaum-Feldman (Eds.), p. 406, 1963.

Moles Robert N, *Logic Programming – An Assessment of its Potential for Artificial Intelligence Applications in Law,* in Journal of Law and Information Science, Vol. 2, No. 2, 1991.

Moles Robert, *Expert Systems – The Need for Theory,* in Proceedings Jurix 92, Koninklijke Vermande, 1992.

Morrise Mark, *Emerging Computer-Assisted Legal Analysis Systems,* in Brigham Young University Law Review, Vol. 16, p. 116, 1980.

Mowbray a., Greenleaf G. & Tyree A., *Legal Expert Systems: An Introduction,* in Gordon (Ed.) p. 471, 1992.

Mowbray, Greenleaf & Tyree, *The Privacy Workstation,* in Yearbook of Law Computers and Technology, Vol. 6, p. 178, 1992.

Munday Roderick, *Case Law and the Computer,* in Yearbook of Law Computers and Technology, Vol. 1, p. 136, 1984.

Nagel S., *Legal Ethics and Decision-Aiding Software,* in Martino (Ed.), 1992.

Newell A., Shaw J., & Simon H., *Empirical Explorations with the Logic Theory Machine: A case study in Heuristics,* in Feigenbaum-Feldman (Eds.), p. 109, 1963.

NUNN-PRICE NORMAN, *The Context System: A New Concept in Legal Information Retrieval,* IN COMPUTER LAW & PRACTICE, p. 25, September/October, 1986.

OLOWOFOYEKU ABIMBOLA, *Computing for Lawyers, the Keel Experience,* in YEARBOOK OF LAW COMPUTERS AND TECHNOLOGY, Vol. 8, 1994, p. 59.

OSKAMP A. & VANDENBERGHE G.P.V, *Legal Thinking and Automation,* in MARTINO & SOCCI-NATALI (Eds.), North Holland 1986.

OSKAMP ANJA, *Knowledge Representation and Legal Expert Systems,* in VANDENBERGHE (Ed.), Kluwer, Computer/Law Series, 1989.

OSKAMP A. & VAN DEN BERG PETER H., *Legal Expert Systems and Legal Text Retrieval Systems:How About Integration,* in KASPERSEN & OSKAMP (Eds.), Kluwer, Deventer, 1990.

OSKAMP ANJA, *Model for Knowledge and Legal Expert Systems,* in ARTIFICIAL INTELLIGENCE AND LAW, Vol. 1, No. 4, 1993, p. 245.

PALIWALA ABDUL, *The Technology of Clinical Legal Education,* in YEARBOOK OF LAW COMPUTERS AND TECHNOLOGY, Vol. 3, p. 181, 1987.

PALIWALA ABDUL, *Creating an Academic Environment: The Development of Technology in Legal Education in the UK,* in YEARBOOK OF LAW COMPUTERS AND TECHNOLOGY, Vol. 5, p136, 1991.

PATERSON ALAN & SUSSKIND RICHARD, *Technology, Lawyers and the Atlantic Divide,* in LAW TECHNOLOGY JOURNAL, Vol. 3, No. 2, May 1994, p. 43.

PEARCE PENELOPE, *Directories to Databases: Bringing the Law into the Information Age,* in LAW TECHNOLOGY JOURNAL, Vol. 2, No. 2, p. 5, May, 1993.

PHILIP JUDITH, *Education in English Law Firms: Challenges, Trends and Opportunities,* IN INTERNATIONAL YEARBOOK OF LAW COMPUTERS AND TECHNOLOGY, VOL. 8, 1994, p. 41.

PLOCH D., DUMAS B., GRAY G., MACLENNAN B. & NOLT J., *Readability of Law: Forms of Law for Building Legal Expert Systems,* in JURIMETRICS JOURNAL, Vol. 33, p189, Winter 1993.

PRAKKEN HENRY, *A Tool in Modelling Disagreement in Law: Preferring the Most Specific Argument,* in PROCEEDINGS OF THE 3RD INTERNATIONAL CONFERENCE ON ARTIFICIAL INTELLIGENCE AND LAW, Oxford, 25-28 June 1991, ACM Press, 1991.

POPP W.C. & SCHLINK B., *JUDITH a Computer Program to advice Lawyers in Reasoning a Case,* in JURIMETRICS JOURNAL, p. 303, Summer, 1975.

POPPLE J., *Legal Expert Systems: The Inadequacy of a Rule-Based Approach,* in AUSTRALIAN COMPUTER JOURNAL, Vol. 23, No. 1, p. 11, February, 1991.

QUINTANA LINCOLN, *Making our Way into the Coming Age of Electronic Casebooks,* in INTERNATIONAL YEARBOOK OF LAW COMPUTERS AND TECHNOLOGY Vol. 8, 1994, p. 131.

RAZ JOSEPH, *On the Autonomy of Legal Reasoning*, in RATIO JURIS, Vol. 6, No. 2, p. 16, July, 1993.

REED CHRIS, *Expert Systems and Legal Expertise,* in COMPUTER LAW & PRACTICE, Vol. 5, p. 122, 1989.

REISINGER LEO, *Strukturtheorie des Rechts und EDV*, in DATENVERARBEITUNG IM RECHT, Vol. 2, p. 271, 1973.

RISSLAND EDWINA & ASHLEY KEVIN, *HYPO: A Precedent-Based Legal Reasoner*, in VANDENBERGHE (Ed.), Kluwer, Computer/Law Series, 1989,.

RISSLAND EDWINA, *AI & Law: Stepping Stones to a Model of Legal Reasoning*, in YALE LAW JOURNAL, Vol. 99, p. 1957, 1990.

RISSLAND EDWINA & ASHLEY KEVIN, *A Case-Based System for Trade Secrets Law*, in PROCEEDINGS OF THE FIRST INTERNATIONAL CONFERENCE ON ARTIFICIAL INTELLIGENCE AND LAW, Boston, ACM Press, 1987.

SARENPÄÄ AHTI, *Computers and Legal Life, The Use of Computers in Legal Life and their Role in Legal Thinking*, BLUME (Ed.), Kluwer, Computer/Law Series, 1991.

SAMUEL GEOFFREY, *The Challenge of Artificial Intelligence: Can Roman Law Help us Discover whether Law is a System of Rules ?*, in LEGAL STUDIES , Vol. 24, p. 25, 1992.

SARTOR GIOVANNI, *Normative Conflicts in Legal Reasoning*, in ARTIFICIAL INTELLIGENCE AND LAW, Vol. 1, No. 2, p. 209.

SAXBY STEPHEN, *Information Technology: A Strategy for Higher Legal Education*, in YEARBOOK OF LAW COMPUTERS AND TECHNOLOGY, Vol. 1, p. 88, 1984.

SAVOY JACQUES, *Searching Information in Legal Hypertext Systems*, in ARTIFICIAL INTELLIGENCE AND LAW, Vol. 2, No. 3, 1994, p. 205.

SCOTT BRENDAN, *Legal Expert Systems, A Practitioner's Perpsective*, IN JOURNAL OF LAW AND INFORMATION SCIENCE, VOL. 5, No. 2, 1994, P. 227.

SCOTT COLIN & WIDDISON ROBIN, *Law Courseware: The Next Generation*, in LAW TECHNOLOGY JOURNAL, Vol. 3, No. 2, May 1994, p. 7.

SEIPEL PETER, *Computerisation of Judicial & Administrative Activities: Educational Consequence*, in YEARBOOK OF LAW COMPUTERS AND TECHNOLOGY, Vol. 1, p. 26, 1984.

SEIPEL PETER, *Computers and Information Power*, in BLUME (Ed.), Kluwer, Computer/Law Series, 1991.

SERGOT M, SADRI F.,KOWALSKI R., KRIWACZEC F., HAMMOND P.,.& CORY H.T., *The British Nationality Act as a Logic Program,* in COMMUNICATIONS OF THE ACM, Vol. 29, p. 370, 1986.

SERGOT M, CORY H.T., HAMMOND P., KOWALSKI R., KRIWACZEC F.& SADRI F., *Formalisation of the British Nationality Act*, in YEARBOOK OF LAW COMPUTERS AND TECHNOLOGY, Vol. 2, p. 40, 1986.

SERGOT M., *The Representation of Law in Computer Programs,* in BENCH-CAPON (Ed.), Academic Press, 1991.

SHAPIRO FRED, *Linguistic Applications of Lexis and Westlaw,* in JURIMETRICS JOURNAL, Vol. 30, p. 147, Winter, 1990.

SCHARTUM DAG WIESE, *Information Technology and Administartive Systems: Presentation of a New Study Option and some of its Challenges*, in YEARBOOK OF LAW COMPUTERS AND TECHNOLOGY, Vol. 8, 1994, p. 81.

SIGLER DAVID, *Computers in Litigation*, in GORDON (Ed.) p. 485, 1992.

SKALAK D., *Taking Advantage of Models for Legal Classification*, in PROCEEDINGS OF THE SECOND INTERNATIONAL CONFERENCE ON ARTIFICIAL INTELLIGENCE AND LAW, Vancouver, 1989.

SKALAK D. & RISSLAND E., *Arguments and Cases: An Inevitable Interwining*, in ARTIFICIAL INTELLIGENCE AND LAW, Vol. 1, No. 1, 1992, p. 3.

SKALAK D. & RISSLAND E., *Using Case-based Reasoning to Extend the Expertise of Expert Systems*, in MARTINO (Ed.), 1992.

SLADE MICHAEL & GRAY ROSEMARY, *Automated Retrieval Systems in British Legal Education*, in YEARBOOK OF LAW COMPUTERS AND TECHNOLOGY, Vol. 1, p. 45, 1984.

SMITH J.C., *The Application of Expert Systems Technology to Case-Based Law*, in PROCEEDINGS OF THE FIRST INTERNATIONAL CONFERENCE ON ARTIFICIAL INTELLIGENCE AND LAW, Boston, 1987.

SMITH J.C & GELBART D., *Legal Reasoning, Legal Theory and Artificial Intelligence*, in THE PROCEEDINGS OF THE INTERNATIONAL CONFERENCE ON COMPUTERS AND LAW, RESEARCH, DEVELOPMENT AND EDUCATION, Association Quebecoise Pour Le Development de L'Informatique Juridique, Montreal, 1992, Vol. C2.2 , p. 1-11..

SMITHSON DAVID, *An Overview of Information Retrieval*, in LSE TUTORIAL ON OFFICE AUTOMATION, 1990.

SMITHSON DAVID, *The Functional Approach to Information Retrieval*, in LSE TUTORIAL ON OFFICE AUTOMATION, 1990.

SMITHSON DAVID, *The Information Seeking Behaviour Approach,* in LSE TUTORIAL ON OFFICE AUTOMATION, 1990.

SOCIETY FOR COMPUTERS & LAW, *Tomorrow's Lawyers: Computers and Legal Training*, in Paper prepared by the SOCIETY'S LEGAL EDUCATION COMMITTE, March 1981.

SOPER PAUL & BENCH-CAPON TREVOR, *Coupling Hypertext and Knowledge Based System,* in ARTIFICIAL INTELLIGENCE AND LAW, Vol. 2, No. 4, 1994, p. 293.

SPAN GEORGES, LITES: *an Intelligent Tutoring System Shell for Legal Education*, in YEARBOOK OF LAW COMPUTERS AND TECHNOLOGY, Vol. 8, 1994, p. 103.

SPROWL JAMES A., *The Scrivener's Tools – Developing Computerised Practice Aids for Tomorrow's Law Office*, in YEARBOOK OF LAW COMPUTERS AND TECHNOLOGY, Vol. 2, p. 105 1986.

STAMPER RONALD, *Modellimng Legal Rules by Computer,* in NIBLETT (Ed.), Cabridge University Press, 1980.

STAMPER RONALD, *A Non-Classical Logic for Law Based on the Structures of Behaviour*, in 2ND INTERNATIONAL CONGRESS: LOGICA, INFORMATICA, DIRITTO, 1982.

STAMPER RONALD, *Key Issues in Formalising Legal & Other Social Norms: A Comparison of PROLOG and an Early Version of LEGOL*, in REPORT FOR LSE, 26 February, 1986.

STAMPER R., *Expert Systems, Lawyers Beware*, in NAGEL (Ed.), Quorum Books, New York, 1991.

STAUDT RONALD, *Practical Applications of Document Assembly Systems*, in NAGEL (Ed.), Quorum Books, New York, 1991, p. 51.

STAUDT RONALD, *Legal Mindstorms: Lawyers, Computers and Powerful Ideas*, in JURIMETRICS JOURNAL, Vol. 31, p. 171, Winter, 1991.

STAUDT RONALD, *An Essay on Electronic Casebooks: My Pursuit of the Paperless Chase*, in INTERNATIONAL YEARBOOK OF LAW COMPUTERS AND TECHNOLOGY, Vol. 8, 1994, p. 149.

STONE JULIUS, *Man and Machine in the Search of Justice*, in STANFORD LAW REVIEW, Vol. 16, p. 515, May, 1964.

STOYLES ROBERT L., *The Unfulfilled Promise: Use of Computers by and for Legislatures*, in COMPUTER/LAW JOURNAL, Vol. IX, p. 73, 1989.

SULZ J. & BAUMANN R., *LEX-Ein juristisches Expertensystem mit natürlichsparchlichen Dialog*, in INFORMATIK UND RECHT, no,11-12, p. 465, 1988.

SUMMERS ROBERT, *A Formal Theory of the Rule of Law*, in RATIO JURIS, Vol. 6, No. 2, p. 127, July, 1993.

SUSSKIND RICHARD, *Detmold's Refutation of Positivism and the Computer Judge*, Reviewing M.J.DETMOLD's *The Unity of Law and Morality: A Refutation of Legal Positivism*, in THE MODERN LAW REVIEW, Vol. 49, p. 125, January, 1986.

SUSSKIND RICHARD, *Expert Systems in Law and Data Protection Adviser*, in OXFORD JOURNAL OF LEGAL STUDIES, Vol. 7, No. 1, p. 145, 1987.

SUSSKIND RICHARD, *Pragmatism and Purism in AI and Legal Reasoning*, in AI & SOCIETY, Vol. 3, p. 28, 1989.

SUSSKIND RICHARD, *The Latent Damage System: A Jurisprudential Analysis*, in PROCEEDINGS OF THE SECOND INTERNATIONAL CONFERENCE ON ARTIFICIAL INTELLIGENCE AND LAW, Vancouver, 1989.

SUSSKIND RICHARD, Book review: A.GARDNER'S *An Artificial Intelligence Approach to Legal Reasoning*, in YEARBOOK OF LAW COMPUTERS AND TECHNOLOGY, Vol. 4, p221, 1989.

SUSSKIND RICHARD, *Systems Based on Artificial Intelligence in the Legal Field*, in REPORT TO THE COUNCIL OF EUROPE, January, 1990.

SUSSKIND RICHARD, *Lawyers Fail to Plead the Full Case for Computers' Potential*, in FINANCIAL TIMES, LEGAL COLUMN, 22 October, 1990.

SUSSKIND RICHARD, *Time to Unravel the Myths of Information Technology*, in FINANCIAL TIMES, LEGAL COLUMN, 22 October, 1990.

SUSSKIND RICHARD, Critical Note: A.GARDNER'S *An Artificial Intelligence Approach to Legal Reasoning*, in THE KNOWLEDGE ENGINEER REVIEW, p. 213, 1990.

SUSSKIND RICHARD, *The Theoretical Foundations of Expert Systems in Law*, in CURRENT LEGAL PROBLEMS, 1992, p. 169.

SUSSKIND RICHARD, *Expert Systems in Law: A Jurisprudential Approach to Artificial Intelligence and Legal Reasoning*, in ESSAYS ON LAW AND AI, COMPLEX 7/93, NRCCL, Oslo, 1993.

SUSSKIND RICHARD, *Artificial Intelligence, Expert Systems and the Law*, A European Appraisal, in ESSAYS ON LAW AND AI, COMPLEX 7/93, NRCCL, Tano, Oslo, 1993.

SUSSKIND RICHARD, *Electronic Communication for Lawyers – Towards Rengineering the Legal Process*, in COMPUTERS AND LAW, Vol. 4, No. 4, Oct/Nov, 1993.

SUSSKIND RICHARD, *The Importance of Commercial Case Studies in Artificial Intelligence and Law*, in ARTIFICIAL INTELLIGENCE AND LAW, Vol. 2, No. 1, 1994, p. 65.

SUSSKIND RICHARD, *Electronic Information Highways for Lawyers*, in LAW TECHNOLOGY JOURNAL, Vol. 3, No. 3, October 1994, p. 42.

SUSSKIND R. & CAPPER P, *Latent Damage Act – The Expert System*, in unpublished leaflet, 1989.

SUSSKIND R. & CAPPER P., *The Latent Damage System, A First Generation Expert System in Law*, in MARTINO (Ed.), North Holland, 1992.

SUSSKIND R. & TINDALL C., *VATIA: Ernst & Whinney's VAT Expert System*, offprint, p. 97, 1989.

TAPPER COLIN, *Lawyers and Machines*, in THE MODERN LAW REVIEW, Vol. 26, p. 121, March, 1963.

TAPPER COLIN, *World Co-Operation in the Mechanisation of Legal Information Retrieval*, in JURIMETRICS JOURNAL, p. 1, September, 1968.

TATA C., WILSON J. & HUTTON N., *Representations of Knowledge and Discretionary Decision-Making by Decision Support Systems: the Case of Judicial Sentencing*, in JOURNAL OF INFORMATION LAW AND TECHNOLOGY, Issue 2, 1996.

TISCORNIA DANIELA, *Meta-Reasoning in Law: A Computational Model*, in JOURNAL OF LAW AND INFORMATION SCIENCE, Vol. 4, No. 2, 1993, p. 368.

TREW A. & ARMSTRONG H., *Information Policy and Legal Technology*, in YEARBOOK OF LAW COMPUTERS AND TECHNOLOGY, Vol. 1, p126, 1984.

TURING ALLAN M., *Computing Machinery and Intelligence*, in FEIGENBAUM-FELDMAN (Eds.), p. 11, 1963.

TURLEY TOD, *Expert Software Systems: The Legal Implications*, in COMPUTER/LAW JOURNAL, Vol. VIII, p. 455, 1988.

TYREE ALAN, *The Logic Programming Debate*, in JOURNAL OF LAW AND INFORMATION SCIENCE, Vol. 3, No. 1, 1992, p. 111.

VALENTE A. & BREUKER J., *A Model-Based Approach to Legal Knowledge Engineering*, in PROCEEDINGS JURIX 92, Koninklijke Vermande, 1992.

VALENTE A. & BREUKER J., *Ontologies: the Missing Link Between Legal Theory and AI & Law*, in PRAKKEN, MUNTJEWERFF & SOETEMAN (Eds.), Proceedings of the Jurix 94 Conference, Koninklijke Vermande, Amsterdam, 1994.

VANDENBERGHE GUY P.V., *Software Oracles, in* KASPERSEN & OSKAMP (Eds.), Kluwer, Deventer, 1990.

VANYO JAMES P, *The Legal System: Can it Be Analyzed to Suit the Scientist?*, in JURIMETRICS JOURNAL, p. 100, Winter, 1973.

VERNON LILLIAN MALLEY, *Financial Conciderations and Feasibility*, in ABA AUTOMATED LAW RESEARCH, p. 163, 1973.

VERNON WESTON JR., *User Acceptability and Training*, in ABA AUTOMATED LAW RESEARCH, 1973.

VOSSOS, DILLON, ZELEZNIKOW & TAYLOR, *The Use of Object Oriented Principles to Develop Intelligent Legal Reasoning Systems*, in THE AUSTRALIAN COMPUTER JOURNAL, Vol. 23, No. 1, p. 2, 1991.

VRECION VLADIMIR, *Zur Anwendungsmöglichkeit der Informationstheorie im Bereich des Rechts*, in DATENVERARBEITUNG IM RECHT, Vol. 2, p. 76, 1973.

VRECION VLADIMIR, *On Possibilities of Exact Analysis and Computing of Decision-Making Processes in Law*, in CIAMPI (Ed.), North Holland, 1982.

WAHLGREN PETER., *Legal Reasoning: a Jurisprudential Description*, in PROCEEDINGS OF THE SECOND INTERNATIONAL CONFERENCE ON ARTIFICIAL INTELLIGENCE AND LAW, Vancouver, 1989.

WAHLGREN PETER, *The Concept of Legal Expertise*, in SEIPEL (Ed.), Kluwer, Computer/Law Series, 1990.

WAHLGREN PETER, *Hypertext and Legal Structures*, in MARTINO (Ed.), 1992.

WAHLGREN P., *A General Theory of Artificial Intelligence and Law,* in PRAKKEN, MUNTJEWERFF & SOETEMAN (Eds.), Proceedings of the Jurix 94 Conference, Koninklijke Vermande, Amsterdam, 1994.

WALL DAVID, *Revenge of the Cyborg Trolls Part Two: Putting IT into the Law Curriculum*, in YEARBOOK OF LAW COMPUTERS AND TECHNOLOGY, Vol. 8, 1994, p. 65.

WALL DAVID & REID KIRON, *The Electronic Lawyer: from Quill to Computer*, in LAW TECHNOLOGY JOURNAL, Vol. 2, No. 2, p. 16, May, 1993.

WALKER R, ZEINSTRA P.G.M & VAN DEN BERG P.H., *A Model to Model Knowledge about Knowledge or Implementing Meta-Knowledge in PROLEXS*, in VANDENBERGHE (Ed.), Kluwer, Computer/Law Series, 1989.

WALSH RAYMOND, *The "Appropriate Information System": User versus Provider?*, in YEARBOOK OF LAW COMPUTERS AND TECHNOLOGY, Vol. 1, p. 102, 1984.

WARNER DAVID R.JR., *Toward a Simple Law Machine*, in JURIMETRICS JOURNAL, Vol. 29, p. 451, Summer, 1989.

WARNER DAVID R.JR., *The Role of Neural Networks in the Law Machine Development*, in RUTGERS COMPUTER & TECHNOLOGY LAW JOURNAL, Vol. 16, p129, 1990.

WATERMAN D.A., PAUL J. & PETERSON M., *Expert Systems for Legal Decision Making*, in EXPERT SYSTEMS, Vol. 3, No. 4, p. 212, 1986.

WEIKERS R. & SHELTON D., *Computerized Representation and Common Law Reasoning*, in COMPUTER/LAW JOURNAL, Vol. IX, p. 223, 1989.

WESSEL MILTON R., *What is "Law, Science and Technology" anyway?*, in JURIMETRICS JOURNAL, Vol. 29, p. 259, Spring, 1989.

WIDDISON JOHN, *A Practicioners Guide to Expert Systems*, in LAW SOCIETY'S GAZETTE, Vol. 86, No. 32, p. 14, 13 September, 1989.

WIDDISON ROBIN, *Computerising Law Schools: The Jackson Report*, in COMPUTERS AND LAW, Vol. 2, No. 5, November, 1991.

WIDDISON ROBIN, *Expert Systems: the Forgotten Dimension*, in COMPUTERS AND LAW, Vol. 3, No. 1, March, 1992.

WIDDISON ROBIN, *Computers in the Classrom*, in COMPUTERS AND LAW, Vol. 3, No. 3, July, 1992.

WIDDISON ROBIN, *Surviving Information Overload,* in COMPUTERS AND LAW, Vol. 4, No. 2, June, 1993.

WIDDISON ROBIN, *Virtual Law School*, in YEARBOOK OF LAW COMPUTERS AND TECHNOLOGY, Vol. 8, 1994, p. 185.

WIDDISON ROBIN, *Building Second-generation Contract Courseware*, in COMPUTERS AND LAW, Vol. 5, No. 2, June/July, 1994.

WIDDISON ROBIN, *Internet Opportunities for Law Schools,* in COMPUTERS AND LAW, Vol. 6, No. 2, June/July, 1995.

WIDDISON ROBIN, *Lawyering in the Internet,* in WEB JOURNAL OF CURRENT LEGAL ISSUES, 1995.

WIDDISON ROBIN & PRITCHARD FRANCIS, *The EC Competition Adviser,* in COMPUTERS AND LAW, Vol. 2, No. 1, February, 1991.

WIDDISON R., PRITCHARD F., & ROBINSON W., *Expert Systems meet Hypertext: The European Conflicts Guide,* in JOURNAL OF LAW AND INFORMATION SCIENCE, Vol. 3, No. 1, p. 83, 1992.

WIDDISON R., PRITCHARD F., & ROBINSON W., *The European Conflicts Guide,* ARTIFICIAL INTELLIGENCE AND LAW, Vol. 1 No. 4, p. 291, 1993.

WIDDISON ROBIN & PRITCHARD FRANCIS, *An Experiment with Electronic Law Tutorials,* in LAW TECHNOLOGY JOURNAL, Vol. 4, No. 1, May 1995.

WILSON EVE, *Automating Computer Based Learning Packages for Law Design, Interface and Implementation,* in LAW TECHNOLOGY JOURNAL, Vol. 2, No. 2, p. 24, May, 1993.

WRIGHT VON G.H., *Truth and Logic,* in MARTINO (Ed.), NORTH HOLLAND, 1982.

WRÓBLEWSKI JERZY, *Operative Models and Legal Systems, in* CIAMPI (Ed.), North Holland, 1982.

WRÓBLEWSKI JERZY, *Representation Models of legal Systems and the Problems of their Computerisation,* in MARTINO & SOCCI-NATALI (Eds.), North Holland 1986.

WRÓBLEWSKI JERZY, *Computers and the Consistency of Law,* in INFORMATICA & DIRITTO, No. 1, 1990.

WRÓBLEWSKI JERZY, *Legal Expert Systems and Legal Reasoning,* in MARTINO (Ed.), North Holland, 1992.

YOUNG MAX, *Information Technology a Role in Legal Education?,* in COMPUTERS & LAW, No. 62, p. 25, December, 1989.

YOUNG MAX, *Information Technology a Role in Legal Education?,Where are we now?* In YEARBOOK OF LAW COMPUTERS AND TECHNOLOGY, Vol. 8, 1994, p. 75.

ZELEZNIKOW JOHN, *Building Intelligent Legal Tools – the IKBALS Project,* in JOURNAL OF LAW AND INFORMATION SCIENCE, Vol. 2, No. 2, 1991.

ZELEZNIKOW JOHN & HUNTER DANIEL, *Rationales for the Continued Development of Legal Expert Systems,* in JOURNAL OF LAW AND INFORMATION SCIENCE, Vol. 3, No. 1, p. 94, 1992.

ZELEZNIKOW JOHN & HUNTER DANIEL, *Deductive, Inductive and Analogical Reasoning in Legal Decision Support Systems,* in PROCEEDINGS OF THE FOURTH NATIONAL CONFERENCE ON LAW, COMPUTERS & AI, University of Exeter, 1994.

ZELEZNIKOW JOHN, VOSSOS GEORGE & HUNTER DANIEL, *The IKBALS project: Multi Modal Reasoning in Legal Knowledge Based Systems*, in ARTIFICIAL INTELLIGENCE AND LAW, Vol. 2, No. 2, 1994, p. 169.

III. SPECIAL REFERENCES FOR THE N-A PROTOTYPE.

BASILI R,. PAZIENZA M.T. & VELARDI P., *Computational Lexicons: the Neat examples and the Odd Exemplars*, in 3RD CONFERENCE ON 'APPLIED NATURAL LANGUAGE PROCESSING', Trento, Italy, 1-3 April, 1992.

CODICE IMPOSTA VALORE AGGIUNTO, Selected papers from the periodical on the interpretation of article 7 of the Italian VAT Law, including case-law and bibliography.

DECRETO DEL PRESIDENTE DELLA REPUBLICA, (DPR) N.633, 26/10/72 - *The Italian Text of the VAT Law.* (see also in the appendices).

DIRECTIVE (6TH OF 17 MAY 1977), *on the harmonisation of VAT Law*, OJ L 145, 13/06/77 .

ESPRIT-DOC II, *AREA 1,5,4, Technical Annex, amendement I*, November 1991.

ESPRIT DOC IL-31-50-01, *Annex II, Representational Issues Concerning Art.7* (Final Results of Annex I), 20-Mar-92.

ESPRIT DOC SG-11-40-06, *Type Hierarchy for the Italian Domain*, 20-Mar-92.

ESPRIT DOC SG-31-50-01, *Legal Knowledge Engineering: A Case Study* (by GIANNETTI A.), First Results, 15-Sep-91.

ESPRIT DOC SG-51-40-01, *Requirements Capture and Archtectural Details for Nomos Italian Application*, 2-Jun-92.

ESPRIT DOC TE-10-40-01, *Normative Field Selection Domain Analysis* (WP1 - IRETIJ), 16-Jul-91.

ESPRIT DOC AS-10-40-02, *Normative Field Selection, Part II: System Architecture*, 1-Mar-91.

ESPRIT DOC AS-10-40-02, *Hardware and Software Choice*, 10-Mar-91.

ESPRIT DOC TE-31-40-01, *Design of ILAM module for NOMOS*, 16-Sep-91.

ESPRIT DOC TE-33-40-03, by BASILI R., *ILAM, Taxonomic Relation Acquisition within the SLAT subsystem.*

329

FARGUES JEAN, *Conceptual Graphs for Natural Language Semantics and Deduction, a Text Analysis and Query/Answer System Based on Conceptual Graphs* in ACAI'89, Neuchatel.

FARGUES J., LANDAU M., DUGOURD A. & CATACH L., *Conceptual Graphs for Semantics and Knowledge Processing*, IBM JOURNAL, Vol. 30, No. 1, Jan, 1986.

GUENTHNER F., LEHMAN H. & SCHÖNFELD W, *A Theory for the Representation of Knowledge*, IBM JOURNAL, Vol. 30, No. 1, Jan, 1986.

HARTLEY-COOMBS, *Reasoning with Graph Operations* in SOWA (Ed.) *Principles of Semantic Networks*, Morgan Kaufmann, California, 1991.

ILAM OUTPUT, *The ILAM output in ASCII format* (see also in Appendices I & II).

KAMEL. M & QUINTANA. Y., *A Graph Based Knowledge Retrieval System, IEEE Conference on Systems, Man and Cybernetics,* Nov. 4-7th 1990, Los Angeles, California.

KONSTANTINOU V., MORSE P., *Electronic Documentation System: Using Automated Hypertext Techniques for Technical Support Services*, ACM SIGDOC '92, August 1992 Ottawa, Canada.

LANDAU MARIE-CLAUDE, *Solving Ambiguities in the Semantic Representation of Texts,* IBM France Scientific Center, 1991.

LANZARONE et al., *Programmazione in Logica della Legge sull' IVA*, Dipartimento di Scienze dell' Informazione, Universita degli Studi di Milano, 1991.

MOULIN-ROUSSEAU, *A Knowledge Acquisition System for Analysing Prescriptive Texts*, in THE 5TH AAAI-SPONSORED KNOWLEDGE ACQUSITION FOR KNOWLEDGE BASED SYSTEMS WORKSSHOP, Banff, Canada, November 1989.

MOULIN B. & ROUSSEAU D., *Designing Deontic Knowledge Bases from Regulation Texts*, in KNOWLEDGE BASED SYSTEMS, Vol. 3, No. 2, June 1990.

MOULIN B. & ROUSSEAU D., *Extracting Logical Knowledge from Prescriptive Texts in order to build Deontic Knowledge Base*, in PROCEEDINGS OF THE 6TH BANFF KNOWLEDGE ACQUISITION FOR KNOWLEDGE-BASED SYSTEMS WORKSHOP, Banff, Canada, 6-11 October 1991.

MUSSETTO et al., *A Multi Layered Architecture for Automatic Knowledge Acquisition from Legal Texts*, TESCIEL & SOGEI GROUP for *Nomos*, 1991.

QUINTANA. Y, KAMEL. M & LO. A., *Graph-Based Retrieval of Information in Hypertext Systems*, ACM SIGDOC'92, 157-168, 1992.

SEMANTIC LEXICON, *The Nomos Sematic Lexicon*, Version 15-Jun-92.

SMITH J.C., GELBART D. & GRAHAM, *A Procedure for Creating Expert Systems in Law*, in COMPUTERS AND LAW, Vol. 3, Issue 3, July 1992, p. 23.

SOGEI GROUP, *A Qualification Assistant for the VAT Law, A Proposal for Nomos Application*, Rome, 18-Jun-92.

SOWA JOHN F., *Definitional Mechanisms for Restructuring Knowledge Base* in RAS (Ed.) *Methodologies for Intelligent Systems* 5, North Holland, 1990.

SOWA JOHN F., *Toward the Expressive Power of Natural Language* in SOWA (Ed.) *Principles of Semantic Networks*, Morgan Kaufmann, California, 1991.

SOWA JOHN. F., *Conceptual Structure: Information Processing in Mind and Machine*, Addison Weshley 1984.

SOWA J.- WAY E., *Implementing a Semantic Interpreter Using Conceptual Graphs*, IBM JOURNAL, Vol. 30, 1, Jan 86.

UW-AIRG, *Knowledge Base (in English and Italian) for article 7 for the Nomos project*, Version 26-Oct-92 (see also in Appendix I, p. 263 & Appendix II, p. 283).

VELARDI P., PASIENZA M., DE GIOVANETTI M., *Conceptual Graphs for the Analysis and Generation of Sentences*, IBM Journal, Vol. 32, March, 1988.

WALKER ADRIAN, *Knowledge Systems, Principles and Practice*, IBM JOURNAL, Vol. 30, January, 1986.

INDEX

ABSTRACT

Computerised applications in law (expert systems, information retrieval, document assembly etc.) are usually built around a specific piece of legislation. The main observation of this research is that such a fragmentary approach to the law cannot produce legally 'correct' results because it ignores the effect of other connected parts of the law and, therefore, researchers must adopt an extended view of the legal phenomenon. Practically, this entails that the analysts of these applications must be legally educated and continuously aware of both the theoretical differences and the practical consequences that different legal theories and methodologies impose. Furthermore, the analysis must be undertaken in the light of the legal system as a whole, trying to create an integrated legal sub-system that can support practical problem solving. The main argument of the thesis is that in order to implement applications following these guidelines, _some_ kind of model representing the legal decision process as a whole must be followed. If this methodology is not applied, as several examples show, legally erroneous results may arise from otherwise technically 'perfect' computer applications.

In **Chapter 1**, out of these findings, a model of the legal decision process, encapsulating a *'minimum requirements configuration'* for building Information Technology Applications in Law from a jurisprudential point of view, is undertaken. This model endeavours to be used as a 'checklist' that can depict a compact picture of the full course of the Legal Decision Process and can provide a clearer view of the methodological rules so that future researchers, especially non-Lawyers, will avoid the omission of important elements of the process.

In **Chapter 2**, feedback from the *Nomos-Advisor* implementation is used to reduce the scope of the model to the application of legal expert systems. An attempt is made to find possible points for insertion of expert systems in the model and to elucidate specific complications which arise when using the model for this purpose. The analysis is extended to explain basic terminology, methodologies and technical characteristics of expert systems.

In **Chapter 3**, the whole process of implementing the fully functional prototype legal expert system *Nomos-Advisor,* which constituted the empirical testbench of the thesis, is described. This prototype used the Italian VAT Law as a source and was tested with real life cases.

In **Chapter 4**, conclusions derived from the implementation and the consultation sessions are used to confirm the theoretical assumptions and the main argument of the thesis, and, consequently, to evaluate the proposed model.

KEYWORDS:

Law | Legal Methodology | Computers | Artificial Intelligence |
Information Technology | Computer Applications in Law | Computers and Law

Law and Electronic Commerce

1. V. Bekkers, B-J. Koops and S. Nouwt (eds.): *Emerging Electronic Highways*. New Challenges for Politics and Law. 1996   ISBN 90-411-0183-7
2. G.P. Jenkins (ed.): *Information Technology and Innovation in Tax Administration*. 1996   ISBN 90-411-0966-8
3. A. Mitrakas: *Open EDI and Law in Europe*. A Regulatory Framework. 1997
                   ISBN 90-411-0489-5
4. G.N. Yannopoulos: *Modelling the Legal Decision Process for Information Technology Applications in Law*. 1998   ISBN 90-411-0540-9

KLUWER LAW INTERNATIONAL – THE HAGUE / LONDON / BOSTON